CASANOVA'S WOMEN

BY THE SAME AUTHOR

Non-fiction

Soho
A History of London's Most Colourful Neighbourhood

The Empress of Pleasure
The Life and Loves of Teresa Cornelys, Queen of
Masquerades and Casanova's Lover

Fiction

Dear Sister

I, Gloria Gold

Crime and Ravishment

Frogs and Lovers

CASANOVA'S WOMEN

The Great Seducer and the Women He Loved

JUDITH SUMMERS

BLOOMSBURY

EASTON AREA PUBLIC LIBRARY
515 CHURCH STREET
EASTON, PA 18042-3587

Copyright © 2006 by Judith Summers

All rights reserved. No part of this book may be used or reproduced in any manner whatsoever without written permission from the publisher except in the case of brief quotations embodied in critical articles or reviews. For information address Bloomsbury USA, 175 Fifth Avenue, New York, NY 10010.

Published by Bloomsbury USA, New York
Distributed to the trade by Holtzbrinck Publishers

All papers used by Bloomsbury USA are natural, recyclable products made from wood grown in well-managed forests. The manufacturing processes conform to the environmental regulations of the country of origin.

Library of Congress Cataloging-in-Publication Data has been applied for.

ISBN 1-59691-122-0
ISBN-13 978-1-59691-122-2

First U.S. Edition 2006

1 3 5 7 9 10 8 6 4 2

Typeset by Hewer Text UK Ltd, Edinburgh
Printed in the United States of America by Quebecor World Fairfield

For Donald

CONTENTS

Throughout my life, cultivating the pleasures of my senses was my main occupation; I have never found any other more important. Feeling that I was born for the opposite sex, I have always loved it, and I have done everything I could to make myself beloved by it.

Giacomo Girolamo Casanova

AUTHOR'S NOTE

By his own estimation Giacomo Casanova made love to several hundred women during his lifetime, of whom around 150 are separately mentioned in his twelve-volume memoir. Any book about the women in his life must therefore either be extremely long or extremely selective. I have taken the latter option and made a very personal choice, which is to write about those women who were most important to him or most colourful, and those who achieved something in their own right. Since Casanova disguised the names of many of his lovers, their real identities are often a matter of conjecture. In some cases the proof seems overwhelming, but in others the jury is still out. I have chosen to go with the person I consider to be the most likely candidate; others will of course disagree with me.

It would not have been possible to write this book without the Robert Laffont/Bouquins edition of Casanova's autobiography, *Histoire de ma Vie*. Brilliantly edited by Francis Lacassin, it contains almost everything anyone interested in Casanova wants to know, including the integral text of the memoirs. It is this Bouquins three-volume paperback edition that I have referenced in my endnotes, referring to each quotation by the Bouquins volume number, followed by the page number.

Past and present Casanova scholars have trawled scrupulously through the archives of Europe before me in order to pin down the adventurer and his women, and I am deeply indebted to their research. I would particularly like to thank Helmut Watzlawick; Jean Louis André for his articles on Henriette; Furio Luccichenti;

Ted Emery; Pablo Günther; and most of all Marco Leeflang for his help and encouragement throughout this project.

Many thanks to my agent Clare Alexander; to Alexandra Pringle, Rosemary Davidson, Mary Instone, Victoria Millar and Erica Jarnes at Bloomsbury Publishing in London, and Kathy Belden in New York. I am indebted to Dr Jiri Wolf of the Casanova Study Room at the Museum Duchcov for his kind help; Matteo Sartorio of the Museo Teatrale alla Scala, Milan; Filippo de Vivo for his advice on eighteenth-century Venice; André Maire of the Archives Municipales de Lyon; Bernard Terlay of the Musée Granet in Aix-en-Provence; Ann-Marie Hodgkiss and Heather Baim of the Princess Helena College, Hertfordshire; Donald Clarke; Gabriella Massaglia; the staff of the Biblioteca Spadoni at La Pergola Theatre in Florence; Enrico Tellini of the Teatro San Carlo in Milan; the staff of the British Library and the London Library; and Roy Harrison of the City of Westminster Archives. Very special thanks are due to Martin L. Thompson, for generously taking the time to photograph Sophia Williams's portrait, and to Martina Vaclavkova, the most thorough, uncomplaining Czech–English translator one could ask for.

Without the kindness and unstinting hospitality of my friend Eva Kolokova I would probably still be lost somewhere on the road between Prague and Duchcov; I simply could not have coped without her help. And without the support of my sister Sue Summers and brother-in-law Philip Norman I might still be floundering in mid-book despair: as always, I'm deeply indebted to them for their criticism and advice. Many thanks to Donald Sassoon for his constant advice and encouragement from start to finish and for acting as a French and Italian dictionary and occasional translator, always at the end of a telephone; and last but by no means least to my son Joshua for putting up with my erratic moods and preoccupations with such good grace and for reminding me, when necessary, that there is more to life than books.

Judith Summers, London, April 2006

2 April 1798

IT IS A PERFECT setting for love, or at least seduction: a bench in an ivy-covered arbour in the grounds of a French château. A fountain of cherubs stipples the surface of a stone carp pool, while swallows swoop above, fishing the air for gnats. Beyond the water, an avenue of yew trees leads the eye between velvet lawns towards distant hills. Hidden somewhere in the foliage, a blackbird serenades the approaching dusk with his clear sweet melody.

The late evening sunlight pours over Giacomo Girolamo Casanova de Seingalt, gambler, adventurer and self-confessed libertine. It warms his long muscular limbs through his lace-trimmed shirt and silk knee breeches and glints off his diamond coat buttons and the jewelled buckles on his shoes. He feels relaxed and light-headed, and is experiencing a moment of exquisite happiness. For sitting beside him in this bucolic idyll is a young dairymaid, the most alluring he has ever seen. Emerald eyes and rose-pink lips smile shyly at him from a face every bit as well-chiselled and delicate as that of a French princess. A mass of long raven hair, fastened on top of her head with a single hair pin, tumbles loosely on to her shoulders in suggestive disarray. Two well-formed breasts, each the perfect size to fit in one of Casanova's large palms, strain against the bodice of her calico dress, and her hands and arms, which are bare up to the elbows, are as flawless and pale as cream.

Casanova breathes in the faint odour of the dairymaid's sweat, a

smell as fragrant as cut grass. He has been aching to possess this treasure from the first moment he saw her two days ago. Since then he has paid her assiduous yet very correct attention, treating her not at all like the servant she is but like the grand lady she was obviously born to be. She has responded with commendable humility and discretion which has redoubled his feelings for her, and he can tell by the way she blushes when she looks at him that she is as smitten by him as he is by her.

He expected no less. Unusually tall, as handsome as a prince and as dark-skinned as a North African, Casanova is aware that he has the kind of presence that stops both men and women in their tracks. At the age of thirty, he is a vital predatory animal in his prime. Coupled with his larger-than-life personality he has a surprising sensitivity, and an unquenchable thirst for all that life has to offer, good or bad. With one notable, damaging exception – his own mother – women like, love or adore Casanova, and one has only to spend a few minutes with him to understand why. As well as good looks he possesses the rare gift of befriending women. He has the knack of addressing them as if they were his equals, and undressing them as if they were his superiors. Unlike many men of his day, he knows what motivates and pleases women and is in tune with their fears, hopes and desires. Sometimes cannily, sometimes unconsciously, Casanova uses his instinctive understanding of the female sex to get what he wants from them. In his long career as a womaniser he learned early on that he has only to be a sympathetic listener to worm his way into a heart or underneath a skirt.

But this evening Casanova wants only one woman, this lovely and innocent dairymaid. A connoisseur of virgins, he is certain she still is one. Furthermore he is convinced that she is the woman he has been searching for since his childhood, the one being who can fill the gnawing hollow inside him and enable him to live at peace with himself. He is not inventing this simply in order to bed her. At this particular moment – the moment preceding seduction – Casanova truly believes that he is in love with her. And since she does not know any better, she is convinced of it as well.

Casanova's practised eye can tell by her smile that she is as ripe for picking as the apricots weighing down the espaliered fruit trees trained against the château walls. He murmurs an endearment in her ear. He tells her how much he feels for her, and squeezes her hand. When she insists that she is saving her maidenhood for marriage he spontaneously and sincerely declares, 'Then let us be married without delay!' Though it is engraved upon Casanova's heart that marriage is the tomb of love, a union between himself and this delectable creature must certainly be the exception. To make an honest woman of her and save her from a life of servitude is to be his happy fate.

'But let us not wait for formalities!' he says. 'Let us seal our union before God right now, and go to the priest later!' As he pulls the girl towards him she smiles up at him with complete trust. With a speed born of years of experience he unties the apron fastened around her waist and casts the garment on to the grass. Casanova does this so naturally, and with such abandon, that instead of resisting him she just laughs. Next, he manoeuvres an arm around her plump shoulders, draws her face towards his and inhales her violet-petal breath. For the first time he kisses her lips – not a passionate or probing kiss that might set her running away in fear, but lingeringly, softly, with a tantalising expertise, so that her lips feel nothing more threatening than the delicate caress of butterfly wings. While he is doing so, Casanova inches her on to his lap. Before she can protest, before she is even aware what he is about, he has unlaced her bodice, slipped his hand inside her chemise and freed her straining breasts from their linen prison.

His treasure sighs deeply and mutters in a guttural voice, 'Come on, sir! Hurry up and open your mouth. I don't have all day to muck around doing this.'

Gaunt, sallow-skinned and propped up in a chintz armchair in his bedroom in Dux Castle in Bohemia, Giacomo Girolamo Casanova, septuagenarian, blinks open his eyes, lets go of this memory of a seduction long past and does what he is ordered to. He has been seriously ill for some weeks and is too feeble to feed himself. However, since the local doctor, fool that he is, has

ordered that Casanova must take some form of nourishment he is having to undergo the indignity of being fed.

Magda, the pasty-faced and entirely charmless kitchen maid who has been allotted this onerous task, dips a spoon into the bowl of soup balanced in her lap and transports the contents up to Casanova's lips. The old man grimaces. On the day before his birth, his mother had had a strong desire to eat crayfish, and consequently a soup made of the creatures has always been one of his favourite dishes. But lately he has lost his taste for it. This batch is particularly unappetising: oily, over-salted and, since it has been carried up here from the far-off kitchen, cold and viscous to the point of being congealed. Casanova can scarcely bring himself to swallow it. As it sits unpleasantly in his mouth, a drop dribbles down his chin where it hangs like spittle until Magda swats it away with a napkin and a disapproving curse.

Today is Casanova's seventy-third birthday, and he is already suffering from the debilitating painful bladder disorder which will claim his life in two months' time. Considering how many deceived husbands and women must have wanted to kill him during the course of his long life it is ironic that he is destined to die of a urinary infection in the safety of his own bed.

Casanova barks out a reprimand. Has Magda no manners or finesse? Does she not know who he is? She wipes her nose on the back of her hand and stifles a laugh. If she has heard this once she has heard it twenty times over. 'Of course I know who you are, sir,' she retorts, trying to keep a straight face as she raises another spoonful of soup to his lips. 'You must think I'm simple. You're Monsieur Casanova, the librarian. You work here at Count Waldstein's castle. Just like me.'

If there is one thing that rouses Casanova to anger it is insolence. Weak as he is, he dashes Magda's hand away from his face. Soup splatters over her apron and across the floor, and recriminations and insults fly from both sides. Leaping up, Magda bangs the soup bowl back on to the tray, flounces out of the room and runs down to the kitchen in tears, less upset than she is looking forward to sharing the story with the other members of the castle's staff.

Left alone, Casanova throws himself against the back of his chair in a paroxysm of anger directed as much against Fortune as against the stupid, ugly girl. He rails against the poverty which has forced him to accept a position in service. He curses his pain, his loneliness, his fate. Why has he ended up living among uneducated strangers who despise him? Why does no one in this godforsaken town appreciate the calibre of man he is?

The crayfish soup, however unpleasant, is easier to stomach than old age, a humiliating state Casanova has been reluctantly but inexorably embracing for the past three decades. Once, he had felt invincible. Born into the despised milieu of a poor theatrical family at a time when class was the defining feature of a man's existence, he reinvented himself as the equal of any aristocrat and rose to become one of the most erudite intellectuals of his age. No high-born philosopher could outwit him, no titled duellist touch him with their point, no wealthy gambler get the better of him at cards, and no woman, however sophisticated, resist his advances for more than a week. Striking-looking, brilliant, vain and proud, Casanova talked his way into all the best drawing-rooms of Europe and under many of the finest lace-trimmed silk petticoats. Senators, empresses and princes invited him into their salons. King George III of England received him at St James's Palace. Frederick the Great discussed taxation with him. Pope Clement XIII joked with him, and conferred on him the Papal Order of the Golden Spur. Paris's wealthiest widow kept Casanova in diamonds. Madame de Pompadour favoured him. Voltaire and Rousseau talked with him, Benjamin Franklin sat next to him in the Louvre, and he had not one but three interviews with Catherine the Great, Empress of all the Russias.

Women – scores and scores of beautiful women whose names have been lost to history – welcomed him into their beds.

Equally at ease in a palace, a merchant's house or a brothel, and most at home between a woman's legs, Casanova successfully straddled the worlds of the high life to which he aspired, and the low life into which he had been born. Steering a course through both, but putting down roots in neither, he followed only one

precept in his life – to go where the wind blew him – and he criss-crossed the continent of Europe as often as the migrating birds. En route he plied a good number of professions, but although he was a polymath with infinite capabilities he had little staying power, so in the end he became master of none. At one time or another he was a priest, a spy, a soldier, a playboy. In Rome he became secretary to a famous cardinal. In Paris he talked his way into becoming a financial adviser to the French government, founded a highly profitable national lottery for them and, on his own account, opened a factory that made hand-painted wallpaper. In the business centre of Amsterdam he dealt in shares as well as cards, and had equal success in both. Addicted to gambling from an early age, he frittered his fortunes away like sand in the wind. He was generous to a fault and fatally extravagant, especially when the money he was spending was not his own.

An historian, philosopher and writer, Casanova published books and pamphlets in Paris, Prague and Dresden, edited a literary journal in Venice, wrote a history of Poland and translated Homer's *Iliad* into his native dialect. Although he had no particular talent for music, he once took a job as a violinist in a theatre, work that he found humiliating but which nevertheless led to his greatest-ever stroke of luck. Somehow able to turn almost any situation, however unpromising, to his own advantage, he was an adventurer whose imprisonment and subsequent escape from the most secure prison in Europe, Venice's I Piombi, earned him fame and admiration as well as notoriety. Strangers of all classes were as captivated by the intriguing, impressive figure he cut as they were enchanted by his magnetic personality and witty conversation; as one female stranger wrote breathlessly after dining with him in Lyon, 'We hung on his lips.' Although he had an extraordinary gift for intimate friendship, if someone dared to slight him he would become their enemy for life. Unable to fathom his character or to pinpoint his exact position in the world, his acquaintances gossiped about him from Salerno to London, sometimes admiringly, at other times critically. Was Casanova a pauper or a millionaire, a man of principle or a

dishonourable, dishonest rogue? At ease with his own contradic-
tions, he worshipped the truth and yet was happy to be a consummate conman whenever it suited him, claiming that he
deceived the foolish only in order to make them wise. He became
a Freemason, a Rosicrucian and a freethinker whilst remaining at
heart a Christian. Though he derided the superstitions of others, he
studied alchemy and the Kabbalah, and led people to believe that
he was a mystic and a sage. Countesses asked him to predict their
future, and duchesses consulted him on intimate matters of health.
Even intelligent men fell for Casanova's clever deceptions and
unwittingly enriched his purse; and he easily convinced the credulous that he could turn base metal into gold.

All in all, Casanova reflects from his armchair in Dux Castle,
these things are substantial achievements for a cobbler's grandson
whose own uneducated mother dismissed him as an imbecile.

But by far Casanova's greatest achievement has been as a
womaniser. He has had women in almost every city, town and
port on his remarkable 64,000-kilometre journey around Europe,
and sometimes on the coach journeys in between. He has slept with
actresses and opera singers, housekeepers and shopkeepers, a slave
and a serf, lawyers' wives and businessmen's daughters, noble
women and fallen women, high-class courtesans and common
whores. He has made love to experienced married ladies and he
has deflowered countless virgins. He has enjoyed sex with women
in their late fifties, and – a particular predilection of his – girls as
young as eleven years old.

Ancient taboos have proved an aphrodisiac rather than a barrier
to Casanova, who has made love to two nuns, his thirteen-year-old
niece and his own grown-up daughter, an encounter that, very
probably, led to him siring his own grandson. No sexual or
romantic challenge has proved too great for him: once, quarantined
in a lazaretto in Ancona, he indulged in heavy petting with a female
slave through a hole in a balcony floor, and, on another memorable
occasion, with a young schoolgirl through the iron bars of a convent
grating.

In his active days Casanova enjoyed a conquest as much as a victory. Relegating the possibility of failure to the realm of impossibilities, he refused to take no for a final answer. If he had the will to woo someone, he would find a way. There was not one woman in the world, he believed, who could resist the attentions of a man determined to make her fall in love with him, and experience taught him that in ninety-nine out of one hundred cases he was right. Scores of women from Amsterdam to Zurich who initially refused to sleep with him later willingly defied their fathers, husbands, lovers or convention in order to throw themselves at his feet.

Yet Casanova was seldom satisfied with winning a woman's body. What he wanted, far more than sexual satisfaction, was to win her heart. And more often than not, he claimed that prize as well.

Casanova was born into an age of intrigue and gallantry, an age when love is the prerogative of the rich, and sex one of the few pleasures available even to the poor. The Church preaches abstinence outside marriage, but few people take any notice of its sermons, even the priests and bishops, many of whom lack religious vocation and have only embarked upon a clerical career at the behest of their families. Since enlightened minds see sex as a natural, pleasurable act which leads only to happiness, male philandering is acceptable and male chastity is almost non-existent· as the Methodist preacher John Wesley writes, 'How few can lay claim to it at all?'

Love is a widely available commodity, and attitudes to sex are liberal. Pornographic engravings are on display for all to see in the windows of London's print-shops and female armies made up of thousands of whores patrol almost every European city. They range from desperate streetwalkers who will pull up their skirts in a doorway, on a bridge or behind a tree for only a few pennies to well-bred prostitutes who demand courtship and high fees. In the Swiss city of Berne, ladies of pleasure step naked into the spa baths with their clients. In London, where there are more than one hundred brothels within the vicinity of Drury Lane alone, pub-

lications such as *Kitty's Atlantis*, the *Whoremonger's Guide* and the *Covent Garden Magazine or Amorous Repository* list the women's names and whereabouts, along with their prices and sexual specialities. Paris has its own such publication: the *Almanack des Adresses des Demoiselles*.

Rich men who want more than relief sex – or sex with less risk of disease – can look for a lover among the better class of courtesan, or the virgin daughters of the working classes, or among their servants, or even among their peers. In the second half of the eighteenth century every woman seems open to their approaches, from highborn duchesses to the wenches who wait on them. For to have a lover is considered a status symbol in sophisticated European circles where marriage is usually little more than a business arrangement forged by one's family, and where only the female servants of the rich, who build up their own dowries from their wages, have the freedom to choose their own spouses. As Lord Chesterfield advises his son, '*Un arrangement*, which is, in plain English, a gallantry, is at Paris as necessary a part of a woman of fashion's establishment as her house.' No king is a king without at least one official mistress, and no prince or duke can hold up his head in public if he does not have a beautiful courtesan in tow. Even the Russian empresses take lovers, Catherine the Great at least twelve of them.

Love is an art, seduction a thrilling, sometimes dangerous sport played by both sexes. Flirtation, subterfuge, refusal, pursuit and final surrender are the basic moves of the game, and the board is anywhere you choose to conduct the affair: a field, a bosky park, a covered carriage or a day-bed in a candlelit room. The absence of any male and female undergarments other than long linen chemises, and the growing fashion for less formal dresses, make success in the sport easy to achieve. As the stiff French manners of Louis XIV's late reign recede into memory, women have lowered their necklines, sometimes as far as their nipples, and loosened their padded whalebone stays in order to push up their breasts without compressing their waists too much. Fabrics are soft and light; more

than ever before they cling to a woman's curves. Held out from the body by rigid panniers and hoops, the new wider skirts allow a hem to be easily lifted to gain access to the stockinged legs and naked flesh underneath. Men's knee breeches, whilst hugging the thighs, are baggy in the seat and speedily unbuttoned at the front.

The game of love has many sets of rules: two for aristocrats, two for their servants, two for country peasants, one of each for men and women. To acknowledge that you have a lover might be acceptable among high society or servants in the capitals of Europe, and in the theatrical profession where actresses like Casanova's mother regularly favour their admirers, but it is distinctly less so among Europe's peasant classes, where couples are more likely to marry for love rather than money or position, and respectability is often the only thing of worth that a girl possesses. A nobleman's daughter who is known to have lost her virginity might still make a marriage with a man of the second rank because she has a dowry. A peasant girl loses her entire value if she is deflowered, and faces an inevitable downward slide into prostitution, destitution and an early death from disease.

The price of love is high, and in most cases it is women who pay it. Pregnancy is the worst disaster. Childbirth, with its possible consequences of haemorrhaging and septicaemia, is so dangerous that women in France face a one-in-ten chance of dying in the process. Abortion is a mortal sin likely to end in a serious internal infection, yet to have a baby out of wedlock brings disgrace on one's person, one's family and one's offspring, who will forever bear the stigma of illegitimacy. Women of means can get away with having an illegitimate child by taking refuge in a country village or convent for their confinement, and afterwards paying for their baby to be brought up by a foster mother whilst they return to their former lives as if nothing had happened. But if a poor woman brings a bastard into this world her reputation, and her life, are ruined.

Though contraception is absolutely forbidden by the Church, it is increasingly used, both within marriage and outside it. It is becoming more possible to separate pleasure from procreation,

and birth rates across Europe are beginning to fall, dramatically so in France. Women douche with astringents after sex or insert sponges or golden balls into their vaginas to stop themselves from conceiving, but such devices are expensive and hard to come by, and since most seductions take place away from the home and without warning, a douche is unlikely to be to hand at the moment when a woman needs it. *Coitus interruptus*, a more reliable method of contraception if practised correctly, is beyond a woman's control. The male contraceptive – *la capote anglaise* or English overcoat as the French called it – has been around since Egyptian times, fashioned out of linen, but it is rarely used outside the better brothels of Paris or London, where it re-emerged during the reign of King Charles II made out of animal gut. Secured to the penis by a gathered ribbon at one end, its texture is often so thick and uneven that it is bound to cool all but the very hottest ardour. Rather than using them to prevent their lovers from getting pregnant, men usually wear the overcoats, if at all, to preserve themselves from disease.

'The malady with which Venus not infrequently repays those who worship at her Shrine', as Scottish writer James Boswell describes venereal disease, is an embarrassing and potentially life-threatening penalty paid by most players of the game of love. No one wants to own up to syphilis, a plague which has devastated the Old World since the discovery of the New in the late fifteenth century and which is mistakenly believed to be part and parcel of the same affliction as gonorrhoea, a sexually transmitted disease which has been around since medieval times. The English call the illness the 'French Disease', Spaniards call it *El Morbo Ingles* and the French *La Maladie Espagnole* or even the *Mal de Naples*. The pox affects the brain if left untreated. It causes pain and ulcers and a putrid discharge that leaves sufferers with 'scandalously soiled' clothing and sheets. Newspapers, particularly in England, are full of quack remedies for sufferers, many of which do more harm than good. They include syringes to wash out an infected urethra, the famous Italian Bolus pill, Velno's Vegetable Syrup, Keyser's Pills,

and Dr Rock's Royal Patent. People will do anything for a cure. Boswell, a sex addict who suffers from venereal disease on nineteen separate occasions, travels from Italy to London just to get hold of Dr Gilbert Kennedy's Lisbon Diet Drink, an anti-venereal tonic containing sarsaparilla, liquorice and guaiac wood, an ingredient used by the natives of the Caribbean island of San Domingo to some good effect. But at half a guinea a bottle, the Lisbon Diet Drink is exorbitantly expensive, particularly since the recommended dose is two bottles a day.

Since the early sixteenth century, the main cure for the pox has been treatment with the liquid metal mercury, administered orally, by injection, as an inhalation or as a topical ointment mixed with animal fat. The high fever and copious saliva that these treatments produce are believed to help the patient sweat out the disease, but they do far worse than that. Mercury poisons the system, causing terrible pain as well as damage to the liver, brain and kidneys. It makes one's teeth fall out and turns one's breath foul. Administered by an unskilled physician, a mercury 'cure' can easily result in chronic weakness or even death. Wary of bad medical practitioners, in all but his most severe cases of the pox Casanova treats himself by avoiding alcohol, sticking to a rigorous diet and drinking a solution of saltpetre; this cure takes him between six and eight weeks. Though in his youth he finds venereal disease humiliating and degrading, by old age he has grown so used to it that he regards the physical scars it has given him as badges of honour won with pleasure on the battlefields of romance.

Casanova is no ordinary player in the game of love, but a past-master at it. What is his secret? For he must have one. Although he does not keep an exact tally of the women he seduces, he estimates in old age that more than two hundred lovers have passed through his practised hands. The love of women dominates his existence from the moment he comes into the world to his dying days, when his female correspondents flirt with him through their pens.

Where does his almost pathological need to be loved and admired stem from? Casanova's mother does not appear to love

him. She all but ignores him and, when he is only twelve months old, she abandons him to pursue her acting career. After his father dies, she exiles her nine-year-old son to Padua and leaves him with a hideous and cruel hag he does not know. Six months later, neglected and half-starved, he is rescued by his grandmother and sent to live at his schoolmaster's house, where he falls into the sexually curious hands of his first love, Bettina.

By the time Casanova returns to Venice, a precocious fourteen-year-old with a university degree in clerical law and an addiction to gambling, he is, like most youths of his age, at the mercy of his hormones and desperate to lose his virginity. In common with many well-educated young men who lack a private income, he is headed for the priesthood, but in the Serenissima or Serene One, as his native city is known, the temptations of the flesh assail him at every turn. Impressed by his sharp brain, an elderly Venetian senator with a penchant for young women takes Casanova under his wing and teaches him the ways of the world. Senator Alvise Malipiero II instructs the novice priest in the invaluable art of discretion. He lets him bear silent witness to his own torment at the hands of a flirtatious seventeen-year-old minx, and introduces him to the cream of Venetian society. Before long, the young Casanova – extremely tall at just under six feet, with large soulful eyes, dark olive skin and, despite the fact that he has taken the tonsure, a head of glorious curls – becomes the confidant and plaything of some of the most well-connected women in the city.

And so his career as a womaniser begins. Dispensing with formalities, these *nobile donne* allow Casanova to visit their palazzi unannounced, at will; and even to mingle with their unmarried daughters at the gratings of the convents where they are enrolled as *educande*, or schoolgirls. Casanova is in his element being their trusted pet. Understandably he would much rather be made a fuss of by a room full of rich sophisticated beauties than kneel on a cold church floor all day long saying his prayers. As he joins in with their small-talk he discovers what women think and feel about life, literature, love and men. He learns how to talk to women, how

to make them laugh and how to befriend them. He learns to like women as much as they like him.

One night when he is sixteen years old, Casanova discovers the joys of sex in the arms of two sisters: above all he desires one-to-one contact with a woman, but after this first experience he is never averse to increasing the ratio to one-to-two, as long as he is the only man. It proves such a pleasurable purusit that, while he is not bisexual, he will not turn down the very occasional opportunity in the future to experience it with a member of his own sex. Women, however, are his overwhelming interest. They are never mere bodies, but always individuals to him; the idea of taking part in an anonymous orgy does not turn him on. Casanova likes to get to know a woman before he makes love to her. For a woman is like a book to him: good or bad, pretty or ugly, she excites his curiosity, his desire to discover and read. If he is to enjoy sex with her, there must be some emotional or intellectual *frisson* between them. Casanova requires a woman to like him, to desire him, even to love him. And for sex to reach its zenith, he needs to love her with the same intensity.

Addicted not to sex, but rather to making an endless succession of conquests – a trait that, in a non-sexual context, extends to his relationships with all those he wishes to impress – Casanova goes out of his way to court women's affection and friendship, both in bed and out of it. He charms them with his intellect and disarms them with his looks. He gets them to talk about themselves, and listens to them with keen interest. He spoils them with the best food, the best accommodation and extravagant presents. When making a move, he seldom oversteps the mark but instinctively knows when to keep silent and when to flatter, when to retreat and when to pounce. He knows how to manipulate a situation to his own advantage, and very few can resist his persuasive arguments. Taking no for answer is not something he does willingly. If a woman tells him that she will not sleep with him, he can make her see in a few easy steps that she means quite the opposite.

His tactics in the game of love can breach the most impenetrable

fortress, and once the walls are down Casanova has full confidence in his ability to please the defeated one who lies physically and emotionally naked at his feet. In bed, he seeks something more than simple sexual satisfaction – a mutual climax that is like death in each other's arms, the kiss that unites two souls. He hints that his penis is large and that his self-control is exceptional, but he also admits to having his insecurities. Able in his youth to perform several times a night with the same lover, and to prolong his performance until she is satisfied, he nevertheless lives in permanent fear of failure. As he admits with disarming candour, 'I have all my life been dominated by the fear that my steed would flinch from beginning another race.'

Sexually uninhibited himself, Casanova believes that the slightest inhibition spoils enjoyment for both parties. He spontaneously does delicious things to women that they would not dare ask a man to do to them, and he shows them sexual practices that they had no idea existed. The link between clitoral stimulation and the female orgasm is well known in the eighteenth century: *Onania – Or the Heinous Sin of Self-Pollution*, an English sex manual first published in 1710, describes in detail how 'the necessary and unavoidable Friction of the *Penis*, against the *Clitoris*, in the Act of Coition, causes those excessive Ticklings and transporting Itchings to each Sex, that are not to be describ'd, so well as felt';[1] and, after being initiated early on into this open secret, Casanova takes pleasure in enlightening the unenlightened among the female sex. In bed he enjoys giving even more than he does receiving, and he claims that his partner's pleasure makes up four-fifths of his own. Since he cannot understand how a woman can enjoy herself with a man if the threat of pregnancy hangs over her – it would certainly put him off sex if he were a woman – he often spares his lovers by practising *coitus interruptus*, and on occasions wears a condom.

Sex and love, if not indivisible for Casanova, are closely linked, and the search for love dominates his life. He himself is shot through by Cupid's arrow almost as often as he plunges one through a woman's heart. Though some of his encounters are

mere passing fancies that gratify his senses for a night or so, others lead to lasting friendships, or change a woman's life for ever, or deeply touch his soul. He enjoys countless lighthearted love affairs, and suffers over a handful of destructive infatuations. He is once so hopelessly besotted by a woman that he secretly eats the split ends of her hair. He experiences true love, 'the love that sometimes arises after sensual pleasure: if it does, it is immortal; the other kind inevitably goes stale.' He knows the delights of living in perfect harmony with a woman who is his soul-mate and his intellectual equal. He tastes the bitterness of unwanted separation before an affair has run its course: 'The pain seems infinitely greater than the pleasure we have already experienced . . . We are so unhappy that, in order to stop being so, we wish we had never been happy in the first place.'[2]

But after falling in and out of love countless times, Casanova is still no clearer as to what love is. 'For all that I have read every word that certain self-styled sages have written on the nature of love, and have philosophised endlessly about it myself as I have aged, I will never admit that it is either a trifle or a vanity,' he writes of it. 'It is a kind of madness over which philosophy has no power at all; a sickness to which man is prone throughout his life and which is incurable if it strikes in old age. Indefinable love! God of nature! Bitterness than which nothing is sweeter, sweetness than which nothing is more bitter! Divine monster which can only be defined by paradoxes!'[3]

'I have loved women even to madness,' he admits in a more prosaic mood. 'But I have always preferred my freedom to them. Whenever I have been afraid of sacrificing it, only chance has saved me.' The thought of marriage has always been as disagreeable to him as the idea of settling down in one place. However deeply Casanova has loved, however strongly he is attached to a woman, his amorous feelings inevitably give way to claustrophobia and the need to escape. Somehow he manages to find a valid reason why the affair must end: the woman's old fiancé turns up unexpectedly; her father locks her away in a convent; Casanova gets himself

thrown into prison or exiled from the town she is in; the girl is unfaithful to him, or she puts her career before him. Eager to leave with an easy conscience, he sets her up with a more reliable partner. He finds her a husband and, generous to a fault, provides her with a dowry. If no substitute suitor is available he gives his lover his own private carriage as a present so that she can return to her parents in style. At the least, he ensures that she is in a position to survive without him. Casanova sees nothing questionable in this pattern of behaviour – in fact, he believes he is acting extremely honourably – and he scoffs at women who accuse the male sex of being perfidious: 'They would be right if they could prove that when we swear to be true to them we do so with the intention of tricking them. Alas! We love without consulting our reason, and reason has no more to do with it when we cease loving them.'[4]

Perhaps Casanova ceases loving once too often. For along with professional success and security, he ultimately sacrifices his happiness in order to follow the path of freedom; at least, that was what he believes he has been doing all these years. Few, if any, men of his time travel quite so much or squander so many golden opportunities, many of them handed to him on a plate. Is he searching for something, or running away from himself? Is no woman, no city, no mode of employment ever good enough for the proud adventurer? Or does the actress's son from Venice secretly feel that, no matter what he does and no matter who loves him, he never quite passes muster? That *he* is never good enough? Although, like Socrates, Casanova believes that 'the unexamined life is not worth living', this is one question he does not choose to ask himself.

In the end Casanova's rootless and peripatetic existence extracts a heavy price from him. Careless of the future, he burns his bridges as fast as he crosses them and makes bitter enemies en route as well as loyal friends. In old age he is *persona non grata* as far afield as Madrid, Vienna, his native Venice and his beloved Paris. He has nothing: no spouse, no lover, no legitimate children, no property, no place he can even call home. Everything of material value he once possessed – the

diamond rings that graced his fingers, his valuable watches, his jewelled chains, his enamelled snuffboxes, even the relic of a saint given to him by his beloved schoolmaster as a parting gift – is sold off to pay his debts. Casanova even loses his laurels, along with the respect of many of the people whose good opinion he once went out of his way to seek. As one ex-admirer puts it, Casanova becomes a 'glorious butterfly, transformed into a worm'.[5]

His life-long travels finally come to an end in 1785 at the château of Count Joseph Carl Emmanuel Waldstein, the wealthy seigneur of Dux Castle, Bohemia, and a fellow Freemason and gambler thirty years Casanova's junior. Here the adventurer remains until his death. Out of kindness and liking for him Waldstein pays the sometime adventurer a modest pension of 1,000 florins to take care of his 40,000-volume library, but Casanova is far from grateful for what is in reality a sinecure. His precious freedom has given way to a life of glorified servitude to which, after more than twelve years, he still finds it nigh impossible to reconcile himself. But however much he hates his situation in Waldstein's grand baroque palace, and however much he loathes life in Dux, a small provincial town on the road between Prague and Toplitz, Casanova cannot afford to leave and, besides, he has run out of places to go.

'They say that this Dux is a delightful spot, and I see that it might be for many,' he scrawls on a scrap of paper on his desk. 'But not for me. What delights me in my old age is independent of the place I inhabit. When I do not sleep I dream, and when I am tired of dreaming I blacken paper, then I read, and most often reject all that my pen has vomited.'[6]

Casanova blackens a lot of paper while he is at Dux. To relieve the terrible boredom of being stuck here, he throws himself wholeheartedly into the literary pursuits which have always been one of his main interests. From being a compulsive womaniser, he becomes a compulsive writer: all the power and energy he once expended in sexual congress now concentrates itself into his pen. He maintains a lively correspondence with past friends and literary acquaintances. He writes and publishes numerous full-length

books and pamphlets: *Icosameron*, a philosophical five-volume romance; *Soliloque d'un penseur*, a polemical tract against his fellow-adventurers; *Histoire de ma Fuite*, the true story of his escape from prison; and *A Leonard Snetlage*, a criticism of the vocabulary that has infiltrated the French language since the Revolution destroyed the country he once loved so much. Casanova also publishes various works on mathematics and algebra, and it is rumoured that he collaborates with his friend, Lorenzo da Ponte, on the libretto of Mozart's opera *Don Giovanni*.

Dwarfing all of these substantial achievements, which Casanova is justly proud of, is a huge manuscript for which he fails to find a publisher. Entitled simply *Histoire de Ma Vie Jusqu'à L'An 1797 – Story of My Life Until the Year 1797* – it is Casanova's autobiography. And it is a masterpiece, all 4,545 pages of it.

Story of My Life absorbs all of Casanova's pent-up creativity from the day in 1789 he begins writing it as an act of desperation, 'the only remedy to keep from going mad or dying with grief'. Unable to break out of his Bohemian prison in the same way he once famously broke out of Venice's Leads, he escapes in the only way possible: by time-travelling through his past. It is a past he has carried with him into the future in his phenomenal memory and written down in notebooks and ledgers which, by the time he arrives in Dux, fill a good third of his travelling trunks. Old correspondence, descriptions of places he has visited, images of friends and acquaintances, journeys he has taken, the dates he arrived and departed from cities, what he saw there and where he stayed, his thoughts on life and literature, skirmishes he has been caught up in, gossip he has been told, adventures he has enjoyed, the misdeeds he has committed, the women he has loved – the road-map of his life is all there, an array of colourful fragments.

Working ten to twelve hours a day year in, year out, Casanova pieces these fragments back together, reliving every breathtaking moment of his existence, both good and bad. Committed to telling the truth as he experienced it, he spares nobody, least of all himself. *Story of My Life* is not intended to be a rose-tinted portrait of its

hero and his world but, on the contrary, as accurate and well-rounded a picture of his flawed life and times as he is able to set down. His cast of hundreds includes rogues, aristocrats, bishops, kings, actors, servants, children, shopkeepers, desperate women and outright crooks (among them one of his own brothers). Although they leap off every page they are all overshadowed by one towering presence: Casanova himself. For his razor-sharp pen dissects his own character with the same ruthlessness and psychological insight with which it slices apart that of everyone else.

The result is astounding. Casanova is both hero and villain of the piece, an observer and a participant, at once the circus performer, the audience and the ringmaster who puts himself through the hoops. He speaks of his own love of truth, and at the same time admits to deceit and lying. He praises his virtues, and also brags about his many vices. He boasts of his insufferable pride and intelligence, and yet strips bare his soul to reveal his deepest insecurities. He confesses to being both the architect of his fortune and the man who undermined its foundations, to taking advantage of other people's stupidity, and to letting others get the better of him. He tells of giving away his last penny to help a woman in need, but also of emptying his friends' purses to satisfy his own, transient, selfish whims.

Most revealing of all, Casanova recounts in detail and with great relish and feeling, how he wooed, seduced, loved and parted from some hundreds of women. Descriptions of his love affairs take up a good third of the work.

Angela and Marta. Manon and Donna Lucrezia. Nanetta, Caterina and Marina. Bellino, Bettina and Teresa. Sophia and Lucia. Leonilda and Marcolina. The Charpillon and the Corticelli. Jeanne Camus de Pontcarré de la Rochefoucauld de Lascaris, otherwise known as the Marquise d'Urfé. Henriette. These women will go down in history as among the most important of his conquests. But there are scores and scores of others too numerous to mention in detail, many of them all but obliterated by the dense mist of the past. Madame Dubois. Doña Ignacia. Hedwige. Sara. Esther.

Signora F. Rosalie . . . Their names – sometimes real, at other times invented – are scattered two-deep across the one hundred and forty-three chapters of Casanova's manuscript. For the most part theirs are not famous names like Voltaire's or Catherine the Great's. But neither are they trophy names inscribed in some roué's little black book.

On the contrary, Casanova's women are unforgettable human beings whose own histories are sometimes as vividly and lovingly recounted as the adventurer's own. Just as Casanova the lover once kissed their dewy skin with breathless abandon, Casanova the writer breathes life into their shadows. He describes what they looked like and where they came from, what they did for a living, if anything, and how much they enjoyed themselves in bed. Where they have grown old Casanova rejuvenates them. When they are dead he resurrects them. Changing nothing in most cases but their identities – discretion remains one of his greatest virtues – Casanova undresses his women on paper just as he once undressed them before taking them to bed, and he exposes their private thoughts and most intimate moments to the public gaze.

Angela is a prissy virgin and stubbornly intends to remain so until the day she is married. Nanetta and Marta are disobedient sisters with a healthy sexual curiosity. Bellino forsakes her sex in order to make a living. Marina is a nun with a libido that far outstrips her religious conviction. Bettina's attempts to express her sexuality are destined to end in disaster, and Lucia's naïve belief that men actually mean what they say leads to her downfall. Manon is a clinging vine, Donna Lucrezia a sexually liberated wife who is lucky to have the most understanding husband in the world. Teresa is the female impresario of an exclusive and successful night club, and an appalling mother whose daughter excites Casanova even though he happens to be her father. Marianne de Charpillon will all but destroy the adventurer, and Marianna Corticelli will make the mistake of retaliating when he tries to double-cross her. Jeanne Camus de Pontcarré de la Rochefoucauld de Lascaris, the Marquise d'Urfé, is as credulous as her name is long. Henriette is refined,

beautiful, daring and clever. She is the love of Casanova's life, and the woman who describes him – after she leaves him – as 'the most honourable man I have ever met'.

In the future Casanova's biographers will accept his version of his relationships with these women. But in any love affair there are at least two versions of the truth. What do Casanova's women really think of the great seducer? How is he different from the other men they encounter? And what effect does meeting him have on their lives? Read between the lines of *Story of My Life*, or search deep in the archives, and it is possible to hear some of their voices, voices which have been silent until now. They speak of a man who undoubtedly loves women but who plucks virginities as light-heartedly as if they are wildflowers in the field, regardless of the consequences. A man whose behaviour often passes the loose boundaries of eighteenth-century sexual decorum. A man who preys on the vulnerable, who uses coercion and emotional black-mail to get what he wants. A man of forty who manages to convince himself that a twelve-year-old Russian virgin whom he buys off her peasant parents for a hundred roubles is passionately in love with him. A man who treats women with the utmost respect – unless he does not deem them worthy of it. A man who claims to abhor violence towards women yet on occasions resorts to it. A man who will fake an orgasm rather than lose face. A man who promises women the world, yet consistently flees after failing to deliver, leaving behind him a mountain of broken pledges, a lake brimming with despair. A seducer who, if he was operating today, might well be in prison for breach of promise, incest, fraud, paedophilia, grievous bodily harm and rape.

Each of Casanova's women is entirely different from the others. Each experiences another side of his character, and only a few of them ever meet. What they have in common is that they are all seduced in one way or another by Giacomo Casanova, and it is upon their naked backs that he will build his reputation as the greatest womaniser who has ever lived.

ONE

Zanetta

*There are certain situations in life to which I have
never been able to adapt myself. In the most
brilliant company, if but a single member of it looks
me up and down, I fall apart; I become bad-
tempered and foolish. It is a weakness.*[1]

ON THE EVENING of Friday 2 April 1734, Giacomo Casanova
followed his mother Zanetta out of the family's tall, narrow house on
Venice's Calle della Commedia, past the back of the theatre where
she worked, across the large *campo* where he often played with his
brothers and sisters and into the network of quays and passages that
led towards the Piazza San Marco. In front of them strode a porter
carrying a small travelling trunk on his shoulder. In it were all
Giacomo's clothes and possessions. That day the boy had celebrated
his ninth birthday, and now his childhood was to end for ever.

As always, Venice looked magical at night. The inky canals
danced with golden reflections, white mist swirled under the

bridges, and the doorways of the grand palazzi were guarded by blazing orange flambeaux. Here and there shutters were thrown open up above, and music and laughter drifted from the lighted windows. Although the Lent Carnival had officially ended a few weeks earlier, the party atmosphere in Venice always continued for a good six months of the year, and revellers wearing white masks and black tricorn hats still swarmed through the streets, sweeping past the child in their full-length cloaks and lending a sinister air to the fairy-tale scene. Some glided silently, like ghosts stalking the living. Others stood in the shadows of doorways, locked in embraces with other masked figures, their curved papier-mâché noses clashing like buffalo horns. Yet others lurched along arm-in-arm with groups of friends, smelling strongly of drink and singing and laughing as if they did not have a single care.

One day Giacomo would be one of these happy-go-lucky, pleasure-seeking adults. For the present, he lived in a frightening world over which he had no control. A few months previously he had seen his father collapse in agony from what the doctors could only diagnose as an abscess in his head. Two physicians had administered medicines which had sent thirty-six-year-old Gaetano Casanova into agonising convulsions, and his horrible screams had torn through the neighbourhood. The powerful authoritarian figure who had only recently threatened to beat Giacomo for stealing a prism from his optics workshop on the ground floor of the house had suddenly been reduced to a bedridden invalid upstairs. Realising that he was dying, he had summoned the entire family to his bedside, along with Zuane, Alvise and Michele Grimani, the three patrician brothers who were his family's patrons. Between convulsions, Gaetano had blessed all of his children and made the noblemen promise to protect them after his death. Then he had made his wife Zanetta swear that she would never allow any of them to go on the stage as they had both done.

After a week of intense suffering, Gaetano Casanova had died on 18 December 1733. Two months later his widow had given birth to yet another child. Zanetta already had three sons – eight-year-old

Giacomo, six-year-old Francesco and three-year-old Giovanni – and two daughters – two-year-old Faustina and one-year-old Maria-Maddalena – so now there were six little fatherless Casanova children, and since Giacomo was the eldest no one, not even his beloved grandmother Marcia, paid much attention to him any more. Everything around Giacomo had changed, and not for the better as far as he was concerned. His mother now headed the household, and it was she who suddenly decided that he should be sent away from Venice to school. Giacomo had always suspected that she did not like him very much, for she never seemed pleased by anything he did, often ignored him and rarely spoke to him except in an impatient tone. Now here was the proof, if proof were needed, that Zanetta favoured his younger brothers and sisters over him: out of the six children, he alone was being exiled from Venice. His grandmother told him that it was for his own good, but how could this be true?

As his mother strode ahead of him down the busy Salizzada San Moisé, a beautiful but determined figure swathed in a black cloak with a black lace *zendale* draped over her head, Giacomo struggled to keep up with her so as not to anger her any more than he must already have done. But there was little point: his fate was sealed; he was doomed. Giving up, he trailed slowly after her into the wide open plain of the Piazza San Marco, Venice's pulsing heart. Lit by scores of flambeaux, the huge square was as bright and crowded at night as it was at midday. Grand patrician gentlemen in embroidered coats and wigs, drunken English milords clutching winebottles in their hands, merchants from the East, Jewish businessmen from the ghetto – the cosmopolitan crowd that assembled here every night, as if in a vast ballroom, all turned to look at the beautiful actress, even the masked women milling around the open-air haberdashery stalls or sitting at tables in the crowded cafés underneath the colonnades, where fiddlers strode among them, playing scratchy tunes on their violins.

Walking fearlessly past the towering campanile that loomed over the far end of the square, Zanetta Casanova turned into the

Piazzetta and walked purposefully over to the waterfront, where the porter was waiting for them with Giacomo's trunk. Here she shooed Giacomo aboard a houseboat built in the form of a large gondola. This *burchiello* would sail overnight across the lagoon and down the Brenta Canal to Padua, she explained in a strained voice, and Padua was the city where he was to live from now on. Inside, the vessel was like a small but sumptuous house. There were chairs and even sofas, and drapes of heavy brocade, and mirrors made of Murano glass suspended between the large windows. Two people Giacomo knew were already on board: Alvise Grimani, the priest who had presided over his father's deathbed; and his late father's friend, poet Giorgio Baffo, the man who had advised Zanetta to send Giacomo away.

The *burchiello* set sail and the glimmering lights of Venice faded into the distance. Once the sailors had fastened the shutters across the large windows, Grimani and Baffo retired to sleep in the back cabin, while Giacomo climbed into a narrow bed in the saloon with his mother. At first he felt awkward, lying so close to her. But, lulled by the rocking of the boat and couched in her unfamiliar scent, he was soon overwhelmed with a feeling of peace and fell fast asleep. In what seemed like no time at all the first rays of the morning sun shone through the trees, across the bed and on to his closed eyelids. He opened them to see his mother standing by the window, while the tops of trees marched past behind her. Puzzled by this odd sight, Giacomo asked her what was happening. Why were the trees walking along beside the boat? He could tell by her expression that, as usual, he had said something stupid, but before she could scold him Baffo and Grimani entered the saloon, and seeing how astonished he looked, they asked him what was wrong. Giacomo repeated his question: why were the trees walking past the boat? 'It's the boat that's moving, and not the trees,' Zanetta snapped impatiently, and told him to hurry up and get dressed. Instead of doing as he was told, a look of enlightenment crossed Giacomo's face. 'Then it's possible that the sun does not move either,' he exclaimed, 'and that it's we who turn from the east to the west!'

One glance at his mother was enough to make Giacomo realise that he had made a fool of himself again. But to his astonishment Signor Baffo gathered him up and kissed him. 'You are right, my child,' he said. 'The sun does not move! Take courage, always reason logically, and let others laugh.' Baffo was mad to put such ideas into the boy's head, Zanetta said with an angry smile, but he ignored her, and instead proceeded to explain to Giacomo Galileo's theory that the Earth did indeed move around the sun; and the walking trees he had spotted were the proof of it. The boy's face lit up with the glorious knowledge that, for once, he knew better than his mother did. Zanetta might think him a fool, but his was in fact the superior intellect.

Eight hours after it had left Venice, the *burchiello* docked at Padua, where Grimani led the small party to the home of an apothecary he knew. Everyone shook hands jovially, and a nice woman clasped Giacomo to her breast and smothered him in welcoming kisses. But instead of staying here with her, soon it was time to leave for another house where they said Giacomo was to live from now on. The building they entered was cold and gloomy. The apartment was up two flights of steep, dark miserable stairs. On the second landing a door was opened by a woman so tall, stern and hideous that Giacomo was almost too frightened to look at her. Built like a soldier, Signora Mida had lank greasy hair, sallow skin, a miserable expression and unsmiling eyes which were thrown into dark relief by thick, masculine, bushy eyebrows. Strands of wiry black hair sprouted from her chin, and a stained and shabby dress hung limply from her broad shoulders with the front unbuttoned almost to the waist, revealing two pendulous breasts which hung down her naked chest like long empty sacks separated by a deep furrow.

This frightening gorgon stood aside and let the party into a filthy kitchen. Giacomo clung to his mother's skirt hoping that they would soon leave. He simply could not believe it when Signor Baffo told him that he was a lucky boy because from now on he was always to live in this house. Instead of his mother and

grandmother, Signora Mida was to be in charge of him in future. She would wash him, tend him if he felt poorly, feed him, put him to bed at night and see that he got up in the morning. Why, she was even going to find a schoolteacher for him, and make sure that he studied hard.

Giacomo gave a quick surreptitious glance up at the bearded monster with her deep scowl and dirty clothes. What Signor Baffo had just said could not be true; his mother would never leave him here! He waited for her to assure him that this was so, but Zanetta said nothing, even when he tugged at her skirt. Too shocked to speak, Giacomo watched as his trunk was brought in and opened up and an inventory was made of the contents: breeches, shirts, shoes, stockings, a small crucifix, a set of silver cutlery that his grandmother had given him as a going-away gift.

The monster muttered something about money. With her delicate pale hands Zanetta opened her pretty purse and counted out six gold sequins into Signora Mida's large oily palm. These, she said, were for Giacomo's keep for the next six months. She could never feed a growing boy on that amount, never mind keep him in clean clothes and pay for his schooling, Signora Mida grumbled. Well, she would just have to manage, Giacomo's mother told her, for that was all the money she had.

Then, without even asking to inspect the room where he was to sleep from now on, Zanetta bent down and peremptorily kissed the nine-year-old goodbye. Firmly detaching his clenched fingers from her skirt, she warned Giacomo to obey Signora Mida in every way, and then, without so much as a backward glance at him, she walked out of his life.

'Ce fut ainsi qu'on se débarrassa de moi.'[2] So, on this bitter note, ends the first chapter of the first volume of Casanova's memoirs: *That was how they got rid of me.* He did not see any member of his family again for six months, or his mother for a year. Her abandonment of him in Padua was to prove a defining moment in his relationships with the opposite sex. Never again would Casanova

willingly let a woman he loved walk out on him. In future he would make sure that he was the one to leave first.

What prompted the widowed Zanetta Casanova to banish her eldest child from his home on his ninth birthday? With her new baby, whom she had named Gaetano after the father he would never know, she now had eight mouths to feed, including her mother and herself – a daunting responsibility for any woman. Of her seven dependants, only Giacomo was a real worry to her. As her eldest he should have been of help to her at this terrible time, but instead he was her greatest burden. 'I was very weak, lacked an appetite, was incapable of concentrating on anything, and appeared to be an imbecile,' was how he later described himself.[3] Instead of living, he merely vegetated. Communication seemed beyond him. Slow to learn to read, Giacomo walked around in a dream world, and although his mouth hung open all the time he rarely spoke. Physically, he was thin, frail and prone to terrible, frequent nose-bleeds when blood dripped steadily from his nostrils like water from a faulty pump, leaving him exhausted.

The physicians reckoned that Giacomo lost two pounds' weight of blood through his nose every week, and argued interminably over the cause of it. One maintained that the milky fluid in Giacomo's intestines turned to blood; another that the volume of his blood increased with the amount of air he breathed. Since none of their recommended cures worked, about four months before his father's death his grandmother had secretly spirited Giacomo out of the house during one of his nosebleeds and taken him by gondola to consult an elderly witch on the island of Murano. Sitting on a bed in a small hovel, an old black cat perched on her lap, the witch listened intently as Marcia Farussi told her about Giacomo's illness, then put out a withered hand and accepted a precious silver ducat from her. Shooing the cat off her lap, the witch opened a large chest, picked the boy up and pushed him into it. As she closed the lid on him, trapping him in the pitch-dark, she told him not to be afraid. So insensible to his surroundings was Giacomo that he did not cry out or protest even when the witch

banged on the sides of the chest with a stick; and when she eventually pulled him out he was still meekly holding his red-spattered handkerchief to his nostrils, which had at last stopped dripping. The witch was not yet finished with him. She undressed him, stroked his body, then burned medicinal herbs on the fire, collecting the smoke they produced in a sheet and wrapping him in it. After rubbing a special ointment on his temples and neck, she dressed him again and assured him that he would now get better – but if he told anyone what had happened to him that day he would certainly die. Sweetening this bitter warning with five sugared almonds, she told him to expect a visit from a beautiful woman that evening; his future happiness would depend upon her.

In the middle of that night, Giacomo awoke to see a dazzling beauty appear in the fireplace of his room. Dressed in magnificent clothes and wearing a crown of fiery stones on her head, she sat down beside him on his bed. When Marcia woke him the following morning he tried to tell her what had happened, but she stopped him: hadn't the witch said that his very life depended on his silence? Giacomo shut up. But something profound had happened to him. From that morning on he became more aware of his surroundings. The beautiful woman, and his visit to the witch, became his first precise memories.

His nosebleeds, however, did not stop. And after his father's death it was decided that, with all this loss of blood, something drastic had to be done to stop the boy following his father to an untimely grave. Gaetano's friend Giorgio Baffo consulted Knipps-Macope, a famous physician and professor of medical botany and practical medicine at Padua University, about his condition. The professor diagnosed that the root of the boy's nosebleeds lay in the unusual density of his blood, a condition which was caused by the quality of the air that he breathed. If Giacomo was to survive he must be removed from Venice immediately, for only a complete change of air could save his life.

Given this advice by the revered professor, Zanetta had no alternative but to send her eldest son away from home. Death

had stalked her marriage from the very beginning, and God only knew when it would strike again. Her own parents had been simple working people. Her father Girolamo Farussi was a cobbler from the lagoon island of Burano. His wife Marcia had been a childless widow when she met him; and by the time their only child was born she was thirty-seven years old. Although the couple did not take their marriage vows until little Zuanna Maria, as Zanetta was baptised, was one year old,[4] they regarded themselves as respectable people, which was more than could be said of many of their fellow-Venetians.

There was simply nowhere else on earth as extraordinary as the Republic of Venice, nor a people as amoral as its citizens. Built at the point of the globe where the East met the West, and situated in the middle of a lagoon on an archipelago of more than one hundred islands, the exotic city was one of the wonders of the known world, famed for its music and wild social life as much as for its magical beauty. Between the eleventh and the sixteenth centuries its rulers had been sinister, fierce and ruthless, qualities that had enabled them to establish a supremacy over their neighbours, to conquer Corfu, Cyprus, Constantinople and Crete, to control the trade routes to Asia Minor and turn the Republic into the most powerful shipping and trading nation in the Mediterranean. At its height the Arsenale, Venice's walled port some two miles in circumference, had employed sixteen thousand men and housed the world's greatest shipping fleet. Fired by single-minded self-interest, Venice's government, which was made up entirely of its ancient patrician families, had crushed its competitors, spied on its residents and tortured its dissident citizens mercilessly.

By 1707, however, the year of Zanetta Farussi's birth, Venice was all but bankrupt, its trading empire had crumbled, the Arsenale lay almost empty of ships and the Council of Ten, the Republic's once-feared ruling body, was reduced to issuing sumptuary laws preventing the importation of French fabrics or the wearing of too many jewels. The most feared power in the Mediterranean was now little more than a tourist attraction – but it was a most glorious

one. Venice's ancient and dilapidated palaces appeared to float on water like the wooden galleons which jostled for space along its famous Grand Canal. Its magnificent basilica, San Marco, threatened to sink into the lagoon under the great weight of the plundered gold it contained, and its centre of government, the massive Doge's Palace, was constructed on such a scale that it dwarfed the human race.

Despite the difficulty of crossing the Alps to reach Venice, foreigners from Northern Europe arrived there in their tens of thousands every autumn, and stayed for months on end. Their purpose was partly to explore the maze of canals and the architectural jewels of the city, but more than anything else they came to enjoy themselves. For despite the seeping damp, the finger-numbing wind that blew off the Adriatic and the occasional flurry of watery snow, wintertime in Venice was one long, wild, hedonistic masquerade ball to which everyone from the most lowly servant to the most exalted patrician was invited. The tiny city boasted more theatres than Paris, its churches and even its orphanages reverberated with the music of professional orchestras, and its Carnival season, when everyone donned masks and cloaks, extended to six months of every year instead of the meagre two weeks celebrated elsewhere. Venice was a party city *par excellence*. It partied all night long week in, week out, and held more public fêtes, civic processions and religious festivals than any other city in the world.

Most alluring of all its attractions, perhaps, were the Republic's women, who were not only beautiful but famously flirtatious and as free with their favours as the men who pursued them. Nowhere in Europe was the game of love played with more relish than within Venice's watery borders. With its winding canals, mysterious dark passages and damp musty smells, the city reeked of sex and promised romance, torrid affairs or quick casual encounters – whatever one wanted, given freely in what the English traveller Lady Mary Wortley Montagu called an atmosphere of 'universal liberty'. Venice was quite simply the sex-tourism capital of Europe,

the place where young male aristocrats on the Grand Tour congregated to scatter their wild oats. Its maze of dead-end alleys, canals, quays and narrow bridges seemed to have been designed specifically with intrigue in mind, as did its anonymous black gondolas with their discreetly curtained cabins just big enough to hold two lovers.

Alla mattina una massetta, al dopo dinar una bassetta, alla sera una donnetta ran a local Venetian proverb – a little Mass in the morning, a little game of cards after dinner, a little woman in the evening. Venetian women were renowned for being beautiful, well-dressed and available. They bleached their hair a streaky blonde by pulling strands of it through the crowns of wide-brimmed straw hats and sitting out on their roof terraces all day in the sun. They adorned themselves with dresses made of sumptuous imported fabrics and wore fabulous pearls and precious stones around their long slender necks. A surprising number of women of all classes were sexually available. The city had been overrun with courtesans for more than a hundred years, and although young unmarried virgins of the patrician classes were safely cloistered away from sexual predators in the Republic's fifty-odd convents, their mothers and even their maids enjoyed an unprecedented amount of freedom. Allowed out all day either on their own or with their *cicisbeo*, a male companion or lover who was officially sanctioned by their families, they moved freely about the city on foot or by gondola, at liberty to do whatever they pleased. Anonymous in their carnival masks, androgynous in their floor-length black cloaks, these liberated wives played cards in the back rooms of theatres, frequented low-life taverns and smart cafés, and even visited male friends in their private *casini*, the small, luxuriously-appointed houses or apartments used by the wealthy for gambling and secret liaisons. No one knew exactly where they went to or what they got up to, and in most cases no one cared. Even God, it appeared, smiled upon love affairs in the Serenissima, where 'Christ Defending the Woman taken in Adultery' was one of the favourite subjects tackled by the city's painters.

Marcia and Girolamo Farussi had to accept that Venice's tourists, thespians and the ruling class behaved as if they were living in Sodom and Gomorrah. However, ordinary working folk such as themselves lived by higher standards, and they expected their only daughter to do the same. When Zanetta fell in love with an actor from the local theatre, they were outraged. For actors were despised beings in their eyes, and rumoured to have no morals at all. 'Remember you are persons whom God abhors, tolerated . . . only for the sake of those who enjoy your sinful antics,'[5] a member of Venice's Council of Ten had once warned the city's acting profession and, though the Farussis were materially worse off than many actors, they held themselves to be superior to them. If Zanetta married an actor, she would inevitably go on the stage herself, and actresses were no better than glorified whores who freely granted their male admirers whatever they desired. The prospect was unthinkable.

That their daughter's suitor, twenty-six-year-old Gaetano Casanova, had slipped into a theatrical career by chance and came from a good family made absolutely no difference to them; nor did the fact that, when he had first fallen in love with an actress himself, his own parents had been as outraged as the Farussis now were. Gaetano had only been nineteen years old when, in his native city of Parma, he had met Giovanna Balletti, an actress popularly known as La Fragoletta after the strawberry-shaped birthmark on her breast. La Fragoletta had not only been a despised thespian but a married woman some thirty-five years Gaetano's senior; both her son and her daughter were older than her lover was. When the senior Casanovas had objected to the patently unsuitable liaison, their son had impulsively run away from home in order to live with the actress, and in retaliation his father had cut him off. With no other means of support, Gaetano had left Parma and joined his lover on the road, first as a dancer and later as an actor in the same theatrical company. Sometime before 1723, the two of them came to Venice where La Fragoletta, who was then approaching sixty but still behaved as if she was a young star, shone playing *soubrette* roles.

Given the age gap between them, it was almost inevitable that the ill-matched lovers would part one day and, predictably, it had been Gaetano Casanova who had eventually left La Fragoletta (years later, when she was an old lady with ill-fitting false teeth and a wig, she still considered that he had never fully appreciated her). Unwilling or unable to return to the bosom of his family and admit that he had made a mistake, Gaetano had stayed on in Venice where he had joined the highly acclaimed company of Commedia dell' Arte players at the San Samuele theatre, a building owned by nobleman Michele Grimani. By late 1723, Gaetano had fallen in love with Zanetta, the beautiful cobbler's daughter who lived close by, and she had fallen for him too.

Ironically there was about as much chance of Girolamo and Marcia Farussi agreeing to the match as there had been of Gaetano's parents condoning his relationship with La Fragoletta. But like her lover before her, Zanetta refused to bow to her parents' wishes. Young, headstrong and displaying some of the determination and strength of character that would stand her in good stead in later life, she eloped without their consent. Provided with the necessary certificates and accompanied by two witnesses, she and Gaetano threw themselves at the mercy of Venice's Patriarch, Pietro Barbarigo, and were married on 27 February 1724 at the parish church of San Samuele.

There was a high price to pay for Zanetta's behaviour. Her mother went hysterical when she found out what had happened. Her father was so distraught that he literally died of grief within the month. By following her heart Zanetta had unwittingly killed her father and made a widow of her mother. The Casanovas' marriage was mired in guilt. When their first child was born on 2 April 1725, the couple named him Giacomo after his estranged paternal grandfather, and Girolamo after his late maternal one.

Had Zanetta known that her firstborn Giacomo Girolamo would posthumously become one of the most famous men ever to have lived, she might well have taken more interest in him, but she appears to have had little maternal instinct as far as he was

concerned. When her husband was invited to join a troupe of actors travelling to England at the beginning of 1726, she accompanied him, leaving her ten-month-old infant in her widowed mother's care for an indefinite period.

Invited to London by the Dukes of Montague and Richmond, the *Comédie du Théâtre de Gherardi*, as the Italian troupe were called after seventeenth-century harlequin Evaristo Gherardi, arrived in the sprawling metropolis of London in mid-March, and opened at the New Theatre in the Haymarket on the twenty-fourth with *La Fille à la Mode ou le Parisien Dupe*, an Italian comedy in spite of its French name. Despite a rather mixed reception, the following autumn they moved across the street to the grander and more famous King's Theatre, a building owned and designed by playwright and architect John Vanbrugh and managed by the charismatic if notoriously ugly Swiss impresario Johann Heidegger. Heidegger staged opera at the King's in conjunction with court composer George Frideric Handel. He also threw lavish masquerade parties there for the aristocracy, thus earning himself the reputation among churchmen as England's 'principal promoter of vice and immorality' and ensuring that his premises became the epicentre of fashionable London society. Eager to exploit any new scheme to make his theatre pay, Heidegger booked the Gherardi players to perform at the King's on nights when no other entertainment was being held there.

After his father-in-law's death, Gaetano had promised Marcia Farussi that he would never force her daughter to appear on stage, but Zanetta needed little encouragement. Although she had had no musical training, she a fine actress with good taste, a true ear and perfect execution. When the Gherardi troupe opened at the King's Theatre on 28 September with a performance of *The Faithful Wife, or Arlequin Strip'd*, the young 'Mrs Casanova' was among the cast. The first night's performance was a grand society event attended by King George I and the Prince of Wales, and despite the presence of his formidable wife, Caroline of Ansbach, forty-two-year-old

Prince George Augustus took an immediate fancy to the ravishing fledgling actress.

'Repetitive' and 'foolish' was how Nathaniel Mist, the publisher of *Mist's Weekly Journal*, described the Commedia dell' Arte season at the King's Theatre that autumn. The Prince of Wales, however, was sufficiently impressed to attend at least five more performances, though it appears he was more interested in one of the players than in the plays. For by early October, Zanetta Casanova, the twenty-year-old romantic heronie of *The Faithful Wife*, was with child. And ironically, far from her being faithful to her real-life husband, rumour had it that the Hanoverian prince was responsible for her condition.

By 26 April 1727, when she took one of the leading roles in a harlequinade called *La Parodia del Pastor Fido*, Zanetta was seven months pregnant. Six weeks later, on 1 June, she gave birth to her second child, a baby boy who was baptised Francesco. Ten days after that, King George I died in Osnabruck, Germany, and George Augustus, Francesco's putative father, became King George II of Great Britain and Elector of Hanover.

Sadly the royal connection was of little benefit to the Gherardi players, who were not proving the box-office draw that Heidegger had hoped for, so the following summer the entire company disbanded and the Casanovas undertook the long return journey to Italy. They arrived back in Venice between eighteen months and two years after they had left it, proudly toting Francesco, the brother whom Giacomo would resent all his life. Flush with the money they had earned on the London stage – and perhaps enriched by a secret pay-off from the new King George II – they rented a house in the parish of San Samuele from Zanetta's patrician godfather, Count Tribù Savorgnan.[6] The three-storey building in the Calle della Commedia was just around the corner from the theatre where, from now on, Zanetta worked as an actress, while Gaetano plied a second trade, that of making optical instruments.

His parents' homecoming was a rude shock for three-year-old

Giacomo who, during their long absence, had been the sole object of his grandmother's attention. Marcia Farussi was indulgent, warm-hearted and as motherly as her daughter was disinterested in her eldest son. Giacomo adored her, and although he was in many ways an unrewarding child to look after, out of all her grandchildren he remained her special pet. However, now that there was another infant in the house Marcia could no longer spend so much time with Giacomo, who suddenly found that he was of secondary importance compared to his new sibling and the three others that soon followed at yearly intervals. As for his parents, they were strangers to him, remote figures who appeared to pity rather than like him. Presuming, perhaps, that their sickly eldest son was an idiot who would not be long for this world, they ignored him most of the time.

Working in London had transformed Zanetta Casanova into a sophisticated actress as confident of her physical charms as of her acting talent, and after Gaetano's death in December 1733 she resolved to remain independent rather than marry again. From now on she would be the family's sole breadwinner. In the winter, autumn and spring there was plenty of work for actors in Venice, but in the hot summer months the tourists returned to their homes in the cooler climates of Northern Europe and the Venetian noble class took refuge in their country houses in the nearby region of Friuli and along the Brenta Canal. Suddenly Venice was empty of all but its poorest citizens. The Matter of Fact and Queen of the Sea cafés in the Piazza San Marco were virtually deserted, the streets and squares no longer echoed to the sounds of late-night revelry, and the theatres were forced to close. Desperate to make a living, Venetian actors packed their costumes and props into hampers and travelled to the mainland in search of new audiences, and during the first summer of her widowhood Zanetta had no choice but to go with them. Leaving her children with Marcia, she followed the San Samuele theatre company to Verona, where they were booked to perform at an annual theatre festival in the city.

Given that he was a sickly child thought to be in danger of dying, it is a mark of her lack of feeling for nine-year-old Giacomo that Zanetta left for the summer without first visiting him in Padua, even though she had not seen him since the day in April when she had left him there. If she imagined that her son was happy living with his foster-mother Signora Mida she was mistaken. At home in Venice he had been mollycoddled by his grandmother, but in Padua he was forced to fend for himself with a vengeance. Signora Mida was as cruel, neglectful and sluttish as she was hideous. Under her roof Giacomo shared a filthy attic room with three other boys, bullies whose beds, like his own, were infested with fleas and lice. Rats ran riot in the darkness at night, scurrying across the floor and even leaping terrifyingly on to the beds. No one ever changed the blood-flecked sheets or washed the children's filthy clothes, and no one ever saw to it that they washed themselves or even brushed their hair. If he did not die from the squalor in the house, Giacomo feared that he would die of starvation. Although he had never had much of an appetite before, at Signora Mida's he was always ravenous, for there was never enough to eat, and what little there was tasted disgusting. Since there were no separate plates or glasses to drink from, he was forced to fight his room-mates for spoonfuls of the foul-smelling soup which was dished up in a single, communal tureen. The lovely silver cutlery which his grandmother had given him had been locked away, and the only utensils available were a few old wooden implements. Whenever Giacomo complained to Signora Mida that things were not as they should be in the house, she scolded him violently and beat the maid.

After six months of torment, in which the only saving grace of his life proved to be Dr Antonio Gozzi, the young, dedicated school-teacher whom Signora Mida had found for him, Giacomo wrote three desperate letters home: one to Giorgio Baffo, another to the priest Grimani, and a third to his grandmother. Since she was illiterate, Marcia Farussi asked Baffo to read the letter to her. She was appalled by what it said. Although she was far from wealthy

herself she had always been house-proud and kept a decent table. In her home, as in most houses belonging to the labouring classes in Venice, 'cleanliness and honest sufficiency reigned'.[7] Never before in his life had her sickly grandson gone hungry, or been treated unkindly. Now the little weakling was living in squalor with strangers, and being treated worse than an animal! And this was supposed to be good for his health? Since Zanetta was in Verona, Marcia took matters into her own hands and boarded the next *burchiello* down the Brenta Canal, determined to see for herself exactly what was going on in Padua.

The following noon she arrived unannounced at Signora Mida's house, took one look at the hideous hag and demanded to see her grandson. So changed and filthy was Giacomo that for a moment Marcia did not recognise him among the scruffy urchins fighting for food around the kitchen table. However, the moment he saw her he flung himself at her neck and burst into tears. Weeping herself, Marcia sat down and drew the boy on to her lap, where he sobbed out a woeful tale of starvation and abuse. Controlling her fury, she inspected the house. There in the attic were the unwashed sheets Giacomo had complained of, crawling with the vermin which had bitten him.

Marcia took the boy away from Signora Mida's immediately. Back at the inn where she was lodging she watched in astonishment as Giacomo devoured plate after plate of food. In the past few months he had grown taller and skeletally thin, and the curls she had once tended with care were so matted that they were beyond saving and had to be cut off. Yet, undernourished as he was, he glowed with good health. For the first time ever he appeared lively and talkative, as if his brain had at last woken up from its long sleep. Marcia summoned his schoolteacher, Antonio Gozzi, who had suggested that his pupil lodge at his parents' house in future. The handsome twenty-six-year-old priest and teacher immediately impressed Marcia with his good sense, his modest, respectful manners and his literal interpretation of the Bible, which was so similar to her own: in his opinion 'the Flood had been universal,

before the disaster men had lived for a thousand years, God conversed with them, Noah had taken one hundred years to build the ark, and the earth, suspended in the air, remained fixed at the centre of the universe, which God had created out of nothing.'[8] Equally impressive was the fact that Gozzi was plump and cleanly dressed, indicating that in his parents' home her grandson would be well-looked-after and properly fed. When Gozzi told Marcia that he had a younger sister who could help care for Giacomo, and that his father was a cobbler, the same trade as her own dear Girolamo had plied, Marcia agreed to pay the Gozzis double the boarding fees that her daughter had paid Signora Mida, and she immediately handed over a year's money in advance.

Marcia stayed on in Padua for another three days. She fed Giacomo all that he could eat, bathed him, and bought him a wig and new clothes. Only when she was satisfied that she had done everything she could for him did she return to Venice. Her heart was at peace. Her daughter had acted irresponsibly by abandoning Giacomo to an unspeakable monster, but she, his grandmother, was leaving him in trustworthy hands.

Unaware of the drama that was taking place nearer to home, Zanetta was still in Verona. Just over sixty miles west of Venice, the ancient city was a lively cultural centre dominated by its ancient Roman arena, a well-preserved oval amphitheatre surrounded by forty-five rows of marble steps capable of seating 25,000 spectators at their ease. For most of the year, this vast edifice was used for jousting, races and bull-baiting. During the summer months, however, a temporary wooden stage was erected in the centre of the arena, simple plank benches were constructed around it, and the best theatre companies in Italy took turns in displaying their talents there. That year it was the turn of the San Samuele actors to perform at this prestigious open-air venue, and the company's highly talented actor/manager, Giuseppe Imer, was delighted to have Zanetta Casanova with him. With her ravishing looks and skilful acting she had become a favourite with his audiences who

flocked to see her play the romantic leads in the innovative musical interludes that he had introduced into his plays.

There was a more personal reason, too, why the stout, charismatic and scrupulously polite Imer was glad that Zanetta had accompanied the players to Verona: he was in love with her. He had known her at least since her marriage, and neither maturity nor motherhood nor her recent sorrows had dimmed her attractions in his eyes. That summer, with his own wife Paolina and his daughters Teresa and Marianna far away in Venice, he was finally free to become her lover. Only months had passed since Zanetta had lost Gaetano, but no matter what her feelings were towards Imer it was almost taken for granted at the time that an actress should favour her impresario with her charms. Zanetta dutifully played the part of mistress, though with little enthusiasm.

Their affair was closely observed by a young stage-struck lawyer who would one day become Italy's most revered playwright. Born in Venice six months before Zanetta, although in more prosperous and enlightened circumstances, Carlo Goldoni had been obsessed with the theatre ever since he was a child; in contrast to the Farussis who had forbidden their daughter to have anything to do with it, his father had encouraged his son's interest by building a puppet theatre for him and asking his own friends to write plays for it. After dropping out of medical school, Goldoni had qualified as a lawyer, but his heart had not been in the work, for he lived only to write. Success did not come immediately to him: his first carefully-composed lyrical tragedy, *Amalasunta*, had been derided by a group of actors in Milan; and in despair Goldoni had set fire to the manuscript that he had formerly regarded as his 'treasure'. Soon afterwards Casali, a leading romantic actor at Venice's San Samuele, had asked Goldoni to write a drama on the subject of the sixth-century Byzantine count, Belisarius. The play was to change both Goldoni's life and the future of Imer's theatre company.

During the summer of 1734, Goldoni was passing through Verona with his new manuscript rolled up in his luggage when he noticed a play-bill for *Harlequin struck mute through fear*, to be

performed by the San Samuele players in the Roman arena. To his astonishment the first actor to come out on stage was Casali, the very man who had commissioned his new play. The actor introduced Goldoni to Imer, who invited the young lawyer to dine with them the following night. Goldoni found the entire theatrical company, including Zanetta Casanova, assembled at Imer's lodgings. 'The dinner was splendid,' he later wrote, 'the gaiety of the comedians charming. They made up couplets, and sang drinking songs. They anticipated my every wish, as if they were whores who wanted to seduce me.' After they had eaten, Goldoni nervously read out *Belisario* in front of a rapt audience, and to his relief their applause at the end was genuinely enthusiastic. 'Imer took me by the hand, and in a magisterial tone said to me: *Bravo*,' he reminisced later in his *Memoirs*. 'Everyone complimented me; Casali wept with joy.'[9]

Goldoni ended up spending the remainder of the season with the company. Imer's talent as an impresario inspired the deepest respect in him. 'He contrived the introduction into comedy of musical interludes which had long been inseparable from grand Opera, and had at last been suppressed to make way for Ballets. Comic opera had had its origins in Naples and Rome, but it was unknown in Lombardy and in the State of Venice, so Imer's project succeeded, and the novelty produced much pleasure, and was highly profitable to the Comedians.' Imer's personal qualities also impressed him: 'Without having had much of an education, [he] possessed wit and intelligence; he loved Comedy with a passion; he was naturally eloquent, and would have been very well-suited to play the extempore lover, following the Italian fashion, if his height and his face had matched his talent. Short, thick-set, without a neck, with small eyes, and a flat nose, he appeared ridiculous in serious roles, and exaggerated characters were not in fashion.'[10]

There was one part, Goldoni noted, which Imer played to perfection: that of Zanetta's admirer. 'I perceived that he had a decided inclination for his friend the widow; I also saw that he was jealous of her.'[11] When Imer commissioned him to create a short

three-act musical interlude for the troupe, Goldoni wrote *La Pupilla*, basing the plot on the couple's relationship. It was a daring move, and one which Imer instantly noticed. However, Goldoni's interlude 'seemed so well crafted to him, and the attack so honest and delicately put, that he forgave me for the pleasantry. He thanked me, he praised me, and immediately sent off the piece to Venice, to the composer whom he had already commissioned.'[12]

When the players returned to Venice that September Goldoni accompanied them, and on 24 November, the Feast of St Catherine, *Belisario* was premiered at the San Samuele. Venetian audiences, like those throughout most of Europe, were accustomed to talking, gambling and flirting their way through every performance, but Goldoni's naturalistic characters and dialogue reduced them to an unprecedented silence broken only by applause between the acts and the occasional cry of pleasure. At the close of the play the actors took so many curtain calls that they broke down with laughter and tears of joy. And when the principal actor came back out on stage to announce the next day's play, the audience drowned him out with cries of *Questa, questa, questa! – This, this, this!* – signifying that they wanted to see *Belisario* again. In the end, the play was performed every night for three weeks. On the sixth night, Imer inserted *La Pupilla* into the intermezzo, with Zanetta playing the romantic role which had been written for her. This became even more popular than *Belisario*.

Thanks partly to Goldoni, Zanetta had become a star within Venice's close-knit theatrical world. And like many of the Republic's star turns, it was not long before she was talent-spotted. The Republic's exuberant actors and singers were among its most important exports, lured as far afield as the courts of Russia, France and Sweden. One such actor was Pietro Mira, a Venetian clown who had become the favourite of Empress Anna Ivanova in St Petersburg. In 1734 the empress commissioned Mira to assemble a company of Italian players to amuse her, and on a trip back to Italy that year, he recruited Zanetta. Accepting an open-ended position in Russia would mean leaving her six children in Marcia's care for

the foreseeable future. Nevertheless, either out of financial necessity or ambition, Zanetta decided to go.

Before she left for Russia, she asked Dr Gozzi to bring Giacomo to Venice for a few days. Incredibly, it was the first time she had seen her eldest son since his ninth birthday, and she could scarcely believe the change in him. He was almost unrecognisable as the sickly imbecile who had seemed destined to die an early death, for in the care of his Paduan schoolteacher he had metamorphosed into a robust, beautiful eleven-year-old with a pin-sharp brain. Among other subjects Gozzi had taught Giacomo Latin, pure Italian, Geography, History, and even how to play the violin. Zanetta watched in amazement as her son impressed her sophisticated dinner guests with his precocious intelligence, reasoning with them in the Italian language rather than in Venetian dialect, and even making risqué puns in Latin. When asked by an English poet who was at the table to read the ancient couplet *Discite grammatici cur mascula nomina cunnus/Et cur femineum mentula nomen habet* – Teach us, grammarians, why *vagina* (cunnus) is a masculine noun/And why *penis* (mentula) is feminine – Giacomo answered it with a witty pentameter of his own invention: *Disce quod a domino nomina servus habet* – It is because the slave always takes the name of his master. Zanetta, who was ashamed that she spoke no Latin herself, had to get her friend Signor Baffo to whisper a translation to her.

Giacomo lapped up his mother's admiration along with all the praise that was heaped on him. Suddenly he was the centre of attention in a house where he had previously been ignored or despised by everyone except his grandmother. 'It was my first literary exploit,' he later admitted, 'and I can say that it was at this moment that the love of glory which comes from literature was sown in my soul, for the applause sent me soaring to the pinnacle of happiness.' He had won Zanetta's interest at long last, and through sheer brain power. From now on he would make sure that his clever wit and sparkling repartee dominated every important social occasion.

The rapprochement with his beautiful mother had its downside. For four days Giacomo was forced to watch her flirt with his embarrassed school teacher, a simple man who was so overawed by her beauty that he dared not look her in the eye. After that, the two of them were dispatched back to Padua, while Zanetta left for Russia with no idea when she would return. Since the Russian aristocracy spoke French, and did not understand either Italian or the Venetian dialect, this turned out to be sooner than expected, and she came back to Venice the following year, stopping off in Padua en route to visit Giacomo. During her long absence her four-year-old daughter Faustina had died of smallpox but, if Zanetta was grieving for her, her son picked up no sign of it. Their reunion, like their previous one in Venice, was not an intimate occasion but a lively social event witnessed by both Dr Gozzi and his mother's travelling companion and probable lover, the famous Harlequin Carlino Bertinazzi who had been working in St Petersburg with her. After spending just one evening with her son and his teacher, Zanetta continued on her journey.

Beautiful, gregarious, and for ever unattainable, Zanetta came into her son's life, captivated him, and then abandoned him – a pattern of behaviour which he himself would later emulate with many of the women who loved him. Six months after she had turned up in Padua, she summoned him to Venice in order to bid farewell to him yet again. This time she was leaving the Republic for good. Her destination was Dresden, where she had been offered a lifetime engagement in the service of Augustus III, the Elector of Saxony, King of Poland since 1733 and an ally of Anna Ivanova in the war of Polish succession. Though she had been living with her other children since her return from Russia – Francesco was now ten years old, Giovanni seven, Maria five and Gaetano just three – Zanetta had spent less than seven days in total with Giacomo since the night of his ninth birthday. This did not stop him feeling resentful at her departure, particularly when he discovered that she was taking his brother Giovanni to Dresden with her. When they boarded the boat to the mainland Giovanni 'wept like a desperate

man, which made me think that he was not at all intelligent, for there was nothing tragic about the departure,' Casanova recalled bitterly in his memoir. 'He was the only one of us who owed all his fortune to our mother, even though he was not her favourite.'[13]

Zanetta and Giovanni settled happily in Dresden. The city on the banks of the River Elbe was then in its golden age, and housed what her eldest son later described as 'the most brilliant court in all of Europe'.[14] An explosion of baroque architecture had taken place since the dawn of the eighteenth century and, stylistically if not in size, Dresden now rivalled Vienna in magnificence. Here, among Balthasar Permoser's flamboyant sculptures and Matthäus Pöppelmann's elegant buildings, Zanetta made her permanent home, which she would only ever leave to follow the court to Warsaw, or to seek temporary refuge in Prague during the Seven Years War.

She never returned to Venice, not even when her seventy-three-year-old mother fell gravely ill in the first weeks of 1743. Marcia Farussi died on 18 March, having been cared for during her illness by Giacomo and the other grandchildren whom she had looked after so devotedly for so many years. Even then, Zanetta did not visit her bereaved children, the youngest of whom, Gaetano, was still only nine. Instead, a month after her mother's death she wrote to her priest and protector, Alvise Grimani, asking him to sell off the family house in the Calle della Commedia on her behalf, along with all its contents. With the money the sale raised, Grimani was to settle the children separately in respectable boarding houses in the city. Seventeen-year-old Giacomo was outraged by the thought of losing his home. 'When I learned that I would no longer have a house at the end of the year, and that all the furniture was to be sold, I no longer stinted myself in my needs,' he later wrote. His anger boiled over into open rebellion: 'I had already sold some linen, tapestries and porcelain; I now made it my business to sell the mirrors and the beds. I knew that people would disapprove, but this was my father's inheritance, upon which my mother had no claim; I regarded myself as the master of the house. As for my brothers, we could discuss it later.'[15]

Casanova's fury towards his mother is evident in every word. If she had a favourite among her children it was clearly not he. Other women would later fall at his feet, but Zanetta had never shown him much affection. Perhaps she now sensed her eldest son's anger or felt guilty for her lack of maternal feeling, for from the safe distance of Dresden she used her influence to procure him a good position in the Church. Bernardo de Bernardis, a Calabrian by birth, was a Minimite monk she had met in the city. He had 'great qualities [that] made me think of you every time he honoured me with a visit,' she wrote flatteringly to Giacomo a few months after his grandmother's death. 'I told him, a year ago, that I had a son who was headed for the priesthood, whom I hadn't the means to keep. He replied that my son would become his if I could get the queen to appoint him to a bishopric in his own country.'[16] What Bernardo wanted was the bishopric of the town of Martirano, near Naples, where the Polish monarch's daughter was married to the king. 'Trusting in GOD,' Zanetta's letter continued melodramatically, 'I threw myself at Her Majesty's feet, and I found favour. She wrote to her daughter, and she had him elected by Our Lord the Pope to the bishopric of Martirano. True to his word, he will take you with him the middle of next year . . . He will set you on the road to the highest dignities of the Church. Imagine my comfort when I see you in twenty or thirty years from now a bishop at the least.'[17]

This behind-the-scenes manoeuvring was as near as Zanetta ever got to expressing love for Giacomo, whom she did not see again until 1752 when he was twenty-seven years old and came to visit her in Dresden with his brother Francesco. By then Zanetta had lost her looks, a tragedy for an actress used to playing romantic roles. 'She is around forty years old,' a German critic wrote of her in 1750. 'Her body is stout, tall, her face looks aged in spite of the theatrical perspective. She would have portrayed a villainous woman, a real demon of a woman, more accurately than a lover. She takes the role of Rosaura; for a young romantic lead her voice is too husky.'[18] Aware that she was no longer in her prime, Zanetta

had already tried her hand at writing for the theatre: on 6 November 1748 her *Le Contese di Mestre e Malghera per il Trono*, an operatic parody, had been staged at Warsaw.

In 1756, due to the start of what would become known as the Seven Years War, the Italian Theatre in Dresden closed and Zanetta was temporarily pensioned off with an income of 400 thalers. When the city came under fire, she fled to the safety of Prague with many of her compatriots. Short of money (she did not always receive her pension during the war), she appealed to Giacomo for financial aid. Always generous by nature, he sent her what he could spare. Zanetta may not have been much of a mother to him, but, as he told an acquaintance at the time, 'I do not forget my duty as a good son.'[19]

Whilst most of her colleagues made their ways back to Italy at the close of hostilities, Zanetta returned to Dresden, the city she now thought of as home. Unexpectedly, it was at this later stage in her life that she at last began to enjoy something of a domestic life. Around 1751, her nineteen-year-old daughter Maria had joined her in Dresden. Breaking the promise she had made to her dying husband, Zanetta had allowed the girl to join her on the stage, and in February 1752 the two Casanova women acted together in *Zoroastre*, a French play written by Cahusac and translated into Italian by Giacomo, presumably at Zanetta's instigation (it was his first theatrical work). Maria later married musician Peter August, the court harpsichordist in Dresden, and gave birth to a daughter, Marianne.

Then, in the autumn of 1764, Zanetta's third son Giovanni, who had been living with her intermittently since her arrival in Saxony, returned to Dresden from Rome, where he had been studying painting for five years under the artist Anton Raphael Mengs. He brought with him a Roman wife, Teresa Roland. Giovanni was appointed director of Dresden's Academy of Fine Art that year, and the couple's first son, Carolus Xaverius, was born in Dresden in 1765.

When Giacomo visited Dresden for a second time in 1766,

Zanetta's family was more complete than it had been since she had first left Venice. Only Faustina, Francesco and Gaetano were missing: Faustina had died in infancy; Francesco was following a successful career as a painter of battle scenes in France, where he had become a respected member of the Paris Academy; and Gaetano, her youngest – then thirty-two years old – was pursuing a lacklustre career in the church. Financially, Zanetta was comfortably off, and divided her time between a country house just outside the city and a fourth-floor apartment 'on the great square' in Dresden.

Here Casanova took refuge from the social whirl by renting a second-floor apartment where he holed himself up for several weeks to cure himself of a dose of venereal disease. And here, on 29 November 1776, Zanetta Casanova died. According to the parish records she was sixty-seven years and three months old. Widowed with six children at the age of twenty-six, the beautiful shoemaker's daughter from Venice had achieved many remarkable things during her lifetime, not least a long and successful theatrical career in which she was never out of work. Despite her lack of maternal feeling, she had given birth to a minor artistic and intellectual dynasty: to two successful painters, an actress and a sub-deacon.

And there was Giacomo.

TWO

Virgins of the Veneto

The more innocent a girl is, the more ignorant
she is of the methods and the aim of seduction.
Without her realising it, the attraction of
pleasure entices her, curiosity mingles with it,
and opportunity does the rest.[1]

BETTINA

SIXTEEN-YEAR-OLD Bettina Gozzi sat on her bed in the small
closet adjacent to her father's room in their house in Padua, and
unpacked the parcel that Signora Casanova, the mother of her
brother's favourite pupil, had sent her from Venice. To her
amazement it contained a dozen pairs of fine gloves and five
lengths of black *zendale*, the silky mantilla-like shawls with which
fashionable ladies covered their shoulders and head. With these
magnificent gifts came a message from the actress to the cobbler's
daughter: would Bettina please take better care of Giacomo's hair
from now on, so that he would soon have no need to wear the awful
wig that his grandmother had bought him?

Bettina unfurled one of the *zendale*, threw it over her head, and
examined her reflection in a tiny fragment of looking-glass. Had
these luxurious presents not sweetened Signora Casanova's request
she might well have felt insulted, for she had been caring for the
boy's hair ever since he had come to live with her family in the late
summer of 1734. The signora paid two zecchini a month for
Bettina's parents, Apollonia and Vincenzo Gozzi, to lodge, feed

and clothe Giacomo, and although Bettina herself naturally saw none of this money it was her duty to wash and dress him in the mornings and to put him to bed at night. Giacomo had taken to his schoolmaster's sister on sight without quite knowing why. In time he would discover the reason. As he later wrote, 'It was she who little by little kindled in my heart the first sparks of a passion which would come to dominate my life.'[2]

Elizabetta Maria Gozzi, as Bettina had been baptised in 1720, was a pretty and vivacious sixteen-year-old, lighthearted, clever and full of fun. By rights her parents should have adored her, but instead they criticised her constantly. When the youths of Padua threw her admiring glances, for instance, Vincenzo and Apollonia scolded Bettina for standing too long at the window. And while they were immensely proud of their son Antonio for becoming a priest, a teacher and a doctor of civil and canon law, they took no pleasure at all in the fact that Bettina had learned to read and write. In enlightened circles women's education was a growing issue: in June 1723, Padua's Academy of the Ricovrati had held a public debate entitled 'Should Women Be Admitted to the Study of the Sciences and the Noble Arts?'; and it was rumoured that in 1732 a female professor of philosophy and physics had been appointed at the University of Bologna. But even among the Italian nobility women's education was usually limited to the odd foreign language, sewing, singing, and the art of polite conversation. In peasant homes like the Gozzis', having a literate daughter was something to be feared rather than welcomed.

The Gozzis were a joyless couple. Born into a peasant family, Bettina's mother Apollonia had had a hard life. The Greek sun god after whom she had been named seldom shone on her. The tragic loss of ten out of the twelve children she had borne had taken its toll, and a life of repeated pregnancies, poverty and suffering had turned her sour and old before her time. Her husband Vincenzo was bad-tempered, taciturn and chronically indecisive, particularly on an empty stomach; Apollonia often remarked that he would never have married her had someone not given him a hearty

breakfast on their wedding day. Bent over the wooden lasts in his workshop for hours on end, a hammer in one hand and a mouthful of iron nails clamped between his teeth, the cobbler rarely spoke, even to his wife, unless he was drunk. Alcohol was his only form of relaxation. On Holy Days he disappeared into a tavern with his friends, and when he lurched home at midnight, wailing sentimental songs in a loud, off-tune voice and with his knees buckling under him, he became violent and aggressive, particularly if his wife and daughter attempted to quieten him down.

Such was life in the Gozzi household. Being blessed with a contented nature and a devout, educated brother to whom she was devoted, Bettina made the best of things. Her main pleasure was reading novels which she bought from the pedlars who passed through the city en route from the print-shops of Venice to Spain, Germany and Russia, or on their way south from Leipzig to Rome. During Padua's regular fairs, Bettina would stand for hours in the piazza listening to these chapmen declaim the stories they sold. Back home, she would lose herself in printed tales of noble bandits, sea-faring adventures and romances, chapbooks of which her strictly religious brother disapproved.

If before she received Zanetta Casanova's gifts Bettina had sometimes rushed Giacomo's morning ablutions, she now redoubled her efforts to look after him. Every morning she went upstairs to the large room he shared with her brother, sat on the big bed where teacher and pupil slept side by side, and carefully combed the boy's hair before he got up. Then, as she washed his face, chest and torso she tickled and kissed him tenderly, just like the older sister she felt she was to him. Soon Giacomo's short curls grew so long and luxuriant that he was able to put away his silly wig for good.

The winter descended on Padua in a blanket of icy mist, and 1736 slipped into 1737. When Giacomo had first moved into the Gozzis' house he had been a half-starved nine-year-old. Three years on, his concave chest was swelling, his childish skin growing swarthier and the lightest dusting of down was casting a shadow

over his prominent upper lip. Giacomo was approaching adolescence. His sexual desire was awakening, and it was Bettina who was rousing it. Instead of looking dully at her as she washed him in the mornings he often shied away in embarrassment from her sisterly caresses. Why, she asked knowingly, did he not return her tickles and kisses? Did he have to be so timid with her?

The following autumn Antonio Gozzi took on three new pupils from the nearby district of Feltre. Vincenzo put them up in a downstairs bedroom of the house, while Giacomo, who continued to be the priest's favourite pupil, continued to share his teacher's big bed in the best room upstairs as he had done since he had moved into the house. Now for the first time there were boys of Bettina's age around, among them Candiani, a robust and good-looking fifteen-year-old country lad. Soon Bettina and Candiani's colluding glances and secretive smiles gave Giacomo his first taste of jealousy, an emotion which always brought out the very worst in him – insecurity, vengefulness and anger. He had already lost his mother and grandmother to his brothers and sisters, and now he was losing Bettina to 'an ignorant, coarse, witless, uneducated farmer's son, unable to match me in anything, whose sole advantage over me was in having reached the age of puberty'.[3] Furious that Bettina could consider him second-best to a stupid yokel, Giacomo pushed her away when she came to dress him. When she gently suggested that he was jealous of Candiani, he retorted that he thought the farmer's son as worthy of her as she was of him.

Amused and perhaps flattered by her charge's jealousy, Bettina hatched a dangerous plan to tease him. One morning she turned up in his bedroom bearing a pair of white stockings that she had knitted for him herself, and insisted on helping him to try them on. When she pulled them up Giacomo's legs she suddenly remarked that his thighs were dirty and, without asking his permission, dipped her sponge into a bowl of warm water and began to wash his loins clean. Higher, higher Bettina washed, with a mixture of curiosity and daring, right to the very top of his legs and under his nightshirt. What happened next shocked both of them: Giacomo

had an erection. 'Seated on my bed Bettina pushed her zeal for cleanliness too far,' he reminisced in his memoirs, 'and her curiosity aroused such a voluptuous feeling in me that it only stopped when it was impossible for it to become greater. When I had calmed down I felt like a criminal, and I believed I had to ask for her forgiveness. Bettina, who had not expected that at all, thought for a while and then told me in an indulgent tone that the fault was all hers, but that it would never happen again.'[4]

The sexual pleasure he had experienced had overwhelmed Giacomo. He was in love for the first time in his life. But to his chagrin Bettina kept away from his bedroom from then on. Deciding that this must be because she loved him back, the twelve-year-old suffered paroxysms of remorse at having committed 'the most heinous of crimes' in front of her. Concluding that the only way to make up for it was to marry her, he wrote her a letter declaring his feelings. One of his first literary works, he considered it 'a masterpiece, more than enough to make her adore me and give me preference over Candiani'.[5] He simply could not understand why Bettina failed to respond to it.

The rivalry between Giacomo and Candiani came to a farcical head one winter's evening when Antonio and Vincenzo were called away overnight. Desperate to talk to Bettina in private, Giacomo asked her meaningfully to come to his room after everyone else had gone to bed. When she failed to turn up he presumed that she had accidentally fallen asleep and, fearful of waking the guard dog which slept in the hall, he crept barefoot downstairs and sat on a step a few paces away from her locked bedroom door, impatiently waiting for her to wake up and let him in. It was snowing, the hall was freezing, and his limbs soon turned to marble. As the hours passed, Giacomo's temper grew as hot as his body grew cold. When, at dawn, he heard the bolt on Bettina's bedroom drawn back, he staggered forward expecting to fall into her welcoming arms at last. However it was not Bettina who came rushing out of the room but his enemy, Candiani. And when the youth saw Giacomo sitting there, he kicked him outside into the snow.

The humiliation and – as Giacomo experienced it – Bettina's betrayal were too much for him. Hungry for revenge, even murder, he attempted to force his way into her bedroom, but she had already bolted the door from the inside. As he kicked at it petulantly the dog began to bark, waking the entire household. Giacomo ran back upstairs before anyone saw him, and as he lay shivering under the covers he thought of ways to avenge himself for having been 'deceived, humiliated, ill-treated, become an object of contempt to the happy and triumphant Candiani'.[6]

Bettina too lay awake, terrified in case Giacomo told anyone what she had been up to. Against the Church's teaching, she had dared to explore her sexuality. If her family found out that Candiani had been in her bedroom all night long her parents would beat her and she would be disgraced in her brother's eyes. Even young Giacomo now despised her. A chaste girl was desirable, pure, and respected by everyone. A sexually active girl, on the other hand, was considered untrustworthy, contemptible and on the road to becoming a harlot. In the words of one anonymous contemporary Englishman, any prospective husband who suspected that his intended was not a virgin should 'discard her with the greatest speed'.[7] 'No charm can supply its place,' advised the writer of *A Letter of Genteel and Moral Advice to a Young Lady*, published in 1740, on the subject of virginity. 'Without it, beauty is unlovely, wit is mean and wanton, quality contemptible, and good breeding worthless. She who forfeits her chastity, withers by degrees into scorn and contrition.'[8] In Catholic countries, where the most revered woman was the Blessed Virgin Mary, virginity had an almost mystical quality. So-called Virgin's Milk, derived from chalky stone from the Bethlehem grotto where the Virgin Mary was said to have breast-fed baby Jesus, was believed to heal wounds, help lactating mothers, and reduce swellings; its properties were considered so extraordinary that, after the Duchess of Urbino smeared Virgin's Milk all over her body, she announced that she had undergone a 'magical rejuvenation'.[9]

'It is one of the superstitions of the human spirit to have

imagined that virginity could be a virtue,'[10] the Enlightenment philosopher Voltaire wrote at the time Bettina was growing up. However, like female education, this idea was very far from being embraced by Padua's working classes. By daybreak, Bettina's anxiety had sent her into a series of terrifying convulsions which made her whole body arch, and her anxious mother stood by her bed with the servants, attempting to hold her down. When Bettina discovered that an incriminating note Candiani had written to her was missing from one of her pockets (Giacomo had stolen it out of jealousy) her convulsions grew even worse. Professional help was summoned: a midwife who diagnosed hysteria, a condition believed to emanate from the womb; a physician who prescribed a regime of rest and cold baths. Apollonia blamed their old maid, who she believed had cast a spell on her daughter. When Vincenzo and Antonio returned home from their trip, the young priest assembled his religious paraphernalia and attempted to exorcise any devils that might be possessing Bettina, but as he approached her his sister stopped breathing.

Over the next twelve days Bettina stayed in bed, at times lucid, at times delirious, fitfully arching her body and clenching her teeth and hands so tightly that no one could separate them. Two more priests tried to exorcise the devil it was believed had infiltrated her body. The first, Father Prospero da Bolvolenta, a Capuchin monk and the most famous exorcist in Padua, decided to argue theology with her, but when she reasoned better than he did he resorted to beating her with his crucifix. The second, Father Mancia, was a handsome young Dominican with a saintly bearing who was reputed never to have failed in exorcising possessed young women. However, although he sprinkled Bettina with holy water and sat quietly with her for hours on end, he too was unable to force the devil from her soul.

Giacomo watched these bizarre proceedings with a detachment that was exceptional in a boy of his age. In adulthood he would describe his feelings at the time in his polemical work *Confutazione della Storia del Governo Veneto d'Amelot de la Houssaie*. 'I was dying

at the least to ask a lot of questions,' he wrote of Bettina's possession, 'but, being so young, I did not have the right to open my mouth; and then my indiscreet questions might have made people suspect me of incredulity, and I could even have been declared an atheist.' In retrospect the possessed girl's behaviour appeared sexual in nature: 'I observed in Elizabetta a great passion for men when the demons tormented her; and I noted that when the demons attacked her throat she indulged in lewdness and indecent contortions.'[11]

Giacomo was secretly convinced that Bettina was putting on an act to draw attention away from her night with Candiani. Perversely, this made her go up in his estimation: since she had the wit to fake a possession in order to escape the consequences of her actions, he felt he could no longer despise her. Bettina had turned herself into one of the heroines of the chapbooks she devoured with such relish: 'This girl seemed more astonishing to me than those who had been presented as marvels in the novels I had read,'[12] Casanova wrote.

As everyone realised a few days later, Bettina really was ill, and dangerously so. For the past twelve days – almost the entire period of her so-called possession – smallpox, the virulent and disfiguring disease which had claimed the life of Giacomo's sister Faustina a few years earlier, had been incubating in her body. Now it broke out in a terrible rash. While Candiani and his fellow-pupils were immediately exiled to a neighbour's house, Giacomo was allowed to remain at home with Apollonia and the patient; presumably he was thought to be immune to the disease, perhaps because he had contracted a mild form of it during his childhood. At Bettina's bedside he developed a life-long passion for medicine, and noted her symptoms with a physician's clinical detachment. Her lovely face, her torso, her legs, her throat, her mouth, even her scalp were soon covered in huge red blisters. Her eyes closed, her body and face all but disappeared under the rash, she smelled of a foul sweat and the only movement Giacomo could discern was the painful rise and fall of her chest.

On the ninth day of Bettina's sickness, Apollonia called the priest and watched as her only daughter received absolution. On the tenth and eleventh days it was feared that she might die at any moment. 'All her rotting pustules had turned black and suppurating, poisoning the air,' Giacomo noted. 'No one could bear it except myself, who was desolate at the poor creature's state. It was in this appalling condition that she inspired in me all the tenderness which I showed towards her after her recovery.'[13] When, on the thirteenth day, Bettina's pustules began to itch violently, Giacomo repeatedly warned her not to scratch them, telling her that if she did she would become so ugly that no one would ever love her again. 'I defy all the physicians in the universe to find a more effective deterrent than this against itching for a girl who knows that she has been beautiful and who realises the risk she runs of becoming ugly if she scratches herself,' he later wrote.[14]

Bettina was kept in bed until Easter, and although the red marks left by her blisters did not fade for a year, thanks to Casanova she miraculously escaped the terrible scarring and pitting which was the usual legacy of smallpox. Giacomo's steadfast support – and the few pox marks on his own face, which he contracted despite his relative immunity – earned him more than her gratitude. From now on, despite the difference in their ages, Bettina loved him 'without feigning, and I loved her without ever seizing a flower which destiny, aided by prejudice, had reserved for her marriage bed'[15] – that is supposing that Candiani had not already seized it.

TERESA

Casanova's feelings for Bettina gave him his first taste of the joys and pains of the romantic life. She made him feel loved but, at the same time, put him through agonies of jealousy. She showed him the importance of persisting when one was rejected, and also gave him his first glimpse of women's wiles. Still having what he termed a kind of virginity himself, Casanova learned through her to love, honour and revere virgins – so much so that in the future he would want to deflower as many as he could.

In the spring of 1739 Casanova was fourteen years old. Although he had outgrown his teacher's schoolroom, he still continued to lodge with the Gozzi family in Padua, where he was now enrolled at the city's ancient university studying for a degree in ecclesiastical law; a career in the Church was often pursued by the impecunious younger sons of the aristocracy, and it was one of the few respectable options open to a boy such as Casanova who, thanks to his mother, had by now been educated far beyond his working-class roots. The Bo' or Boeuf, as Padua University was nicknamed after a nearby inn, had once had a reputation for high standards, but it was now a rather ailing institution. 'Today when universities have declined it is the case of this one still more than others,' Charles de Brosses, writer, philosopher and President of the Parliament of Dijon, wrote of it that year. 'The students, [once] so impressive in number and strength, are now few, and most of the time the professors lecture to empty benches.'[16] Instead of studying, the Bo's students ran wild in the town, gambling, brawling and generally disturbing the peace. They seduced the virgin daughters of respectable families, frequented prostitutes and kept the town awake with their late-night antics. Protected by a bevy of historic privileges, they rarely suffered any consequences for their actions, even when they broke the law, for if the *sbirri*, as the local constables were called, dared to intervene when they caused trouble the students hunted them down and threatened them with pistols.

Casanova experienced his first taste of freedom among these students and soon fell in with a bad crowd, most of them older and from wealthier backgrounds. In order not to lose face he spent money he did not have and joined in many of their japes, including gambling and frequenting brothels; but his continuing relationship with Bettina, which had by now reached the petting stage, made him stop short of having sex with a prostitute. Even though his lodgings were still being paid for by his mother, his extra-curricular activities soon caused him to run up so many debts that he had to sell off all his possessions in order to clear them; and when he ran

out of things to sell, he wrote to his grandmother, asking her for more money. Instead of bailing him out of trouble Marcia arrived unannounced in Padua to see for herself what was going on, just as she had years earlier when Giacomo had appealed for her help from Signora Mida's house. This time the only person her grandson needed rescuing from was himself. Shocked that he had run into debt at such a young age, she immediately pulled him out of the university and took him back to Venice with her. Time would show that, in the long term, he learned nothing from this lesson. For as his beloved teacher Dr Gozzi bade an emotional farewell to the boy he had nurtured for the last five and a half years, he handed Casanova his most treasured possession: the relic of a saint which hung on a chain around his neck. When he was writing his memoirs Casanova admitted that he would still possess the relic 'had it not been set in gold. The miracle it performed was to get me out of trouble in a time of urgent need.' Ironically, he had eventually sold it to pay off more debts.

Back in Venice, Marcia found Casanova a teacher of poetry and pure Italian, a language which was considered more refined than the local Venetian dialect. As she took him around the city, she introduced him to everyone she met with the proud words, *He's just come from Padua, where he's been studying.* The heads of families shook Casanova's hand solemnly, elderly ladies embraced him, and those who were not old pretended to be so in order to be able to kiss him with propriety, for by now he had grown into a tall, extremely handsome youth. Though his heart was set on becoming a physician – a profession in which 'charlatanism is more effective than in the work of a lawyer'[17] as he had observed cynically at Bettina's bedside – Marcia was adamant that he should follow the ecclesiastical career he had been studying for. On 14 February 1740, shortly before his fifteenth birthday, Casanova was formally inducted into the Roman Catholic Church by Giovanni Tosello, the priest at the local parish church of San Samuele; and eleven months later the Patriarch of Venice conferred minor orders on him; these were the first two steps, towards his becoming a fully-fledged priest.

Anxious that his protégé the young novice abbot or *abate* should meet the kind of people who could help him, Tosello introduced Casanova to an important and well-connected senator who lived just across the square from the church. Seventy-six-year-old bachelor Alvise Malipiero II was the head of a patrician family whose name had been inscribed in the famous Libro d'Oro, or Golden Book, of Venetian nobility since 1297. Once, like his ancestors, he had been an active member of the Republic's ruling senate, but by now, due to his advanced age and chronic ill-health, he had lost interest in affairs of state and retired from his civic duties. Malipiero remained extremely sociable, however, and despite regular and severe attacks of gout that left him crippled in every limb he still held court every night to the cream of Venetian society in his vast salon on the *piano nobile* of his Byzantine palazzo on the Grand Canal. No one who saw the senator seated behind his long table talking animatedly to his guests would have guessed that he was in such permanent pain that he could scarcely move. His eyes shone with intelligence and good humour and he relished good company, witty conversation, gossip and, above all, fascinating women. Although he had never married, Malipiero often boasted that he had taken twenty mistresses during his lifetime, and claimed that he had only stopped at that number when he had realised the futility of trying to please yet another one.

Soon Casanova became Malipiero's daily companion, and his unlikely confidant. He spent every day talking with him, often alone; and at night he was allowed to attend his receptions, where he was by far the youngest person present. Instructed by the senator never to speak unless directly spoken to, nor to express any opinions of his own (for at his age he was too young to have any), Casanova quickly became the favourite pet of Malipiero's sophisticated female friends, who trusted him so implicitly that they even let him enter their homes unannounced and mingle with their well-protected unmarried daughters. Instead of steering the young priest down a path suitable for one destined to take a vow of chastity, as Tosello had hoped, the senator was inadvertently

leading him into a life of temptation. In Padua Giacomo had mixed in a predominantly male society. In the sexually liberated circles of the Serenissima, beautiful married women and pretty virgins surrounded him day and night.

Of all the young women he met through Malipiero, the greatest temptress of all was Teresa, the daughter of Giuseppe Imer, the actor/manager of the San Samuele theatre and Zanetta Casanova's erstwhile lover. The Imer family lived around the corner from the Casanovas in the Corte del Duca Sforza, a small paved courtyard situated midway between the senator's palazzo and the theatre where Teresa and her older sister Marianna were both destined to begin their singing careers. Like her short, stout father, the youngest Imer was no great beauty. However, she was pretty, curvaceous and remarkably sexually alluring, and her strong nose and thick, arched eyebrows lent her face an amused, coquettish expression which was enhanced by an outspoken manner and a feisty character. Men found Teresa irresistibly attractive. Well aware of this, she already knew how to get what she wanted from them whilst giving little to nothing in return.

Teresa's mother, Paolina, was the kind of grasping thespian whom Marcia Farussi despised; without doubt it was she who instructed Teresa on how to use her feminine wiles. She was determined to find a rich man to finance the girl's singing career and, since one of their neighbours was a rich, elderly bachelor susceptible to pretty women, she did not need to look far. The back of the Imers' terraced house overlooked the large back garden of Malipiero's palazzo and was situated directly opposite his bedroom window. In her eighteenth year Teresa Imer was frequently to be seen pouting at *her* window – far too frequently for her presence there to be a matter of chance. Malipiero's interest was quickly aroused by her provocative appearance, and they struck up a friendship. Along with Casanova, the Imer women became daily visitors to the palace, where Teresa flaunted her charms and flirted shamelessly with the old man, while at the same time managing to keep him at arm's length.

Old and crippled as he was, Malipiero soon grew obsessed with making Teresa his mistress. Although he was delighted to see her when she arrived with her mother, by the time they left he was always in a rage. He allowed only one other person to be present at their meetings: the novice *abate* Casanova who, as he recorded in his memoirs, was amazed by Teresa's flirtatious behaviour: 'She came to visit him nearly every day, but always accompanied by her mother, an old actress who had retired from the theatre for the good of her soul and who, as one might have expected, had formed a project to unite GOD with the devil. She took her daughter to Mass every day, she demanded that she take confession every Sunday; but in the afternoon she took her up to see the amorous old man, whose anger astonished me when the girl refused to kiss him on the grounds that, having made her devotions in the morning, she could not condescend to offend the same GOD whom she had eaten and might still have in her stomach. What a sight for me then aged fifteen, the only one who the old man allowed to be a silent witness to these scenes! The villainous mother applauded the resistance of her daughter, and dared to lecture the voluptuary, who in his turn dared not refute her maxims which were either too Christian or not at all so, and he had to resist the temptation of hurling anything he could lay his hands on at her. He didn't know what to say to her. His lust turned to anger; and after they left he calmed himself down by having philosophical talks with me.'[18]

It seemed inconceivable to Malipiero that Teresa would not allow him to take even the slightest liberty, never mind relinquish her precious virginity to him – that is, if he had the physical ability to claim it. He was wealthy, noble, generous and well-connected, while she came from the kind of milieu where to offer sex to one's patron was *de rigueur*. And yet, despite being urged on by her mother, the young soprano resisted Malipiero's every advance. Though he attempted to bribe her to become his mistress she insisted that her maidenhead was not for sale at any price; and when, out of desperation, he offered to marry her, she turned him

down, very properly saying that she did not wish to earn the hatred of his relatives, whose name would have been struck from Venice's Golden Book of patrician families if the senator had married a commoner; though sexually liberated, Venetian society was still rigidly divided when it came to class and birth. Frustrated beyond endurance, the senator turned to fifteen-year-old Casanova for some distinctly non-clerical advice on how to seduce Teresa:

'Offer her a huge sum of money, a settlement.'

'From what she says she wouldn't commit a mortal sin to become queen of the world.'

'You'll either have to rape her or throw her out and ban her from coming here.'

'I'm not capable of doing the former, and I can't bring myself to do the latter.'

'Kill her.'

'That might happen if I don't die first.'

'Your Excellency is to be pitied.'

'Do you ever go to her place?'

'No, for I could fall in love with her; and if she behaved towards me as I see her do here, I'd become unhappy.'

'You are right.'[19]

Malipiero was eager to nip in the bud any possible relationship between Teresa and Casanova. Since they were thrown together every day, she was an obvious temptation to the youth, and for her part the handsome young novice was a much more enticing prospect than the withered septuagenarian who was forever trying to talk her into bed. They shared a similar family background in the twilight world of the Venetian theatre where their parents' lives had once been all too intimately intertwined; and given their similarly adventurous spirits, their good looks, their amorous natures and the amount of time they spent together, it was almost inevitable that they would eventually be attracted to one another. The opportunity for them to show their feelings for each other was

not to come quite yet, and when it did it had explosive consequences for Casanova. Left alone in the salon with Teresa one
afternoon while the senator took a siesta, Casanova began to play a
dangerous game with her. 'Being seated close to one another at a
small table,' he wrote, 'our backs turned towards the door of the
bedroom where we supposed our benefactor was asleep, in the
innocent gaiety of our natures we were overcome with the desire to
explore the differences between our bodies.' They were so carried
away that they did not notice the furious Malipiero hobble back
into the room with the aid of his walking-stick: 'We were at the
most interesting part of our examination when a violent blow from
a cane fell on my neck, followed by another, which would have
been followed by more if I hadn't very rapidly escaped from the
hail by making for the door.'[20] This was the last Malipiero saw of
Casanova, whom he banned from his palazzo from then on; but the
senator was so much in Teresa's thrall that he never reproached her
about what had happened.

All this would take place a year in the future. In the meantime,
there were plenty of women other than Teresa to distract the
sexually charged novice priest from his prayers and studies, for the
famous beauties of Venice, with their penchant for the game of
love, were to be found in every corner of the city and, as in the
future, women took to him at first sight. 'So many fine acquaintances with women of the world, as they are called, gave me the
desire to please by the way I presented myself and the elegance of
my dress,'[21] Casanova later admitted. By the tail-end of 1741, he
had grown obsessed with his appearance. He swaggered around the
city in his clerical garb with his face lightly powdered, and his thin
gangly body plastered with jasmine-scented pomade. Even though
the top of his head had been shaved by Tosello when he took the
tonsure, the famous curls once so lovingly tended by Bettina Gozzi
had grown thick and long again, contravening an ancient ecume-
nical edict often cited by his worried priest that *Clericus qui nutrit
comam anathema* – a cleric who grows his hair shall be anathema.
Afraid that his self-love was out of control, the ever-anxious Marcia

let Tosello into his bedroom early one morning while Casanova lay sleeping, and allowed him to cut off all his front curls. When her grandson woke up he was furious, particularly when Francesco, his younger brother, laughed at him ('He was jealous of me all his life,' he wrote of Francesco, 'nevertheless combining envy with fondness, I'm not sure how.') Casanova plotted revenge on Tosello, but calmed down somewhat when Malipiero sent him a fashionable hairdresser who restyled his cropped hair and made him look even more handsome than before.

The proof of this came when, appealing to Casanova's vanity, Malipiero suggested that he should write and deliver the panegyric at the church of San Samuele on 26 December; in the senator's capacity as president of the Confraternity of the Blessed Sacrament, a charitable organisation of laymen, the sermon lay in his gift. Casanova had never thought of becoming a preacher before, but suddenly he had full confidence in his own ability to write and deliver a sermon that would astonish everyone. The occasion restored an uneasy peace between the priest and his novice, for Casanova's first sermon was indeed brilliant. The church received fifty gold sequins in offerings from the impressed patrician audience who had been invited to hear it, Marcia wept with joy, and Casanova's considerable ego was further inflated not only by the praise that was heaped upon him but also by the number of love-letters that the female congregants slipped into the offerings bag along with their coins.

He did not bother to reply to any of them, for by now Casanova was in love for a second time. While rehearsing his sermon at Tosello's house he had met a young girl, Angela Cattarina Tosello, who would exercise an irresistible attraction over him for the next year.

ANGELA AND LUCIA

Angela Cattarina Tosello was the daughter of the priest's brother, painter Iseppo Tosello. Two months younger than Casanova, she was an honest, beautiful girl who had heard the dramatic story of

his haircut from her uncle's lips, and, when Casanova came to the house, insisted on hearing it again from his. Casanova soon became as obsessed with Angela as Senator Malipiero was with Teresa Imer. In order to have a valid excuse to see her, he announced his intention of becoming a full-time preacher and roped in her uncle to help him. On his frequent visits to the Tosello household, ostensibly to discuss the subject of writing sermons, Casanova wooed Angela with all the charm he could muster. But whilst she was happy to encourage him to love her, and even promised to marry him if he gave up the Church, she proved a perfect dragon of virtue. None of Casanova's emotive arguments had the slightest effect on her. Angela was adamant that she was going to save her virginity, and all her other sexual favours, for her marriage bed.

By the following summer Casanova was still pestering Angela like a wasp hovering around a sealed honey pot. It was no use. 'Her meanness in granting me favours irritated me; and my love had already become a torment,' he wrote. 'With my strong instinct I needed a girl more like Bettina, one who enjoyed appeasing the flame of love without snuffing it out.' He began to lose weight out of sheer sexual frustration. Angela was, he claimed, 'drying me up. The pathetic, plaintive speeches I made to her over the embroidery frame at which she worked with two sisters, friends of hers, had more effect on them than they did on her heart, which was too enslaved by the maxim that was poisoning me. If I had not only had eyes for her I would have realised that the two sisters were more attractive than she was; but she had made me stubborn.'[22] Convinced that he would lose interest if she gave in to him, Angela clung on to her principles in the face of Casanova's emotional blackmail. When she insisted that her self-enforced abstinence was as difficult for her as it was for him, he grew even more annoyed with her, and turned his attentions to a country bumpkin, whose downfall he unwittingly caused.

It was the custom of the patrician classes to leave Venice in the hot summer months when the sewage-polluted canals smelled to high heaven and the mosquitoes were at their most vicious, and to

take refuge in their country villas on the cooler mainland, where they enjoyed an idyllic rural lifestyle. Boating parties, afternoon *trottatas* in carriages around the shady countryside, and balls, picnics and dinners galore were all conducted with the kind of lighthearted informality that would have been unacceptable in town.

One of Malipiero's female friends, the Countess of Montereale, owned a large estate at Pasiano in Friuli, where she spent every summer along with her daughter and a large retinue of guests. In September 1740 she invited Casanova to join her there for a few weeks, and she allotted him a bedroom on the ground floor of the villa, next to that occupied by her caretaker's daughter, who was to wait on him. The girl, Lucia, was fourteen years old, an innocent uneducated country lass with an all-too-trusting and generous nature. Childish almost to the point of being simple-minded, as her parents' only child she was 'their darling, the consolation of their old age'. She was obedient, devout and healthy, these good people told Casanova; in fact, her only fault was that she was 'too young' – a subtle warning to their employers' teenage houseguest to respect her honour. They had good reason to warn him off, because physically Lucia was as mature as many seventeen-year-olds. Her skin was fashionably but naturally pale, her eyes were smoulderingly dark, her breasts were 'two rocks made to shipwreck the most experienced of pilots'[23] and she wore her long black hair pinned up in an untidy style that was uniquely hers. So unconscious was Lucia of the power of her beauty that she walked about in a state of semi-undress: Casanova's first view of her was when she appeared barefooted in his bedroom early one morning clad only in a skimpy chemise. Far from being embarrassed by the situation, Lucia looked at the young priest as serenely as if he had been an old friend, unaware that her appearance had put him into a state of violent sexual excitement and wiped all thoughts of Angela, Teresa and even Bettina from his mind.

Casanova found it inconceivable that any well-brought-up young girl, 'virtuous and not at all stupid',[24] could behave as freely as Lucia did and still be strait-laced enough to repulse him. He was

certainly not the first man to take an interest in her: the countess's elderly husband had made so many advances towards her that Lucia now ran away whenever she saw him approaching. By contrast with this archetypal lewd old man who was fond of making rude jokes at her expense, the young *abate* was somehow safe, 'well-behaved, and what's more a priest', as Lucia put it when, determined to find out whether or not she would be open to his advances, Casanova managed to entice her under his bedcovers on the second morning of his stay in Pasiano. Her uninhibited response to him, he concluded, was entirely innocent in nature. 'Her naïvety, her vivacity, her curiosity, her frequent blushes when she guile-lessly said things that made me laugh, everything convinced me that she was an angel incarnate who could not fail to fall victim to the first libertine who should take her in hand. I was certain that it would not be me.'[25] It was self-esteem rather than disinterested respect for Lucia that made Casanova determined not even to attempt to lose his own innocence with her; for he did not wish to be shown up in front of his wealthy friends as the kind of man who would betray Lucia's parents' confidence.

What did Lucia think of the young priest who asked her into his bed every morning, chatted with her for three hours without so much as holding her hand, and then disappeared off to spend his days entertaining her parents' wealthy employers with his witty repartee? Did she suspect that during their time together he was torturing himself with desire or that, night after night, he resorted to what he called 'the schoolboys' remedy' and masturbated with her image in his mind? When, at the end of twelve days, Casanova warned Lucia to stay away from him in future for her own good, she made a fatal error very common among women who were new to the game of love: she mistook his lust for love. She was in love with him too, she declared, but instead of making her miserable, as it did him, love made her happy. Could it be that Casanova was not born to love women? Begging him to think of some plan, and touchingly telling him to 'Trust in Lucia', the caretaker's daughter fell into his arms.

If threatening never to see her again had been a tactic designed to seduce her it could not have been more successful. From now on, Lucia spent the early hours of every morning, the late evening hours, and often all night, in bed with Casanova, and she swore that she would love him for ever. Angela had refused him everything; too generous for her own good, Lucia refused him nothing. Although their sexual relationship stopped short of actual pene-tration – or so Casanova later insisted – by the time he left Pasiano at the end of the month, her virginity, if it still existed, was a nebulous technicality.

His feelings for Lucia lasted until the moment he returned to Venice and saw Angela again. Intent on obtaining the clearly unobtainable – a trait that would continue throughout Casanova's adult life – he visited the recalcitrant virgin every day at the embroidery school where she was now studying, but she still resisted him. Instructed by her uncle the priest not to spend so much time at the school, Casanova enlisted her fellow-students and close friends, Nanetta and Marta Savorgnan, to help him towards his goal.

NANETTA AND MARTA

The noble-born Savorgnan sisters were in every way delightful girls. Nanetta, the older at sixteen, was clever, quick-thinking, adven-turous, literate and well-read. Her sister Marta, who was just one year younger, was quieter and perhaps less intelligent, but she had a gentle, artless nature which made her happy to follow her sister's lead. Both girls, whilst entirely inexperienced, were bursting with sexual curiosity. They simply could not understand why their good friend Angela persisted in repelling her gorgeous admirer, parti-cularly when she had already confessed to them that she liked him; when she stayed overnight with them and shared their large bed, she even made Marta play the part of her 'dear *abate*' in their kissing games.

The patrician Savorgnans had long-established links to the Far-ussi family: Tribune Savorgnan had been Zanetta's godfather,[26] and

the actress and her husband had rented their house on the Calle della Commedia from one of his relatives. By the time when Casanova met Nanetta and Marta their mother was dead, and the girls were living in a large but dilapidated palazzo with their aunt, Caterina Orio, a noble lady who had fallen on hard times. Dependent on a small pension from her brother, the secretary of Venice's ruling Council of Ten, Signora Orio coveted one of the grants handed out to needy windows by the charitable Confraternity of the Blessed Sacrament (the recipients' names were selected by lot twice a year) but she lacked an influential person to put her name forward for the draw.

When Casanova asked Nanetta and Marta to intervene with Angela on his behalf, the sisters threw themselves into the task with the gusto of professional matchmakers. Compared to their fun-loving, mischievous natures, prim Angela soon seemed rather dull. As Nanetta's first letter to Casanova made clear (she smuggled it to him at the embroidery school), the intrigue was to be delightfully complicated and risky and involve all sorts of subterfuge, and *she* was to organise everything. Since there was nothing in the world that she was not prepared to do for Angela, she wrote, she had devised a plan that would benefit all of them. Casanova's first task was to get into their aunt's good books by recommending to Senator Malipiero that her name be entered into the lottery for a grant from the Confraternity of the Blessed Sacrament, of which he was president.

'Last Sunday Angela told her that you enjoy this gentleman's affection,' Nanetta wrote, 'and that the best means of gaining his support would be by committing you to ask him for it. She foolishly told her that you're in love with me, that you only go to the embroidery school so that you can speak to me, and that consequently I would be able to engage your interest on her behalf. My aunt answered that since you were a priest there was nothing to fear, and that I could write and invite you to her house; but I refused. The lawyer Rosa, who's my aunt's soul-mate, said that I was in the right, and that it wasn't proper for me to write to you;

but that she herself must ask you to come and see her on an important matter. He said that if it was true that you liked me you wouldn't fail to turn up, and he persuaded her to write you the note that you'll find when you get home. If you want to find Angela at our house, don't come until the day after tomorrow, Sunday. If you can obtain the favour that my aunt desires from Signor Malipiero you'll become the pet of our house. Forgive me if I treat you badly when you come, for I told them that I didn't like you. You'd do well to flirt with my aunt, even though she's sixty years old. Signor Rosa will not be jealous, and you'll endear yourself to everyone here. I'll arrange things so that you can speak to Angela alone. I'll do everything to convince you of my friendship. Farewell.'[27]

Nanetta's plan ran like the mechanism of a well-oiled clock. Casanova visited the palazzo, and Signora Orio handed him her application for the Blessed Sacrament's grant. Since he had less influence over Malipiero than Teresa Imer did, Casanova decided to enlist her help. Tracking Teresa down at her parents' home, he found her in her bedroom with another of her admirers, a local doctor named Leonardo Doro. Though they were both fully dressed, the situation was compromising enough for Teresa and Doro to be flustered, particularly since the jealous senator had made the young soprano promise never to receive the doctor alone. All this was very much to Casanova's advantage. Once Doro had hurriedly left, he told Teresa what he wanted from her and, at the same time, delicately assured her of his discretion. In return, she promised that she would present Signora Orio's case to the senator.

Two days later, Teresa handed Signora Orio's application back to Casanova, endorsed by Malipiero. Casanova duly returned it to Signora Orio on the next feast day, when Angela was due to stay overnight with her girlfriends. The moment Casanova arrived at her aunt's house, Nanetta slipped him another note and told him to read it before he left. Since an urgent need to relieve himself was the only excuse he could think of to be alone, he took it to the water closet. 'My aunt will beg you to stay for supper, but you'll

decline,' the breathless note instructed him. 'You'll leave when we sit down to eat, and Marta will light you as far as the street door, which she'll open; but you won't go out. She'll shut it and come back up. Everyone will believe that you have left the house. You'll go back up the staircase in the dark, and then up two other flights to the third floor. The steps are good. You'll wait for all three of us there. We'll come up after Signor Rosa has left, and after we've put our aunt to bed. It will rest with Angela to grant you the private interview that you desire, even all night long, and I hope it makes you very happy.'[28]

After pretending to leave the house later that evening, Casanova crept upstairs and waited excitedly for the girls to join him. At last all three of them appeared carrying a single candle. Nanetta and Marta sat quietly in a corner, while Casanova sat close to Angela, anticipating the pleasures that he presumed lay ahead of him during the next few hours. But while he talked endlessly to her of his love, she repulsed his roving hands 'with the most disagreeable gentleness'. He grew impatient. When the candle burned out, plunging the room into total darkness, he reached out to grab Angela, only to find that she had slipped away. Though he spent the next hour doing his best to coax her back, she only giggled at him through the darkness. After a while Casanova's disembodied voice began to sound aggressive – anger was often his reaction whenever his powers of persuasion failed to work on a woman – and he declared that he would play Blind Man's Buff until he found her. As he stumbled around the pitch-black room, his groping hands stretched out in front of him, Marta and Nanetta threw themselves into his path with joyful relish, but Angela remained out of harm's way.

It was all good, childish fun until an hour before dawn when Casanova's mood suddenly changed. Desperate to get somewhere with Angela before he had to leave, he ignored the sisters and unleashed the full fury of his frustration on Angela. First he pleaded with her. Then he nagged her. Then he begged her to give in, prayed and even wept. When none of these ploys produced the

result he wanted – Angela's willing body in his arms – Casanova resorted to a stream of verbal abuse: 'I showered on her all the insults that scorned love suggests to a furious mind. I hurled fanatical curses at her; I swore to her that all my love had changed into hate, and ended by warning her to keep away from me, for I would certainly kill her the moment I saw her.'[29] The three girls were terrified. As the dawn light gradually seeped through the shuttered windows, bleaching the darkness into a dismal grey light, they dissolved into tears – as did Casanova, who suddenly realised how shamefully he had behaved. As soon as they heard Signora Orio go off to Mass, Nanetta rose to her feet and told him to leave immediately.

This was the last the three girls would see of Angela's temperamental suitor for eight weeks: anxious to avoid them, he immediately left Venice for Padua, where, to his consternation, he found out that Bettina Gozzi was engaged to be married to an unprepossessing cobbler named Annibale Pigozzo. While he was away from Venice, Angela was plagued with doubts about how she herself had behaved, and the Savorgnan sisters and their aunt missed his visits to their house. When he returned after a few months' absence Signora Orio immediately invited him over, and Marta and Nanetta received him with such obvious pleasure that it dispelled Casanova's sense of shame. As in the past, Nanetta was well-prepared for intrigue, and slipped two letters into his hands. One was from Angela, who promised that if he had the courage to spend the night with her again he would not leave disappointed; she loved him, and wished to know 'from your own lips, if you would have continued to love me if I had consented to dishonour myself'. The second letter was from Nanetta who, in her role as go-between, wanted him to know that Angela was in despair over losing him: 'If you still love her, I advise you to run the risk of another night. Maybe she can justify her behaviour, and you'll end up happy. So do come.'[30]

The temptation was too great. After spending an evening at Signora Orio's, Casanova secretly made his way upstairs to the

sisters' bedroom again. But either Angela had failed to turn up that night or she had deliberately not been invited, and Nanetta suggested that Casanova make do with Marta and herself. Almost as if they had been expecting this to happen, they produced Parmesan cheese and bread to add to the wine and meat which their visitor had brought with him, and the three of them picnicked in the bedroom. Slightly tipsy and full of gaiety, they pledged the eternal friendship of siblings, but their innocent embraces soon turned distinctly lustful, and Casanova suddenly realised that the two sisters eclipsed their absent friend Angela in every way.

Guilty at having Casanova to themselves, Nanetta and Marta spent the next hour talking non-stop about Angela. After that, they decided that it was time to go to bed. Casanova sensed that victory was in the offing. Aware that he had to act with great caution if he was not to ruin his chances with both girls, he proceeded slowly and carefully towards his goal. Insisting that he only felt an innocent brotherly love for them, he refused to let them sleep on the sofa in another room as they wanted to, and suggested that all three of them share the same big bed. Next, since he would never be able to sleep if he kept his clothes on, he told them that he was going to undress. If the sisters trusted him – and he would feel insulted if they did not – they must do the same and count on his word of honour that he would not lay a finger on them. Nanetta and Marta conferred with each other for a few minutes and then agreed. Before they could change their minds, Casanova ripped off his clothes, climbed into the middle of their bed, and either fell asleep or pretended to.

By the time he opened his eyes again the candle had been snuffed out, the room was in total darkness and the sisters, dressed only in their loose linen chemises, lay curled up on either side of him, both apparently asleep. His word of honour that he would not molest them, which he had given only minutes earlier, suddenly counted for nothing. He reached out and touched one of them; unknown to him, it was Marta. As she felt his hand slide up her body, she was as overcome with curiosity as he was, and, still pretending to be

asleep, she allowed him to continue his exploration. 'Little by little I spread her out,' Casanova later wrote of this seminal moment in both their lives. 'Little by little she unfurled, and little by little by steady, very slow but marvellously natural movements, she assumed the most favourable position for me that she could without betraying herself. I set to work, but to do the thing properly I needed her to join in openly, and nature at last obliged her to do so. I found this first sister beyond suspicion, and not being able to doubt the pain she must have gone through, I was surprised. Duty bound to religiously respect a prejudice to which I owed this pleasure, the sweetness of which I was tasting for the first time in my life, I let the victim alone, and turned on my other side to do the same thing with her sister, who must have been expecting all my gratitude.'[31] Nanetta was also a virgin. After feigning sleep for a while, as Marta had done, she turned towards Casanova and embraced him passionately. Within the space of an hour Casanova's virginity, and that of both Savorgnan sisters, were things of the past.

Angela was furious when her girlfriends admitted to her what had happened. Hurling insults at them, she stormed out of Signora Orio's palazzo, swearing she would never set foot in it again. The sisters had no regrets: when Casanova came to dine two days later they passed him a piece of bread-dough impressed with an imprint of the front door key, and instructed him to get a copy cut so that he could visit them whenever he pleased. From then on the novice priest stole secretly up to their bedroom at least twice a week. His sexual confidence grew along with theirs, and whilst they remained faithful to him he became more daring. Although he was aware how much his 'little wives', as he called them, were risking by sleeping with him, he was not above trying to seduce other women at the same time: once, during a party which was being thrown in the house where he was lodging, he attempted to seduce the hostess while Nanetta, Marta and their aunt were waiting downstairs (his attempt failed miserably when the hostess, a courtesan named Giulietta, boxed him around the ears). And when, after

Easter, the Countess of Montereale invited him back to her country estate in Pasiano, Casanova eagerly rushed there in the expectation of seeing the beautiful Lucia again.

He was to be disappointed. The caretaker and his wife tearfully informed him that their beloved daughter had disappeared. Soon after he had left the previous summer she had been seduced by L'Aigle, one of the Montereales' couriers. Very soon she was pregnant – an unmitigated disaster for any unmarried woman but particularly for an adolescent peasant living in the countryside where there was no access to illegal abortion and where the scrutiny and scathing words of neighbours and friends could not be avoided. When she could no longer hide her pregnancy, Lucia had eloped with her seducer to Trieste. Her parents, whose pride and joy she had once been, were heartbroken, as Casanova guiltily observed. He was overcome with remorse and, until the end of his life, held himself responsible for Lucia's downfall, though perhaps for the wrong reasons: if he had only had fewer scruples about deflowering her, and had left her sexually satisfied, he believed, she might never have been receptive to the courier's advances.

Lucia's life became an unstoppable downhill slide into eventual ruin, for L'Aigle had no intention of marrying her. Instead he forced her into a life of prostitution from which she never escaped. Six months after their child was born he took Lucia to the picturesque island of Zante, a Venetian possession some eight miles south of Cephalonia in the Ionian Sea. Once they were there, L'Aigle enlisted in the navy and fled, leaving Lucia to fend for herself and their child. About nine or ten years later she managed to get to England, where she presumably joined the tens of thousands of poverty-stricken prostitutes who led a gruelling existence on London's streets. Later she moved to Holland, where she added a smattering of Dutch to the Greek, English and French she had picked up on her long and arduous journey from the Friulian countryside.

In the early weeks of 1760, around nineteen years after he had first met her in Pasiano, Casanova came across Lucia by chance in a

low-class dance-hall-cum-whore-house in Amsterdam. This gloomy *musikhaus* could not have been more depressing, even to a hardened libertine such as himself. It was 'a real cesspit of vice, haunt of the most disgusting debauchery. The very sound of the two or three instruments that made up the orchestra plunged one's soul into sadness. A room stinking of the foul tobacco that was smoked there, and of the stench of garlic from the belches emitted by those who were dancing or seated with bottles or pots of beer on their right side and hideous slatterns on their left, offered up to my eyes and thoughts a desolate reflection of the miseries of life, and the degree of degradation to which brutality could reduce pleasures. The crowd which gave life to the place consisted entirely of sailors and the kind of common people to whom it seemed a paradise which compensated them for all they had suffered on long and tedious journeys.'[32] Prostitutes hung around, each more unattractive than the other, and boorish pimps tried to cajole the customers into dancing with them.

This dreary hell-hole was Lucia's place of work. Eighteen years of the 'accursed trade'[33] had not only crushed the *joie de vivre* out of her, it had made her 'not positively ugly, but something worse: disgusting'.[34] Debauchery and, no doubt, repeated attacks of venereal disease had completely obliterated her natural beauty and vivacity, leaving her with no alternative but to make a living by becoming a pimp herself and procuring customers for younger, prettier girls. When Casanova offered her a drink, she accepted it without even bothering to look up at him, never dreaming that the richly-dressed gentleman had been her first love. He found only a trace in her features of the old Lucia, 'the tender, the pretty, the naïve Lucia, who I had loved so much and spared out of delicacy . . . She was only thirty-two, and I foresaw a terrible future for her.'[35]

On and off, Casanova remained the lover of both Nanetta and Marta Savorgnan for a number of years. Their relative wealth, their patrician birth and their aunt's trusting nature all insulated them

from the kind of dire misfortune that befell poor Lucia. Signora Orio had so much faith both in her nieces and the young *abate* whom she now regarded as a family friend, that on one occasion she even invited Casanova to stay in the palazzo with them, and allowed him to sleep in a bedroom adjoining theirs. In February 1745, on the night before he quit Venice for a long stay in Corfu, Casanova repeatedly made love to both sisters there. The next morning he left them in floods of tears, convinced that they would never see him again.

'This love, which was my first,' he wrote of his relationship with them, 'taught me almost nothing of the ways of the world, for it was perfectly happy, never disrupted by any discord, nor tarnished by the slightest self-interest.'[36] Did they both experience it in the same way? On 2 March 1745, a few days before her father's death, Nanetta married a forty-one-year-old count whom Casanova referred to in his memoirs by the initial R (it has been suggested by one Casanova scholar that the initial stood for Rambaldi). She went to live with him in Guastalla, a city on the River Po in Emiglia-Romagna. Around the same time, her younger sister Marta was confined in one of Venice's convents, in all probability that of Santa Maria degli Angeli on the island of Murano. Being forced to become a nun was a common fate of the unmarried daughters of Venice's noble families, not least because the dowry required to become a bride of Christ was far less than that required to secure a good husband. It was also a convenient way for the nobility to dispose of troublesome daughters. Could Marta possibly have been pregnant with Casanova's child at the time she was banished there? We can only speculate.

In her future life as a nun, Marta wanted nothing more to do with Casanova. She even wrote to him from the convent, where she took the religious name of Mother Maria Concetta, and beseeched him in the name of Jesus Christ and the Holy Virgin never again to appear before her eyes. She had, she said, forgiven him for the crime he had committed in seducing her, since the consequence of that crime was to ensure that she would save her soul by spending

her entire life repenting it. Her tone was unmistakably ironic and bitter, and her last word to Casanova was that she never ceased praying to God for his conversion.

One feast day in the year 1754, Mother Maria Concetta noticed a man standing at the grating of the convent's visiting-room, deep in conversation with a fourteen-year-old girl who had recently been sent to Santa Maria degli Angeli as a boarder. Though nine or ten years had passed since she had last seen her lover, she recognised him immediately. Afterwards she discreetly took the girl aside and warned her to beware of Casanova, for he was a dangerous man. Her advice came too late: Casanova had already made the girl pregnant, and she had suffered a miscarriage that had almost killed her.

By now Mother Maria Concetta was mortally ill with consumption which she had contracted in the cold, damp environment of the Murano convent. She died the following year, at the age of twenty-seven.

Bettina Gozzi, the young woman who first awoke Casanova's lust, eventually married her fiancé, cobbler Annibale Pigozzo. She would have done better to have remained a spinster, for he treated her scandalously and frittered away all her dowry. Poverty-stricken and brutalised by his harsh treatment, she eventually fled back to the safe haven of her family with her two daughters. When Antonio was appointed parish priest of the nearby village of Cantarana in 1750, Bettina went with him to keep house for him. Years later the two siblings moved on to the village of Val San Giorgio, where Antonio had been appointed as the archpriest.

By this time, Bettina was fifty-seven years old and had been ill for at least three years. Over the next months she grew progressively worse. By the summer of 1777 she lay mortally sick within the cool walls of their stone house, while the cicadas serenaded her outside in the baking heat. Was she conscious that the boy whose hair she had once so lovingly tended, whose thighs she had so daringly caressed and who had inadvertently brought so much trouble on

her, now came to visit her? Showing commendable loyalty to the family who had brought him up, Casanova arrived at Val San Giorgio on 28 June 1777, no doubt summoned by his old teacher. At the age of fifty-two, he was by then more sanguine and less hot-headed when it came to love, and still two years away from beginning his most solid, down-to-earth relationship. By contrast, the woman who had inspired his career as a great seducer was a spent force.

'I found Bettina old, ill and dying,' he wrote of the sad occasion in his memoir. 'She expired before my eyes[37] . . . twenty-four hours after I arrived at her home.'[38]

THREE

Donna Lucrezia

*It is impossible to feel only friendship for a
woman one finds pretty, with whom
one can converse, and whom one suspects of being
in love. Friendship at its apogee becomes love,
and, relieving itself by the same sweet mechanism
which love needs to make itself happy, it rejoices
to find itself stronger after the tender act.*[1]

IN A SUN-DRENCHED street in Naples in June 1744, Donna
Lucrezia Castelli climbed into a carriage bound for Rome, and
took a forward-facing seat opposite her husband and next to her
seventeen-year-old sister Angelica. A pretty young woman in her
late twenties, she had light chestnut hair, a neat, clean appearance,
a vivacious manner and a mind of her own. Lucrezia had moved to
the Kingdom of Naples on her marriage ten years previously and,
despite the prospect of the long, uncomfortable trip that lay ahead,
she was excited at the prospect of returning home to Rome, where
Castelli had business to pursue and where Angelica was due to be
married in a few months' time.

While the driver secured their luggage to the roof with ropes, the
three travellers spread themselves out over the upholstered seats,
pleased to have a little extra space. Lucrezia fanned herself en-
ergetically, raised the dusty window blind and looked out into the
street, hoping that no one else was going to join them. The *vettura*
was a small, slow-moving vehicle pulled by a single team of mules,

and the journey north would take six days and entail five overnight stops at rustic coaching inns along the way. If a fourth passenger were to appear they would not only have to share the hot, airless carriage with him or her, but also their meals and their bedrooms too: for a flat fee a *vetturino* made all the sleeping and eating arrangements for his passengers, whoever they were, and in order to make as much profit as he could from the trip he would hire only one room for all of them at each inn, as was customary. Just as Lucrezia was congratulating herself for being lucky, a portly red-faced man with a hefty laugh strolled up to the vehicle, accompanied by a young man and a tall, youthful novice priest. After they had tearfully embraced on the roadside and sworn eternal friendship to each other, it was the priest who climbed up into the carriage and squashed his long limbs into the seat opposite hers.

His arrival put paid to any privacy Lucrezia and her family might have hoped to have enjoyed on the way to Rome. As the carriage lurched off down the long Strada di Toledo, past the rows of busy market stalls, she glanced surreptitiously at the fellow who was now seated next to her husband with his back towards the driver and his knees jammed against hers, and who, like it or not, was to be their constant companion and even their bedfellow from now on. He was a large youth some ten years her junior with a high forehead, tanned skin and a chin softened by a shadow of down. Dark brown curls cascaded from under his cap, and his thin face was imprinted with the hunger of burning ambition. Although he was simply dressed in the clothing of a novice *abate* he clutched an expensive gold and tortoiseshell snuffbox in one hand, and sat as erect as any nobleman. Off to Rome to make his fortune in the Church, one would have guessed, and rightly so. But as he gazed resolutely out of the window, tears of emotion welled up in his big, limpid eyes and Lucrezia was suddenly intrigued by him.

Content to be en route at last, she settled back in the corner of the seat as the *vettura* passed through the city gates and took the road towards Capua. She was totally unaware that she was embarking on a journey that would transform her life. The young

priest sitting opposite her was Giacomo Casanova, and Lucrezia was about to have a liaison with him which would have far-reaching consequences for her. In the future Casanova would not only name her as one of the greatest loves of his life, he would write about their love affair in intimate detail. Had she known that, more than two centuries after her death, scholars would be discussing her licentious sexual behaviour in terms of the social mores of the times, Lucrezia might well have jumped down from the carriage before it left Naples.

Casanova, too, stared out of the window, and contemplated his future with mixed feelings. Since his beloved grandmother had died in March the previous year he had been seized with a restlessness that would never leave him. At nineteen years old he was still at heart the same carefree young man who had romped with abandon in the Savorgnan sisters' bed, but he had known difficult times, too, and was now at a crossroads in his life. Now that the family house in the Calle della Commedia had been sold he no longer had a permanent base in Venice, where his wild behaviour after Marcia's death had landed him in a seminary for two brief weeks, and later in the Republic's Fort of Sant' Andrea, where he had caught his first dose of venereal disease from a lieutenant's wife. On his way to Rome in the suite of Venetian ambassador Andrea de Lezze, Casanova had stopped off in Chioggia, a fishing port where he had caught a second dose of the shameful illness, and when his ship had landed at Ancona, he had been put in quarantine for the plague along with the other passengers. After a brief stay in Rome, Casanova had returned to Venice, and from Venice he had travelled south again, this time to Martirano, to take up the position with the city's new bishop, Bernardo de Bernardis, which his mother had obtained for him through her influence in Dresden.

Before he had arrived there Casanova had imagined Martirano as a prosperous city with a sparkling social and intellectual life, the kind of place where he could build a glittering future for himself. He could not have been more mistaken. To his horror Calabria had turned out to be a poverty-stricken region, Martirano a charmless

city, and the bishop's house so dilapidated and sparsely furnished
that there was not even a clean mattress for him to sleep on. It had
taken Casanova only hours to work out that Bishop Bernardis was a
simple man and no match for him intellectually, and for him to
dismiss the local aristocracy as an uneducated bunch of provincials.
To make matters worse, all the women and girls he had seen in
Martirano had been ugly. Accustomed as he was to the female
beauties of Venice and the Republic's glittering social life, Casanova had had no intention of building his future, or even spending a
matter of months, exiled in some rural backwater 'without a good
library, a social circle, an equal, a literary connection'.[2] After
spending all of sixty hours in Martirano he had obtained Bernardis's
permission to leave, and had travelled to Naples where, by leading
others to believe that he had an aristocratic lineage, he had made
valuable and influential connections. The Neapolitan friends who
had just seen him off had no idea that he was the son of two actors.
They had made Casanova feel loved and appreciated, and he was
leaving them with regret to return to Rome where, armed with
letters of introduction to two of the most powerful men in the
Vatican – Father Antonio Giorgi, the Procurator General of the
Augustinian order, and Cardinal Acquaviva, the Protector of Spain
– he was determined to build the brilliant career in the Church that
he had been educated to pursue.

What would he find to do in Rome, and how would he acquire
the kind of well-paid, interesting position he so wanted? Casanova
silently ruminated on these questions as the *vettura* rumbled along
the stones of the most famous of all Roman roads, the Via Appia,
which cut through the countryside like a knife blade pointing
towards Rome. In ancient times, travellers had looked out of their
chariots on to lines of crucified prisoners. Now they saw flat fertile
wheat fields, and grape-vines strung between poplar trees. Respecting his quiet mood, Casanova's fellow-passengers chatted amongst
themselves, Lucrezia talking to her sister in the Roman dialect, and
to her husband in Neapolitan. At dusk the *vettura* stopped at
Capua where they were to spend the night – a far from enticing

prospect, for Italian inns were notoriously uncomfortable and primitive. Even if there was a welcoming fire in the dining-room the bedrooms were more often than not cold and damp, for there was seldom any glass in the windows and only simple wooden shutters to keep out the rain. As for the sleeping arrangements, the beds were mostly simple cots consisting of rough-hewn wooden bases covered with straw-filled mattresses, and they were set close together with no thought for the privacy of the occupants, many of whom were strangers to one another. 'Often times they can find neither beds nor provisions when the company is too numerous,' remarked Englishman Thomas Nugent of Italian inns in his 1749 book *The Grand Tour*, he recommended that travellers take with them their own 'light quilt, a pillow, a coverlet and two very fine bedcloths', if not an entire bed.[3]

That night the travellers' room contained two large beds. Propriety required that Lucrezia and her sister should sleep together in one of them. 'So, I shall have the honour of sleeping with the signor *abate*,' Castelli said jovially to their taciturn companion. 'I leave it to you, signor,' the young priest replied coldly, which made Lucrezia smile. He retired early and went straight to sleep, a polite gesture which allowed the two women a degree of seclusion in which to prepare themselves for bed, and by the time they awoke the following morning, he had discreetly gone out for a walk. When he returned, the barber who had come to the room to shave Castelli offered to do the same to Casanova's downy chin, but to everyone's amazement the young priest flew off the handle and told the barber in no uncertain terms that he had no need of a shave. A beard was an unclean thing, the disgruntled barber muttered. Back in the coach, Lucrezia's husband tried to calm down their fellow-passenger by remarking that barbers were an insolent lot, and, as Casanova later recorded, she joined in.

'The question is,' said the beauty, 'if a beard is, or is not, an unclean thing.'

'Yes it is,' said the advocate, 'for it is an excretion.'

'That may be so,' I told him, 'but one doesn't regard it as such; does one call hair an excretion, which on the contrary is nourished, and admired for its length and beauty?'

'In that case,' the lady resumed, 'the barber is a fool.'

'But aside from that,' I asked her, 'do I have a beard?'

'I believe so.'

'In that case I'll start to get myself shaved at Rome. This is the first time I've been accused of needing it.'

'My dear wife,' said the advocate, 'you should have held your tongue, for it could be that the abate was going to Rome to become a Capuchin.'[4]

This sally made me laugh, but I did not want him to have the last word. I told him that he had guessed right; but that the desire to become a Capuchin had left me the moment I had seen his wife. Laughing too, he answered that his wife was mad about Capuchins, so I should not abandon my vocation.[5]

The ice was broken and the flirtatious tone of Lucrezia's relationship with Casanova was set. For the next five days the four travellers would enjoy an easy companionship in the cramped, hot carriage and at the inns where, as in the town of Garigliano that evening, their 'amusing conversation compensated for a poor supper'.[6] Lucrezia could not help but be flattered by the amount of attention the young *abate* paid her, for he carried himself with the air of a wealthy nobleman and talked with a self-confidence and breadth of knowledge that were truly astounding in one so young. His past friendships with the elite of Venice's women, coupled with his sexual experiences with the Savorgnan sisters, had given Casanova a veneer of sophistication, an ability to flatter and flirt and an ebullient self-confidence which went way beyond his years. 'It is not beauty, but something better that I had, but I can't quite define it,' he wrote of himself at this period of his life. 'I felt that I was capable of anything.'[7]

Previously Casanova had kept away from married women out of fear that he would feel jealous of their husbands. This time, he

could not avoid one. Cooped up with Lucrezia in the close physical proximity of the tiny *vettura*, and even sharing a bedroom with her, he became ever more captivated by her. Her very ordinariness seemed to excite him. Though she appeared to be both respectable and happily married, he nevertheless sensed that she desired him, and her husband's presence gave the potential intrigue an added piquancy.

Unknown to him, Casanova had awoken Lucrezia's dormant sexual feelings. Sexual passion and romantic love seldom entered into the equation between a husband and a wife, at least on the woman's side, at a time when most middle- and upper-class marriages were arranged by one's parents for financial or dynastic reasons. However, Lucrezia willingly did her duty towards Castelli, who was a jovial, hard-working, plain-speaking fellow in his forties, a nice man, and in many ways a typical Neapolitan. As an advocate he was well respected in his native kingdom, where years of rule by different nations had resulted in a complex legal system that was a mishmash of Roman, Byzantine, Swabian, Angevin, Aragonese and Spanish laws. The resulting muddled legislation was a perfect medium for roguery and corruption to fester in, and since there was no shortage of rogues in Naples, Castelli, like other Neapolitan lawyers, could not afford to rest on his laurels. Built on the flat plain at the foot of Mount Vesuvius, his city was neither as smart nor as relaxed as Rome, Lucrezia's birthplace, but it was one of the largest cities in Europe and it teemed with life day and night. The cafes were always packed, the long crowded *strade* echoed with the clatter of thousands of small brisk carriage horses, and the huge port was one of the busiest in the Mediterranean. 'Naples proclaims herself from the first as gay, free and alive,' wrote Goethe, who visited the Campagna Felice, or Happy Country, as the kingdom was called, in February 1787. 'The Neapolitan firmly believes that he lives in Paradise and takes a very dismal view of Northern countries.'[8] From the sweet perfume of its fragrant tomatoes and the salty stench of its fish market, to its multicoloured flora and the azure blue of its gulf, Naples sang with smells and colours. Great

wealth, in the shape of marble-clad palazzi, existed side by side with terrible slums, and the streets teemed with ne'er-do-wells, bandits and beggars who flocked into the city from the surrounding towns and hills. 'The most abominable, the most disgusting vermin that have ever crawled on the earth,' Charles de Brosses called them. 'These people have no habitation; they live in the streets, do no work, and are kept from starving by alms given them by the convents. Every morning they cover the steps and the ground of the Monte Oliveto, which they make impassable; they form a truly sickening sight.'[9]

Despite the ubiquitous beggars and paupers, Naples was much loved by its people. *Vedi Napoli e poi muori!* went the local saying even then: see Naples and then die! Neapolitans, Castelli included, were an earthy lot: robust, tireless and bellicose. They worked hard and played hard, took long siestas in the afternoons, and indulged themselves in the evenings by consuming an inordinate quantity of chocolate. The atmosphere at their assemblies might be formal, even somewhat constrained compared to that in Rome, but 'the chat in private companies is quite Grecian, that is, very free, and very merry'.[10] As in many sophisticated European cities, married women of the merchant and noble classes enjoyed an exceptional degree of liberty, but the freedom of the Neapolitan women shocked even some Parisians. 'Women of quality go about more less indifferently with anyone,' remarked the French astronomer Jérôme de Lalande of Neapolitan women. 'It is by no means against normal behaviour for women to visit bachelors in their homes.'[11] Love was pursued with volcanic recklessness, and 'Mount Vesuvius, which overlooks the city, is the nearest emblem under which it can be represented in this respect.'[12]

'In Italy there are husbands who willingly tolerate the gallants of the wives, and who even become their confidants; but there are others extremely jealous, who bear the strongest ill-will to those singular beings who are the second masters in an ill-regulated family,' Goldoni wrote in his memoirs.[13] According to Charles de Brosses, Neapolitan men were the worst offenders, 'for all the

old Italian jealousy of women seems to have concentrated itself here.'[14] Castelli, however, was neither jealous nor possessive of his pretty young wife, whom he trusted implicitly and loved dearly, despite the fact that in ten years of marriage she had failed to provide him with an heir. Instead of resenting Casanova's flirtation with Lucrezia, he openly joked about it. In fact, he seemed almost to encourage it.

On the third day the *vettura* reached the ceremonial wooden gate which marked the end of the Kingdom of Naples and the beginning of the Papal Territories. A Swiss Guard waved them through. From here, the road was cut into the rock and rose precariously above the sea to a height of 120 feet. With every jolting, dangerous turn of the way Lucrezia felt ever more attracted to the young man sitting opposite her, and when the *vettura* finally stopped that night at the whitewashed hilltop village of Terracino an opportunity finally arose for her to signal discreetly that she was interested in him. At the inn they were allotted a room which contained one large bed with two narrow ones on either side of it. While the men turned their backs, the women removed their dresses and, wearing only their linen shifts, climbed into the big bed together. But before she did so, Lucrezia quickly put Castelli's nightcap on the narrow bed on her sister's side, leaving the bed on her side free for Casanova. The significance of the carefully-placed nightcap was certainly not lost on her admirer who 'was already burning for her'.[15]

Soon Lucrezia was lying in bed in the darkness, longing for the young man who was lying a mere arm's length away from her. But the gap between them might as well have been a mountain valley, treacherous to cross even after her husband and sister fell asleep. After waiting for what seemed like hours for Casanova to make a move, Lucrezia must have presumed that she had mistaken his intentions for she slipped out of bed, tiptoed around to the other side and climbed in beside the sleeping Castelli. Casanova, who was still awake, fumed with anger. Seeing Lucrezia get into bed with her husband 'displeased me to a supreme degree, it annoyed me,

and it revolted me so much that, turning on my other side, I fell asleep until dawn; I saw the woman in his bed.'[16] Rejected by his mother, displaced by his sisters and brothers, he could never abide competition in the game of love.

Throughout the next day Casanova sulked like a spoiled child in the cramped, stuffy confines of the coach, rarely speaking to Castelli or Angelica and, in marked contrast to his previous behaviour towards her, completely ignoring Lucrezia. When asked if anything was wrong, he complained of having a bad toothache – a malady made to order, as she commented wryly over their dinner. By the time they arrived at their next overnight stop, the medieval village of Sermonetta, his behaviour had become so embarrassing that Lucrezia decided to have the matter out with him. Suggesting they should all take a walk through the cobbled streets, she assertively took Casanova's arm, leaving her husband to take Angelica's, and when they were far enough away from the others Casanova's long silence finally cracked. Without actually saying anything incriminating, both parties laid their cards on the table, and Lucrezia's good sense and delicacy put Casanova's childish petulance to shame. When he impetuously kissed her on the lips, Lucrezia did not resist him.

She had been worried that Casanova's moodiness that day would make her husband suspicious, but Castelli had even more reason to be so that night. For, instead of being sunk in gloom, their travelling companion was suddenly 'drunk with happiness'. Again, the lawyer seemed flattered rather than threatened by the young man's crush on his wife. He even made jokes about the walk that had miraculously cured his toothache.

The desolate, marshy plain they crossed the following day failed to dent the lighthearted spirits of Lucrezia and Casanova, who, sitting opposite one another, 'spoke to each other with our knees more than with our eyes, in this way making sure that our conversation would not be overheard'.[17] Nor did the threat of being caught up in a battle between the Spanish and Austrian armies bother them. Velletri, the town where the party stopped to

dine, would on 11 August that year become the scene of a Spanish victory over the Austrians. The two armies were already massing nearby, and a territorial skirmish between them that very evening was about to turn Casanova's first attempt to seduce Lucrezia into pure farce.

It was the travellers' last evening before they reached Rome and, convinced that Lucrezia would now acquiesce to any demands he made on her, Casanova wanted to take as much advantage of the opportunity as he could. The sleeping arrangements at their inn fitted his purposes perfectly: 'There was one bed in the room where we ate, and another in a small adjoining closet which had no door and which could only be entered by passing through the room where we were. Naturally, the two sisters chose the closet. After they had gone to bed, the lawyer went to bed too, and I last of all; before snuffing out the candle, I put my head into the closet to wish the women goodnight. My purpose was to see on which side the wife was sleeping. I had a plan all prepared.'[18] His plan – to creep into the closet the moment the lawyer fell asleep – was foiled by the rudely-fashioned wooden bed he shared with Castelli, for the planks creaked so loudly that the lawyer woke up every time Casanova moved. He had almost given up hope of getting near Lucrezia when suddenly they were all disturbed by a terrible racket. A detachment of Austrian troops had surprised the Spanish soldiers garrisoned in the town:

'A great noise of people running up and downstairs, coming and going, fills the house. We hear gunshots, the drum, the alarm, there are calls, shouts, knocks on our door, the lawyer asks me what is happening, I answer that I have no idea and beg him to let me go back to sleep. The terrified sisters ask us in the name of God to fetch a light. The lawyer gets up in his shirt to go and look for one, and I get up too. I want to close the door again, and I shut it, but the spring jumps back in a way that I can tell it cannot be opened without a key, which I do not have.'[19]

One can safely presume that this was no accident and that, grabbing the opportunity, Casanova had sprung the lock on pur-

pose. Now he groped his way into the sisters' closet, where, on the pretext of giving them courage, he stumbled over to Lucrezia's side of the bed in the pitch-darkness. Emboldened by her lack of resistance he threw himself on top of her, and the bed collapsed, trapping Lucrezia, Casanova and Angelica between the broken planks and the mattress.

When the lawyer came back he was furious to find himself locked out of his own room. Thoroughly annoyed by the sexual fumblings that were taking place beside her, Angelica clambered out of the broken bed and tried to open the door for him. Lucrezia begged Casanova to let go of her, and they too groped their way towards the locked door. While the lawyer went downstairs again to find a key, Casanova, repeating the game he had once played in Signora Orio's palazzo with Angela Tosello and the Savorgnan sisters, groped his way around in the dark with his arms spread out, hoping to catch Lucrezia, and 'to have time to finish' what he had already begun. Instead, he accidentally caught Angelica who roughly pushed him away. When he eventually found Lucrezia they hurriedly embraced, and by the time her husband came upstairs again, this time jangling a large bunch of keys, Casanova was so excited that he ejaculated over his shirt. Lucrezia pleaded with him to get back into his bed, 'for if her husband were to see me in the appalling state I was in, he would guess everything'.[20] There was a limit to her husband's understanding nature. By the time the lawyer finally opened the door, he found Casanova apparently half-asleep in his bed, and his wife and sister-in-law folded up in their collapsed bed in the closet. Bursting into a peal of heartfelt laughter, he demanded that Casanova come and see what had happened to them.

The excitement of the situation, the humour of it, the exhilarating danger and the sheer wonder of being desired overwhelmed Lucrezia like a narcotic. This was the first time in her life that she had ever experienced such strong sexual feelings for a man, and during the next few weeks she would risk her marriage and her reputation in order to satisfy them. The good sense, loyalty and propriety that she had previously shown now deserted her. The

following morning, in the sweet grip of what Casanova termed the 'divine monster' of love, she watched as he behaved with shameful familiarity towards her husband when they stopped for omelettes at the famous Tor di Mezza Via inn on the outskirts of Rome, hugging and kissing him, calling him 'papa' and even predicting the birth of a son to him and his wife.

When the *vetturino* dropped Casanova off near Rome's famous Piazza di Spagna the bittersweet pain of love must have struck Lucrezia. Her admirer had promised to call on her, but Rome was an easy place to lose a person in. The Aurelian walls, built in the third century AD, still marked the twenty-kilometre perimeter of a city which in ancient times had been home to more than two million people. Now the same area housed less than a tenth of that number, and consequently even the centre of the city had a sprawling, rural feel to it. History rubbed shoulders with modernity, the urban with the rural, the religious with the secular, and the exalted with the everyday. Though wealthy foreigners travelled across Europe to wonder at the remains of Rome's ancient circuses, markets, aqueducts and temples, the locals regarded them as no more than conveniently placed stone-quarries. 'One comes upon traces both of magnificence and of devastation which stagger the imagination,' wrote Goethe. 'What the barbarians left, the builders of modern Rome have destroyed.'[21] Sheep grazed in the Coliseum, which was overgrown with brambles and ivy, the Forum was used as a cattle market, vines were trained up abandoned marble columns, fragments of temples could be found cemented into the walls of new houses, and artisans built their workshops underneath half-buried arches. The ancient Romans had been famous for their road-building skills, but now the city's roads were unsurfaced, unswept and unlit. The long straight avenues with their plashing fountains gave way to twisting alleyways which led in turn to open spaces where exuberant baroque churches and luxurious palazzi built by generations of extravagant popes stood cheek by jowl with lowly shacks and tumble-down cowsheds. The result was a charming, unplanned hotchpotch of a city that was both relaxing and uplifting to live in.

'Imagine a population a third of which is composed of priests, who do absolutely nothing; the peasants work little, there is no agriculture, no commerce, no manufactures,' wrote Charles de Brosses of Rome's laid-back atmosphere. The city was so pleasant because of 'the extreme freedom prevailing in it, and the civility of its inhabitants, who, if not cordial, are full of good breeding, and are more obliging and accessible in Rome than in any other part of Italy.'[22] Romans were the most friendly and delightful of all Italians, and if the city itself was not as colourful as Naples, its floating population certainly made up for it. The fashionable cafés overflowed with tourists, local noblemen, pilgrims on their way to the Vatican, English lords discussing their private audiences with the Pope (as essential an ingredient of any Grand Tour of Europe as being carried over the Alps or taking a ride in one of Venice's gondolas), effeminate castrati employed to sing in the churches, and richly-dressed clerics on the make.

Casanova now unashamedly became one of the latter. His whole life had been leading up to this one moment. Everything was in his favour: 'Rome was the one city where a man, starting out from nothing, had often risen very high; and it was not surprising that I believed I had all the requisite qualities; my currency was an unbridled self-esteem, which inexperience forbade me to doubt.' He had every chance of succeeding, for he was 'well turned out, provided with enough money, with a fair amount of jewellery, with enough experience, with good letters of recommendation, perfectly free, and at an age when a man can count on good fortune, if he has a little bit of courage, and a face which disposes those whom he approaches in his favour'. To forge a career in the Vatican, a man needed political skill rather than faith, to be 'flexible, insinuating, a great dissembler, inscrutable, conniving, often base, insincere, always seeming to know less than he does, having only one tone of voice, patient, in control of his features, as cold as ice when another in his place would burn; and if he is unfortunate enough not to have religion in his heart, he must have it in his mind, suffering in silence, if he is an honest man, the mortification of knowing that he is a hypocrite'.[23]

Single-mindedly pursuing his goal – a good position in the Church – within hours of his arrival in Rome Casanova went to see Father Antonio-Agostino Giorgi and talked his way into a job as secretary to Cardinal Acquaviva who, as the Protector of Spain, was one of the most powerful men in the Vatican. From now on he would receive a salary of twenty Roman scudi a month, take private French lessons from a local advocate, Signor Delacqua, and lodge in beautiful rooms on the fourth floor of the Palazzo di Spagna, the extremely grand residence of the King of Spain's ambassadors. As soon as his future was settled he called at Lucrezia's mother's home near the Dominican church of Santa Maria sopra Minerva. Lucrezia scarcely recognised him. The impetuous youth who had courted her on the journey from Naples seemed to have matured within the last twenty-four hours. His simple clothes had been replaced by a smart Roman wardrobe, and his impetuous behaviour had vanished. Towards her mother, Donna Cecilia Monti, Casanova was modest and respectful, and he took a lively interest in everyone around him, including Lucrezia's fifteen-year-old brother. When guests arrived that evening, Casanova's witty repartee dominated the conversation. He put himself out to charm his hostess and he succeeded: when he finally left late that night, Donna Cecilia sent her son-in-law running after him to tell him that, from now on, he was to regard himself as 'a friend of the house, free to call on them without ceremony at any time'.[24]

Donna Cecilia's son-in-law may not have suspected Casanova's motives, but Father Giorgi, his mentor in Rome, certainly did. Gossip travelled fast in the city, and by the following day Giorgi had already heard of his protégé's visit to the Minerva district; Rome was full of spies, and from now on every move the lovers made would be discreetly monitored. Giorgi warned Casanova against going to visit Donna Cecilia too often, even though hers was 'a very respectable house frequented by people of integrity'.[25] The unspoken message was that Casanova must put his career before pursuing women. He was outraged at this reining-in of his liberty. Deferring gratification went against his very nature. 'To ensure the

would-be happiness of my future life, I was to commence by becoming the executioner of that which I already had, and the enemy of my heart,' was how he justified his defiant attitude. 'I could only accept this logic by becoming a base object of contempt in my own eyes.'[26] Still, he attempted to comply. Lucrezia had to wait two days for his next visit, and on that occasion he stayed for only an hour. Despite his meteoric professional rise he seemed sad, and the reason, Casanova told her meaningfully, was that his time was no longer his own. When Castelli joked that the real reason he looked so miserable was because he was in love with Lucrezia, Donna Cecilia told her son-in-law not to be so sure of himself. He might be blind to the sparks that were flying between the priest and her daughter, but she was not. The following morning, when Casanova sent the lawyer a poem he had written, everyone in the house with the possible exception of the recipient knew for whom it was really intended. Over the next few days Lucrezia read the lines so often that she could recite them by heart.

When Casanova absented himself from the house for some days, the unaware Castelli was dispatched to invite him to a family outing to Monte Testaccio, a small hill to the south of the city that was the scene of local festivities every October. Lucrezia knew that if she was ever to have the opportunity of being alone with Casanova it would happen then, and her excitement as they discussed the trip together was obvious. Casanova, too, was gambling on having the opportunity to seduce Lucrezia that day, and on the morning of the outing he deliberately arrived at the family's house in a hired *carrosse-coupé*, a covered four-wheeled carriage that seated only two people. In case Castelli became suspicious, he insisted on taking Donna Cecilia in it on the outward journey, leaving the lawyer to take his wife, Angelica and her betrothed, Don Francesco, in his large carriage. Continuing the ruse, Casanova openly flirted with Donna Cecilia all day long, so much so that her son-in-law insisted on driving her home himself, leaving Casanova to take Lucrezia in the two-seater. As an exercise in manipulation the plan had worked perfectly. The cuckold had fallen neatly into the trap.

The trip back to the Minerva district took half an hour, and Casanova and Lucrezia did not waste a moment of it in conversation. As soon as the others drove off ahead of them, they fell into each other's arms under cover of the dark night. The journey passed in a flash of delirious heavy petting and, perhaps, actual intercourse. The element of danger, coupled with their sexual chemistry, elevated their love-making to a different emotional level than either of them had ever experienced before. Interrupted by their return home, both parties quickly straightened their clothes and went into the house where Lucrezia somehow mustered enough sangfroid to spend the rest of the evening acting as if nothing untoward had happened.

Fearful of ruining his career prospects by seeing too much of his lover, Casanova avoided the Minerva district for the next few days. Lucrezia was not afraid to express her feelings of disappointment, as she had proved once before on the journey from Naples. It was impossible, she reprimanded him gently when he eventually called at her mother's house four days later, that Casanova had not had time to come and see her before now. Already skilled in the art of talking his way out of trouble, her lover swore that he had only kept away because their love was so precious to him that he would rather die than have it discovered. He proposed another family outing, this time at his expense to fashionable Frascati, a town famous for its lovely gardens and private villas, where he hoped they would be able to spend more time alone.

On the following Sunday, the Feast of St Ursula, Casanova arrived at Donna Cecilia's house at seven o'clock in the morning with two carriages: a phaeton seating four and a *vis-à-vis*, a light but well-upholstered carriage designed for two people to sit face to face in. As on the excursion to Testaccio, Donna Cecilia travelled with him on the outward journey. Crammed into the phaeton with her husband and the rest of her family, Lucrezia boldly declared that she would have her turn in the *vis-à-vis* on the way back. The fifteen-kilometre trip took two hours – there would be plenty of time for love on the return journey – and once they had arrived at

Frascati the party split up into small groups to explore the gardens of the Villa Ludovisi before lunch.

'Frascati is a Paradise,' wrote Goethe when he visited the town in 1787. 'The town lies on the slope of a mountain, and at every turn the artist comes upon the most lovely things. The view is unlimited; you can see Rome in the distance and the sea beyond it. The hills of Tivoli to the right, and so on.'[27] These beautiful vistas enchanted the rest of Lucrezia's family, but she and Casanova only had eyes for each other. In the beautiful water gardens of the Villa Ludovisi they quickly wandered away from the others and threw themselves down on a grassy bank, overcome with a mixture of lust and emotion. This did not feel like a fleeting affair to either of them. In tears, Casanova told Lucrezia that she was the first woman he had truly loved; she was unique. He was her first love too, she confided, and he would certainly be her last. Sexual desire made her both reckless and fearless. Although she was usually terrified of snakes, when she spotted one close by she was convinced it was no danger to them, and even though her mother, husband and siblings were strolling in the vicinity she abandoned herself to Casanova there and then.

After meeting up at an inn for a fine lunch at Casanova's expense – the adventurer always entertained over-generously, perhaps out of fear that he would be found wanting – the party set off to explore the grounds of the famous Villa Aldobrandini, a massive sixteenth-century house which was the highlight of the area. Did Lucrezia's husband suspect nothing when his wife wandered off with their host down yet another tree-bordered walkway? She was convinced that Castelli either did not believe they were in love or made very little of their flirtation. Her mother, she suspected, knew everything but was minding her own business, while Angelica, who had been party to the collapsed bed, 'is discreet, and besides, she has decided to pity me. She has no idea of the nature of my passion.'[28]

Passion certainly took hold of Lucrezia and Casanova that day. It was an insatiable hunger, and the constant threat of discovery only heightened their appetites. Luckily the gardens of the Villa Aldo-

brandini had been laid out for lovers to lose themselves in: behind
the house was a carefully-designed wilderness perfect for illicit
idylls, and amid the formal terraced gardens at the front and the
innumerable water features were endless paths, hidden grottos and
dark leafy corners decorated with statues. In the middle of one
particularly long and secluded tree-lined walkway, Lucrezia and
Casanova found an arbour filled with turf seats, the most striking of
which resembled a bed upon which were set two turf 'bolsters', one
at the head, the other parallel to it an elbow's length away. They
both looked at this 'eloquent bed'[29] and laughed. Though it could
be seen clearly from either end of the avenue of trees it would take
anyone who approached it a good fifteen minutes to reach it. They
unloosened their restrictive outer garments to get access to the
naked flesh underneath their chemises: 'Standing face to face,
serious, looking only into each other's eyes, we unlaced, we
unbuttoned, our hearts palpitated, and our quick hands hastened
to calm their impatience. Neither of us having been slower than the
other, our arms opened to tightly clasp the object of which they
were to take possession. Our first combat made the beautiful
Lucrezia laugh and swear that, having the right to shine everywhere, genius was never out of place. We both applauded the
happy effect of the small bolster. After that our adventures varied,
and they were all good but all, despite that, rejected to make way
for others. At the end of two hours, enchanted with each other and
looking into each other's eyes most tenderly, we said in unison
these exact words: *Love, I thank you.*'[30]

No sooner had they dressed and walked on than they stopped to
make love again, this time on a long narrow bench which they
straddled as if on horseback, and although they were forced to
break off through exhaustion and lack of time, they resumed their
love-making in the *vis-à-vis* on the two-hour journey back to Rome.

Lucrezia would not have another opportunity to be alone with
Casanova until the end of November, when Angelica's fiancé Don
Francesco invited him to join the family on an overnight trip to his
country house in Tivoli. Here she and Angelica shared a bedroom

leading off a pretty orangery, and Casanova manoeuvred himself into the small intercommunicating chamber next door. While the sisters prepared for bed, he spied on them through the keyhole, and when he saw the seventeen-year-old virgin strip off her linen chemise, walk across the room stark naked and climb into bed beside her older sister, 'I believe,' he confessed in his memoirs, 'that I have never undressed more quickly.'[31] As soon as they extinguished the light he burst in on the two women and threw himself into Lucrezia's arms. With their unwilling witness lying naked beside them, they made love in a fast and furious manner, and after a short rest, began again. This time neither of them wished the act to end; luckily Casanova 'excelled in the art of prolonging it', or so he boasted.[32] Awaking at dawn, they made love for a third time, and only afterwards spared a thought for Angelica who had passed an embarrassing and sleepless night in the same bed. According to Casanova Angelica watched them make love for a fourth time, then Donna Lucrezia thrust her lover towards her sister and watched as he deflowered her.

It is at this point in his *Story of My Life* that Casanova's all-too-convincing account of his affair with Donna Lucrezia suddenly moves into the realms of fantasy. For did Lucrezia really feel so little for her sister that she was willing to jeopardise her entire future on a whim? 'I have enlightened her,' Casanova reports her as saying to him after the event. 'Instead of pitying me, she has to actually approve of me, she must love you, and since I am about to depart, I leave her to you.'[33] Would a virgin on the point of being married really allow her sister's lover to take away her chastity just weeks before her wedding night, in her fiancé's house, under his very nose, and with her mother and brother-in-law sleeping close by? Forced to collude in the affair against her will, Angelica had already made her distaste for her sister's lover apparent: the very day before, at Tivoli, she had told Casanova, 'As soon as I am the mistress here, signore, the first person I will order my doors closed to is you.' Perversely, the adventurer interpreted this as a declaration of love. If he did indeed deflower Angelica at Tivoli the

chances are that, at best, he took advantage of her, and at worst, he did so against her will. Eighteen years later, Angelica still bore a grudge against Casanova: when he called on her at her marital home in Rome she gave him short shrift, and told him that she scarcely remembered ever having met him.

Several months later, on 17 January 1745, Angelica and her fiancé were married at the church of Santa Maria sopra Minerva. Pointedly, Casanova was not invited to the wedding. Nor was Lucrezia present. A week after their visit to Tivoli, her husband had concluded his business in Rome and taken her back to Naples. It was the end of their pleasures, she told Casanova sadly before she left.

Lucrezia would never be able to forget her young lover, for within weeks of returning to Naples she realised that she was pregnant, and that the child she was carrying was his. With her usual frankness, she admitted as much, and Castelli accepted the situation with such generosity and good grace that one could almost believe that, after years of failing to produce an heir himself, he had planned the entire affair. When Lucrezia's daughter was born in July 1745, her husband stood at the font and himself named her Leonilda Giacomina – the feminine form of Giacomo. Even though she was not his biological child, he brought her up as his own; and little Leonilda never suspected otherwise.

Castelli died a few years later. The widowed Lucrezia was now more in control of her own destiny than she had ever been. In her thirties, and still as beautiful and youthful as ever, she moved to the countryside outside Naples to live near some friends. This was no place to bring up Leonilda, however, who by the age of ten was a precociously clever, beautiful cherub of a girl. Given the appropriate education and contacts, she might well make an advantageous marriage, but this was not something that her mother felt able to handle by herself.

Money was an issue. While disposing of some of her late husband's assets Lucrezia came in contact with Carlo Caraffa,

the Duke of Maddaloni and head of one of the most powerful and
prominent aristocratic families in Naples. The duke had inherited
his father's title and vast fortune at the age of fourteen. Now in his
early twenties, he lived in his family's imposing sixteenth-century
palazzo on the corner of the Strada di Maddaloni and the Strada di
Toledo, where he indulged his passion for art, the theatre, opera
and forbidden books. Rich, generous, kind and intelligent, Maddaloni was a young man who seemed to have everything; his one great
sorrow was that he was impotent, and everyone in the Kingdom of
Naples knew about it.

Maddaloni was so enchanted by young Leonilda that he made
Lucrezia an offer. In exchange for an annual allowance of 600
ducats, he would adopt the little girl as his nominal 'mistress'; since
he was impotent, this title was for appearance's sake only; a man in
his position had to be seen to have a mistress. In reality Maddaloni
would bring the girl up as his daughter, have her educated to his
own taste, equip her with a fine wardrobe and diamonds, and install
her in her own house in Naples. Furthermore, he would settle a
large dowry on her, find her a suitable husband and ensure that she
was a virgin on her wedding night.

If Lucrezia had any misgivings about handing over her pre-
pubescent daughter to this freethinking twenty-one-year-old aristocrat, they did not stop her from doing so. Her duty as a mother
almost demanded it of her. Being a widow with limited means she
could never offer her daughter the social advantages that Maddaloni could. But was the duke really impotent? The same year that
he adopted Leonilda he married Vittoria Guevara, the daughter of
the Duke of Bovino and 'a charming woman who had the talent to
make him into a man'.[34] As testament to this, three years later
Vittoria bore him a son, leaving all Naples agog.

Under Maddaloni's unconventional tutelage Leonilda grew up
into a vivacious young woman who resembled her mother in both
looks and spirit. By the age of fifteen 'she was a beauty; her hair was
light chestnut, a colour above suspicion, and her beautiful black
eyes listened and questioned at the same time . . . when she told a

story she spoke with her hands, her elbows, her shoulders and often with her chin. Her tongue was not sufficient for her to be able to express all that she wanted people to understand.'[35] Leonilda's character was as striking as her appearance, an intoxicating mix of sophistication and total innocence. Maddaloni's education had freed her from convention and prejudice, but her knowledge of sexual matters far outstripped her actual experience by a long way. The duke was a father-figure and mentor to her, and no more, but nevertheless there was a sexual element to their relationship: he had decorated one of the rooms in her house with Chinese erotic prints which they often studied together, although the subject-matter aroused neither of them; and, Leonilda was accustomed to receiving him while sitting in bed wearing only a ribbon-trimmed dimity corset, and she unabashedly dressed and undressed in front of him.

Lucrezia could relax in the knowledge that her daughter was living in luxury and had a secure future in front of her. She herself was now lodging as a paying guest with friends in Sant' Agata, a picturesque spot in the hills behind Naples. Life there was not as quiet as it sounded: the town's stunning views of Mount Vesuvius and the gulf made it a popular stopping-off point on the Grand Tour, and Lucrezia's friend, the Marchesa Agnese Galiani, had three young children to liven up the place. It was at Sant' Agata that, one day in January 1761, Lucrezia received startling news from Naples: within the next few days Leonilda was to be married to a man old enough to be her father and then she was to leave with him for Rome. Needed in the city to sign the marriage contract and give her blessing to the match, Lucrezia set off for Naples immediately, arriving there in the evening, and going directly to Leonilda's house, where her daughter excitedly told her about the debonair thirty-five-year-old whom she adored and who had settled a generous dowry of 5,000 ducats on her.

The moment Lucrezia saw her future son-in-law she gave a cry and sank down on to the nearest sofa. Leonilda's betrothed was not only old enough to be the girl's father, he *was* her father. The

sixteen years since Lucrezia had last seen Giacomo Casanova had treated him kindly, or so it appeared. Then he had been a young ambitious cleric with nothing to his name. Now, he was – or rather he appeared to be – a wealthy aristocrat who passed by the French name of the Chevalier de Seingalt. When he saw Lucrezia he rushed over to greet her as a long-lost friend, but, when she informed him pointedly that he was to marry her daughter, Casanova sank down next to her, and the look on his face showed that he understood everything.

Rather ungallantly, the adventurer left it to a frightened and embarrassed Lucrezia to explain what he called the 'unpleasant mystery' of his real identity to Leonilda and her protector. The young girl immediately threw herself at her mother's feet and swore that she had never loved Casanova 'except as a daughter'[36] – exceptionally for the adventurer, their relationship had yet to be consummated. Lucrezia's courageous confession had averted a disaster. Incestuous relationships were known to happen, particularly between siblings – Cardinal Guerin de Tencin, one of the highest figures in the Roman Catholic world, was credited by his enemies with committing incest with his sister, novelist and courtesan Claudine Guerin de Tencin – but to knowingly proceed with an incestuous marriage between a father and a daughter was unthinkable, even to freethinkers such as Maddaloni and Casanova, who knew that there was so much prejudice attached to such a union 'that one would have to have an entirely depraved mind to trample it underfoot'.[37] Nevertheless, the idea of committing incest with one's young and beautiful daughter was far from repugnant to him, as he would later demonstrate, not only with Leonilda but with another of his illegitimate daughters. As he wrote, shocking us even today, 'I have never been able to conceive how a father could tenderly love his charming daughter without have slept with her at least once.'[38]

By the following morning Maddaloni had come to the conclusion that, to save face, they should all treat Casanova's short betrothal to Leonilda as a joke, and that the adventurer should renew his affair

with Lucrezia instead. The idea soon awoke the pragmatist in Casanova. If he could not marry his daughter, he would marry her mother, and that way he would possess both of them. As they all dined together two days later, he publicly proposed to Lucrezia, or rather he told her he would marry her and take both women to Rome. Instead of eliciting the delighted, grateful response he expected, his proposal met with a suspicious silence. Lucrezia might still love Casanova, but she distrusted his motives, and with good reason.

While her daughter and the duke went to the opera that evening, Lucrezia visited Casanova in his room, where they made love with the ease of old friends. Afterwards they lapsed into silence. 'Here I am again,' he joked eventually, 'in the charming country which undid me, to the sound of gunfire and drums, the first time I dared to travel up and down it in the dark.'[39] Lucrezia could not help laughing at this witty reference to the skirmish between the Austrians and Spanish that had reduced their first attempt at love-making to a farce. The passing years had made Casanova even more charming and attractive, but to give up her independence for him was a risk she was unwilling to take for her daughter's sake as much as her own. For where did his newly-found wealth and name come from? And what were his motives in wanting to marry first her daughter, and now herself? When he repeated his proposal of marriage, she told him that her dearest wish was to live with him until her death, but instead of going to Rome with him she would like him to 'stay in Naples, and leave Leonilda to the duke. We'll frequent society, we'll find her a husband worthy of her, and our happiness will be perfect.'

That Casanova fell at this hurdle was no accident. During his lifetime he proposed marriage to many of his lovers, and wriggled out of it successfully every time. Having escaped from marrying Leonilda because she was his daughter, he proceeded to backtrack as fast as he could from marrying her mother, a woman whom he nevertheless regarded as one of the great loves of his life. He could not possibly settle down in Naples, he told her, adding reproach-

fully, 'Your daughter was ready to leave with me.' The subtle nuance of his language was not lost on Lucrezia: 'Say our daughter. I see that you wish you were not her father. You love her.'

'Alas! I am very sure my passion will subside so long as I am living with you; but I answer for nothing if you are not there. She is charming, and her mind captivates me even more than her beauty.'[40]

Lucrezia now knew for certain that Casanova could never be trusted with Leonilda. From that moment on, she entertained no more thoughts about marrying him. Still, she had no objection to making the most of their remaining time together. Not averse to sleeping three in a bed – that is, if Casanova's tale of seducing her sister Angelica at Tivoli is true – Lucrezia allowed her daughter to climb naked under the bedcovers with them that night, as if she was trying to prove, to herself as much as to Casanova, that her own powers of attraction were as strong as ever. For Casanova, who with good reason counted himself 'the happiest of mortals' to have both beauties in bed with him, the moment was so exciting that he lost his usual exceptional self-control. Forced to withdraw before he ejaculated, he left Lucrezia unsatisfied. 'Moved to pity, Leonilda helps her mother's soul on its flight with one hand, and with the other she puts a white handkerchief under her gushing father,' he later wrote with such attention to detail that we are convinced that the event actually took place.[41] Leonilda then demanded that Casanova look at her while he kissed her mother. This three-sided, doubly incestuous combat continued until late in the night and resumed at dawn, and although Casanova stopped short of having coitus with his daughter, in the end nothing else was forbidden. Incest was only an abhorrent crime, it seemed, if it entailed actual penetration.

Two days later, Casanova left Naples. Generosity towards the women he loved was always one of his greatest virtues, and he insisted that Leonilda should keep the dowry of five thousand ducats he had promised her – only now he was giving it to her as a father. Well satisfied by the outcome, Lucrezia returned to

Sant'Agata. To her surprise, Casanova was already waiting for her there. His carriage had overturned on a nearby road, an almost too convenient excuse (and this was not the only time in his life he would use it), and her friend the Marchese had offered to put him up overnight. Since Lucrezia had no wish to become the centre of gossip in the small community where she now lived, when Casanova asked if he could sleep with her she told him that it was out of the question. Although he pleaded that he would marry her in the locality that instant, she called his bluff by repeating that if he really loved her he had only to buy an estate in the Kingdom of Naples and she would live with him there without asking him to commit to marriage. That was the end of the matter. Casanova would regret it in his old age, but at the time there seemed no alternative. As he put it himself, 'I should have lived happily with this charming woman, but I abhorred the idea of settling down anywhere. I would have been able to buy an estate at Naples which would have made me rich, but it would have meant adopting a prudent course of conduct which was absolutely opposed to my nature.'[42]

Imprudence was certainly one of Casanova's greatest faults. One of his finest character traits, however, was his sense of discretion, a trait that had been cultivated in him by his first mentor, Senator Malipiero. It created many problems for him when he was writing his memoirs. As he wrote to his friend J. F. Opiz in 1791, 'What afflicts me is the duty I am under to conceal the names as I have no right to publish the affairs of others.'[43] Although he had few scruples about naming his social acquaintances, the rogues he had encountered and the actresses he had slept with (women in the theatre were seldom bashful about their love affairs), he took pains to disguise the identities of private individuals, particularly women, who might be embarrassed or even harmed by his disclosures. Sometimes, as in the case of Nanetta and Marta, the Savorgnan sisters, Casanova used only Christian names. Elsewhere he wrote down a woman's initials, or identified her by mysterious initials that did not belong to her: one finds in his memoirs a

Signora F, a Mlle X.C.V., a Mme . . ., and even a Mme X.

In the case of Donna Lucrezia, however, Casanova gave her and her family false names. Never dreaming that scholars would comb through the archives of Rome centuries after his death, in search of their real identities, he did not look far for inspiration but instead adapted their real names. Cecilia Monti, Lucrezia's mother, was identified in the early 1960s by the academic J. Rives Childs as Cecilia d'Antoni, who, like her namesake in *Story of My Life*, lived in Rome's Minerva district in the 1740s. In 1745 Cecilia d'Antoni had a fifteen-year-old son and two daughters, as had Casanova's Cecilia Monti. Her elder daughter was named Anna Maria, and the younger was named Lucrezia.

Born in 1725, the real Lucrezia d'Antoni was nineteen years old in 1744 – around the same age as Casanova's Angelica Monti. In common with his Angelica, Lucrezia d'Antoni was married in the church of Santa Maria sopra Minerva in January 1745. Hers was the only marriage to take place in the church that month, and she and her husband, Filippo Tomassi (Casanova's Don Francesco), later named their first child Angelica, as Casanova was well aware when he was writing his memoirs.[44]

The real Lucrezia's older sister, Anna Maria d'Antoni, was the 'Donna Lucrezia' of the memoirs. Born in 1715 in Rome, Anna Maria was married in 1734 to a man named Alessio Vallati – 'Donna Lucrezia's' lawyer husband Castelli. When she met Casanova in 1744 Anna Maria was in her late twenties and had been married for ten years, long enough for her and her husband to have settled into a comfortable relationship devoid of jealousy. After so long a period of childlessness, the birth of a daughter must have been a blessed event that might, perhaps, have solved the Vallatis' inheritance problems. No matter who her biological father was, Leonilda was wanted by both her parents.

Her biological father never stopped wanting her. And what Casanova wanted, he usually got eventually, as we shall see later.

FOUR

Bellino

The duty of a lover is to force the
object of his love to surrender to him.[1]

HE WAS NEITHER a son nor a daughter to his mother. He bore no
relation to his sisters. The boy he called brother was his son, but he
was no father to him. The youth who called him brother wore a
dress, but was no brother to him. In short, he was a man who was
not a man and whose purpose in life it was to be a woman.

Bellino's life was a riddle that is believed to have inspired Balzac to
write *Sarrasine*, a novel about mistaken sexual identities, and Casanova was as confused by it as anyone else. Entranced by Bellino's
beauty, he was nevertheless deeply disturbed by the desire he felt for
him. For although underneath his skirt Bellino was built like a man,
his face, hands and even his tiny breasts were utterly feminine.

Casanova was in no mood for conundrums when he met Bellino
in February 1745. Just weeks away from his twentieth birthday, he
had stopped off at the Adriatic port of Ancona on his way back to
Venice from Rome. To his dismay, almost his disbelief, he had had
to leave the city only a few months after arriving there in Donna
Lucrezia's company. The great Cardinal Acquaviva, in whose suite
the young priest had planned to build his future, had sacked him
from his post as a secreatary.

The cause of his dismissal had been a woman – Barbaruccia
Dalacqua, the daughter of his French teacher, whom he had got to
know when he had visited her father's house as a student. For once

this was not a romantic liaison, for Barbaruccia was involved with another of her father's pupils, who was not in a position to marry her. When Dalacqua found his daughter in bed with her lover, he banned the student from the house, and that might have been the end of the affair had not Barbaruccia discovered that she was pregnant. The lovers decided to elope, but at the last minute their plan was discovered and the young man was arrested. Pursued by the authorities herself, Barbaruccia fled in disguise to Casanova's rooms in the Palazzo di Spagna and threw herself on his mercy. Since he could never resist a tearful woman in distress, particularly when she was a beauty like Barbaruccia, Casanova hid her overnight and arranged for her to plead her case in front of the cardinal the following morning. Since nothing could be kept secret for long in Rome, the affair soon became the talk of the city and, although Acquaviva recognised that his protégé had acted entirely honourably, Casanova's position was compromised to such an extent that the cardinal had no alternative but to let him go.

This was the account of his departure from Rome that Casanova included in his memoirs, but it may well have hidden a less flattering, more truthful version of the event. His friend the Prince de Ligne, one of the few people to read the manuscript of *Story of My Life* before its publication, noted of the affair that Casanova 'takes away the mistress of the nephew of the Pope and, about to be assassinated, makes his escape'.[2] So had his irrepressible sexuality, rather than his disinterested kindness, led to his downfall? Whatever the real reason, overnight Casanova's meteoric rise in the Catholic Church had become a catastrophic fall. The nineteen-year-old novice was 'in despair, for I loved Rome, and being on the great road to fortune I saw myself thrown off it without knowing where to go and bereft of all my hopes'.[3] When Cardinal Acquaviva generously offered him letters of recommendation to any city in the world he chose to go to, Casanova named Constantinople on the spur of the moment. Armed with the cardinal's letters, plus a generous pay-off of one hundred gold Spanish doubloons, he left for Venice, where he planned to set sail for the East.

Reaching Ancona at the tail-end of the carnival season, Casanova checked into the best tavern; he may have lost his job, but since he still had money in his pocket he saw no reason to sacrifice his newly-acquired sense of self-importance. The inn was crowded with visitors, his temper was frayed, and within minutes of his arrival he became embroiled in an argument with the innkeeper. To calm him down a Castilian army officer named Sancho Pico invited Casanova to accompany him to one of the rooms where they could listen to music and meet a person he described as the 'first actress' or *prima donna* at the local theatre. Sancho Pico was being ironic: Bellino was no *prima donna*, he was a young castrato engaged as *primo uomo*, or first man, at Ancona's La Fenice opera house.

Italy's castrati were the celebrities of their time, flamboyant and often temperamental singers who dominated the popular genre of *opera seria*. The leading male and female roles were written for them, they were treated with the deference of modern divas, and were paid the highest salaries of any performers in the operatic world. Revered as they were, the very existence of castrati was an anachronism, for the removal of the testicles was an illegal operation in Italy. Even so, it was carried out hundreds of times every year to preserve the high singing voices of poor boys whose parents sold them to the music masters or conservatories that trained them. Due to the high penalties for performing a castration – death to the surgeon, excommunication to anyone associated with it – the mutilations usually took place in secret, or using the excuse that they were medically necessarily. No one wanted to own up to removing a young singer's testicles, as musicologist Dr Charles Burney discovered when, on a trip to Italy in the early 1770s, he attempted to discover the centre of the practice: 'I was told at Milan that it was at Venice; at Venice that it was at Bologna; but at Bologna the fact was denied, and I was referred to Florence; from Florence to Rome, and from Rome I was sent to Naples.'[4] The two main centres of castration were rumoured to be Naples and Bologna, and it was from Bologna that Bellino and his family hailed.

Due to a strict interpretation of St Paul's interdict that *mulier taceat in ecclesia* – women should be silent in church – which had almost certainly been intended to prevent women from taking part in theological discussions, women had been banned from singing in church services or performing in public theatres since at least the sixteenth century. So whenever a female voice was called for in a musical score, impresarios had to employ a young choir boy or, better still, a male singer who had been castrated before puberty to prevent his voice from breaking. The castrato voice was said to be superior to that of a baritone, a tenor and even a female soprano, for it melded the high vocal range and angelic sweetness of a young boy's voice with the power and resonance of a fully-grown man's. In acting ability, too, many audiences felt that castrati were superior to the women they were impersonating. 'A double pleasure is given, in that these persons are not women, but only represent women,' wrote Goethe of them. 'The young men have studied the properties of the female sex in its being and behaviour; they know them thoroughly and reproduce them like an artist; they represent, not themselves, but a nature absolutely foreign to them.'[5] Frenchman Charles de Brosses had a far more down-to-earth opinion of Italy's castrated singers: 'Except for one or two, all I have heard seem to be miserable,' he wrote of them. 'It is not worthwhile forfeiting one's personal property for the right to chirp like that.'[6]

During the seventeenth century the strict rules regarding female performers had relaxed in much of Italy. In the sexually-liberated climate of the Venetian Republic, for instance, actresses had taken part in plays as early as the 1630s, and one hundred years later singers such as Senator Malipiero's favourite Teresa Imer regularly performed alongside the castrati whenever operas were staged. In the Papal States, however, the large band of territories across central Italy which fell under the direct authority of the Pope and which included Ancona, the ban against women performers remained very much in force. Given a choice between employing actresses with loose morals or turning a pragmatic blind eye to the illegal mutilation of male singers, the latter option was considered

the lesser evil, even in the Vatican: as late as the 1780s more than two hundred castrati were employed in Rome's churches, and they even performed in the pope's private chapel.

Far from discouraging immorality in the Papal States, the presence of so many castrati had the opposite effect of encouraging homosexuality, a sexual practice that was tolerated far more in Italy and France than it was in England, the American colonies, Spain and, in particular, the Dutch Republic, where those suspected of committing sodomy were ruthlessly persecuted, tried, and put to death. In Rome, a city where thousands of unattached male clerics lived without women, a cardinal could share his bed with another man without arousing suspicion or disapproval, and the soft features, smooth skin and curvaceous bodies of the castrati cast their spell over even heterosexually-inclined men. Often exceptionally tall and handsome, with unusually long legs and arms, castrati combined the beauty of male youths with the voluptuous figures and grace of women. Well aware of their special charms, they did not hesitate to make full use of them: when Casanova mistook one beautiful castrato he spotted in a Roman café for a woman, he reported that 'the impudent fellow looks at me, and says that if I want to spend the night with him, he'll serve me equally well either as a girl or a boy.'[7] On another occasion the adventurer found the well-known castrato Giovanni Osti as seductive-looking as any woman: 'Squashed into a tight-fitting corset, he had the figure of a nymph, and one saw few women with breasts as firm and sweet as his. The illusion he created was irresistible. One was stopped in one's tracks, overcome with admiration . . . It was evident that, as a man, he wanted to encourage the love of those who loved him as such, and who would perhaps not have loved him if he had not been a man; but that he also wished to inspire love in those who, to fall in love with him, needed to think that he was a real woman. Rome, the Holy City, which thus makes pederasts of all humanity, neither wishes to admit it nor to recognise an illusion which it does everything in its power to create in the minds of the audience.'[8]

The perks of being a castrato could almost be said to outweigh

the obvious disadvantages. At the musical conservatories they received a rigorous education, and since they were thought to be more susceptible to illness than ordinary boys they were given better food and allowed more heating in their dormitories. Once a castrato was trained his potential earning power was without equal. In 1738 in Naples the castrato Senesino received four times more than the composers' salaries, even though he was a painfully wooden actor; and in 1769 *alto castrato* Gaetano Guardagni – famous for stopping mid-aria to lecture his inattentive audiences on their behaviour – was paid a phenomenal £1,150 by the King's Theatre in London, and dared to ask for a rise of £450 the following year. Castrati were in demand at the courts and theatres of London, Vienna, Dresden, Berlin and Paris, where they were fêted by dukes, duchesses and government ministers. Even royalty bowed down before them: in 1772 it was said that the ex-Electress of Saxony visited Bologna expressly to have lunch with seventy-year-old Carlo Farinelli; and after he had played the harpsichord and sung for her, the Electress kissed him and 'told him that henceforth she could die happy'.[9]

In 1745 Bellino was about fifteen years old. Taking advantage of his relative inexperience, the impresario at Ancona's La Fenice theatre paid him only a pittance for performing during the Carnival. By late February, the singer's family, who consisted of his mother, two younger sisters and a younger brother who was employed at the all-male theatre as a 'ballerina', had spent everything they had earned on their living expenses, and feared that they would have to walk back to their home in Bologna when the Carnival was over, begging for alms along the road. But far from being crushed by their terrible poverty, the family compensated for it by being vivacious, gregarious and affable. As theatre people they were used to charming money out of wealthy strangers, and when Sancho Pico brought Casanova, who was still dressed in his smart Roman *abate*'s clothes, to their room in the inn they took him to be a rich man. No one could have known from his wardrobe, his conversation and the self-important way he carried himself that the

highly-educated young priest was an actors' son himself with no money in the world other than the pay-off his ex-employer had recently given him.

Bellino's family enchanted Casanova from the first moment he entered their room. The mother was jolly and welcoming, her eleven- and twelve-year-old daughters, Marina and Cecilia, were pretty, unselfconscious children who were both studying to go on the stage, and their brother Petronio was a cheeky, effeminate youth. The castrato eclipsed them all in Casanova's eyes: though less gregarious than the others he was 'ravishingly handsome' and so feminine-looking that Casanova found it difficult to believe that he was really of the male sex. When Bellino sat down at his harpsichord and began to play and sing with an angelic voice embellished with enchanting *fioriture*, his black eyes sparkled with a fire that scorched the young priest's soul. Casanova's desire for Bellino disturbed him, but only mildly, for he was convinced that there must be a woman's body hiding underneath the youth's male garments.

In modern times there has been much speculation about Casanova's so-called bisexuality. In his memoirs he admits to having the very occasional homosexual encounter (most notably with Ismail Effendi, the ex-Minister of Foreign Affairs in Constantinople, and with Lieutenant Lunin in St Petersburg) but these usually occur in situations where he has been aroused by a woman. A note which was found among his possessions in Dux after his death hints at several other homosexual experiences that he left out of the final draft of his memoirs: it includes the short phrases '*Mes amours avec Camille (en prison); le Duc d'Elboeuf; Pédérastie avec X. à Dunquerque*'. (Camille was a male as well as a female name in eighteenth-century France, and the Duc d'Elboeuf was a well-known sodomite.) A libertine by nature, Casanova had no strong moral objection to homosexuality nor, it seems, to having the occasional sexual experience with someone of his own sex, but to have sexual feelings for men did not, he insisted, come naturally to him.

His interest in Bellino did not go unnoticed by the singer's

mother. But was the young cleric heterosexual or homosexual? Did he desire Bellino because he was an effeminate-looking castrato, or did he hope, as many men did, that her son might secretly be a woman? Anxious to make money out of him whatever his sexual leanings, she dispatched Bellino to Casanova's room the following morning to offer him Petronio's services as a manservant during his stay in Ancona. Certain that Bellino was a woman, Casanova was about to make a pass at 'him' when his younger sisters Cecilia and Marina came running in. 'I could only be delighted with the appealing tableau in front of me,' he wrote of them. 'Gaiety, unadorned beauty of three different kinds, sweet familiarity, the verve of the theatre, pretty banter, little Bolognese facial expressions with which I was unfamiliar and which pleased me excessively. The two little girls were real living rosebuds, and worthy of being preferred to Bellino, if I had not got it into my head that she was also a girl.'[10] On offer before him, or so he presumed, were an irresistible and vivacious trio: a beautiful youth of indeterminate sex who looked about seventeen years old, and two pubescent children. And when he tipped Petronio for bringing him some coffee the boy thanked him with an open-mouthed kiss, leading Casanova to believe that he, too, could be his for a small price.

If he had money in his pocket a man believed he had the right to buy sexual favours from anyone. And, although he had no idea how he would live in the future, compared to the poverty-stricken theatrical family Casanova was wealthy. Using money as his weapon of power, he set out to discover the true sex of the castrato in the hope that, if Bellino *was* a woman, he could make love to him – or rather, to her. A large tip to the mother elicited the information that Bellino had indeed been certified as a castrato by Ancona's bishop (intimate inspections of castrati by the authorities were commonplace, in order to prevent female singers from slipping through the net and performing illegally). This conclusive-sounding evidence did not satisfy Casanova, who then generously tipped Bellino's sisters to stay away from his room. Left alone with the

castrato, he offered Bellino a gold doubloon to let him examine his genitals. When he rejected this crude offer, Casanova refused to take no for an answer. Exhibiting the bullying streak he usually kept hidden, he attempted to grope the youth, who firmly pushed his hand away.

Bellino's 'obstinacy' in refusing him what he wanted threw Casanova into the kind of childish sulk he had already exhibited on part of the journey between Naples and Rome with Donna Lucrezia, for he had already spent fifteen or sixteen golden sequins to satisfy his curiosity, and had so far failed to get anything in return. Determined to get his money's worth somehow, he began to fondle little Cecilia and Marina when they returned. 'With all three of us seated in front of the fire eating chestnuts, I began to distribute kisses,' he wrote. 'And Bellino, in turn, shows no lack of compliance. I touch and I kiss the budding breasts of Cecilia and Marina, and Bellino, smiling, does not stop my hand from slipping inside his ruffled shirt and grasping hold of a breast which leaves nothing to doubt.'[11]

'Girl, or boy, what does it matter!' laughed Sancho Pico when Casanova told him of his dilemma. As long as the castrato was pretty, who cared what sex he was? Casanova clearly did care. Desperate to know Bellino's real sex, he bribed Cecilia to reveal it, but she claimed that she had never seen her oldest brother naked. The sexually frustrated Casanova then let Cecilia satisfy him in another way – by spending the night in his bed. She was twelve years old, physically undeveloped and, she claimed, a virgin. 'I did not quibble with her,' Casanova wrote in his memoirs. 'Love is the divine sauce that makes that particular little morsel delicious. Cecilia was charming, but I had not had time to desire her; so I wasn't able to say to her, you have made me happy; it was she who said it to me; but I wasn't much flattered by it.'[12] The child's compliance earned her the generous sum of three doubloons. Not wanting to be outdone, her sister Marina – only eleven years old but, Casanova noted, more physically developed and sexually experienced than Cecilia – earned a similar sum to have full intercourse with him the following night.

In the eighteenth century, Casanova's behaviour, which today would be regarded as criminal, was not that unusual. The concept of childhood as we know it scarcely existed at the time. In France there were no laws to prevent the rape or sexual abuse of children. In England, the age of female consent, which in 1275 had been fixed at twelve years old under canon law, had in the late sixteenth century been lowered to just ten. Child prostitution was a common fact of life among the desperately poor, for destitute parents regarded their daughters as a potential source of income, one of the few commodities they had to sell. And wealthy men were willing to pay a high price for the privilege of deflowering a young virgin, partly due to the widely-believed myth that it would cure them of venereal disease.

However, even by the standards of the time there was something distinctly unsavoury about the fickle ease with which Casanova switched from pursuing the fifteen-year-old castrato to seducing both his pubescent sisters, and it earned him Bellino's contempt. Contempt turned to disgust a few days later when the castrato accompanied Casanova to Ancona's port. Here they boarded a Turkish vessel, and were left alone in the captain's cabin for a few minutes with a beautiful Greek slave girl. Without exchanging a single word with the slave, Casanova immediately unbuttoned his breeches, pulled her on to his lap and had sex with her. And, to Bellino's amazement, the slave complied 'like a bitch which only listens to its instinct'.[13]

As Casanova had perhaps intended, Bellino was deeply shocked by this behaviour, which ran completely contrary to his own romantic nature. Or rather, to *her* romantic nature. For, as Casanova suspected, Bellino was in reality a young woman disguised as a castrato. Her name, he tells us, was Teresa Lanti, and she was born in Bologna around 1730.

Although Casanova rarely, if ever, disguised the names of his thespian lovers, there has always been speculation about Teresa Lanti's identity. She has been named as any number of eighteenth-century sopranos, the most popular being Angiola Calori, a

Milanese singer who achieved fame in London in the late 1750s and early 1760s. There was, however, a real Teresa *Landi*, born in Bologna on 15 May 1731 to parents Luigi Landi and Flavia Gambarini.[14] Furthermore, a sumptuous portrait of a singer bearing her name hangs today in the theatre museum of the famous La Scala Opera House in Milan, although no one has ever been sure of the painting's real provenance.

Whatever her true identity, Teresa told Casanova that she grew up as the only daughter of a poor widower who worked for the city's Institute of Science, where several men bearing the name Landi are known to have been employed at the time. When she was twelve, her father took in a lodger, a talented castrato in his late twenties who was to end Teresa's lonely childhood and transform her life. In his memoirs Casanova identified him as the celebrated singer Felice Salimbeni, but it is far more likely from the date and place of his death that he was Salimbeni's direct contemporary, the Milanese castrato Giuseppe Appiani.

On the verge of great success in Bologna in 1742, Appiani, as Teresa later told Casanova, took on as his protégé a local youngster named Bellino, and sent him to study with a singing teacher in the nearby city of Rimini. At the same time he fell in love with his landlord's eleven-year-old daughter. Entranced by Teresa's beauty and wonderful singing voice, he taught her everything about music that his own singing teacher, Nicola Porpora, had taught him.

His reward, Teresa said, 'was such as his affection forced him to ask of me; I did not feel humiliated to grant it to him, since I adored him'.[15] In short, she became his lover. Castrated men were widely presumed to be impotent and have no sexual desires, but this was not necessarily the case. Many castrati were far from sexless. The great Salimbeni smiled knowingly when people pitied him for having been castrated; the famous Farinelli fell passionately in love with his nephew's young wife; and in 1766 *primo uomo* Ferdinando Tenducci caused a scandal by eloping with Miss Dora Maunsell of Limerick, a well-connected young Irishwoman whom he later married in Cork. Tenducci was a star in both England and Ireland:

his voice, immortalised by Lydia Melford in Tobias Smollett's novel *Humphry Clinker*, published in 1771, was said to be 'neither man's nor woman's; but it is more melodious than either; and it warbled so divinely, that, while I listened, I really thought myself in paradise'. His fame did not stop Dora's outraged family from kidnapping her and having him thrown into prison. Despite this, Mr and Mrs Tenducci stayed together, had two children and later published a full account of their relationship and subsequent persecution.

Teresa worshipped her father's lodger. Although she later re-assured Casanova that 'men like yourself are, without doubt, to be preferred over those who resemble my first lover' (one can presume that this was a great relief to the great seducer) Appiani was the exception. 'His beauty, his mind, his manners, his talent and the rare qualities of his heart and soul' made her prefer him to all the whole men she had met up until that time. In addition, he was modest and discreet, rich and generous. Castration had turned him into a 'monster of adorable qualities'.[16] But within a year of arriving in Bologna, he was offered engagements to sing in Ferrara and Venice, and Teresa was heartbroken at the thought of parting from him. When, just before his departure, her father suddenly died of a malignant fever, she was inconsolable. Unable to leave her all alone in Bologna, her lover took her with him as far as Rimini, where he planned to board her with the same music teacher who was currently training his young protégé Bellino.

Tragically, Bellino had just died. Appiani immediately hatched a daring plan that would allow Teresa to continue her musical education and ensure that they would eventually be able to live together without incurring society's disapproval. From now on, she must pretend to be Bellino. In this guise he would take her back to Bologna and board her with the real Bellino's mother, whom he would pay to look after her while she continued her musical training. In future, Teresa would have to sleep and dress alone to prevent her true sex from being discovered, and when her breasts developed people would think nothing of it 'for having

too much bosom is the usual defect of our sort'. In four years' time
her lover would send for her to join him, and from then on they
would live together as two castrati and no one would be able to
criticise them for it. In short, in exchange for publicly renouncing
her sex, Teresa would have a lucrative singing career and the man
she depended on

From that moment on, Teresa effectively became Bellino. It was
a complicated, risky and often humiliating deception for a girl who
was little more than a child. Dressed in the dead boy's clothing, she
returned with her lover to Bologna, where the real Bellino's younger siblings – Petronio, Cecilia and Marina – were tricked into
thinking that she was their real brother whom they had not seen
for some years; only Bellino's bereaved mother knew the truth.
Since it was common practice for castrati to have to undergo
intimate examinations by priests or theatre owners anxious to
avoid prosecution by the Church for unwittingly employing a
female singer, Appiani supplied Teresa with a small prosthesis
that would give her the appearance of having a penis. It was 'a kind
of cat-gut, long, limp and as thick as one's thumb, pale, and of very
soft leather' surrounded by an oval of transparent skin five or six
inches long. Teresa quickly learned to attach it to her own genitals
with gum tragacanth, a glue made from a shrub.

Once he had settled Teresa with her new family, the castrato left
Bologna and Teresa had a premonition that she would never see
him again. She was right: thirty-year-old Appiani died soon afterwards in the nearby city of Cesena, of erysipelas, a disfiguring skin
disease known as St Anthony's Fire. For the second time in a few
months, Teresa was bereaved. Since she had no other means of
support she continued to live with Bellino's mother who thought it
best to continue the deception in the hope that her new 'son' might
one day make the family's fortune on the stage. In the meantime
the woman found a singing engagement for 'Bellino' in the city of
Ancona, where her surviving son, Petronio, was employed as a
female dancer.

A precarious, almost farcical existence on the road began. While

Petronio put on a ballet dress and danced in the female chorus of the theatres they worked for, Teresa donned breeches during the daytime and, at night, put on a dress and sang castrato roles. Her reputation soon grew. By the time she was fourteen her alter ego Bellino had engagements in Ancona and Rimini and even in the Holy City itself, and since 'he' looked so feminine, each time 'he' performed in a new city Teresa had to glue on her false penis and endure a degrading examination by the priests before she could work. She was risking disgrace, prosecution and a severe punishment by breaking the law against women performers, and her life was made even more unpleasant by the men who constantly molested her in the hope of procuring 'illicit and dreadful favours' in return for the money she and her family so badly needed. Homosexual men who believed that she was a boy and wished to use her as such made Teresa so angry that she feared she would stab one of them. Heterosexual men who were convinced that she was a woman pestered her with terrifying requests to inspect her mutilated genitals.

Casanova appeared to fall into the latter category. Though the fifteen-year-old was revolted by his coarseness towards her and her adopted sisters, her feelings were complicated by the fact that she was secretly attracted to him. However, his crude behaviour with the Greek slave girl on board the Turkish vessel was the final straw for her. Unaware that Giacomo and the slave had encountered each other months before in Ancona's lazaretto where, locked up on separate floors of the building, they had attempted to have sex through a large hole in a balcony floor, Teresa decided to teach him a lesson. At a supper party laid on that night by Sancho Pico, she appeared as she did on stage: as a castrato disguised as a woman. Casanova was set on fire by her feminine beauty. He could not rest until he had discovered Bellino's secret. In his opinion the singer had obviously set out to arouse and confuse him, and he now demanded that he satisfy his curiosity. When Bellino refused to expose his genitals, Casanova held him down and forced up his skirt. One quick glance was enough to enlighten and shock him:

for, perhaps anticipating that this would happen, Teresa had glued on her false penis. 'Astonished, angry, mortified, disgusted, I let him go,' Casanova wrote. 'I'd seen that Bellino was a real man; but a man to be despised as much for his degradation as for the shameful calm which I had observed in him at a moment when I should have seen proof of his emotions.'[17]

The following morning, still furious at having mistaken the singer's sex, Casanova left Ancona for Venice. Since he had already promised to take the castrato as far as Rimini, where his next theatrical engagement was, he did not renege on this, so Bellino/Teresa accompanied him on the journey north while the rest of the family followed on. Teresa had perhaps supposed herself safe from Casanova's prurient interest now that he had glimpsed her genitals, but she was wrong. He still 'could not look into (her) eyes without burning with desire'[18] and as soon as the carriage left Ancona he began a long, vicious tirade against her in the hope that it would shame Bellino into letting him touch with his hands the evidence he had seen:

I told him that since his eyes were those of a woman and not a man, I needed to convince myself by touch that what I had seen when he had run away was not a monstrous clitoris . . . I no longer care to see it; I only ask to touch it, and you can be sure that, as soon as I am certain, I'll become as gentle as a dove, for as soon as I've acknowledged that you're a man it will be impossible for me to carry on loving you . . . If it turns out that you truly are a castrato, permit me to believe that, knowing you perfectly resemble a woman, you have hatched a cruel plan to make me fall in love with you in order to drive me mad by refusing me that proof which can alone restore my sanity . . . You must also be aware that your obstinate refusal to give me the clarification that I ask you for forces me to despise you as a castrato. The importance you attach to the thing is puerile and malicious . . . If you have a human soul you cannot persist in this refusal. . . . With my mind in such a state you must finally realise that I

must resolve to use force, for if you are my enemy I must treat you brutally as such . . . What has infuriated me is the display you have made of your charms, the effect of which, you must understand, you cannot ignore. You did not dread my amorous fury then, and do you expect me to believe that you fear it now, when all I ask of you is to let me touch an object which can only disgust me?[19]

This was Casanova at his most manipulative. Years of being indulged by his grandmother had led him to believe that he could get what he wanted at the instant he wanted it, and his bullying threats and guilt-provoking arguments in the carriage reduced the young impostor to tears. Still she would not give in to him. He was not her master, Bellino/Teresa reminded him, in fact she – or rather he – was travelling with Casanova on the strength of a promise he had made that he would leave him alone. If he persisted in persecuting him, Bellino would get out of the carriage and walk all the way to Rimini. Bellino assured Casanova that, had 'he' been a woman, he would have loved him in return, but since he was a man he would not give in to his demands, 'for your passion, which is now only natural, would all of a sudden become monstrous'. Casanova might perpetrate a brutal act of anal rape, or even murder 'if I stopped you from penetrating an inviolable temple, whose gate wise Nature only made to open outwards'.[20]

By late afternoon Casanova had been shamed into submission. But his relentless onslaught had finally worn down the girl. When they reached the city of Senigallia, where they were to spend the night at an inn, Bellino/Teresa suddenly capitulated and offered to share his bed that night. The outcome was predictably passionate. Overjoyed to get his way – and hugely relieved to find out, once they were in bed, that the beautiful castrato he so desired was indeed a woman – the angry bully of the last few days instantly metamorphosed into a tender, thoughtful lover and confidant; Casanova at his best. He listened to Teresa's life story attentively, then asked her to show him how she glued on her cat-

gut penis. As the contraption 'offered no obstruction to the well of her sex'[21] it made Teresa even more sexually alluring to him, but their attempts to make love whilst she was wearing it were hopelessly comical.

During the course of that night Casanova fell deeply in love with Teresa. Donna Lucrezia, the great love he had parted from a matter of weeks ago in Rome, was now forgotten in favour of the fifteen-year-old singer. The following morning he impulsively asked Teresa to marry him. A civil ceremony could only increase their feelings and respect for one another, he reasoned to himself. It would also be necessary for them to marry if they were to be accepted by good society, and although he had been thrown off his original course of a clerical career in Martirano and Rome, he was still hungry for professional success and the approbation of his social superiors.

No sooner had he popped the question, however, than Casanova began to have misgivings. Did he really want to marry at such a young age, or indeed to marry Teresa? Her talent would ensure that they 'would never lack the necessaries of life'[22] but the idea that he had no job and might have to live off her terrified him. He decided to give her a starkly honest analysis of his position in life to test her out. Contrary to appearances he was not a rich man, he confessed. All he owned was 'youth, health, courage, a modicum of intelligence, a sense of honour and integrity, and a few attempts at a literary career. My great treasure is that I am my own master, that I am not dependent on anyone, and that I am not frightened of misfortunes. My nature tends towards being a wastrel. That's your man.'[23]

Casanova was perhaps hoping to discourage Teresa, but instead his confession that she had not been the only one perpetrating a deception came as a relief to her. She was glad that Casanova had neither money nor rank because it put them on a more equal footing. She would travel with him anywhere he wished, she swore, and would marry him if he wished to have legal rights over her, although she assured him that the marriage ceremony would make her love him no more than she already did – a surprisingly emancipated attitude. Teresa would also give him a present which,

if he loved her, he would not be too proud to accept: the present was to be herself. She was all his, and from now on she would take care of him. 'Hereafter think only of loving me; but only me,'[24] she pleaded.

Her last words sounded the death knell of their love affair. Although Casanova swore he would marry Teresa in Bologna 'day after tomorrow, at the latest' he must already have been looking for a way out of what he could only see as a claustrophobic relationship that would limit his future prospects. In truth he had no intention of getting married, certainly not at this stage in his life. Marriage was 'the tomb of love' in his opinion and, as he said of the institution, just months later, 'I hope never to find myself compelled to contract that tie.'[25] But how was he to renege on his promise without dishonouring himself in his own eyes as well as in Teresa's? The answer was as simple as it was devious: he mislaid his passport.

In eighteenth-century Europe, as in modern times, passports – quite literally documents which allowed the bearer to 'pass through a port' – had to be carried on most long-distance journeys, and travellers lost them at their peril. For identification purposes they contained a detailed description of the bearer. 'It is commanded to safely and freely let pass: Jacques Cazanua Italian thirty-two years old, five foot ten and a half inches tall or Thereabouts Face long, plain Swarthy. Heavy long nose. Large mouth. Brown, highly intelligent eyes. Who is going to Flanders' read the passport issued to Casanova by the Duc de Gesvres in Paris in 1757.[26] Usually issued by government ministers, the military, or the Church or city authorities, such documents were essential when travelling through disputed territories such as central Italy, where the Austrians and Spanish were still battling over their possessions. When he set off from Senigallia with Teresa, Casanova placed his passport safely with his other papers, or so he claimed. Just four hours later, when a non-commissioned officer of the Spanish Army stationed in Pesaro asked to inspect it, he found that it had mysteriously disappeared.

Casanova was instantly arrested and told that he could go

nowhere until he obtained a replacement passport from Rome. Until then, he was to be imprisoned in a Spanish guard house on the edge of Pesaro while Teresa was allowed to walk free. She was distraught at the thought of parting from him. 'She wanted to stay in Pesaro,' he later wrote, adding tellingly, 'but I would not allow it.'[27] Instead, he had his trunk untied from their carriage, gave Teresa a generous one hundred sequins and sent her on to Rimini alone.

Having glimpsed a more secure existence free from deception, Teresa could no longer carry on living as a castrato. The moment she reached Rimini she confided her secret to the impresario who had hired her as 'Bellino'. The impresario congratulated her on her brave decision. Luckily for her Rimini fell within the ecclesiastical province of Ravenna, where the bar against female singers was no longer in force, so Teresa could legally perform as a woman. She was an immediate success, and not only with the audiences: by the time Casanova turned up ten days later, she already had a new male admirer in tow: an Austrian, Baron Weiss.

Casanova kept his promise to meet up with Teresa in Rimini, but by his hot-headed behaviour he ensured that he could only stay with her for one night. Although his time in captivity in Pesaro had been boring rather than unpleasant – he had whiled away the long hours playing faro and piquet with the soldiers – he impulsively escaped on a stolen horse before his passport arrived, and turned up in Rimini on the run, disguised as a muleteer. After spending only a few passionate hours with Teresa, he fled at dawn, promising that he would meet up with her again in Bologna in May and marry her then.

We shall never know if he intended to keep his promise. For within weeks of her debut as a female performer, Teresa was introduced to fifty-six-year-old Francesco d'Eboli, the Duke of Castropignano and Captain General of the Spanish Army in Naples. Castropignano instantly fell in love with her, and offered her a lucrative contract at the San Carlo theatre in Naples. Built in 1737, the magnificent San Carlo with its blue and gold décor was

regarded as one of the most prestigious opera houses in the world, and to be offered a year's contract there was a fabulous opportunity for any singer. Nevertheless, Teresa hesitated to accept it until she had consulted Casanova by sending him two letters. The first told him of her good luck, and contained the unsigned contract for the San Carlo theatre. The second contained a pledge to serve him all her life. 'She said that if I wanted to go to Naples with her she would meet up with me wherever I wished,' he reported, 'and that if I felt an aversion to returning to Naples I must disregard her good luck, and be certain that she could conceive of no fortune and no happiness other than to do everything within her power to make me content and happy'[28] – an impossible task, had she but known it.

By putting her fate into Casanova's hands, Teresa reduced him to a state of the 'greatest irresolution' in which his genuine feelings for her battled against his own needs and pride. It was a defining moment for him. He neither wanted to lose his latest passion nor to stand in the way of her success, yet he was not prepared to follow her to Naples without having first made his own mark in the world. Like his own mother Zanetta, Teresa was in the theatrical profession, a despised lower-class milieu which Casanova had always tried to distance himself from. And, like Zanetta, Teresa would soon be surrounded by male admirers – in fact, she had already had two in tow, Weiss and the powerful duke. Casanova knew he could never cope with competition from other, richer admirers, nor with the ignominy of living off a woman's earnings. Then there was his position to think of. During his previous stay in Naples he had made well-connected friends who believed him to be of high social rank. If he were to reappear in the city he had left with such high hopes only months previously as the penniless husband or lover of an actress, 'a coward living off his wife or his mistress',[29] he would feel disgraced, and rightly so. More than anything else Casanova was ambitious to rise in the world, and an alliance with an actress – one of his own kind – would inevitably lead to his social downfall: 'Sharing her lot, whether as a husband or lover, I should find myself

degraded, humiliated, and forced by my position and profession to grovel. The reflection that in the fairest time of my youth I would have to renounce all hope of the high fortune which it seemed to me I had been born for gave the scales such a strong jolt that my reason silenced my heart.'[30]

Marrying a singer was out of the question for Casanova. And now that he had enjoyed Teresa's charms, even associating with her was losing its attraction. Playing for time, he returned her contract by post, warning her to engage a respectable chambermaid as a chaperone and to conduct herself in such a way 'that I could marry her without blushing', and promising to join her in Naples as soon as he could. Teresa replied poignantly that she would 'wait for him until such time as he wrote and told her he no longer thought of her'. In another letter, written in early May, she informed him that Castropignano had offered to escort her personally to Naples. The duke was old, she reassured him, but even if he had been young Casanova would have had nothing to fear, for she would always remain faithful to him. If he needed money, she added, he should draw bills of exchange in Bologna on her name, 'and she would pay them even if it meant her having to sell everything she had'.[31]

This loving, generous, passionate letter did Teresa no good at all. It is doubtful if Casanova even replied to it. While she went to Naples and threw herself into her career, he returned to Venice and the welcoming arms of his two upper-class 'wives', as he called them, Nanetta and Marta Savorgnan. It was not so easy for Teresa to forget him: she was pregnant. With no one else to turn to, she confided her predicament to Castropignano who was fast becoming her father-figure and saviour. Unwilling to lose her, the duke arranged for her to give birth in secret, then sent her child – a boy – to a wet-nurse in Sorrento where he was baptised in the name of Cesare Filippo Lanti and looked after and educated until he reached adulthood.

For the next fourteen years Castropignano's generosity to Teresa was boundless. He let her spend his money at a ruinous rate, settled

20,000 ducats on Cesarino, as Cesare was familiarly called, and arranged for both mother and son to be placed under the protection of the Prince della Riccia in the event of his own death. Teresa had accidentally fallen into clover. Her only regret was that her son was brought up believing that she was his sister rather than his mother. Deception was set to be a permanent fixture of her life.

Casanova stopped writing to Teresa soon after she settled in Naples, so she never told him that they had a son. Nevertheless she regarded Cesarino, who grew up bearing an uncanny resemblance to his father, as 'a sure pledge' of their union, and she remained convinced that she and Casanova would marry if they ever met up again. When they did meet by chance sixteen years later, her position was very different. It was late November 1760, Castropignano had died two years previously, and Teresa was now a self-confident, independent thirty-one-year-old with her own substantial private means. She owned to having 'fifty thousand *ducati del regno* and the same amount in diamonds';[32] and she travelled from city to city with a strongbox containing all her precious stones and silver plate plus fifty thousand ducats in securities. During the summer of 1760 she had married Cirillo Palesi, a poor but extremely handsome Roman some ten years her junior who was her delight and her plaything. Though he now had legal rights over her, Teresa sensibly intended to retain control of her money; she neither told him the full extent of her wealth nor informed him of her real relationship with Cesarino. She even lied to him about her age, which she claimed was no more than twenty-four.

As well as her own income, Teresa also received the interest on Cesarino's inheritance from Castropignano. With so much money at her disposal, there could have been scant financial incentive for her to work. However, she continued to perform as a soprano, and in the autumn of 1760 travelled with her husband and fifteen-year-old 'brother' to Florence, where she was engaged to sing at the Pergola Theatre (the name *Artemisia Lanti* appears in the Pergola's records of the time). One night in November, Teresa glanced into the audience and saw Casanova staring back at her. He was no

longer the impulsive young priest she had known in her youth, but a sophisticated man in his thirties, bewigged, bejewelled and richly dressed in the style of a French aristocrat.

Teresa was so surprised to see Casanova at all, never mind so richly attired, that her eyes never left his during the rest of her aria, and when she walked into the wings she beckoned for him to meet her backstage. Without hesitating for a moment she introduced Casanova to her husband as her 'father', and the man to whom she owed all her good fortune in life. While Palesi was with them Teresa behaved with strict propriety towards Casanova, and when he left them alone together she would only grant her old lover a single passionate clinch. Her attitude to him was clear-cut: 'It is all over,' she said of their relationship. This was the perfect cue for Casanova to express his undying love for Teresa. For years he had carried the guilt of not replying to her last letter from Naples, and now that she was rich and in love with someone else he could indulge himself in regrets and pass the responsibility for their continuing separation on to her. 'I find you bound, and I am free,' he told her. 'We would never have parted again; you have just rekindled all my old passion; my feelings are unchanged, and I am happy to have been able to convince myself of it; and unhappy not to be able to hope to possess you; I find you not only married but in love. Alas! I have delayed too long.'[33] His regret increased when he met Teresa's so-called 'brother', his own son Cesarino whose existence he had been unaware of until this point. Casanova was flabbergasted: the vivacious boy was his mirror-image; nature had 'never been more indiscreet'.[34]

The day that Casanova spent with Teresa and their son was, he later wrote, 'one of the happiest of my whole life'.[35] It gave him a taste of the domestic felicity he might perhaps have enjoyed had his nature been different. But his restless spirit would never change. When he ran into Teresa again two years later in Milan, he was disturbed to discover that she was free again. Her honeymoon period with Palesi had ended, and with it their marriage. In an arrangement similar to modern-day alimony payments Teresa, as

the wealthier partner, had paid her husband off with a handsome annuity which allowed him to live independently of her.

Despite the years that had passed Teresa still nursed a small hope that she and Casanova might even at this late stage resume their love affair and marry. Or perhaps she was just playing a trick on him when she told him that there was nothing to stop them staying together for the rest of their lives. Nothing, she might well have added, except Casanova's nature. Now that he could finally have Teresa, he no longer wanted her, except for casual sex.

'I went home in love with her,' the serial seducer wrote after they had spent the night together, 'but my passion found too many diversions to last long.'

FIVE

Henriette

*There is a happiness which is perfect and real
as long as it lasts; it is transient, but its end does
not negate its past existence and prevent he who
has experienced it from remembering it.*[1]

HE MET HER at an inn in Cesena in the late autumn of 1749. She
was in bed with another man at the time. At first all that Casanova
could see of her was a shape huddled beneath the sheets. He
presumed that whoever she was, she was hiding herself out of
modesty or embarrassment, but when at long last she stuck her
head out from under the covers she did not seem at all ashamed of
her predicament. In fact, the opposite was true. Her face was as
fresh and sunny as a spring morning, and although she was wearing
a man's shirt and her tousled hair was cut in a male style, her
bewitching smile left Casanova in no doubt that she was all woman.

This was Casanova's first glimpse of Henriette, the greatest love
of his life. She was everything he could possibly desire in a woman –
courageous, intelligent, witty, beautiful and sexually liberated
while at the same time being extremely cultivated and refined.
She was also, most importantly, a grand aristocrat, and literally in a
different class to the other women he had known. If a woman such
as Henriette loved him, Casanova must be worth loving. Through
loving her, the needy child rejected by his mother at last began to
value himself.

Henriette asked nothing of Casanova except a pledge of no

commitment. This alone made her the ideal romantic partner for a man with an aversion to being tied down. But there was much more to their relationship than that. Casanova admired Henriette. He was in awe of her. She alone out of all his women was his soul-mate. Just being in her company gave him a feeling of contentment he had never experienced before. 'Those who believe that a woman is not enough to make a man equally happy all the twenty-four hours of a day have never known an Henriette,' he wrote of her. 'The joy which flooded my soul was much greater when I conversed with her during the day than when I held her in my arms at night.'[2]

At the time they met, Casanova was ready to fall in love again. Twenty-four years old and wandering aimlessly through Italy with a surprising amount of money in his pockets, he was almost unrecognisable as the penniless novice priest who had fallen in love with fifteen-year-old Teresa Lanti four years previously. Just before parting from Teresa in Rimini he had abandoned his ecclesiastic garb and with it all thought of making a career in the Church. Donning an officer's uniform, he had returned to Venice, entered the service of the Republic as an ensign, and sailed for Corfu as adjunct to Giacomo da Riva, the governor of the Venetian galley slaves there. After several months working for da Riva, Casanova had made his way to Constantinople, where good fortune and happiness had continued to evade him. By January 1746, he was back in Venice, unemployed and rootless. The family house on the Calle della Commedia had been given up long ago, his sister Maria had moved to Dresden to join their mother, and his brother Francesco was temporarily imprisoned in the fortress of Sant'Andrea, where he was whiling away his time by painting battle scenes, an occupation at which he later earned a good living. As for the Savorgnan sisters, Nanetta had left Venice with her new husband, Marta was locked away in a convent on the island of Murano, and Signora Orio, their all-too-trusting aunt, had married an admirer and closed up her huge palazzo.

Casanova was homeless and penniless. Desperate for money, he managed with the help of nobleman Michele Grimani, his family's erstwhile patron, to get a job as a violinist at the San Samuele

theatre, which Grimani owned and where his parents had once been employed; though Casanova could not have cared less about music, Dr Gozzi had taught him a rudimentary knowledge of the violin during his schooldays, and he now put it to use. To work as a humble fiddler was the ultimate humiliation for a brilliant university graduate who had been given every opportunity to better himself and of whom great things had been universally expected. Ashamed of the level he had sunk to, Casanova avoided his old acquaintances, particularly those among the nobility, and his self-esteem, which was always so important to him, spiralled downhill along with his behaviour. In the company of a group of fellow-musicians and a dissipated young member of the patrician Balbi family, he frequented Venice's least salubrious taverns after the performances, then roamed drunkenly through the city committing crimes of vandalism and playing malicious practical jokes. The gang set gondolas loose on the canals, rang alarm bells in the church towers and broke into houses in the early hours of the morning, terrifying the occupants. Sexual predators who thought of nothing but their own immediate needs, they snatched whores away from their clients in the brothels, made them submit to brutal sex acts and then left without paying them.

These misdeeds and crimes culminated in a premeditated gang-rape during the February 1746 carnival. While several members of the gang kidnapped a weaver and stranded him on the island of San Giorgio Maggiore, opposite San Marco, the others abducted his pretty young wife to an inn in the Rialto district. Here they took her to a private upstairs room, plied her with wine and then took turns raping her. When Casanova wrote about the affair years later, he was still convinced that the woman had enjoyed 'her happy fate'[3] as he described the ordeal of being forced to have sex with seven drunk men (the one gang member who refused to take part was Francesco Casanova, who had been freed from imprisonment only to be led into bad ways by his older brother). The city authorities offered a large reward for anyone who denounced the rapists, but since the ring-leader was a nobleman no one did.

Casanova knew that he was going to the dogs. However, he trusted in a stoic Latin maxim taught to him by his erstwhile mentor Senator Malipiero that *Fata viam invenient* – Fate will find the way – and counted on the goddess Fortune to rescue him. Miraculously, she did. Just before dawn on the morning of 21 April 1746 he was on his way home from playing the fiddle at a smart wedding when he saw a middle-aged senator drop a letter as he was getting into his gondola. When Casanova handed the letter back to him, the senator, wealthy fifty-six-year-old bachelor Matteo Giovanni Bragadin, offered him a lift home. During the short journey the senator suffered from what appears to have been a stroke. Casanova quick-wittedly summoned a surgeon, took Bragadin back to his palazzo, stationed himself at his bedside and refused to leave until he had recovered. His own childhood experiences at the hands of Venice's doctors, coupled with the vigil he had kept at Bettina Gozzi's sickbed, had given Casanova a healthy disrespect for the medical profession, and when he observed that the mercury poultice which the physicians had applied to Bragadin's chest was making him worse rather than better he took it upon himself to scrape off the poisonous ointment. From then on, he treated the senator himself.

Once Bragadin was back on his feet he regarded the young fiddler as his saviour and his oracle. He and his two male companions, Marco Dandolo and Marco Barbaro, with whom he shared his family's ancient palazzo, secretly dabbled in the occult arts – a practice regarded as heretical at the time. With just a little encouragement from Casanova all three were soon led to believe that their young friend had supernatural gifts, knew all about alchemy and possessed the key to the Kabbalah, an ancient system of thought and knowledge based in Jewish mysticism. Sensing that he was on to a good thing, Casanova was reluctant to disillusion the three men. To do so seemed almost unkind – or so he persuaded himself – for 'with me at their command they saw themselves possessed of the philosopher's stone, the universal medicine, communication with the elemental spirits, and all the celestial

intelligences and the secrets of all the governments of Europe'.[4] Although he knew he was being dishonest he enjoyed the public notoriety that the trio's hero worship soon brought him. When Bragadin offered to adopt him as his son – to provide him with a servant, an apartment in the palazzo, his own private gondola and a moderate income of ten gold sequins a month – and told him to think of no career in future other than that of enjoying himself, Casanova lacked the moral strength to turn down what was, by any standards, a remarkable and unprecedented stroke of good fortune for a young man without status or means of his own.

Overnight Casanova was transformed from a homeless musician scraping a living on the margins of society into a rich nobleman's son, a position he felt he had been born for. For the next three years, while he was nominally employed in the office of a Venetian lawyer, in reality he lived a hedonistic, dissolute lifestyle which consisted mostly of gambling, womanising and meddling in other people's love affairs. It did his character little good but, since Bragadin continued to support and house him, Casanova ignored the criticism aimed against him by almost every level of Venetian society: 'Wealthy enough, empowered by nature with a striking appearance, a resolute gambler, a spendthrift, a great talker with a sharp tongue, lacking all modesty, fearless, pursuing pretty women, supplanting rivals, thinking no company any good other than that which amused me, I could only be hated. Since I was always prepared to risk my own skin, I felt that I was entitled to do anything I wanted, for it seemed that anything which got in my way deserved to be rudely attacked.'[5]

By the beginning of 1749, Casanova's cocky arrogance had earned him many enemies, particularly among the nobility who, not without good reason, viewed the actors' son as a young upstart on the make. Accused of raping and beating a young virgin (having attempted to 'buy' the girl's virginity from her mother, Casanova admitted to the beating but not to the rape), he was summoned to a special court presided over by four magistrates. A charge of blasphemy was also laid against him. The reason was either a grisly

practical joke Casanova had played which had involved digging up a corpse, cutting off its arm and hiding it under a man's bed (the victim of the so-called joke was so shocked that he had a stroke and never recovered) or his rumoured dabbling in the Kabbalah with Bragadin. Before he could be imprisoned for either offence Casanova quit the Republic on the senator's advice.

Exiled from his beloved Venice for the first time, Casanova roamed aimlessly through Italy using his mother's maiden name, Farussi, as a pseudonym and supplementing the private income which Bragadin continued to send him by gambling and committing petty fraud. His brilliant intellect was wasting away; he was doing nothing with his life. By March he was in Milan, where he ran into Teresa Lanti's younger sister, Marina. The child he had slept with when she was eleven was now fifteen or sixteen years old and working as a comic dancer and a prostitute. Casanova took her away from her violent pimp and became her lover himself. Together they met Antonio Stefano Balletti, a dancer from a famous Parisian theatrical family who was due to partner Marina in a subsequent engagement in Mantua. Balletti remained Casanova's friend and eventually introduced him to his influential parents and younger sister, an innocent beauty whom, as we shall see later, Casanova made miserable for years.

Since his affair with Teresa, Casanova had enjoyed the sexual charms of many women but had fallen deeply in love only once, during his spell working for Giacomo da Riva, the governor of the galleys, in Corfu in 1745. The object of his desire had been Andriana Longo, the wife of his superior officer, Foscarini. An expert in prolonging an intrigue without ending it, Signora F . . ., as Casanova discreetly referred to her in his memoirs, refused to give in to him, with the result that he became so obsessed with her that he collected the split ends of her hair, had them made into comfits and secretly ate them. Casanova was on the point of consummating the affair when he caught venereal disease from a courtesan – his fourth such infection. When he confessed this to Signora F . . . she refused to have anything more to do with him.

Soon after his encounter with Marina, Casanova caught venereal disease yet again, this time during a drunken encounter with a whore. Disgusted by the sordid nature of the affair, he pined for a relationship of real substance. Mere sex, though readily available, was not enough for him, for by the age of twenty-four he had already discovered that 'the pleasure of love without love is insipid.'[6] To really enjoy sex, Casanova needed to be in love. Hoping perhaps to recapture something of his old raw ambitious spirit and to re-ignite either, or even both, of his two greatest passions so far – those for Teresa Lanti and Anna Maria Vallati, the 'Donna Lucrezia' of his memoirs – he decided to head for Naples, unaware that he now had not one but two children living there: Leonilda, his daughter by Anna Maria; and Cesarino, his son by Teresa. Without knowing it, Casanova was on the brink of the most meaningful relationship of his life. For en route to Naples, he broke his journey in the city of Cesena and encountered Henriette.

On the morning of his intended departure from Cesena he was awoken at daybreak by a terrible hullabaloo in the inn where he was staying. A crowd of *sbirri* were clustered in the corridor outside the open door of the next bedroom. Inside it, an elderly grey-haired man was sitting up in bed in a nightcap yelling angrily at the constables in Latin, of which they did not understand a word. The innkeeper explained to Casanova that the problem was one of suspected immorality: the *sbirri*, in practice the moral police of the strict Papal States, were trying to discover whether the person sharing the man's bed was actually married to him, but since he spoke only Latin they could not communicate with him. If the woman who was hiding under the covers was married to this man, the two of them needed to produce some sort of certificate to prove it. If, on the other hand, they were not married, 'he'll have to put up with going to prison with the girl; but that won't happen to him because I'm trying to settle the thing amicably for two or three sequins. I'll speak to their captain, and all these men will go away. If you speak Latin, go in and make him see reason.'[7]

Casanova had learned fluent Latin as a schoolboy, and since he

loved to meddle in an intrigue he immediately sorted out the affair to the satisfaction of the bed's occupant, who turned out to be a Hungarian officer in the service of Austrian empress Maria-Theresa. The person lying beside him remained hidden under the covers until later that morning, and when she finally popped her head out from under the sheets she was sporting a male haircut and a man's nightshirt. The Hungarian indicated that, despite her obviously feminine features, Casanova was to address the ravishing cross-dresser as a man.

It was love at first sight. Henriette's form and bearing immediately captivated Casanova. Whilst the other cross-dresser in his life, Teresa Lanti, had actually pretended to be a man, Henriette carried off her male disguise with all the elegance and panache of a fashionable woman at a masquerade. Later that day, outfitted in 'a blue riding-coat, with her dishevelled hair arranged like a man's', her womanly beauty amazed Casanova. Dressed for supper that evening in a fantastical soldier's uniform of her own invention she looked even more feminine, and 'the beauty of this girl instantly enslaved me'.[8] The situation was made even more intriguing by the fact that, whilst the elderly Hungarian spoke only Latin, Henriette, who was in her early twenties, spoke only French; they could not exchange a single word unless Casanova acted as their interpreter. Since this odd couple were heading for Parma, on the spur of the moment Casanova decided to change his plans and go with them. He wanted Henriette so badly that he had to have her, and would sacrifice anything to get her. His desire to reconnect with his Neapolitan friends and lovers had completely vanished.

It was soon apparent to him that, despite her situation as the lover of a man she could scarcely communicate with, Henriette was well-brought-up and educated to the highest degree. She was also the first Frenchwoman Casanova had ever met, and as such she was a revelation to him. Never before had he encountered such sophistication, allied with such charm and ease of manner, and her sparkling conversation that evening at the house of a local general set the seal on his feelings. It was as if, with her soldier's

outfit, Henriette assumed the freedom to talk like a man. When a prudish lady remarked that it was peculiar to live with a man with whom one could not converse, Henriette quipped that words were unnecessary for the business she and the Hungarian officer conducted together. When asked what this business could possibly be, she answered that they gambled: 'Nothing else. We play faro; and I keep the bank', and the stakes were 'so small that it was not worth counting up'.[9] Casanova was entranced by her lighthearted and risqué tone. Since he assumed Henriette was a high-class adventuress, he was convinced that he could easily win her from the Hungarian. With this in mind, the following morning he impetuously offered them both a lift to Parma in his private carriage; impetuously, because he did not own a carriage. When they gratefully accepted his offer Casanova immediately ran out and bought a beautiful English *coupé* at a cost of two hundred sequins, twenty times his monthly allowance from Bragadin. He would spend whatever it took in order to impress Henriette.

It says much about Casanova's attitude to sexual equality that he thought no less of Henriette for being the lover of a man she obviously did not know very well, a man, it soon emerged, whom she had picked up by chance a few days previously. Her mysterious story began to emerge in Bologna, where the travellers spent their first night en route to Parma. With Casanova acting as interpreter, Henriette gave the Hungarian full permission to explain how he had met her. When visiting the ancient port of Civitavecchia near Rome, he recounted, he had spotted Henriette, dressed in men's clothing as she was now, disembarking from a small tartan[10] in the company of another elderly officer. Later that day Henriette and the officer had checked into the same inn where he was staying and were given the room opposite his, and from his window he had observed that they were scarcely on speaking terms. Presuming, as Casanova now did, that the female masquerader must be a courtesan, he had sent his guide and interpreter to offer Henriette ten sequins for an hour's meeting. She had sent him back the message that she was about to leave for Rome, and that if he wished to see

her again he should contact her there. Once back in Rome himself, he had thought nothing more of Henriette until three days before he was due to leave for Parma, when he had suddenly found out where she was staying. In answer to his urgent note asking to see her before he left the city she had volunteered to meet him two hundred paces outside the walls. There she had climbed up into his carriage and, by gestures and with great difficulty, had given him to understand that she would travel with him all the way to Parma. She had become his lover that day.

What was a young, well-brought-up Frenchwoman doing running around the strictly religious Papal States in breeches, passing herself from man to man as if she were a bag of sweetmeats? Who was the old man with whom she had arrived in Civitavecchia, and what had motivated her to run away from him in Rome and entrust herself to a stranger she could scarcely communicate with? Why did she want to go to Parma? When asked by the two men if she cared to explain her side of the story, Henriette was evasive. The same principle that prevented her from lying to them did not permit her to tell them the truth, she answered carefully, adding that when they arrived in Parma her lover must promise to let her find lodgings by herself, and to pretend not to know her if he saw her by chance in the street.

Mystery enveloped Henriette like a heady perfume, and Casanova was intoxicated by it. Unable to sleep, he spent the night pacing up and down his room talking out loud to himself. Who was this woman who combined 'the most elevated feelings with an appearance of the greatest libertinism'? Why did she insist on being left to her own devices once they reached Parma? How did she imagine she would survive alone in that city since she spoke no Italian and appeared to possess neither money nor clothing of her own? Alongside these questions ran a current of desire for Henriette so strong that it bordered on anger. Henriette must realise that Casanova was determined to have her, and that he would not let her make a dupe of him!

When he finally fell asleep, Casanova had a vivid dream that he was making love to Henriette. When he awoke, he went directly to

see the Hungarian and, in what was regarded at the time as a civilised, gentlemanly fashion, discussed the possibility of taking Henriette over; his dream had to be turned into reality with the utmost haste. Since the Hungarian seemed more than willing to pass her on, Casanova then approached Henriette herself with a desperation that took the form of a furious harangue. Did she want him to take her to Parma or not? he demanded. She should understand that since he was her friend – since he actually loved her – he could not, as the Hungarian had done, promise to abandon her in the city 'without money, and with nothing to sell, in the middle of the street in a city where you cannot even talk to anyone . . . *Forget me* is soon said. Know, madame, that a Frenchman may be able to forget, but an Italian, to judge by myself, has not that singular power.'[11] It was a matter of honour, even of national pride, that Casanova would stick by her. If Henriette did not want him, he would immediately leave for Naples and do his best to forget her. But if she agreed to let him take her to Parma, she must promise to make him happy by the possession of her heart; nothing less would do. Casanova wished to be her only lover, and to enjoy her favours only when he had deserved them 'by my services and my attentions and by everything I will do for you with a submission of which you will never have seen the like.'[12]

A weaker, more emotionally involved woman might have felt coerced or upset by Casanova's harangue, but the self-assured Frenchwoman was merely amused by it. Did he understand, she laughed, 'what it is to say to a woman in a declaration of love, which should be all tenderness, *Madame, one or the other, choose this instant*'?[13] Casanova persisted in the same vein: this was an extremely serious matter to him. By giving Henriette an ultimatum, he was honouring, even empowering her by making her the arbiter of both their fates. He was not in a rage but at a pivotal moment in his life, and if he was railing, it was not at her but 'at my bizarre fortune and those accursed Cesena *sbirri* who woke me up, for had it not been for them I should never have seen you'. So Casanova was sorry he had met her? Henriette teased.

'Have I not reason to be?'

'Not at all, for I have not yet chosen.'

'I'm beginning to breathe. I wager you will tell me to come to Parma.'

'Yes – come to Parma.'[14]

With these four words, Henriette made the choice for both of them, in control of their relationship from the very beginning. From then on, fearful of revealing her full story – perhaps because it painted her in a bad light – she was careful to tell Casanova only as much as she wanted him to know about herself. All she would say was that she came from an aristocratic family in Provence, that she was convent-educated, and married, and that she had committed three follies in her life, the last of which – running off with the Hungarian officer – 'would have ruined me, but for you. Delightful folly, the cause of my knowing you,'[15] she added charmingly. If she had taken a wrong turning in her life it was not she herself but her husband and father-in-law who were to blame, for they were monsters. At times Henriette may well have lied to Casanova in order to protect herself, for instance when she told him that the man she had arrived in Civitavecchia with had been her father-in-law, who had brought her to Italy with the intention of locking her away in a convent; it was unlikely that he would search for her, she added, as he would be all too pleased to see the back of her. This was a highly implausible story on every level. No strict Frenchman would have travelled with his daughter-in-law dressed as a man when both the Church and civil authorities considered such behaviour scandalous. And, if he had wanted to imprison her in a convent, he would have been unlikely to have taken her to Italy when there were plenty of suitable convents in France.

With admirable discretion – or perhaps blind faith or naïve credulity – Casanova accepted Henriette at her word. From the very beginning, discretion played an important part in this, the greatest of all his love affairs. Having passed Henriette on to Casanova, the Hungarian tactfully rode ahead to Parma, leaving the new lovers to spend their first night together in the town of

Reggio, where they supped in an awkward silence before going to bed. 'We knew that we were going to sleep together,' Casanova wrote of the moment, 'but we would have thought it indiscreet to say so to each other. What a night! What a woman was this Henriette, whom I loved so much! Who made me so happy!'[16] When they reached Parma they both checked into an inn under false names, Casanova as Giacomo de Farussi, Henriette as *Anne d'Arci, Frenchwoman* – a pseudonym which has given rise to speculation that she was born under the astrological sign of Sagittarius, termed *l'Arcifère* at the time.[17] From then on, Henriette kept a low profile, rarely leaving her room where, on the rare occasions Casanova went out, she passed her time with the chambermaid and the Italian teacher her lover had generously engaged for her (she mastered the language within a month). She received only two visitors: the Hungarian officer, whom she now addressed as 'papa'; and Baron Michel Dubois Chatellerault, a hunchbacked French artist and medallion-engraver in the service of the Duke of Parma. When Henriette did venture outside it was only to ride through the city in a closed carriage with Casanova. And when he finally persuaded her to accompany him to the opera she insisted on taking an unlit box in the less fashionable second tier, where she appeared without rouge, a cosmetic very popular in France at that time. During the performance Henriette never once looked at the other spectators, but kept her gaze resolutely on the stage – behaviour which, perversely, was bound to get her noticed in an age when the main purpose of attending an opera was to gossip about other members of the audience and to be gossiped about in return.

Enclosed in his private world with Henriette, Casanova was completely happy. Sex was by no means the most important element of their relationship, and he gave no details of their intimate relations in his memoirs – a mark in itself of how much Henriette meant to him. He could not praise Henriette enough: she was adorable, generous, noble and divine; she was intelligent and shrewd, widely read and had innate good taste and acute judge-

ment. Despite his relatively modern attitude to women's sexuality, Casanova did not necessarily approve of female education, for in his opinion too much knowledge compromised the essence of the female sex. Henriette, however, was the exception for she 'never said anything important without a laugh which, giving it a veneer of frivolity, put it within reach of the entire company. In this way she bestowed intelligence on those who did not know they had it, and who, in return, adored her for it. In the end, a beautiful woman who does not radiate intelligence has nothing to offer her lover once he has enjoyed her physical charms. An ugly woman with a brilliant mind makes a man fall so much in love with her that she leaves him wanting nothing. So what must I have been with beautiful, witty, cultivated Henriette? It is impossible to conceive of the extent of my happiness.'[18]

'I was very happy with Henriette, as she was with me,' Casanova wrote elsewhere of their time together in Parma, time he would later describe to another lover as *four months of perfect and continuous joy*.[19] 'Never a moment's griping, never a yawn, never did a rose leaf bent in two come to disturb our contentment.'[20] One must suppose that Henriette felt the same way. In the past she had lived in such fear of her husband and father-in-law that she had risked her reputation, perhaps even her life, to get away from them. On the run, and not without shame for the situation she was in, she had stumbled upon a man who not only did not judge her but who treated her with the utmost tenderness and tact. Casanova was brilliant company. He was never violent towards her. He was a thoughtful lover who aimed to please his partner in bed. He respected Henriette's privacy, and asked nothing of her except to be allowed to adore her, spoil her, and enjoy being with her. He loved her for the person she was, and moreover respected her despite her 'missteps', as she described the misdemeanours by which she had nearly ruined her life.

Henriette brought out the very best qualities in Casanova – selflessness, kindness, empathy and generosity. Though his finances were by no means unlimited – his income from Bragadin was just ten sequins a month – he looked after her with the lavishness of a

wealthy prince, renting rooms for them at the best inn in Parma, hiring servants for her, and secretly taking it upon himself one day to go out shopping on her behalf. He returned carrying yards of fine linen to make chemises, dimity to make corsets and petticoats, silk and cotton stockings, dress fabric, handkerchiefs, hats, mantles, and with a seamstress and a shoemaker in tow. Henriette received all these unasked-for gifts without the kind of ingratiating thanks which would have made Casanova think less of her. Days later, when her first new clothes were ready, she banished him from the inn while she changed into them. When he returned, Henriette was transformed. The boisterous bravado she had adopted along with her male clothing had been dropped along with her breeches. Dressed as a woman, curtseying before him, Henriette was all femininity, composure and aristocratic grace – a Frenchwoman of the very highest rank. The actors' son was in awe of her, and quite intimidated by her metamorphosis. That day he fell in love with her all over again.

Though this grand lady now looked as if she would never put a foot wrong, Henriette was still capable of surprising Casanova by her impulsive behaviour. Persuaded by him to attend a private concert at Dubois Chatellerault's country house, she received the attentions of the all-male guests with 'an ease unknown outside France'. At first she kept a relatively low profile, but after listening to a cello concerto she suddenly rose to her feet, congratulated the young soloist and confidently took the instrument from him. Without daring to meet Casanova's eyes, Henriette asked the orchestra to begin the concerto again. Like the rest of her shocked audience, Casanova looked on in silence. The cello, like its close cousin the viola da gamba, was simply not perceived as a woman's instrument because it had to be held between one's open legs, a distinctly unladylike position. Never dreaming that Henriette could actually play the instrument, Casanova presumed that she was either joking or had gone mad, and his heart palpitated with a 'deathly fear' for her. To his amazement she could play, and very well indeed. Unusually for the time, Henriette's mother had been a

fine cellist; and at her father's insistence she too had learned to play the instrument at her convent school (although the Mother Abbess had objected strongly on the grounds that the young girl 'could only grasp the instrument by assuming an indecent posture'[21]). Keeping her eyes firmly on the music stand in front of her, Henriette sight-read the concerto she had just heard without making a single mistake, and when her performance was greeted with rapturous applause she played alone another five times. Casanova was overcome with love for her, and overawed by the huge difference in status between them. He rushed out into the garden and burst into tears, unable to believe that this talented jewel was his. The following day, he bought Henriette a cello of her own from one of Parma's skilled luthiers.

In 1749 Parma was on its way to becoming one of the most active musical centres in Italy. It was also becoming an outpost of French culture. Fought over during the War of the Austrian Succession, the city had been granted to the Bourbon monarchy in 1748 by the Treaty of Aix-la-Chapelle, and it now fell under the rule of the Infante Don Filippo, second son of the late King Filippo V of Spain and his powerful wife, Elizabetta Farnese, the niece of the old Duke of Parma. Don Filippo and his ministers had arrived in the city on 7 March 1749, and when Henriette and Casanova took up temporary residence that autumn preparations were underway for the imminent arrival (on 23 November) of Don Filippo's wife, 'Madame de France' Louise-Elizabeth, the eldest daughter of King Louis XV. Consequently there were Frenchmen on every street, in every café, and in every government building.

Henriette's presence and behaviour in Parma speak volumes about her wishes at the time. Although she claimed to be in hiding from her French father-in-law, she had deliberately chosen to go to the most French of all Italian cities. Once there, she expressed a strong desire to stay at Andremont's, a popular French-style inn overrun by her fellow countrymen; and her attentive lover made sure that she got her way. Henriette was well aware that her appearance at the opera, and her music recital at Dubois Chatelle-

rault's house, were guaranteed to get her talked about, for it was impossible that such a remarkable Frenchwoman could remain unnoticed by Parma's small, mainly male French community. Contrary to what she said – that she did not wish to be found – Henriette clearly wished to recognised. Her objective was to return to France and to be reunited with her family; if not with her monster of a husband then perhaps with her parents and siblings. Without doubt this had been her intention when she set out for Parma; and meeting Casanova along the way had not altered her resolve. For a short while she was content to live in the present and to teach Casanova to do the same. Although her emotional lover begged her never to leave him, Henriette knew that she soon would, and she never promised him otherwise.

Henriette was marking time, waiting for the right opportunity to make contact with her family. Like Casanova she trusted in the maxim that *Fata viam invenient*. It happened on a December night at the royal palace of Colorno, twelve kilometres outside the city, where Don Filippo was holding a fiesta for his newly arrived wife. Anxious not to miss the grand occasion, even though they were aware that the entire French community would be there, Henriette and Casanova drove out to Colorno with Dubois Chatellerault and took rooms at a local inn. As the three of them strolled around the illuminated palace grounds, Henriette was noticed by Don Filippo's friend and courtier, François-Antoine d'Antoine-Blacas, a knight of the Order of St Louis and a native of Provence. When this man approached Henriette she politely denied knowing him, but their encounter left Casanova so uneasy that he suggested that they leave immediately for Genoa. She reassured him that there was no need for them to depart in a hurry; if Fate had at last found its way she clearly had no desire to confound it.

Was Henriette already aware that d'Antoine-Blacas was not only acquainted with her situation but actually related to her husband's family through marriage? Had she herself made moves to contact him? This was the opportunity to be reunited with her family that she had clearly been hoping for. A few days after the court returned

to Parma the knight sent a note to Andremont's asking Casanova
for a private meeting with him. In Don Filippo's garden he handed
him a sealed four-page letter addressed to *Madame d'Arci*, and
asked Casanova to deliver it to her unopened. Though they had
been lovers for months, Henriette kept the contents of this letter to
herself, claiming that the 'honour of two families' prevented her
from showing it to Casanova. She needed to consult d'Antoine-
Blacas, she said, for he knew 'my whole story and my mistakes, but
also my reasons, which oblige him as a man of honour to protect me
from all affronts, and he will do nothing except in agreement with
me, and if he tries to deviate from the conditions I will dictate to
him, I will not go to France.'[22]

Casanova was devastated at the thought that he might have to
part from Henriette – 'So the last act begins,' he commented
theatrically – but she was strangely resigned. As in control of
her emotions as she was of the relationship, she had known from
the start what she wanted: to return to her family on her own
terms. Just as she had used the Hungarian officer and later
Casanova, to help her get to Parma and make contact with an
appropriate go-between, she now used d'Antoine-Blacas to open
up negotiations with her Provençal family. During a six-hour
meeting she and the knight struggled over the wording of a letter,
or letters, which would seal her fate, while her distressed lover was
forced to sit alone in an adjoining room.

Parma had suddenly lost its magic. While Henriette waited for a
reply to come from France – it would take at least two weeks for the
messenger to reach her home and return to Italy – she went with
Casanova on an excursion to Milan; their servants followed them in
another carriage, bringing with them their trunks and Henriette's
cello. Even though he knew he was losing his lover, Casanova
continued to lavish money on her and, with a delicacy which
pleased him, she continued to accept his generosity. Although they
attempted to enjoy themselves a certain sadness invaded their
hitherto carefree existence, and sadness was 'a disease which
eventually kills love'.[23]

Casanova's most exquisite, most memorable love affair was drawing to a close. By the time he returned to Parma with Henriette a fortnight later, d'Antoine-Blacas had received an answer from her family: all her conditions had been met, and she was to leave for France in a few days' time. Holding the reins of power until the very end, Henriette asked Casanova to find her a respectable maid and to escort them both across the Alps as far as Geneva, from where she said she would continue her journey alone.

A few days later, the lovers left Parma at dusk in Casanova's English *coupé*, along with Henriette's new maid. After stopping at Turin to engage a manservant for Casanova they drove to the foot of Mount Cenis, where they were to cross from Piedmont to Savoy over the mountain's 2,090-metre-high pass. Since there were no roads across the Alps, Casanova's *coupé* had to be dismantled and loaded on to mules along with their trunks in preparation for the ascent. The Mount Cenis pass was a favourite route with aristocrats on the Grand Tour. Shrouded in clouds even during the summer months (and it was now midwinter), it was dangerous and exciting at the best of times, even for a seasoned traveller, as English aristocrat Horace Walpole had discovered several years earlier when his King Charles spaniel puppy ('the prettiest, fattest, dearest creature!') was carried off by a wolf on the same route. Like Henriette and Casanova, Walpole and his party had been carried up the narrow paths 'in low armchairs on poles, swathed in beaver bonnets, beaver gloves, beaver stockings, muffs and bearskins . . . The dexterity and nimbleness of the mountaineers is inconceivable; they run with you down steeps and frozen precipices, where no man, as men are now, could possibly walk.'[24] At the top of the pass, Henriette and Casanova, their dismantled carriage, trunks and servants were all transferred from sedan chairs on to sledges for the slow, steep, uncomfortable descent to the village of Lanslebourg nestling in the snow far below them. Neither Casanova nor Henriette was in the mood to enjoy the thrilling trip. Ahead of them lay a parting that weighed heavily on both of them.

Five days after leaving Parma they finally reached Geneva and checked into the best inn, L'Hôtel à la Balance – The Scales – on the Place de la Bel-Air. The following day Henriette contacted Tronchin, the Genevan representative of a firm of Lyonnais bankers of the same name, requesting a carriage, two reliable male servants and the considerable sum of one thousand louis in cash. Demonstrating just how wealthy and well-connected her family must be, Tronchin himself brought the money to the inn the very next day and assured Henriette that she would have everything else she had asked for within twenty-four hours.

'Glum and pensive, as one is when the most profound sadness overwhelms the spirit',[25] Henriette and Casanova sat together in a grim silence, which he finally broke by offering to exchange his luxurious English *coupé* for the less comfortable vehicle the banker was due to supply her with. She responded by pushing five rolls of one hundred louis each into Casanova's pockets. The money, he felt, was but 'a poor consolation for my heart, only too overcome by so cruel a separation'.[26] Nevertheless, and quite out of character, he accepted it. Ever the realist, Henriette offered Casanova no illusory hopes to make their parting easier. On the contrary, she asked him never to make enquiries about her, and furthermore made him promise not to acknowledge her if they should ever meet by chance in the future.

With her maid sitting beside her, and accompanied by two footmen – one sitting at the front of the *coupé*, the other standing at the back – Henriette left Geneva at dawn the next day. She had asked Casanova to remain at the Scales until he received a letter which she would send him from the first post-station she stopped at, Châtillon. Genuinely grief-stricken at her departure, he took to his bed and let sorrow overwhelm him. If he was hoping that Henriette's letter would offer some explanation for her behaviour or tell him where she was headed he was disappointed. When the postillion delivered it the following day, Casanova found that it contained only one word from her: *Farewell*.

Henriette had also written Casanova a longer letter which he

received the following day from d'Antoine-Blacas. He copied it out word for word in his memoirs: 'It is I, my only friend, who had to abandon you. Do not make your sorrow greater by thinking of mine. Let us imagine that we have had a pleasant dream, and let us not complain of our fate, for never was so pleasant a dream so long. Let us congratulate ourselves on having had three whole months of perfect happiness; there are few mortals who can say as much. So let us never forget each other, and let us often recall our love in our minds in order to renew it in our souls, which, though parted, will enjoy it even more intensely. Do not enquire about me, and if chance brings you to find out, be it as if you did not know. You should know, my dear friend, that I have put my affairs in such good order that for the rest of my days I shall be as happy as I can be without you. I do not know who you are; but I know that nobody in the world knows you better than I do. I will have no more lovers in all my life to come; but I hope that you will not think of doing the same. I wish you to love again, and even to find another Henriette. Farewell.'[27]

This was not Henriette's only message to him: with the point of a small diamond ring he had given her she had scratched four words into the window-glass of their room: '*Tu oublieras aussi Henriette.*' – You will forget Henriette too. Although in many ways such a wise judge of Casanova's character, Henriette was wrong in this one thing. 'No, I have not forgotten her,' he wrote some forty years later, 'and it is balm to my soul every time I remember her.'[28]

From the post-station at Châtillon, Henriette's carriage took the road to Lyon. There we, like Casanova, lose sight of her. It seems almost certain that, at Lyons, the English *coupé* bought in haste by Casanova in Cesena to impress her turned south down the Rhône valley towards the prosperous city of Aix-en-Provence, where Henriette's family owned a house in town and a pretty country château six to ten kilometres outside the city, near the Croix d'Or crossroads on the Marseille road.

Whatever difficulties she had expected to encounter when she

returned to France, Henriette faced them without a backward glance. Though it is unlikely that she ever lived with her husband again, she was certainly accepted back into the bosom of her parental family, and eventually resumed life as a *grande dame* of Aixoise society. She had got what she had wanted by running away: not passion, but rather independence and peace of mind and, most importantly, freedom from her husband's tyranny. She never told anyone the details of her Italian adventure. Her love affair with Casanova and her fling with the Hungarian officer belonged to a brief, desperate period of her life that was best kept secret. By her own admission, Henriette was blessed with a natural *joie de vivre* and possessed the ability to live for the moment. A quiet life was perhaps enough for her.

By the spring of 1763, Casanova was just a memory to thirty-seven-year-old Henriette, one that was unexpectedly revived towards the end of May, when she was staying with members of her family at their country estate on the Marseille road. Shortly after half-past five one afternoon, a French manservant knocked at the château door asking for help. He introduced himself as Clairmont, and said that his master the Chevalier de Seingalt's carriage had broken down at the end of the drive; they were in need of a cartwright to mend the vehicle and some help in pulling the carriage off the road. Carriage breakdowns were a habitual feature of long-distance travel, particularly in France where, according to Laurence Sterne's *Tristram Shandy*, 'a French postillion has always to alight before he has got three hundred yards out of town',[29] and two servants from Henriette's château were dispatched to bind up the carriage's broken shaft. At the same time, an invitation was extended to the travellers to take shelter in the château until the carriage was mended. Henriette put on a hooded cloak and walked with her relatives down the long tree-bordered drive that led to the public road. At the end of the drive she could see a broken Berlin being pulled slowly through the gates by a team of four rather restive horses. In front of it walked a man who appeared at first to be a well-dressed French aristocrat, arm-in-arm with a tall, natural

beauty some twenty years his junior whose long dark loose hair streamed out behind her in the wind. As these two figures drew nearer, Henriette became aware that the so-called Chevalier de Seingault was in fact the Venetian she had known in Parma as Giacomo de Farussi.

Henriette shrank back under her hood, while one of her male relatives offered Casanova and the young woman, who everyone at first presumed was his daughter, the hospitality of the house. When she spotted one of the family's mastiffs chasing a pet spaniel, Henriette seized the opportunity to get away and ran off to rescue it, but she accidentally tripped and fell. Before Casanova could help her up she struggled to her feet unaided and, claiming a sprained ankle, limped back to the house on her brother's arm and took refuge in her bedroom. She could only wonder what Casanova was doing there. Had he found out where she lived and come there deliberately with the purpose of seeing and perhaps embarrassing her, or was his carriage breakdown directly outside the gates of her house an extraordinary coincidence?

Casanova claimed it was the latter. He was travelling from Marseille to Lyon with Marcolina, a feisty Venetian beauty he had recently stolen from under the nose of his detested youngest brother Gaetano ('a blasphemer and a fool, a barbarian who deserves no pity' as the adventurer generously described him).[30] A league beyond the Croix d'Or, a well-known crossroads near the village of Bouc-Bel-Air, a fastening on the pole of their carriage had accidentally broken, leaving Casanova no alternative but to send his servant Clairmont to approach the nearest house for help. That it turned out to be Henriette's house was, he insisted, the work of destiny. *Fata viam invenient*. Once again in their relationship, Fate had shown the way.

Casanova and Marcolina would have made an extraordinary impression on Henriette's family – just how extraordinary we can gauge from a description of them written by a young Frenchwoman, Marie de Nairne, who met them by chance just three days later. 'This stunning traveller arrived in a Berlin at the Hôtel du

Parc in Lyon towards five o'clock in the evening,' Mademoiselle de Nairne wrote to her fiancé Baron Michel de Ramsay in a letter of 28 May 1763. 'He immediately created a hullabaloo because he was not given the room he claimed he had booked in advance. His servant, like himself, had the same threatening manner . . . But at table, once the hors d'oeuvre had been served, he was in charming humour, expounding enthusiastically upon a thousand different subjects. We hung on his lips . . . He was tall, with a dark complexion, richly dressed with heavy jewelled rings on his fingers. His foreign accent was highly comical.[31] A very attractive young woman, dark and with dazzling teeth, and the same foreign accent, who had arrived with him in the coach, laughed ceaselessly at the stories related for our amusement . . . It was M. de Casanova, a Venetian nobleman.'[32]

Casanova's behaviour outside her house showed Henriette that either he had not recognised her beneath her hood or, as in the past, he was behaving like the consummate gentleman. She was curious to talk to him, but reluctant to reveal who she was if he had not already guessed. When she learned that her brothers had invited him to stay for supper she sent down a message inviting the entire company to join her in her room before they ate, but she made sure to arrange herself in a dark alcove. 'She was lying in a big bed at the back of an alcove made even darker by crimson taffeta curtains,' Casanova wrote of going up to her bedroom. 'She was not wearing a cap; but it was impossible to see her to the point where one could not make out whether she was ugly or pretty, young or of a certain age. I told her that I was in despair at having been to blame for her misfortune, and she answered me in Venetian Italian that it would amount to nothing.'[33] Henriette would not show her face in the light but she was not above giving Casanova a hint as to who she was. Though she had never been to Venice, she explained, she had often talked with Venetians. Delightedly, Casanova introduced her to Marcolina who, since she spoke no French, was thrilled to have someone to talk to in her native language. From then on, Henriette did nothing but talk in the Venetian dialect to her guests. The only

personal detail that she deliberately let slip about herself was that she was a widow – a term used to denote both bereavement and separation at a time when divorce was virtually unknown in France.

Since their carriage would not be ready until the following day, the travellers were invited to spend the night at the château. It was Marcolina, not Casanova, who shared Henriette's bed, and, according to the salacious description the young girl gave him the following day, the two women committed 'all the follies that you know that two women who love each other do when they sleep together . . . I saw all of her this morning, and we kissed each other all over.'[34] Henriette had lost neither her youthful beauty nor her libertine attitude to sex. Marcolina had pleased her, and the proof of it lay in a beautiful jewelled ring that Henriette presented her with the following morning. This valuable gift (Casanova estimated its worth as 200 French louis) may have obliquely been intended for the man who had once behaved with such generosity towards her.

Perhaps Henriette was hurt that the lover who had once adored her to distraction had conversed with her for so long without even responding to the timbre of her voice. Alternatively, she may have presumed he was respecting her position by giving no sign that he knew her. After delicately quizzing Marcolina about the nature of her relationship with her companion, Henriette wrote out a note for him, sealed it, gave it to her and made her promise not to hand it to him before they reached Avignon. She wanted Casanova to know that she, at least, had recognised him, but she clearly had no desire for a potentially embarrassing reunion under her family's roof.

In Avignon, Marcolina gave this letter to Casanova along with a message from Henriette that, if he were to return to Aix at some future time, either alone or with a companion, he would be welcome to call on her. Casanova opened the letter with a pounding heart. At the top was written in Italian: 'To the most honourable man I have met in the world'. The rest of the sheet was blank except for the signature. *Henriette*. The knowledge that he had been in the company of the woman whom he still regarded as

the love of his life and yet had failed to recognise her plunged Casanova into a state of numb shock.

To his knowledge, Casanova never again came face to face with Henriette, though six years later he would turn up in her life one last time, as we shall see presently. Discreet until the end, he did not reveal her true identity in his memoirs, and consequently it has intrigued generations of his readers. The facts we know about his greatest love are so few that they can be written down on half a sheet of paper. They are these: Henriette came from Aix-en-Provence where she or her family had a house in the city and a country house situated at the end of an alley of trees either a league or a league and a half north of the Croix d'Or crossroads on the Aix–Marseille road. She was of noble birth. Her family was wealthy and well-connected. She had been educated to a very high standard in a French convent. Like her mother before her, Henriette played the cello, an unusual instrument for women to take up at the time. D'Antoine-Blacas was related by marriage to her husband's family. In the autumn of 1749 she left her husband under threatening circumstances and travelled by boat to Italy where, on one occasion, she signed herself into an inn under the name Anne d'Arci. In February 1750, Henriette returned to Provence via Geneva, where she stopped to collect a substantial amount of money from the Tronchin bankers. Once she was back home, Henriette either lived alone or under the protection of her family – probably her father or brothers, one of whom Casanova refers to in his memoirs as a 'chevalier' or knight.

By her own admission, Henriette committed three follies in her life, the last of which was absconding from her travelling companion in Rome. Her first folly was presumably her marriage to a man who treated her badly; the second may have been an extramarital affair; her third running away with the Hungarian officer. A possible scenario is that Henriette was mistreated by her husband, was unfaithful to him and ran away to Italy, probably with her lover and wearing his clothes. When their relationship turned sour, she realised the impossibility of surviving indefinitely on her wits and

sought reconciliation with her family. Thereafter Henriette lived separately from her husband, wintering in Aix and spending the summers at the family château near the Croix d'Or with her parents and/or her siblings.

There have been three main contenders for Henriette's château, and three possible candidates for the woman herself. Charles Samaran, author of an authoritative early twentieth-century biography of the adventurer, believed that Henriette's house was a château at Luynes, three and a half kilometres from the Croix d'Or, and that Henriette herself was Jeanne-Marie d'Albert de St Hippolyte, the owner's niece, who at the time of Casanova's affair with Henriette was married to Jean-Baptiste Laurent Boyer de Fonscolombe, a lawyer in Aix's parliament. According to the contemporary Casanovist Helmut Watzlawick,[35] Henriette was Marie-Anne d'Albertas, the spinster daughter of a well-connected Marseille businessman whose family owned the Pavillon d'Albertas, a pretty hunting lodge close to the Croix d'Or and the village of Bouc-Bel-Air, and whose family motto was *Fata Viam Invenient* – an expression which Casanova uses several times when describing his affair with Henriette.

The third château in the area, and the third candidate for Henriette, were discovered by the Casanova scholar Jean-Louis André in the 1990s, and they remain far and away the most likely candidates.[36] At the Croix d'Or crossroads, just before the Pavillon d'Albertas, the Marseille – Aix road splits into two. The old Route Royale heads directly north towards Aix, while the road branching off to the right follows the path of an ancient track through the villages of Bouc-Bel-Air and Gardanne to Luynes, where it rejoins the main road. Three kilometres north of the hilltop village of Gardanne lies the Domaine de Valabre, a large estate upon which is built a sixteenth-century hunting lodge known as the Pavillon de Valabre or the Pavillon des Quatre Tours, and a pretty two-storey seventeenth-century château, restored in the Italianate style in 1733 and set at the end of an avenue bordered with oak trees.

From the late nineteenth century onwards, the Château de

Valabre was an agricultural college; since 1967 it has been the
headquarters of the Centre Interrégional de Formation de la
Securité Civile. Until the 1880s, however, it was a private home
and the property of the de Gueidans (or de Gueydans, as the name
was sometimes spelled), an ancient family whose links with French
royalty went back to the eleventh century when Baron Guy de
Gueydan participated in the First Crusade. By the early eighteenth
century, the baron's descendants, led by Aix resident Pierre de
Gueidan and his son Gaspard, had become one of the most
prominent families in Provence. For sixty years Pierre held the
post of president of the local Chambre de Comptes. From 1714
onwards his son Gaspard was Aix's most distinguished magistrate
and advocate general; and in 1740 King Louis XV nominated him
president of the local parliament, a post he retained until 1766.

Gaspard and his wife, Agélique de Simiane, owned a large house
in Aix's grand Cours Mirabeau, and in the summer months they
retreated to the village of Gardanne, where his father Pierre had in
1683 acquired the ancient Valabre estate. Together Gaspard and
Agélique produced at least six children: there were four sons –
Joseph, Pierre, Etienne and Timoléon, three of whom became
Chevaliers de Malte (Knights of the Maltese Cross) – and two
daughters: Anne-Thérèse-Adélaïde born on 14 December 1725;
and her younger sister Catherine-Polyxène-Julie, who was born in
1734. Gaspard was justly proud of his beautiful wife and daughters,
who appear to have been as musically talented as he was himself. In
1730 he commissioned a portrait of his wife (as 'Flora') by the
fashionable artist Nicolas de Largillière, and five years later he had
himself portrayed by Hyacinthe Rigaud playing the bagpipes. This
was followed by a painting of his daughters, whose joint portrait
Adélaïde de Gueidan and her sister Polyxène on the harpsichord now
hangs with those of their parents in Aix's Musée Granet.

Originally attributed to Largillière but now to the Aixoise artist
Claude Arnulphy, this is a gorgeous portrait of two innocent, well-
brought-up young girls with pink cheeks and powdered hair. Both
are dressed in elaborate embroidered gowns that show off their

status as the daughters of a wealthy, highly-respected member of society. Catherine-Polyxène is seated at a harpsichord, her hands hovering above the keys while her older sister Adélaïde stands on the left, clutching a rolled-up scroll, presumably of music. What instrument does she play? In the foreground leans what appears to the modern eye to be a violoncello but is in fact a viola da gamba. If Adélaïde is the one who plays this instrument, her talent cannot be illustrated in the picture. For the viola da gamba had to be held between the knees, and to paint a young virgin in such an unlady-like pose was unthinkable.

The six-stringed viola da gamba (the name literally means 'leg viol') was a precursor of the violoncello, and it is almost certainly the instrument played by Casanova's Henriette: for while the violoncello usually took only a supporting role in orchestras in the early eighteenth century, the viola da gamba was regarded as the solo virtuoso instrument. Louis XIV loved its sound so much that he employed two rival viola da gamba players at his court: the prodigious Marin Marais, who composed around 650 works, and Antoine Forqueray, a bizarre, violent man who seldom wrote any of his compositions down. After Forqueray's death his son Jean-Baptiste, a famous player in his own right, collected about thirty of his father's works together and published them in a volume, *Pièces de Viole, avec la Basse Continuë*, which came off the Paris presses in 1747. Since the viola da gamba was losing popularity at the time, Jean-Baptiste dedicated the book to his most illustrious pupil in the hope that she might do something to revive the instrument's popularity. The dedication on the frontispiece reads, 'A Madame Henriette de France'.

Forqueray's Madame Henriette was none other than Anne-Henriette de Bourbon, one of Louis XV's eight daughters (another of whom was named Adélaïde) and the twin sister of Louise-Elizabeth, whose arrival in Parma to join her husband, the Infante Filippo, coincided with Casanova and Henriette's visit to the city. Around the same age as Casanova's Henriette, and justly proud of her talent on the bass viol, the sophisticated Madame Henriette de

France unabashedly had herself painted several times (by the Parisian court painter Jean-Marc Nattier) with the instrument clearly placed between her legs.

Since Casanova's Henriette and her mother both played the cello or, more likely, the viola da gamba, it is possible that they had acquired Forqueray's book of music; alternatively, Casanova may have bought Henriette a copy of the book when he purchased an instrument for her in Parma. If Henriette was looking for a heroine whose name she might adopt during her flight from home – or if Casanova was searching for a pseudonym for her when he wrote his memoirs – surely Madame Henriette, a royal princess who shared a passion for the same musical instrument and whose sister bore the name Adélaïde, would have been she?

Could Adélaïde de Gueidan have been Casanova's Henriette?

The Château de Valabre, the de Gueidan family's country house, is in the right location near the Croix d'Or crossroads. An inventory of 1734 described the upstairs layout of the buildings as 'a mass of rooms and dark alcoves'[37] which ties in perfectly with Casanova's description of Henriette's bedroom. Born on 14 December 1725, making her eight months younger than Casanova, Adélaïde de Gueidan grew up both at this château and in Aix, where, like Henriette, she was educated at a convent. It appears from her joint portrait with her sister that one of the skills she acquired was playing the viola da gamba. In January 1745, just weeks after her nineteenth birthday, she was married to twenty-nine-year-old Pierre-Louis de Demandolx, the Marquis de Meireste and a moderately well-off nobleman from La Palud in the Alpes de Haute Provence. Interestingly, one of the witnesses to the marriage was the same d'Antoine-Blacas who later recognised Casanova's Henriette in Parma and claimed that he was related to her husband's family. D'Antoine-Blacas, as it turns out, was indeed related by marriage to the Demandolxes of La Palud.[38]

After her marriage Adélaïde, now the Marquise de Meireste, moved to La Palud to join her husband. It must have been something of a shock for her. Though her in-laws were in her own

father's words 'a distinguished, even illustrious family,'[39] she was far away from her loving parents, in a remote mountainous region where life was far more primitive than it had been in sophisticated Aix. With no relative of her own to protect her, Adélaïde was now at the mercy of her husband and his family. She must have missed her father as much as he obviously missed her. From a distance, Gaspard did what he could to ingratiate himself with his daughter's in-laws by using his influence to secure a place for one of her brothers-in-law in the marines, but for Adélaïde this was not the same as having her father near her, and when he was taken ill she wrote begging him to visit her in the mountains for the good of his health. 'I know very well that a few doses of the air in La Palud, and above all an embrace from my precious would do me more good than a drink of liquid gold,' Gaspard wrote back to her. 'I am too far away to apply these panaceas. But whatever wishes I have in this regard I can no longer think of them effectively. The next month will decide it. I do not very much like to delude myself with pandering ideas only to have the displeasure of having them taken away . . . As for me, my darling daughter, I can make no better use of the remaining paper than to protest that it's for ever, and without either end or limit, that I am yours.'[40]

Between 1746 and 1749 Adélaïde gave birth to three children at La Palud: a daughter, Angélique-Anne-Louise, born in October 1746; a son, César-Amable, born in November 1747; and another boy, born in February 1749. Blessed in haste by his paternal grandmother, this third child was not officially baptised until July 1752, when he received two names from his maternal family – Jean, the name of Adélaïde's uncle, and Gaspard, that of her father.

Why was there such a long delay in baptising Jean-Gaspard? And why did the otherwise loving Gaspard de Gueidan, a doting grandfather to Angélique and César, take such a dislike to this grandson? His negative feelings towards little Jean-Gaspard were so out of character that they prompted a letter from his friend Canon Dulard, who simply could not understand his attitude. 'I do not know why you are so prejudiced against that child,' Dulard wrote

to de Gueidan on 29 December 1758. 'As for I, who have seen him with totally disinterested eyes, to whom your own feelings had even given an unfavourable impression before the examination, I swear to you, Monsieur, that he pleased me in all respects, and I persist in saying that he is fit to see the light. For the future, if on your side you persist in not valuing him as highly as I do, you can exercise the right that paternity gives you over this boy whom you treat as illegitimate, but I will not hide from you that my heart will bleed over it.'[41]

If Jean-Gaspard was indeed illegitimate, who then was his real father? In December 1746, Provence had been invaded and occupied by Austro-Hungarian forces. They remained in the area of La Palud until the following year. Born in February 1749, Jean-Gaspard could possibly have been the child of a Hungarian officer who had remained in the area – the same officer, perhaps, with whom Casanova's Henriette absconded by sea to Civitavecchia later that year.

Gaspard de Gueidan was a methodical man who kept detailed accounts of his day-to-day expenses. His records show that Adélaïde returned to Aix from La Palud in March 1749, just weeks after giving birth to Jean-Gaspard. She remained in the city until the following October, without her husband or any of her children. Then, for the three months commencing on 11 November, when Gaspard mentions the expenses of a journey in his ledger, Adélaïde appears to have been missing from the city. On 18 December her father notes down a payment made to 'the coach driver who carried the trunk to Cannes'.[42] Thereafter, several crucial pages of the ledger are missing.

Gaspard's housekeeping records further indicate that Adélaïde returned to Aix on or just before 14 February 1750, St Valentine's Day. The period when she was away – November 1749 to February 1750 – corresponds exactly with the dates of Casanova's love affair with Henriette. Wherever Adélaïde was during this period, we know from a letter written by her brother-in-law that she was not with her husband at La Palud. Nor would she be again. From then

on, she resided in Aix, without her husband or her children. The reason remains a mystery, for although Gaspard de Gueidan preserved the letters of his other children, Adélaïde's are missing, either lost or deliberately destroyed.

The jigsaw pieces of Adélaïde de Gueidan's history – her skill on the viola da gamba, her abortive marriage, her suspected illegitimate son, her absence from Aix over the winter of 1749/1750 – fit together to create an almost perfect image of Casanova's 'divine Henriette', a woman who withheld her real identity from Casanova for many years. Only one piece of the jigsaw does not fit. When he wrote about her in his memoirs, Casanova claimed that Henriette was still alive, content with her life and in contact with him. But Adélaïde de Gueidan had died at La Palud on 2 December 1786, some two years before he started work on *Histoire de Ma Vie* in 1789.

More than two and a half centuries after her love affair with Casanova, Henriette, the most romantic of all his women, still remains as she always wanted to be – an enigma, as intriguing to us now as she was to Casanova on the day he first fell in love with her.

SIX

M.M. and C.C.

Nothing is more certain than that a devout girl,
when she does the work of the flesh with her
lover, experiences a hundred times more
pleasure than one without prejudices.[1]

IT IS FIVE O'CLOCK on the morning on 1 November 1753. An icy mist hangs over the black Venetian lagoon. The terns, ducks and gulls that live in the marshes have not yet awakened the day with their cries, but there is life already within the glass factories on the island of Murano, where the furnace fires which have been kept burning all night cast their demonic red glow into the sky. At the mouth of the Canale degli Angeli a light flickers behind the barred window of an ancient convent. Inside, a twenty-two-year-old woman sits shivering at a desk in an unheated bedchamber, writing a letter to a man she has never met.

Sunk in thought, M.M. twists a lock of long golden hair around fingers so blue with cold that her skin appears to be translucent. She knows virtually nothing about the intended recipient of her letter, not even his name. All she knows is that he is a tall, darkly tanned nobleman, with an imposing physique, a head of raven curls tied neatly with a ribbon at the nape of his neck, and large soulful eyes that smoulder with passion. Since August, he has put in an appearance at the convent's church on every feast day – the Transfiguration of the Lord, the Day of the Assumption, the Birth of Virgin Mary – as if he is the Holy Spirit made flesh, and today

being All Saints' Day, M.M. is hoping that he will turn up again. Although he has never once looked in her direction, something about this man intrigues and excites her. She is overwhelmed with the desire to make contact with him, even to touch him. As delicately as she can under the circumstances, but in terms that will leave little room for doubt, she is going to suggest to him that they become lovers.

Discreetly using the French language, which she believes he understands, M.M. sketches out in her letter the possible trajectory of a liaison between them. If he wishes, the recipient can first come to visit her with one of her friends, to whom he should not tell his name even if, once he has seen her, he decides that he does not want the matter to proceed. Alternatively, M.M. will send him the address of a private casino on Murano 'where you will find her alone at the first hour of the night, on the day you indicate to her; you can stay and sup with her, or you can leave after a quarter of an hour in the event that you have business'. If he prefers to offer her dinner in Venice, he should 'Tell her the day, the hour of the night, and the place where she should surrender herself, and you will see her leave a gondola masked, provided you are on the quay alone, without a servant, masked, and holding a candle.' Impatient to know his answer, M.M. ends by begging the stranger to give his reply to the same serving-woman who delivers this letter to him, and who will be waiting for him an hour before midday tomorrow in the church of San Canziano, near the Rialto bridge.

M.M. puts down her pen and reads through what she has written. Then, with a burning feeling inside her chest, she clutches at the heavy crucifix that hangs like a stone around her neck. What will the man think of her for propositioning him so brazenly? What if she has misjudged his character? What if he finds out who she is and publicly shames her? For she is suggesting the unthinkable to him: that the two of them commit a crime against God, by making a cuckold of the most Holy of husbands – Lord Jesus Christ.

M.M. is a nun.

She hesitates for a moment, then dips her pen in the silver-

topped inkpot once more and scrawls a final mitigating sentence at the bottom of the page. 'Consider,' she writes, 'that if I had not assumed you to be good and honourable, I should never have resolved to take a step that might make you form a dreadful opinion of me.'[2] After blotting these words dry, she folds the unsigned letter into a small rectangle, melts some bronze-coloured wax in the flame of her candle and firmly fastens the paper shut with her seal, which bears the imprint of a running knot. Before she can change her mind and tear the letter up she rings for her serving-woman and hands it to her with a large tip, instructing her exactly to whom, and when, the thing should be delivered.

A bell tolls, summoning M.M. to Prime. Terrified by what she has done, and yet at the same time exhilarated, she hides her tousled hair under a modest head-dress, slips a plain habit over her lace-trimmed shift, and rushes to the chapel in time to join her sisters for morning prayers.

In the autumn of 1753 M.M., the most enigmatic of all Casanova's lovers, was a twenty-two-year-old *monacha da coro*, or choir-nun, in the Augustinian convent of Santa Maria degli Angeli on the Venetian island of Murano. She was 'an absolute beauty, tall, with a complexion so white that it verged on pallor, a noble and decisive demeanour that was at the same time shy and reserved, large blue eyes; a sweet and smiling face, beautiful lips moist with dew, which allowed a glimpse of two superb rows of teeth'.[3] Like her glorious knee-length hair, which instead of cutting off as nuns were supposed to she kept hidden under her head-dress, her arched eyebrows were of the lightest chestnut colour. Her hands and forearms – the only parts of her flesh visible to the world apart from her face and throat – were plump, dimpled and as flawlessly white as the purest Carrara marble.

Who was this beautiful, libidinous nun? For obvious reasons, Casanova was very much concerned to disguise her identity, and in his manuscript he originally gave her the name *Mathilde*.[4] When he wrote to his friend the Prince de Ligne about the problem of what

to call her, he received the advice to *'Faites imprimer M.M'*.[5] This must have appealed to Casanova's sense of discretion, for he returned to his manuscript, scored out the original name and replaced it with the two initials. In reality M.M. was almost certainly a young woman named Marina Maria Morosini. Like many Venetian choir-nuns, she came from a patrician family. Her father, Domenico Morosini, was descended from a long line of notable Venetians that included several doges, a sixteenth-century historian, and the seventeenth commander-in-chief of the Republic's vast navy, said to be one of the greatest captains of his time (Francesco Morosini besieged Athens' Acropolis in 1687 and bombarded the Parthenon, almost destroying it in the process).

Born on 11 September 1731, Marina had been sent to Santa Maria degli Angeli days before her eighth birthday when, like many of her contemporaries, she was enrolled as an *educanda*, or temporary boarder. There, behind the convent's high walls and locked gates, she was schooled in subjects thought appropriate for a young woman of her class and, at the same time, kept out of harm's way – that is, away from the temptations of Venice and the sexual advances of predatory young men. When the noble-born *educande* grew up some were married off and left to live in their husbands' palazzi. Others remained in the cloister for the rest of their lives. Due to the Republic's rigid caste system, marriage to a man of a similar or higher social status was considered essential in Venetian society. However, this kind of union required the payment of an extremely large dowry by a girl's father. To avoid bankrupting himself, a nobleman would pour a large proportion of his resources into securing a prestigious marriage for his oldest or prettiest daughter, and rather than let her younger sisters marry beneath them he would exile them to one of the Republic's fifty convents where, for a much smaller dowry, they could respectably become the eternal spiritual brides of Jesus Christ. In this way the patrician families of Venice sacrificed their children to economics and tradition: while their younger sons were forced to remain bachelors in order not to split

up the family inheritance, their younger daughters were buried alive within convent walls.

In common with her older sister. Marina was destined to spend her life as an 'Angel of Murano', as the nuns in the convent of Santa Maria degli Angeli were known. Being pushed into taking religious vows was a dreadful experience for a young woman who had no religious calling, though girls did not always realise the full consequences of what they were doing until the ceremony of profession had concluded. 'When she first appeared, she looked pale, and more dead than alive,' wrote Dr Charles Burney after witnessing the profession of a beautiful young Roman noblewoman, an event he called a human sacrifice. 'She made a most profound reverence to the cardinal who was seated on the steps of the altar in his mitre and all his rich vestments, ready to receive her. She threw herself upon her knees at the foot of the altar, and remained in that posture for some time . . . She said, that she begged to be admitted into that convent as a sister of the order of St Ursula: Have you well, said the cardinal, considered of what you ask? She answered, cheerfully, that she had; and was well informed of all she was about to do . . . At the altar she changed countenance several times, first pale, then red, and seemed to pant, and to be in danger of either bursting into tears, or fainting; but she recovered before the ceremony was ended, and at the convent door assumed an air of great cheerfulness; talked to several of her friends and acquaintance, and seemed to give up the world very heroically.'[6]

In a furious work which she bluntly entitled *Inferno monacale* – The Nun's Hell – the seventeenth-century Venetian nun Arcangela Tarabotti, who had been a victim of enforced profession herself, described the ceremony from a novice's point of view as like being 'a witness at her own funeral'.[7] Becoming a nun was tantamount to dying. At the convent gates a novice gave up her hair, her worldly possessions, her personal relationships, her desires, her sexuality and whatever freedoms, however limited, she had hitherto enjoyed. The rest of her life would be ruled by a monotonous timetable of prayers, sermons, meals and devotion overseen by

an abbess and the local bishop. She would never know the love of a man, never have a child, never go to the theatre or dance in the streets during carnival, never choose for herself which book to read, never even walk down the street on her father's arm. When her relatives came to visit her she would communicate with them through a heavy iron grating in a public visiting-parlour. Even in church she would be separated from the secular congregants by a locked iron communication window.

'Hope and love keep us in this pleasant prison' read the sixteenth-century inscription above the main entrance to the church of Le Vergini, the convent to which some of the most celebrated Venetian families sent their daughters. But there was little hope for those forced to endure the 'eternal imprisonment' of the convent, even though the older nuns, who had been through the experience themselves and were often relatives of the young novitiates, went out of their way to make the girls' day-to-day existence as pleasant as possible. Upper-class choir-nuns were waited on by *converse*, lay-nuns who only took simple vows and were, in reality, serving-women who went back to their own houses and children at night. Some convent rules – such as those forbidding personal relationships – were simply made to be broken: abbesses frequently turned a blind eye to nuns wearing their own clothes under their habits, keeping valuable personal items in their rooms or forming close, even loving friend-ships with the young *educande*, as Marina did. Older choir-nuns, 'instead of enjoining them to adopt a rigorous silence,' assured their younger sisters 'that they can make as much noise as they like'.[8] Convent visiting-rooms often resembled social salons, with family members and secret masked admirers gathering there with their dogs and children to watch a puppet show or exchange gossip and news with the nuns. But even when Venice's carnival celebrations invaded the quiet of the cloister, the nuns remained locked behind their iron grating, forced to be passive spectators to a way of life in which they were forbidden to participate.

According to one well-informed Venetian gossip, Marina had not been forced to become a nun by her family but, after spending her

childhood at the Angeli as a boarder, she had embraced the conventual life of her own free will. The real enigma was the sudden caprice that had made such a wealthy and cultivated young beauty decide to take the veil. If she had indeed entered the cloister on a whim, Marina had plenty of time to repent of her irrevocable decision. During the four years since her profession the religious life had become anathema to her, and her island convent now seemed more like a prison than a place of refuge. Venice was so close that she could see it in the distance and almost hear its music, yet its multitudinous attractions could have been one hundred miles away. With her questioning mind and her strong sexual drive, Marina yearned for what took place in the city: family life, the theatre, gambling, witty conversation, love affairs and intrigues. Instead, she was marooned on Murano with petty rules, a religion she no longer believed in, and the island's smoke-belching glass industry with all 'the Furnaces and Calcinations, the Transubstantiations, the Liquefactions that are incident to this Art'.[9]

There was only one way that many young Venetian nuns could bear their restricted lives inside the convent, and that was to rebel by escaping now and then, often in carnival costume, and having secret lives outside it. When she had entered Santa Maria degli Angeli Marina had taken vows of poverty, chastity and obedience, but since then she had deliberately and defiantly broken each one time and again. For in the autumn of 1752, at the age of twenty-one, she had taken a lover. The Abbé François Joachim Pierre de Bernis was handsome, witty, sweet-natured, thoughtful and loveable; and, as the new French ambassador to Venice, he was also a man of power and means. The youngest son of an impoverished noble family, he had been educated at St Sulpice in Paris where he had taken the tonsure in his youth in preparation for an ecclesiastical career. In his mid-twenties he had worked under Cardinal de Fleury, tutor and later Prime Minister to Louis XV and one of the guiding lights of the French Church. Fleury had strongly disapproved of his young abbé, and had warned him that he would receive no appointment from him as long as he lived. De Bernis is

said to have replied, 'Very well, Your Grace, I shall wait' – which is exactly what he did. For the next few years, he lived in Paris as well as he could on his limited means, and whiled away his time by writing light poetry and essays. Elected into the French Academy in 1744 at the age of twenty-nine (Cardinal de Fleury had died two years earlier), he was befriended by Voltaire, who, because of de Bernis's florid literary style, nicknamed him 'Babet la Bouquetière' after a famous Parnasse flower-seller. Since a farce entitled *Les Amours de Babet la Bouquetière* was staged in Paris in 1772, by which time de Bernis was a famous cardinal in Rome, he had clearly had a reputation as a ladies' man in his youth.[10] He certainly became a favourite of the future Madame de Pompadour, who received him at her husband's home, the Château d'Etoiles, and, after she became Louis XV's official mistress, secured de Bernis a modest annual pension of 1,500 livres and a grace-and-favour apartment in the Palais du Louvre.

Through Pompadour's influence, thirty-seven-year-old de Bernis was appointed ambassador to Venice in 1752. Although he was sent there that October 'as into a cul-de-sac of little interest', as he admitted in his memoirs, he was determined to make his mark in the Republic: 'I had been announced in Venice as an agreeable man and a younger son without resources. People expected gallantry and a very ordinary style of living. I balked this public expectation on both points.'[11] His new home was a grand palazzo near the Madonna dell'Orto church, decorated with blue and green damask silk and filled with gold ornaments. It had a charming summer house in the garden, painted white and covered with brightly-coloured wooden carvings of flora and fauna, and the main building contained a billiard table at which he played during the long evenings. Seven footmen, two secretaries and a plethora of domestic servants waited on him, and his kitchen was presided over by a wonderful French chef, du Rosier, whom he had probably brought from Paris with him. Keeping this large retinue under control required the imposition of strict discipline: 'I wished my household to be regulated like that of a Carthusian establishment,' de Bernis

wrote, 'I required that silence and order should reign there; that my retinue should be polite and respectful towards all citizens, and that libertinism should be banished.'[12]

Banished it was, to the island of Murano where de Bernis was introduced to Marina in the visiting-parlour of Santa Maria degli Angeli. The intermediary may well have been a scheming friend sympathetic to Marina's plight, or perhaps an unwitting member of her family; although Venice's patricians were forbidden by law from conversing with foreigners, Marina's relative Francesco Morosini had served as the Venetian ambassador in Paris between 1748 and 1751 and would almost certainly have met de Bernis there. With all the finesse that his nation was renowned for in matters of intrigue, de Bernis courted Marina through the iron grating of the communication window. Clever, generous and witty ('Seriousness never excluded jesting on the minister's side, who in this way possessed to perfection the French spirit', Casanova wrote of him)[13] he quickly won over the sexually and intellectually frustrated nun. He was not the first French ambassador to fall under the spell of one of Murano's enclosed women: the Marquis de Froulay, one of his predecessors, had conducted a very indiscreet affair with Maria da Riva, a patrician-born nun from the convent of San Giacomo. The Council of Ten had eventually transferred Maria to a convent in Ferrara, from where she had later absconded with a colonel whom she subsequently married, scandalising society and causing de Froulay to go mad with grief.

As one eighteenth-century observer noted with some sympathy, Venice's reluctant nuns had a reputation for being 'cheerful libertines . . . If they fail to keep up an enforced vow of chastity it is no fault of theirs, but of the parents who pushed them into the cloister and of the people who thought of such a dreary vow to begin with . . . Nuns from the large convents are forever going masked to the play or out to meet their lovers on the Piazza. All they have to do is get round the sister-portress, who never says no to those with noble families or powerful friends and admirers.'[14] The Burgundian President Charles de Brosses was also aware of the nuns' libidinous

reputation: were he to be sent to Venice for a long stay, he remarked, his mind would immediately turn to its *religieuses*.

Seducing a nun was a sacrilegious crime theoretically punishable by perpetual banishment from the Republic, or even death. The inherent dangers made the pleasure even sweeter for de Bernis. Generous, protective and above all discreet, he proved to be Marina's perfect comrade in her rebellion against her religious vows. With the help of his influence and money, with which she bribed the convent's gardener and the lay-nun who looked after her, she was soon escaping from the convent at night through a door in her bedchamber which led on to a side canal. From there she was spirited off in one of the ambassador's five gondolas to a nearby private house or *casino* which de Bernis had rented for her and to which he gave her a key. In this sumptuously furnished apartment he introduced the bride of Christ to sex (to which she soon became addicted), pink champagne and French food served on silver hotplates and Sèvres porcelain. He also passed on to her the enlightened ideas he had imbibed from Voltaire. A small library of books and erotic engravings at the *casino* provided Marina with 'all that the wisest philosophers have written against religion, and all that the most voluptuous pens have written on the subject which is the sole aim of love'.[15]

By reading these books and through philosophical discussions with her lover, the fallen Murano 'Angel' soon lost her remaining religious faith. Her new enlightened perspective made her even more defiant against her religious wardens. When her confessor warned her to stop reading the French moralist Pierre Charron's book, *La Sagesse*, she refused on the grounds that her conscience was untroubled by it; and when the Bishop of Torcello, under whose diocese the Angeli fell, took the matter up with her, she retorted that a confessor's job was to absolve her, not to advise her. Since Marina was unsatisfied by the bishop's ruling that she be left to her own conscience in future, de Bernis wrote to Rome on her behalf and procured a brief from the Pope authorising the nun to confess in future to whomsoever she wished.

There seemed no end to the delight Marina took in rebelling against the Church. During Venice's long carnival season, when everyone went about disguised in cloaks and masks, she allowed de Bernis to take her to the opera and to gamble at the public ridotto. Through him, she acquired a wardrobe of fine secular clothes, and he showered her with diamonds and money which she kept locked up in her desk at the *casino*, a place which soon became her refuge and where she delighted in playing house, making up the day-bed in front of the fire herself and even dressing the salad at table. Everything she could possibly need was thoughtfully provided for her there including a personal maid. There was even a pretty box filled with hand-made condoms to ensure that her lover would not make her pregnant. De Bernis did everything within his power to make Marina happy – and that included facilitating her desire to take a second lover when the stranger she saw in the Angeli's church took her fancy. The idea actually appealed to the ambassador's voyeuristic streak. The *casino* contained a secret chamber that could only be entered through the false back of a cupboard, and twenty holes bored through its walls looked directly into the main chamber. With Marina's consent, de Bernis planned to spy on her and the handsome churchgoer who had caught her fancy. Sexual exhibitionism was about to be added to the list of her crimes against God.

When twenty-eight-year-old Giacomo Casanova left the church of Santa Maria degli Angeli after hearing mass on All Saints' Day, an elderly lay-nun from the convent walked past him and dropped Marina's letter at his feet. Intrigued, Casanova picked it up and, as his gondolier steered him back towards Venice, he broke open the wax seal and read the contents with a mixture of curiosity and amazement. Back at the Palazzo Bragadin, where he was then living as the senator's adopted son, he shut himself up in his apartments while he made up his mind what to do. Although the letter was a work of daring madness on the part of its anonymous author, Casanova nevertheless found a dignity in it that made him respect

her. From its tone he concluded that the nun who had written it must be young, pretty and well versed in the art of intrigue – in short, a delectable prospect. But two things made him hesitate: first, the letter might have been written to entrap him; second, he already had a lover among Murano's 'Angels'. In fact, he had two.

The first was Marta Savorgnan, one of the two sisters with whom he had lost his virginity so many years ago. The second was fourteen-year-old Caterina Capretta (C.C. as he called her in his memoir) who, because of her suspected liaison with him, had been sent to the Angeli the previous June as a boarder.

Casanova had met Caterina at the end of May 1753, just days after returning to Venice from Paris, where he had spent two hedonistic years at Senator Bragadin's expense. Since parting from Henriette he had become a sophisticated socialite and a skilful womaniser. Life in Paris had polished any remaining rough corners off his education and manners. His French, the language of the European aristocracy, had been all but perfected thanks to a year's worth of private lessons given him by the then-famous satirical playwright Crébillon; he had learned the minuet under the well-known dancing instructor Marcel; and, thanks to his friendship with the renowned family of actor Antonio Balletti, whom he had met in Milan, he had insinuated himself into the highest echelons of Parisian artistic society.

Caterina was introduced to Casanova by her older brother Pietro, a ne'er-do-well who was trying to persuade the young adventurer to honour three dubious bills of exchange in return for a share in his business, which was importing beef cattle into Venice from Styria and Hungary. While his father was out of town, Pietro deliberately threw his innocent fourteen-year-old sister together with his sophisticated acquaintance under compromising circumstances, hoping that an intrigue between them would put pressure on Casanova to give him money. Pietro's plan backfired when Casanova fell in love with Caterina. Tall, slim and raven-haired, the girl was a well-protected virgin who knew nothing of the ways of the world. She had never mixed in company before, or

even left her parents' house unless it was on her mother's arm. What impressed Casanova most about her was her fresh candid mind, her unspoiled nature and her youthful exuberance – all so different from the studied airs and graces of Parisian women. Allowed by her brother to visit the San Biagio garden on the island of Giudecca with her admirer, Caterina raced around 'like a young greyhound . . . she runs until she is out of breath, and then laughs at the astonishment which keeps me motionless and staring at her.'[16] Convinced that if he himself did not fall for the bait, Pietro would use Caterina to attract a less scrupulous man, Casanova felt well and truly trapped. He 'could proceed with C.C. neither as an honest man nor as a libertine. I could not delude myself that I might have her as a wife, and I thought that I would kill anyone who dared to persuade me to seduce her.'[17]

These noble sentiments lasted a matter of days – just long enough for Caterina and her mother to grow to trust Casanova, and for him to link up again with his old friend Teresa Imer. The flirtatious young singer who had captivated Senator Malipiero in her youth was now married to a choreographer named Angelo Pompeati, and living with him and their children in the Prussian outpost of Bayreuth. Here she had become an opera star and the adored lover of two important men: the Marquis de Montpernis, the French impresario of Bayreuth's beautiful opera house; and the ruling Margrave himself, Friedrich von Hohenzollern, the brother-in-law of Frederick the Great. Back in Venice in the spring of 1753 to visit her parents, Teresa was at a loose end. Years earlier, Casanova had ruined his relationship with Senator Malipiero by being caught petting with her in his palazzo. Older but no wiser, the two of them now consummated the affair that had been brewing since then. It was a lighthearted fling for both of them: Teresa was soon to return to her husband and lovers in Bayreuth; and Casanova had Caterina's virginity on his mind.

Persuading himself that the only way to save Caterina from being exploited by her brother was to marry her, Casanova moved in for the kill. Having assured Signora Capretta that his intentions to-

wards her daughter were strictly honourable, he spirited the girl away on an afternoon excursion to a private *casino* on the island of Giudecca. One minute Casanova was talking to Caterina about obtaining her father's permission to be wed in ten days' time, and waiting until then to consummate their marriage. The next minute he was piling on emotional pressure designed to make her give in to him straight away. Was Caterina sure that he loved her? Did she believe him capable of failing her? Was she certain that she would never repent of marrying him? If the answer to these questions was yes then they should marry immediately with God as their witness and make themselves happy. A public church ceremony and marriage documents could wait! Carried away by this emotional outburst, Caterina immediately exchanged vows with Casanova. Then, assuring her that they were truly married, her new husband persuaded her to complete their nuptials in bed.

Casanova, who was twice Caterina's age, knew exactly what he was doing. 'An innocent girl who despite her fourteen years has never loved, or mixed with other girls, knows neither the violence of desires nor what it is that gives birth to them, nor the dangers of being alone with a lover,' he wrote of her. 'When instinct makes her fall in love with a man, she believes him worthy of all her trust, and she thinks she can only make him love her by showing him that she has no reservations about him.'[18] She surrendered her virginity in what he described as a heroic manner, and then submitted to six hours of energetic and passionate sex. The experience took its toll on her. By the time Casanova took Caterina home late that night her eyes were 'surrounded by such dark circles that she looked as if she had been beaten up. The poor child had sustained a combat which had positively changed her into another being.'[19]

The amorous combat was resumed several times over the next few days thanks to Pietro, who guessed what had happened and used it to blackmail Casanova into standing surety for his money-making schemes. Since Caterina was convinced that her father would have no choice but to let them marry if she became pregnant, and believed that conception was most likely to occur

if she and Casanova reached orgasm simultaneously, they took every opportunity to work towards this goal.

By the time that Christoforo Capretta returned to Venice a few days later his son Pietro was in prison for debt and, though he did not know it, his previously innocent fourteen-year-old daughter had not only been deflowered by Casanova, she was also pregnant by him (and so, incidentally, was Teresa Imer). Convinced in the heat of the moment that he wanted to legalise his 'marriage', Casanova persuaded Senator Bragadin to grant him a sufficient income to guarantee Caterina's substantial dowry and then despatched him to see Capretta to plead his cause. Astounded by the senator's proposal that his young daughter be allowed to marry an actress's son with no real position in life, and no money other than the income Bragadin gave him, the merchant summoned Caterina and gently cross-examined her. Terrified of admitting the truth, she swore that she had only met Casanova five or six times, and always in her brother's room where he had asked her if she would consent to marry him. Justly suspicious, Capretta immediately bolted the side door that led from his son's room on to the street. Two days later, while his wife lay sick in bed, he summoned one of his sisters, who was a nun at Santa Maria degli Angeli, and ordered her to take his daughter back to the convent, giving Caterina only fifteen minutes' warning that she was to leave the house.

By mid-June Caterina was enrolled as an *educanda* in the Murano convent, where she was destined to remain until her marriage five years later and where the beautiful nun Marina Maria Morosini – or Mother Maria Contarina, as she was known within the convent walls – took her under her wing. She discouraged Caterina from befriending the other girls, gave her French lessons twice a day and showered her with passionate kisses of which, Caterina told Casanova, he would have had a right to be jealous if the nun had been a man. The abbess had been instructed not to let Caterina correspond with anyone outside the convent, and she was threatened with excommunication if she attempted to do so. Nevertheless, by bribing a lay-nun by the name of Laura, she managed to exchange

letters with the man she now regarded as her husband. With Laura acting as a go-between, Casanova smuggled Caterina some money; and with the unwitting help of her mother, whom he persuaded to believe that he was really a pious man, he managed to send her a miniature portrait of himself concealed in a secret compartment of a ring which bore on its exterior a tiny painting of her namesake, St Catherine.

Caterina had already paid a high price for falling in love with Casanova. First she had lost her precious virginity, then her freedom. Worse was to come. The Bellini *Barbarigo Madonna and Child* that hung above the altar in the Angeli's church portrayed a glowing vision of motherhood, but Caterina's pregnancy would have no such happy outcome. At the end of July she had a miscarriage. Forced to hide it from all the choir-nuns except Marina, who helped her to keep the affair secret, she lay propped up in bed on pillows, bleeding copiously into a large wad of linen napkins which Casanova purchased from a Jewish merchant in Venice's ghetto, and which Laura smuggled in and out of the convent underneath her own dress. It was possible, even likely, that Caterina would die, and Casanova knew that he would hold himself responsible if she did. Overcome with guilt, he temporarily moved into Laura's rag-strewn house on Murano in order to be closer to Caterina; and when he saw the number of blood-soaked napkins which the lay-nun pulled out from under her skirt when she came home at night he 'nearly dropped dead. It was sheer butchery.'[20]

Eventually Caterina recovered from the 'illness' that had mystified the entire convent. By the end of August, when Casanova attended a profession at the Angeli church in order to try to catch a glimpse of her, she looked older and yet more beautiful than ever. She seemed so pleased to see Casanova, even from a distance, that he decided to visit the church on every feast day from then onwards. But the sordid miscarriage, and her internment, had already dulled his romantic feelings towards Caterina. Celibacy was definitely not on his agenda: he 'had been born to have a

mistress and to live happily with her'.[21] Unwilling to wait four years to marry the girl whose life he had all but ruined within the space of a fortnight (and he was not finished with her yet), Casanova was already on the lookout for a new relationship.

Marina suspected from the start that Caterina had been sent to the convent because she had a lover. Yet it did not occur to her that he was the same man who had attracted her so strongly in church that she had dared to write to him. When Casanova replied to her anonymous letter he assured her that he was free of ties, and she had no reason to doubt his word. Within days he took up the offer of visiting her in the convent in the company of her close friend the Countess Segura. While the two women chatted through the iron grille in the visiting-parlour, a masked Casanova sat nearby observing the beauty who had propositioned him by letter. By the time he left he was madly in love with Marina, and fully resigned to being unfaithful to Caterina, who, he justified, could only be pleased at a liaison designed 'to keep me alive, and consequently to preserve me for her'.[22]

The following afternoon he returned to the convent alone as the nun had instructed him to if he wished to see her again. Claiming that he was a relative, he asked for Mother Maria Contarina in the countess's name. Suddenly Marina's courage failed her. After keeping Casanova waiting for an hour, she told her elderly lay-nun to inform him that she was ill the whole day. Instead, the woman told him that she was 'busy all day'. Marina was devastated, for she guessed that he would take it as an insult. She was right: always sensitive about his humble origins, Casanova could never bear to be slighted by anyone. Furious at having been trifled with by the fickle nun, he returned Marina's letters to her along with a cold but somewhat restrained note pardoning her folly and at the same time warning her never to repeat it with another man.

It took five or six days for the misunderstanding to be cleared up and for the two would-be intriguers at last to meet face to face in the convent visiting-room, alone and with only the iron communication grille separating them. After fifteen speechless minutes,

and with little time left for preliminaries, Casanova explained that he was a man in easy circumstances: his life in Venice consisted of theatre, society and gambling; and the nun should know that he loved spending money on the woman he adored. For her part, Marina admitted to the stranger – whose name she still did not know – that she already had a lover who gave her money, who was absolutely her master, and from whom she kept no secrets, not even this new liaison. They arranged to meet at Marina's *casino* two days later, and she gave Casanova the key to it. Promising him that her lover would not be present when they met, she reassured him that the man would nevertheless be delighted for her.

Casanova had never been so directly propositioned before, let alone by a nun, and he was intoxicated as much by the danger of the situation as by Marina's manner and beauty. By the time he left the visiting-room he had all but forgotten Caterina as well as every other woman he had ever professed to love. 'It was as if I had never been happy in love,' he wrote, 'and I was about to be so for the first time.' The idea of having illicit sex with the beautiful, sexually-experienced Bride of Christ excited him so much that he could neither eat nor sleep until he next saw her: 'The affair involved a vestal. I was to taste a forbidden fruit. I was to trespass on the rights of an omnipotent husband, seizing from his divine seraglio the most beautiful of all his sultanas.'[23] Any fantasy he had of taking her in her nun's habit would have to wait, for when he turned up at the candle-lit *casino* two days later Marina, who had arrived there earlier, was dressed in elegant secular clothes. Contrary to what she had promised the stranger, her lover was present, but hidden in the secret chamber, from where he watched their every move. By prior arrangement with de Bernis, Marina allowed her new admirer to kiss her and even to uncover her breasts, but she would let him go no further. As a seductive technique, her 'charming refusals' worked magic on Casanova, particularly since they came in the form of 'arguments given in words as amorous as they were energetic and reinforced every moment by loving kisses which melted my soul'.[24] The couple spent the entire night kissing

passionately, and eventually fell asleep half-clothed on a day-bed in front of the fire.

When he next visited the Murano convent Casanova suspected that he was being followed by a spy, so by mutual agreement he and Marina decided that their second private meeting should take place at his own *casino* in Venice. As with his offer to take Henriette to Parma in his private carriage, there was a drawback to Casanova's plan: although he was still being financed by Bragadin, his income was not sufficient for him to own a *casino*. Eager to impress Marina, he rushed out and rented the most expensive one he could find – an elegant five-roomed apartment a hundred paces from the San Moisé theatre, close to the Piazza San Marco. Formerly the property of Robert d'Arcy, the fourth Earl of Holderness and the English ambassador in Venice until 1746, it contained an octagonal room with mirrored walls, floor and ceiling, a salon decorated with painted Chinese tiles depicting erotic scenes, and a boudoir with a bathtub and English-style water-closet – rare novelties in Venice, where plumbing, if it existed at all, was distinctly primitive. Designed to preserve the anonymity of the lovers who met there, the rooms were served by a kitchen hidden behind a revolving dumb-waiter which discreetly blocked off the servants' view of the dining-room. Since he was anxious not to be found wanting in any respect when the nun visited him, Casanova first spent a night there alone and made the servants prepare him a test dinner for two with no expense spared. Always a generous host with a perfectionist's eye for detail, he pronounced the game, truffles, sturgeon and oysters served to him on Meissen dishes faultless, as was the champagne and the fine Burgundy wine. However, he reproached the cook for having forgotten to put out a platter of hardboiled eggs, anchovies, and prepared vinegars for making a salad, and insisted on having bitter oranges to flavour the punch in future as well as all the fresh fruit and ices the man could find. In response, the world-weary cook, who had no doubt seen it all before, rolled his eyes with a contrite air.

Mindful of Marina's safety, it was de Bernis himself, masked and disguised as a gondolier, who conducted her from Murano to

Venice's Campo dei Santi Giovanni e Paolo where she had arranged to meet Casanova behind the famous equestrian statue of the fifteenth-century warrior Bartolomeo Colleoni. The ambassador had disguised her as a masked male masquerader in black satin breeches teamed with a pink velvet coat and matching waistcoat embroidered with gold thread. Marina's hair was arranged in a masculine plait that hung all the way down her back to her knees, her shoe buckles were set with brilliants, her fingers were covered in valuable rings, and the neck of her ruffled shirt was pinned with a heart-shaped diamond brooch. In addition, de Bernis had filled Marina's pockets with all the accessories appropriate for a wealthy young nobleman: opera glasses, scented handkerchiefs, a case of toothpicks, a snuffbox and even a pair of fine English flintlock pistols, presumably so that she could protect herself from Casanova in an emergency. Casanova was overcome by her lover's generosity in presenting Marina to him in this way. Assuring the nun that, although she was not his first love, she would surely be his last, he wined and dined her before making love to her for seven hours, pausing only to engage in the odd fifteen minutes of intimate conversation. Since Marina demonstrated no sexual novelties to him (her experience was limited to one man), Casanova took it upon himself to enlighten her in the mysteries of the female orgasm and, he later hinted, to oral sex: she was 'astonished to find herself capable of so much pleasure, for I had shown her many things which she had believed were fictions. I did to her what she did not believe she was allowed to ask me to do to her, and I taught her that the slightest embarrassment spoils the greatest of pleasures.'[25]

Between November 1753 and May 1755, when de Bernis was recalled to France, the rebellious nun was in the extraordinary position of having two devoted lovers, neither of whom could do enough for her. The French ambassador paid for her *casino*. He watched over her with the care of a doting father, and his money and influence enabled her to escape from the convent as often as she liked. Meanwhile Casanova worshipped her body and under-

stood her troubled soul. He waited on Marina hand and foot when they were together, taking on the role of her maid when they went to bed by pinning up her hair for her, and he even made the ambassador's chef teach him how to cook her favourite dish. This kind of attentiveness was irresistible. Aware that Marina belonged first and foremost to her other lover, whose identity he soon guessed, Casanova complied with all the ambassador's wishes and, instead of trying to compete with him, was happy to take second place. If he unexpectedly turned up at the convent to see Marina when the ambassador was due to arrive there, he immediately left so that there should be no awkward meeting between them. At de Bernis's request, he took care not to make Marina pregnant. And although he had rented his own *casino* in Venice for her, he willingly accepted the fact that she rarely came there, because the ambassador thought it safer for her to stay on Murano, particularly if he himself was out of town. When Marina confessed that her other lover planned to hide in the secret chamber and spy on them making love on New Year's Eve, Casanova obligingly joined her in putting on a display of sexual fireworks for the ambassador's benefit. 'I picked her up, she threw her arms around my shoulders so that she weighed less, and having dropped my muff, I seized her by the thighs and she braced herself on the nail,' he wrote of their exploits that night, 'but after a little walk around the room, fearful of what might follow, I put her down on the carpet, then having sat down and having made her sit on top of me, she had the kindness of finishing the job with her beautiful hand, collecting in the palm the white of the first egg. "Five more to go," she says to me.'[26] Instead of moving into the bedroom where de Bernis would not be able to spy on them, the couple then made love on the sofa. After this they made love again in front of a mirror, and had mutual oral sex in the 'straight tree' posture mentioned by sixteenth-century poet Pietro Aretino in his *Sonetti lussuriosi*: 'I lifted her up to devour her chamber of love which I could not otherwise reach, wishing to put her in a position to devour in turn the weapon which wounded her to death without taking her life.'[27]

For this performance Casanova was rewarded by a love-letter from Marina ('I love you to adoration, I kiss the air, thinking that you are there') and, from the ambassador, a gift of one of his own precious snuffboxes. Made of gold, it contained two concealed portraits of Marina, one depicting her dressed as a nun, the other showing her lying naked next to her habit, upon which sat a cupid with a quiver at its feet.

It seemed that there were no lengths to which Marina and Casanova would not go in order to please de Bernis. This included sacrificing Caterina to the ambassador's wishes. Casanova's so-called 'wife' soon suspected that he was involved with the same Mother Maria Contarina with whom she was now having her own passionate lesbian relationship but, lying through his teeth, he assured her that there was nothing between them but friendship. After that, Caterina kept her suspicions to herself. But when, a few months later, she spotted Marina wearing a medallion of the Annunciation painted by the same artist who had painted the St Catherine ring which Casanova had given her, she drew her own conclusions. Caught lying, but anxious that she should not make trouble between them, Casanova assured Caterina that his feelings for the nun in no way detracted from his passion for her.

He was lying again and she would soon find out in the cruellest of ways. For just after she had guessed the truth about his liaison with the nun, Marina secretly opened the *educanda*'s St Catherine ring and discovered Casanova's portrait hidden within it. Possessing no concept of sexual jealousy herself, she conceived the idea of bringing Casanova and Caterina together again. The surprise meeting was to be a gift to both of them, as well as to de Bernis, with whom she planned to spy on the lovers' passionate reunion from within the secret chamber in her *casino*. The evening involved a great deal of planning on her part. First Marina obtained permission from the abbess for Caterina to sleep in her room, so that she could smuggle her out of the convent whenever she wanted to. Next, she herself arranged to meet Casanova at the Murano *casino* at two o'clock in the morning on a night when a carnival masquerade ball

was being held in the public part of the convent parlour for the amusement of the nuns. After watching the festivities with Caterina through the grating (they laughed most of all at the antics of a male masquerader dressed as Pierrot) Marina took the girl aside and, asking her to trust her, dressed her up in a nun's habit and sent her off to the *casino* in a gondola.

By now it was two o'clock in the morning. While Marina, who had secretly followed her from the convent, watched with de Bernis from within the secret chamber, a perplexed Caterina stood alone in front of the fire in her nun's habit, with no idea of where she was or what she should expect. Suddenly the door opened and the Pierrot from the convent parlour walked in. The moment he saw her he froze. Caterina instantly realised that he was Casanova, and she understood everything: the man she believed was her 'husband' really was her female lover's lover. And, even worse, he was clearly displeased to see her. In truth, he was in a state of shock, for he knew that his lies to both women had been exposed. He felt dishonoured, and 'played with, tricked, trapped, scorned' by both of them. The only way he could understand the situation was to presume that Marina had discovered his duplicity and set out to punish him for it, and he was so overwhelmed with self-pity at the thought of having lost her that he was unable to hide his feelings. To make love to Caterina for form's sake when he was in love with Marina would have made Casanova feel even more contemptible: 'I was her husband; I was the one who had seduced her. These reflections tore at my soul.'[28] With a maturity way beyond her years, Caterina put on a bravura show in the face of rejection: Marina was her worthy successor, she insisted; she loved both of them, and wished them both well.

Marina's plan to give pleasure to all three of her lovers had backfired badly. The evening had turned into a disaster. After eight tortuous hours of tears, explanations and sorrow, which she and de Bernis observed with growing dismay, Casanova handed his key to the *casino* to Caterina with instructions that she should return it to the nun. Then he left, believing that he would never go back there.

It seemed that the heavens were conspiring to punish Casanova for his lies. Since he had arrived on Murano that afternoon a terrible storm had blown up from the west. Freezing cold in his thin linen Pierrot's costume, and with no cloak to protect him from the wind, he barely made it back across the lagoon to Venice even though his gondola was steered by two strapping men. Drenched to the skin, he took to his bed in the Palazzo Bragadin, his fever and delirium aggravated by shame at having lost face, betrayed Caterina and ruined his chances with Marina. In this he was mistaken. Believing for a short while that their mutual lover had drowned in the storm, the two women were now as distraught as he was. By the time Casanova began to recover a few days later there were already two letters on his bedside, one from each of them. Caterina's explained Marina's good intentions in thrusting them together; and enclosed in Marina's letter to him was the key to her *casino*.

Reconciliation with Marina followed. Shortly after that, Casanova entertained both her and de Bernis in his own *casino*: impressed by what he had seen of Casanova's behaviour, the ambassador now wanted to meet him in person. During this bizarre evening, Casanova's attitude to both his guests 'was that of a private individual to whom a king accompanied by his mistress was paying the greatest of all honours'. He fed them the choicest wines and best oysters, and treated Marina as if she were no more than a friend. At length the nun turned the conversation to Casanova's young 'wife', de Bernis expressed his desire to meet Caterina, and Casanova found himself agreeing to invite the girl to join them all for dinner in a few days' time. Although he realised what was happening – that the ambassador was interested in Caterina, and Marina was acting as his procuress in the matter – Casanova felt helpless to stop it. De Bernis had generously shared his mistress with him for months. Now Casanova owed it to him to return the favour. And despite his protective feelings towards Caterina, the idea was not wholly repugnant to him.

Slowly, surely, Caterina was being debauched. Only months ago she had been an innocent virgin. Casanova had seduced her and

made her pregnant. Because of him she had been locked up in the convent, where she had nearly lost her life and where Marina had seduced her. Now, Caterina was being groomed by Marina to become another man's lover, and far from doing anything to stop this happening, Casanova actively participated in the plot. At a dinner he arranged for the four of them he went out of his way to make Caterina shine, even though he despised himself for doing so. At their next meeting, from which the ambassador purposely stayed away, he and Marina showed Caterina books of porno-graphic engravings, and the three of them indulged in a night of sex. By now Casanova felt well and truly trapped into returning all the favours de Bernis had shown him. He knew that if he attended the two women's next meeting with the ambassador Caterina would be safe but he himself would appear niggardly, rude and ungrateful. If he stayed away, however, she would be corrupted and, even though he would hold himself responsible, she would fall in his estimation and he would no longer want to marry her.

Perhaps it was for this reason that the marriage-shy adventurer decided to abandon Caterina to her fate. It was a bitter pill for him to swallow, but he had more than met his match in the libertine nun who had engineered the plot. Caterina's mind 'is now as free-thinking as ours', Marina wrote cheerfully to Casanova after the two women had spent an evening with de Bernis, 'and she owes it to me. I can boast that I have finished training her for you.'[29] Regretful that he had not watched their antics from the secret chamber, she insisted on recounting every lurid detail of the evening when she next saw Casanova. She had misjudged him: instead of arousing him, the tale had the opposite effect of making him fear he would be 'out of sorts to cut a good figure in bed'; and, as the great lover knew, 'to cut a poor figure one only needs to fear it'.[30]

Between 1753 and May 1755, while Christoforo Capretta believed that his daughter was safely out of harm's way in the convent, she was being debauched by Marina Morosini, Casanova and the

French ambassador to Venice. And while de Bernis insisted in his memoirs that Venetians were astonished to find him 'insensible to the charms of women',[31] he was carrying on with a fifteen-year-old school girl and a nun, as we know from a letter he wrote to his friend the Comtesse des Alleurs, wife of the French ambassador at Constantinople. 'Your nun has evaded the walls of her convent to take refuge in Padua,' he wrote on 1 September 1754, 'which is the most sombre cloister that I know. I have been to see her, and she will come to dine in my house in the fields.[32] In speaking of her flirtations, you cast in the most delightful possible manner some stones in my garden; you put to me questions on unfaithfulness which, happily or unhappily for me, can no longer embarrass me. I lead the life of a Carthusian friar and I have all the more merit in that it is quite necessary that I possess some sanctity.'[33]

Discreet as de Bernis was, it was hard to keep secrets for long in Venice. By the time that the new British ambassador, John Murray, arrived in the Republic in October 1754, rumours were rife that the French resident was having an affair with a patrician-born nun at Santa Maria degli Angeli – a situation that was probably tolerated by the Council of Ten for diplomatic reasons as well as to protect the powerful Morosini family. John Murray, a man who delighted in sexual exhibitionism and was 'a scandalous fellow in every sense of the word'[34] according to Lady Mary Wortley Montagu, was soon boasting to his new friend Giacomo Casanova that he himself had enjoyed Mother Maria Contarina, the French ambassador's mistress, for the price of a hundred sequins. When an outraged Casanova investigated this claim, the so-called nun turned out to be an impostor, but the news that she was being impersonated by a prostitute drove home to Marina the precarious nature of her situation.

Casanova's behaviour also attracted unwelcome attention from Venice's Council of Ten. What was the reason for his frequent visits to Murano? Whilst they might close their eyes to the ambassador's liaison with Marina, if Casanova was involved with her it was a different matter. Moreover, why was the upstart actors'

son in cahoots with de Bernis and Murray? In order to prevent spying by foreign powers, any communication between the Venetian patrician classes and the foreign ambassadors living among them was strictly forbidden, and, although Casanova was a commoner by birth, his close relationship with Senator Bragadin cast his friendships with foreigners in a suspicious light. Highly suspicious, too, were Casanova's dealings with Bragadin. Just why had the middle-aged senator taken him under his wing? Why did he support him financially? What was at the root of Casanova's power over him and his two male companions, Dandolo and Barbaro? It was rumoured that the three men dabbled in Jewish mysticism with Casanova's help.

A month after Murray's arrival in Venice, the Inquisitors ordered one of their spies, a jeweller named Giovanni Battista Manuzzi, to keep track of Casanova's activities. Between November 1754 and the following July, Manuzzi stalked his quarry through Venice. He questioned Casanova's old neighbours in the parish of San Samuele and the men who worked at the wine-shops he frequented, he gathered information about his relationship with Senator Bragadin, and he no doubt tailed him on his frequent trips to Murano. Manuzzi even waylaid Casanova himself at an inn, goading him on to boast about his exploits.

Casanova and Marina were unaware that both their situations were about to change, and very much for the worse. For in January 1755 de Bernis was sent to Parma by his government; and from there he was recalled to Paris. Returning to Venice for a brief spell in May to be ordained as a sub-deacon by the patriarch, he finally left Venice for good on the last day of that month. His return to France plunged Marina into despair, bringing on a serious illness, probably depression. She had already lost Caterina, who nowadays slept in her aunt's chamber at the convent. Now she had lost a man who had genuinely loved her, who had enabled her to fulfil her passionate nature, and whose generosity had bought her a degree of freedom. The Murano *casino* which had been her refuge for more than two years was sold along with all its contents, and without the

ambassador to protect her and buy the gondoliers' discretion, escaping from the convent was impossible for her. As in the early days of her confinement at the Angeli, Marina was a prisoner in the house of God. Unable to meet her alone any more, Casanova comforted her as best he could through the iron screen in the visiting parlour. Soon she would lose this bittersweet pleasure too.

Just eight weeks after de Bernis left Venice the Inquisitors moved in on Casanova. By now Manuzzi had compiled at least half a dozen reports on him. They painted a picture of a consummate conman, a sponger and an unbeliever 'who, by his lies and his beautiful words, lives off others'. Money was 'never lacking to him'. He had been the ruin of Senator Bragadin, from whom he had extricated a great deal of money 'and made him believe that he can make the Angel of Light appear'. In addition Casanova had travelled widely posing as 'a man of letters'. He was acquainted with and beloved by many patricians, foreigners and the flower of Venice's youth, whom he bewitched with his clever talk. Casanova was given to mixing with debauched people, Manuzzi claimed, and he led them even deeper into bad ways. He had heard him admit that he cheated at cards and, perhaps worst of all, boast that he was a freethinker who 'believes nothing in the matter of religion'. In a wine-shop called *Al Rinaldo Trionfante* Manuzzi had heard Casanova publicly read out a poem which mocked religion: 'The subject is treated in an astonishing manner for he speaks both directly and indirectly of copulation.'[35] In short, he was a reprehensible character: 'Conversing with and becoming intimate with the said Casanova one sees truly united in him misbelief, imposture, lasciviousness, voluptuousness in a manner to inspire horror.'[36] If Manuzzi had found out about Casanova's relationship with Mother Maria Contarina of the convent of Santa Maria degli Angeli, this information was not included in the report; since the nun was one of the powerful Morosini clan, the resulting scandal would have been too terrible.

On 20 July Manuzzi was ordered by the Inquisitors to get hold of a copy of Casanova's blasphemous, pornographic poem. He broke

into Casanova's rooms but could not find it. Instead, he reported that Casanova 'has many evil books at his place, and at the back of a cupboard, strange objects including a kind of leather apron like those worn by people who call themselves *masons* in what they call loges'.[37] Casanova had indeed been initiated into freemasonry in the French city of Lyon in 1950. On 25 July – ironically the Feast of San Giacomo, his name day – the Inquisitors issued an order to their agent Messer Grande 'to arrest G. Casanova, to take all his papers and conduct him to I Piombi' – the notorious prison under the roof of the Doge's Palace known as The Leads. That evening Messer Grande and his *sbirri* forced their way into Casanova's *casino* looking, so they claimed, for a trunk full of contraband salt. Protective of him as ever, Senator Bragadin advised his adopted son to flee the city immediately, as he had done in 1749, but this time Casanova stubbornly refused to go.

At daybreak the following morning, Messer Grande entered Casanova's chamber in the Palazzo Bragadin, woke him up and arrested him. While his possessions were rifled through and his books seized, he dressed himself in a smart ruffled shirt, a new coat, a floss-silk cloak and a hat trimmed with lace and a jaunty white feather. Guarded by thirty to forty officers, he was escorted to the constables' headquarters, and from there conducted by gondola to the Doge's palace, where he was marched upstairs to the attic cells. Here one of the most restless spirits of the eighteenth century was imprisoned in solitary confinement in a dark, baking hot cell so low that he could not stand upright. The place was bare except for a bucket 'for the needs of nature' and a wooden shelf one foot wide fastened four feet above the floor. Rats the size of rabbits scuffled outside the thick iron grating that separated this tiny hell-hole from the garret that led to it, and an instrument of execution was nailed to the wall.

Casanova was never tried. Neither was he told how long he had been condemned for, nor informed of the reason for his arrest. Nevertheless on 21 August 1755 his offence was recorded in the journal of the Secretary of the Inquisitors: it was 'the grave faults

committed by G. Casanova primarily in public outrages against the holy religion'.[38]

On 12 September it was noted in the Republic's records that Casanova had been condemned to The Leads for a term of five years. This was a light sentence compared to Marina Maria Morosini's. She was still imprisoned within the walls of Santa Maria degli Angeli in 1790, at which time she was listed in the records as the convent's abbess. It is believed that she died there in 1799.

As for Caterina Capretta, she was allowed out of the Murano convent after three years in order to marry a Venetian lawyer named Sebastiano Marsigli. She appears to have born no resentment towards her seducer, for when he returned to Venice from exile in 1774 she renewed her acquaintance with him. Two letters to him bearing the name Caterina Marsigli, written in 1780 and 1781, were found among his papers after his death.

SEVEN

Manon Balletti

*I laugh when I hear certain women call men
whom they accuse of inconstancy 'perfidious'.
They would be right if they could prove that
when we swear to be true to them we have
the intention of failing them. Alas! We love
without consulting our reason, and reason is no
more mixed up in it when we stop loving them.*[1]

MARIA-MADDALENA BALLETTI, known as Manon, was born
into a theatrical dynasty in Paris. Her father was a famous actor, her
uncle an impresario, her aunt Flaminia a playwright, and her
mother was quite simply the most famous actress of her generation
and the idol of all France.

Manon's paternal grandmother, an actress named Giovanna Benozzi, was the same La Fragoletta over whom Casanova's own father,
Gaetano, had run away from his home in Parma back in 1716. Mario,
La Fragoletta's son by actor Francesco Balletti, had followed in his
thespian parents' footsteps, and in 1715 he moved to Paris to join a
new company of Commedia dell' Arte players set up under the
patronage of the Regent, Philip of Orléans (Paris's previous Italian
troupe had been expelled in 1697 for staging *La Fausse Prude*, a play
which made fun of Louis XIV's mistress Madame de Maintenon).
Successful from its very first performance at the Palais-Royal theatre
on 18 May 1716, the new Comédie-Italienne also included Mario's
sister, playwright and actress Elena 'Flaminia' Riccoboni and her

husband, impresario and actor 'Lelio' Riccoboni. From the Palais Royal the players moved to the revamped Hôtel de Bourgogne, where they continued to perform to much acclaim.

Four years later the company was joined by a Toulouse-born actress named Rosa-Giovanna Benozzi, whose own family of itinerant Italian players appears from its surname to have been related to La Fragoletta's. She and Mario fell in love, and were married on 15 June 1720. During the next decade Rosa-Giovanna – now known simply as Silvia after one of the parts she played – became the most outstanding actress in Paris and a revered figure in society. Though no beauty, she appeared to be one by sheer force of personality. In her portrait by Nattier, which depicts her as Thalia, the muse of comedy whose image appeared on the stage curtains of the Comédie-Italienne, Silvia's eyes sparkle with amusement and kindness, and an almost impish smile plays across her lips. Affable, witty, modest, unpretentious and equally charming towards everyone from her fellow thespians to the aristocratic courtiers who fawned on her, Silvia brought all these good qualities to the stage, as well as an innate emotional intelligence. Her acting was so skilful that it always appeared totally natural. Inspired by her talent, Pierre Marivaux wrote plays especially for her.

Apart from being a marvellous actress ('the best in the kingdom' according to Frederick the Great) Silvia was intelligent and deeply pious. A portrait of the Virgin hung in her bedroom, and her personal library of some two hundred books included moral texts, volumes on the English theatre and the works of Molière and Corneille. Unlike most actresses of her day, her morals were impeccable. Famously faithful to Mario, she was also a devoted mother to their three sons – Antonio, Luigi and Guglielmo – and their only daughter, Manon, who was born in April 1740, when Silvia was in her late thirties.

> Toi que les Grâces ont formée,
> Sois sure aimable Silvia,
> Que tu seras toujours aimée
> Tant que le bon goût durera.

(You who the Graces have made
Be certain, kind Silvia,
That you will always be loved
As long as good taste endures.)

read a poem about Silvia published in *Le Mercure de France*. Her
teetotaller husband was equally lauded in the Parisian press for his
good character and talent:

Mario, que chacun renomme
Pour un acteur ingénieux,
Le rôle que tu fais le mieux,
C'est le rôle d'un galant homme.[2]

(Mario, whom everyone admires
As an ingenious actor,
The role you play the best
Is that of a courteous man.)

Success earned the Ballettis the respect of their peers, the adoration of
their audiences and an extremely interesting circle of artistic friends.
Their daughter grew up in a cultured home filled with books and
musical instruments and frequented by all the greatest painters, actors
and writers of the day. The print-hung walls of the dining-room in
their house in the rue du Petit-Lion – a building which the family
shared with the director of Paris's Opéra-Comique, Charles-Simon
Favart, and his wife, writer and light-opera-star Marie Favart – echoed
with the lively talk and laughter of guests at mealtimes. Marivaux was
a frequent visitor, as was Louis XV's painter Carle Vanloo, whose
portrait of Silvia hung in the salon. However, although they entertained constantly and employed a cook, a general servant and a maid,
money was always in short supply in the Balletti household; and when
Mario died in 1762 he left fifty-four unpaid creditors.

Unusually for an actress's daughter, Manon received a first-class
education at the convent of the Ursulines de Saint-Denis, to the

north of Paris. At home she was taught how to play the guitar and the harpsichord by a famous music master and composer, Charles-François Clément, and how to act and sing by her uncle Lelio and aunt Flaminia, and above all by her mother, who from the moment of Manon's birth regarded her as the most important person in her life. The fourth floor of the house was lined with wardrobes stuffed with theatrical costumes, lengths of material, fans and other props which Manon could use to put on plays of her own, and in her mother's bedroom – a delightful refuge boasting wicker armchairs, floral cushions and a four-poster bed – Silvia taught the girl 'everything necessary in the way of talents, graces, good behaviour and savoir-vivre'.[3] Although she herself was embraced by the highest echelons of Parisian society, most actresses still lived on the very edge of respectability, or beyond it, and Silvia did not encourage her precious daughter to follow her on to the stage.

By her early teens Manon had grown far prettier than her famously attractive mother. Innocent, loving and obedient by nature, like all her family she was bilingual in French and Italian, and in addition she could read, write, dance, sing, and accompany herself on the guitar and harpsichord. In short, she was enchanting. When her music teacher Clément asked Mario and Silvia for her hand in marriage, they did not object. Although twenty years Manon's senior, Clément was a family friend and a famous composer of theatrical scores and essays on composition. Marriage to him would provide their daughter with a secure future and keep her close to home. That she was not in love with Clément did not matter an iota: it would have been enough for her parents that she liked him. By now Silvia was already suffering from the consumption that would eventually kill her, and she no doubt wished to see her precious daughter settled before she died.

The marriage was not to be. Giacomo Casanova would disrupt Silvia's plans for Manon, and all but ruin the girl's life.

Manon Balletti caught her first glimpse of Casanova in June 1750 when she was just ten years old. She was driving with her mother

out of Paris towards Fontainebleau to meet her brother Antonio, who was returning home that day from Italy where he had spent the last four four years. After an hour on the road mother and daughter spied a carriage racing towards them. Antonio leapt out of it and flagged them down and, laughing and crying at the same time, Manon and Silvia jumped down from their Berlin and threw themselves at him with little regard for the well-dressed stranger standing beside him in the road. When they had stopped kissing him, Antonio introduced the stranger as his good friend Casanova, a Venetian whom he had met in Milan in 1749. Silvia graciously invited Casanova to dine with them that evening, and Antonio climbed up into the Berlin and returned to Paris with the women, leaving Casanova to complete his journey alone.

From that night on, and for the next two years, Casanova and the Balletti family were inseparable. With his outgoing personality, sparkling conversation and similar background (despite his airs and graces and his income from Senator Bragadin he had been born into a modest theatrical family just like theirs) he fitted in perfectly with their gregarious and artistic way of life. Silvia and Mario looked on Casanova as another son, and Antonio as a brother, while Manon grew to regard him as a glamorous family friend. From Casanova's point of view, he could not have chosen 'company more agreeable and more apt to procure me countless advantages and a quantity of brilliant acquaintances in Paris', and at this point in his life his sole purpose was to improve and enjoy himself. He was in awe of fifty-year-old Silvia – that 'woman of women' as he described her. Age had not made her any less attractive or captivating, and he 'found her above everything that was said of her . . . By unanimous consent Silvia was a woman above her profession.'[4] She was not, however, above being flattered by the attentions of her son's handsome young friend. During the next two years the pair became so close that a police report of 1752 cited Casanova as living 'at the charge of Mlle Silvia, of the Italian Comedy'. Another claimed that 'Mlle Silvia lives with Casanova, an Italian, said to be the son of an actress. It is she who keeps him.'[5] But although he dined and

supped with Silvia almost every day and became acquainted with all her friends, including the playwright Crébillon who volunteered to become his French teacher, it is highly unlikely that anything improper happened between the actress and the Venetian despite the police inspector's innuendo.

Casanova had left Paris in the autumn of 1752. He returned in the first week of 1757 under totally different circumstances – as a penniless exile and fugitive. Since his arrest on 26 July 1755 he had been imprisoned in The Leads under the eaves of the Doge's Palace. The notorious and terrifying prison – 'The Hell of living humanity' as Casanova called it[6] – took its name from the three-foot-square lead sheets covering the palace's roof. They acted as heat conductors, turning the primitive cells underneath them into ice-houses during Venice's cold winters and into sweat-boxes during the sweltering summer months. Casanova either lay on the dusty floor or at times sat stark naked in an armchair, exhausted by the heat and with the sweat pouring off his body and on to the floor. Fleas ate him alive. The silence of his frequent spells in solitary confinement was unbearable to a man who thrived on company. 'I discovered that a man shut up by himself, and in a situation where it is impossible for him to do anything, alone in a place of near darkness, where he does not and cannot see anything other than he who brings him something to eat once a day, and where he cannot stand upright, is the unhappiest of mortals,' he wrote. 'He longs for Hell, if he believes in it, just to have some company. In that place I reached the point of longing for that of an assassin, a lunatic, a man with a foul-smelling disease, a bear. The solitude under The Leads drives men to despair; but to understand it one must have lived through it.'[7] No one ever informed him how long he was condemned to stay there; for all he knew it was for the rest of his life. He was allowed no visitors. Never in his life had he felt so alone. But he was not entirely without friends: Senator Bragadin, his adopted father, went down on his knees before the Inquisitors and begged for his son's release, but to no avail. As soon as he was allowed to – on

New Year's Day 1756 – he sent Casanova gifts of a bearskin bag to put his legs in during the cold weather, a dressing gown lined with fox fur, money and books.

Literature and philosophy consoled Casanova to some extent, but he was desperate for freedom and started planning his escape as early as November 1755. Despite the fact that no prisoner had ever escaped from The Leads before, he was convinced that he could succeed; he had to, the alternative was unbearable. When he was allowed out of his tiny airless cell into the garret next door for exercise, he began to amass objects that might be useful to him, including a long iron bolt and a piece of marble, which he used as a whetstone to fashion the bolt into a pike which he hid in the stuffing of his armchair. His initial plan – to break through the floor and lower himself into the room beneath – collapsed when he was moved to a new, superior cell with windows and a view of the Lido. After he left his old cell, the hole under the bed which he had so painstakingly chiselled away was discovered, and from then on Casanova was placed under constant surveillance by his warder, Lorenzo.

Despite this, using a sharpened fingernail as a pen and mulberry juice as ink, Casanova started a secret correspondence with a Venetian noble-born monk, Marin Balbi, who occupied the next cell and with whom he exchanged messages hidden inside the bindings of books. By this means, he persuaded Balbi not only that he had a failsafe escape plan but also to do most of the preliminary work for him by breaking through the ceiling above the wall of their adjoining cells. Casanova smuggled the priest his pike hidden in the parchment binding of a large folio Bible that he had asked Lorenzo to buy for him, and he even made the unwitting warder carry the book through to Balbi's cell, with a large dish of hot buttery macaroni balanced on top of it.

On the last night of October 1756, Balbi at last broke through the ceiling. Casanova immediately ripped up every bit of material he could find – sheets, napkins, even his mattress cover – and knotted them together into a rope almost two hundred feet long.

Bundling his clothes and lace handkerchiefs into his coat, he squeezed through the hole Balbi had made into the loft above, and hacked a hole through the boards that lined the lead-plated roof. After peeling back one of the three-foot lead squares Casanova put his head out into a bright moonlit night. Anxious of being spotted by Venice's *sbirri*, he waited until the moon set after midnight, then scrambled across the dizzyingly high and precariously sloping roof with his possessions tied around his neck and Balbi in his wake. Missing death by inches when he slipped over the guttering and hung suspended by his arms while the rest of his body dangled in space high above the palace courtyard, Casanova heaved himself back on to the roof, prised off a window-grating on a lower floor, and re-entered the deserted building. Over the next few hours he and the priest, who was complaining bitterly because there was no real escape plan, gradually forced their way through a series of locked doors and worked their way down to the magnificent Stairway of the Giants, just above ground level, only to find that the gates at the top of it were locked and they were trapped inside the building. While Balbi ranted against him, a scratched and bleeding Casanova calmly changed into the faded summer clothes and feather-trimmed hat that he had been wearing on the day of his arrest, bandaged the cuts and scratches he had suffered with his old handkerchiefs, and trusted in destiny to rescue him as it had done so many times in his life. *Fata viam invenient*. Alerted by some idlers in the courtyard, who glimpsed his rather quixotic figure peering out of a window, a lone caretaker came up to see what was going on. The moment he unlocked the gates, Casanova pushed past him and, followed by Balbi, walked swiftly down the ceremonial stairs, through the palace's fifteenth-century royal gateway and out towards the Molo, or wharf, where they jumped into the first gondola they saw.

After one year, three months and five days of torturous and at times terrifying imprisonment Casanova was free. Via Munich, Augsburg and Strasbourg, by boat, on foot and eventually by hitching a lift in a carriage, he made his way to France, and arrived triumphantly in the

French capital on the freezing cold morning of Wednesday 5 January 1757. During his first stay in Paris, between June 1750 and the autumn of 1752, his single-minded goal had been the pursuit of pleasure. Now he was returning under markedly different circumstances, as a penniless thirty-one-year-old with an urgent need to make his fortune. His first stop in the city was the Ballettis' house in the rue du Petit-Lion. Since news of his dramatic escape had already reached the family they had been expecting him to turn up in Paris sooner or later, and he was received with open arms. 'Joy filled the house as soon as my arrival was known,' he wrote. This was as near to a home-coming as the rootless Casanova would ever get. He found the Balletti family much as he had left it four and a half years earlier, with one notable exception: Manon, who had been just twelve years old when he had last seen her, was now a ravishingly pretty sixteen-year-old, engaged to be married to Clément, a man five years Casanova's senior.

As Casanova exploded back into Manon's life, triumphant at having been the first man ever to achieve the impossible and break out of Europe's most notoriously secure prison, he eclipsed everyone around her including her fiancé. For no one could have seemed a more exciting and romantic figure than Casanova at this point in his life. Whatever Manon's feelings for Clément, he did not stand a chance compared to the unshaven, travel-soiled and exceedingly attractive fugitive who proceeded to captivate the entire family – and before long the whole of Paris – with colourful tales of his unwarrantable arrest, his fifteen months of cruel imprisonment and his daring escape. That Casanova visited Versailles on his first day in Paris, just after a disgruntled and disturbed ex-soldier named Robert-François Damiens made an attempt on Louis XV's life, and brought news of the event back to the rue du Petit-Lion that evening, must have made him appear even more of a heroic and dashing figure in Manon's eyes. Before nightfall not only she but all of Paris was in turmoil, for the populace believed that the king had been assassinated when in fact he had only been slightly wounded and soon made a full recovery. Despite this, for the next few weeks

fashionable Parisians dressed only in elegant black as a conspicuous display of grief over the assassination attempt.

As for Manon, she was lost. For the first time in her life she was in love, and the object of her affection happened to be one of the most dangerously seductive men in history. Keeping her feelings to herself at first, she observed Casanova with a mixture of amazement, awe and blind adoration, and tried to persuade herself that she felt nothing but friendship towards him, for what interest could this glamorous friend of the family possibly take in a young girl such as she? 'If you only knew how hard I tried to vanquish the fondness that I felt towards you – when I began to perceive it – now I can say to you for better or for worse I did not succeed,' she later confessed in a rambling letter. 'I enjoyed myself more with you than with anyone else, but I told myself, he's merry, he's intelligent, this isn't surprising, but in the end, I was uneasy when a day passed without you coming to the house; I was sad, dreamy, and I would find that I when I dreamt I thought only of you . . . What should I do, I asked myself; on the point of marrying a man to whom I have been promised. To whom I have promised myself – I go and take a liking for a man I probably will not see for much longer, who does not love me – for at that time I believed in good faith that you did not love me – what will become of me, how imprudent I am, stupid; to love someone who is indifferent towards me, such a thing makes one miserable; but then sometimes I thought that perhaps you might love me but that you dared not show any signs of your love because circumstances did not permit you to.'[8]

Casanova knew women well enough to be able to tell that his friend's sister hero-worshipped him, and he was not shy about flirting with her or paying her compliments, though always in a safely avuncular manner and in her parents' presence. For a few weeks he believed that his intimate relationship with her family was an insurmountable barrier which prevented him from even thinking of pursuing Manon – rather conveniently as it happened, because for once falling in love was not on his immediate agenda. What overwhelmingly concerned Casanova at that moment was his future. In

the past he had wasted almost every opportunity that had come his way, but he could no longer afford to do so. 'I saw that in order to make anything of myself,' he wrote, 'I needed to put in play all my physical and moral faculties, to become acquainted with the great and the powerful, to be the master of my own intelligence, and to play the chameleon to all those whom I saw it was in my interest to please.'[9] Although he was able to live modestly on the small sum that Bragadin continued to send him, modesty was not enough for Casanova. He wanted to be wealthy.

With this in mind, on his second afternoon in Paris he called on François Joachim Pierre de Bernis who, very conveniently for Casanova, had been nominated Minister of State just four days earlier, on 2 January. De Bernis had heard of his friend's arrest and subsequent escape from The Leads through their erstwhile lover-in-common Marina Morosini who, two years after the ambassador had left Venice, continued to correspond with him from the convent of Santa Maria degli Angeli; with no hope left of seeing either of the two men on whom she had once depended, and with no religious faith to sustain her, the nun's life had become a burden to her. Pressing one hundred louis into Casanova's hand, de Bernis signalled that he would be his patron from now on and advised him to try to make his fortune in finance. Two years into seven years of war with Britain and Saxony, the French royal coffers were already depleted, and the First Intendant of the École Militaire Royale, Joseph de Pâris-Duverney, was at that moment trying to find a way to raise twenty million livres to fund his military school. Since his recall from Venice, de Bernis had become a powerful, trusted politician with access to all the top government ministers, and even to the king, and he was still an intimate friend of Madame de Pompadour's. A simple recommendation from him was enough to secure Casanova an immediate audience with Duverney. Although Casanova knew absolutely nothing about making money – all he was good for was spending it – he persuaded Duverney to believe that he had a failsafe secret scheme for raising millions, and this proved enough to secure him a second meeting the following day.

In modern times Casanova is sometimes credited for inventing the idea of the French National Lottery, but in his memoirs he makes no such claim for himself. On the contrary, he recounts how at his second meeting with Duverney, which took place the following day, the idea was literally handed to him. At first, he sat for an hour and a half before a roaring fire with Duverney and seven or eight other finance ministers, unable to join in their conversation for the simple reason that he was totally mystified by their complicated technical language; the only time he opened his mouth was to eat. Later, Duverney took him to another room and introduced him to a middle-aged gentleman named Giovanni Antonio Calzabigi, who was working in Paris as Secretary of the Legation of the Kingdom of the Two Sicilies. Duverney handed Casanova a folio notebook belonging to Calzabigi, and declared that it contained Casanova's own secret money-making plan. Glancing down at the title page, Casanova read the word 'Lottery' followed by a brief outline of how such a scheme would work. Quick to take advantage of the situation, he immediately agreed that this plan was identical to his own. The scheme was Calzabigi's, Duverney said; Casanova had been forestalled. Rather than disillusion him, Casanova played along with the minister's misconception. Though up till now the ministers had been cautious about going ahead with the scheme, the silver-tongued Casanova soon persuaded them to; the king could only profit by financing it, he insisted.

Before long Calzabigi was named administrator of the lottery, and Casanova became its director. Over the next few years he garnered a good share of its profits. The lottery would guarantee him an annual income of 120,000 livres in the future, and gave him immediate access to at least 4,000 francs. As one of its two co-founders, he was granted the right to open six offices selling lottery tickets and paying out prizes. For once Casanova revealed a good head for business. Instead of running all these offices himself, he immediately sold off five of them for 2,000 francs each, and rented luxurious premises in the rue Saint-Denis for the sixth. When the

other ticket-sellers announced that they would pay out the prizes a week after each draw, Casanova printed bills to the effect that any tickets bought from *his* office would be redeemed within twenty-four hours, ensuring that he sold far more tickets than anyone else.

Though the first lottery draw did not take place until April the following year, Casanova was already well on his way to becoming wealthy beyond his dreams. Strutting around Paris in expensive new clothes paid for by de Bernis, or riding up and down the boulevards in his own private carriage, he was besieged by the *haut monde* who, because they accepted him as one of themselves, bought their lottery tickets only from him. Since he looked, talked and behaved like a wealthy aristocrat everyone presumed that he was one, and this allowed him to enjoy unlimited credit with the shopkeepers. 'Paris was, and still remains, a city where people judge everything by appearances,' he remarked. 'There is no other country in the world where it is easier to impress people.'[10] Between the Ballettis, with their wide artistic and literary connections, and de Bernis, with his access to the court and politicians, Casanova soon gained admittance to the best circles in Paris. He knew everyone worth knowing, including Madame de Pompadour, who promised to help him make his way.

Although he resolved to behave well and avoid bad company, Casanova could not resist the temptation to stray. When Count Edoardo Tiretta, a penniless fellow-adventurer, turned up in Paris in February bearing greetings from their mutual Venetian friend Signora Manzoni, Casanova accompanied him to the house of Angelica Lambertini, a wealthy widow famous for her libertine behaviour (she later insisted on telling Casanova all the details of her sexual encounters with Tiretta, whom she christened the 'Count of Six Fucks' after the number of times he had made love to her in one night). At Lambertini's, Casanova exposed himself in front of a well-brought-up, sexually innocent young virgin, to whom he gave the name Mademoiselle de la M-re in his memoirs. On 1 March, he took a party which included her, her aunt, Tiretta and Lambertini to the Place de Grève to watch the horrific public

execution of Louis XV's would-be assassin. During the four hours Damiens was being burned with molten lead, tortured with steel pincers, and torn limb from limb by horses, Tiretta sexually molested Mlle de la M-re's aunt.

Mlle de la M-re was an heiress and 'an angel' whose family had promised her in marriage to a man she had never met. In order to seduce her, Casanova promised to marry her himself – a cynical exercise in getting his own way. Although he swore he would not deflower her, he did so anyway. 'What does one not promise in such moments?' he later wrote of this betrayal. 'But then who is the woman, if she loves well, who charges her lover to keep his promise when love seizes hold of the place which was occupied by reason?'[11] By the following evening he had ceased to desire Mlle de la M-re, just as she had predicted he would. Instead, he turned his attention to Manon Balletti: 'I was in love with this young woman, but Silvia's daughter, with whom I had enjoyed no pleasure other than dining with the family, weakened this love which no longer left me anything to desire.'[12] When Mlle de la M-re's fiancé turned up, Casanova abandoned her to him and at the same time blamed her for forsaking him. The 'angel' had suddenly turned into an inconstant monster, and he wanted revenge.

Instead, he decided to salve his hurt pride by enticing his friends' young daughter-away from her fiancé Clément. By early April he had begun 'to spin the perfect love to Manon Balletti, who every day gave me some new sign of the progress that I was making in her heart'. What was he thinking of in trifling with her heart? He knew from the start that courting her was a terrible mistake: 'The friendship and esteem which I felt for her family kept me from harbouring any idea of seducing her; but falling more in love with her every day, and not thinking of asking for her hand in marriage, I could not conceive what the outcome would be.'[13] Manon was a young beauty, as we can see from the portrait of her painted by Nattier that same year, but she was engaged to be married to another man, and even if Casanova had been in a position to marry her himself he had no intention of doing so. His attitude to the

institution had not changed since he had wriggled out of his engagement to Teresa Lanti. The very idea of marriage 'made me shudder', he admitted. 'I knew myself too well not to foresee that I would become unhappy in a settled relationship, and consequently make my other half unhappy too.'[14] Nevertheless, unable to resist the flattery of being desired by her, he pursued Manon in a series of late-night visits to the house, and in secret love letters that he passed to her via her maid, Madame Obert.

Like a sapling tree in a hurricane, Manon did not stand a chance of withstanding Casanova's artful courtship which, being so inexperienced, she immediately took for a profession of undying love. 'You begin by exaggerating your love greatly to me,' she replied to one of his letters shortly after she had celebrated her seventeenth birthday at the beginning of April. 'I believe that it is sincere, it flatters me and I desire nothing else than to see it last for ever.' However, already exhibiting the lack of self-confidence that would characterise their relationship, she finished off her sentence with a plaintive 'will it last?'[15] If this did not make Casanova feel trapped, then Manon's 'always love me well' at the bottom of the letter must have done so. Her postscript – 'If you want to make me really happy, you will burn our letters'[16] – provided him with his first opportunity to betray her: despite repeated requests from her to destroy the letters she wrote to him during their relationship, Casanova kept them, refused to return them to her when their relationship ended, and even showed them to another woman.

Far from making her happy, Manon's first experience of falling in love was like a painful, unpredictable illness over which she had no control. One moment she felt feverishly elated, the next she was distraught. She fretted that her family would discover what was going on and that Casanova would be 'so sure of my tender feelings that you will neglect to take care of my heart'.[17] She was right: in the middle of May he suggested that her feelings for him would fizzle out within a month. 'Is it possible that you think so little of me to believe such a thing of me?' she replied, confounding his

Venice: The Doge's Palace and the Molo from the basin of San Marco (Francesco Guardi)
Gondolas in front of the palace from which Casanova made his
famous escape on the night of October 31st 1756.

The Parlour of the Nuns of San Zaccaria (Francesco Guardi)
The noble nuns of Venice receive visitors at the parlour grating.

Teresa Lanti (Anonymous)
Possibly a portrait of the false castrato, Bellino.

Manon Balletti (Jean-Marc Nattier)
Seventeen-year-old Manon painted in
1757, at the time of her love affair with
Casanova.

Thalia, Muse of Comedy (Jean-Marc Nattier)
Painted in 1739, this is thought to be a
portrait of Silvia Balletti, Manon's mother
and the most famous actress in
eighteenth-century Paris.

The Marquise d'Urfé
An engraved portrait of the wealthy and
eccentric widow, discovered among Casanova's
possessions at Dux.

Adélaïde de Gueidan and her sister Polyxène at the harpsichord
(eighteenth-century French school)
Adélaïde, standing on the left, could well be 'Henriette', the
greatest love of Casanova's life. Her viola da gamba is on the right.

Teresa Cornelys
Teresa Imer Cornelys, whom Casanova first met in Senator
Malipiero's palazzo in Venice, in her incarnation as the
impresario of Carlisle House, Soho Square, London.

Soho Square, 1731
Carlisle House, the home of Teresa Imer Cornelys and Sophia, her daughter by Casanova,
is on the lower right-hand side, just below the street opening.

Mrs Sophia Williams (Anonymous)
A portrait of Casanova's daughter in later life, commissioned
by her patroness Princess Augusta.

Casanova
The down-at-heel seducer pictured in Prague at the age of sixty-five.

Dux Castle (Anonymous)
The Bohemian palace where Casanova spent his final,
and most unhappy, years.

probable escape plan. 'No, be convinced that I will never change
. . . I believe that I could never stop loving you.'[18]

Perhaps to prove how committed she was to Casanova, Manon
now broke off her engagement to Clément. Since she did not dare
to tell her parents her real reason for ending it – that she was in love
with their friend and believed he would marry her as soon as he was
in a position to do so – Mario and Silvia immediately enlisted their
close acquaintance and patroness the Marquise de Monconseil, the
wife of Louis XV's Lieutenant General, to secure her an alternative
match. The marquise roped in a bachelor named M. Jonel to help
her, but Manon believed she had little to fear in the short term.
Casanova was clearly terrified of the implications of her break with
Clément. Instead of reassuring her of his love he became highly
critical, exacerbating her feelings of insecurity. Rather than blame
him for being nasty to her, Manon blamed herself: 'It is true I
believe your love has lessened, I don't think that's a crime of yours,
no, I have a thousand faults, I know, and the more one knows me
the more one discovers them.'[19] Her self-abasement made Casanova angry, and they were soon openly quarrelling. 'To fall out
with each other all the time makes me despair,' she wrote to him at
the beginning of June, 'it makes me desolate, and I don't want to do
it any more. No, no, no!' She suggested, naïvely, that each of them
should draw up a list of behaviour that they found annoying in the
other so that they could avoid aggravating each other in the future.
Anyone who broke the treaty could be reprimanded, but only in
writing: 'By this arrangement we will always be happy together . . .
My dear friend, would you like things to be this way?'[20]

After two months of courtship – which consisted mostly of secret
kisses snatched in stolen moments, but no actual sex – there was
clearly only one thing that Casanova wanted from his relationship
with Manon, and that was for it to end. But it seemed impossible
for him to get out of the affair without risking a permanent break
with Antonio, Mario and Silvia, friends whom he not only loved
and respected but also found extremely useful. It was now his turn
to become morose and depressed, moods which Manon was quick

to notice. 'Your sadness tonight made me very dejected,' she wrote to him one midnight in early June, after he had picked a fight with Antonio. 'I imagine the cause of it and that makes things worse. We are not happy, my dear friend, I'm beginning to perceive it.' Since her brother was growing suspicious about their relationship, she begged her secret suitor to be more circumspect in his behaviour: 'Don't say anything to him which could shock him for he is a stronsegosse![21] You have an unbounded vivacity and a quarrel between you two is the most distressing thing that could happen to me. B is sometimes pernickety, I admit, but you are also a bit too scathing on a subject that he himself would find really ridiculous if he bothered to think about it . . . I quake lest any of these miseries reach Mama's ear.'[22]

A pattern of psychological abuse was being established which would grow worse in time. Casanova became increasingly fractious and inconsistent towards Manon, and she reacted by abasing herself more and more. 'Your letter which I am reading again makes me see all my faults and eclipses those that I imagine you have yourself,' she wrote to him in July. 'I alone am to blame my dear friend, will you forgive me? I love only you, and I want always to love you, if I am in a bad mood towards you it's because I stupidly suppose that you no longer feel towards me the same tender feelings which makes my happiness, and which is the only thing I desire.'[23] Nothing Manon did improved their relationship, in-cluding indulging in sexual petting with Casanova, though not full sex; that was the only thing she withheld from him. By the end of July, after four months of courtship, Casanova was constantly wrong-footing her, and she still felt tongue-tied in his presence. The idea of being in love with him was proving far more enjoyable than the reality. 'It seems to me,' she confessed, 'that I am more at my ease when I write to you than when I talk to you.'[24]

Rather than face the consequences of breaking off the liaison, Casanova fed Manon just enough affection to keep her hopes alive. But when de Bernis was created Minister of State for Foreign Affairs at the end of June, and asked him to go to Dunkirk on

secret government business (it was to compile a report on French warships), Casanova jumped at the chance, as much to put space between himself and Manon, one suspects, as for the 12,000 francs he would eventually earn from the mission. Manon's letters pursued him from the very moment he left Paris on 28 August – 'It already seems as if I haven't seen you for a month,' she wrote to him that very day[25] – and only his return could make her happy. When she had not heard from him after four days she was in torment. What had become of him? Why had he not written to her? And when was he coming back? she asked. It was impossible that he thought of her as often as she did of him. So little importance did she give her own achievements that, when she sang and played the guitar to great acclaim at a party given by the Marquise de Monconseil on 5 September – the guest of honour was the exiled King of Poland, Stanislas Leszczyński – she did not even mention it in her next letter.

Clingy, obsessive, and chronically insecure, Manon was in many ways typical of a young girl experiencing the pangs of first love. However, her behaviour was guaranteed to bore and alienate Casanova, who continued to play her along when he returned from Dunkirk in the latter months of the year. During his absence Silvia's consumption had taken its toll on her – 'I only wish that her health were as perfect as her heart,' Manon had written to him in September.[26] If the actress found out that her trusted friend had been carrying on with her precious young daughter, the news might well destroy her, and Casanova saw no alternative but to continue to renew his promise to marry Manon at some unspecified future date whilst pursuing his ambitions – and his sexual interests – elsewhere.

There was no shortage of beautiful women treading the *grands trottoirs* of Paris. They ranged from common whores with whom one could rent rooms above the shops at the Palais-Royal by the hour, or even by the minute, to young girls fresh in from the countryside whom Casanova met through his female pimp Brunet, and haughty courtesans who disdained to have liaisons with anyone

less than a wealthy financier or aristocrat. The latter group included actress Giacoma Antonia Veronese, known as Camilla, who lived with the Count of Egreville and worked with the Ballettis at the Comédie-Italienne. Camilla had a number of lovers that year including Casanova and the Comte de la Tour d'Auvergne, who introduced the Venetian to his aunt, the Marquise d'Urfé.

It was with good reason that Manon complained that she was feeling marginalised and neglected. Casanova was preoccupied not only with enjoying himself in the arms of other women but also with securing his future through both legitimate and dubious means. He was too busy to see her. He no longer told her that he loved her. In fact, he gave her every proof that he disliked her. And yet he persisted in stringing her along by telling her, from time to time, that he adored her and would marry her one day. 'Do not keep my heart in perpetual chains,'[27] Manon begged him in February 1758. 'Didn't you promise me yesterday that you would see me today?' she reproached him a few weeks later. 'Not at all, you go and enjoy yourself elsewhere, you just about remember in the evening that you promised someone (who you say you love) to come and see her and you arrive with an indifferent air.'[28]

Insecurity made Manon sulky, moody and jealous. By the beginning of April their mutual reproaches had grown increasingly bitter, and Casanova was turning nastier by the day. He openly insulted her, and afterwards showed neither repentance nor any desire to make peace. 'You have pierced my heart,' she admitted after one terrible quarrel. 'Have you forgotten my dear Casanova that you used to love me (for I dare not flatter myself any longer that you still do).'[29] Her eyes, blinded by love for so long, were now wide open. Even she could see that the abusive relationship was drawing to a close. But when she pleaded time and again for him to return her letters, Casanova consistently refused to do so. 'Oh God, how angry I am towards you, even more towards myself!' she wrote to him in May. 'You are the most ungrateful of men. Adieu Mr.'[30]

The spiralling deterioration of their relationship over the spring and summer of 1758 coincided with a sharp decline in Silvia's health,

and in June, if not before, Manon told her mother of her feelings for their family friend. Her 'nona', as she referred to her in a letter to Casanova, responded 'with all the sweetness and kindness imaginable, how I love her, and how she deserves to be loved.'[31] Her daughter's happiness was paramount in Silvia's mind. Wishing to see her settled, she was on the point of speaking to the Marquise de Monconseil about allowing Manon to marry Casanova when her daughter's relationship suddenly appeared to be over. 'Tell me or write to me what you intend to say to Mama to justify your change of heart, which cannot fail to seem strange to her,' a despairing Manon pleaded with Casanova. 'Farewell, soon you will no longer remember if you ever loved me; as for me, I will remember it for ever!'[32]

Their differences were set aside at the end of August, for Silvia was fading fast. On 1 September the actress summoned her notary and dictated her will. Terrified of being buried alive ('People will think this puerile, but it is a human weakness that they will pardon me for'), she begged not to be interred until a full two days after her death. Although her possessions were to be divided up between all her children, she left a special financial legacy to Manon, saying that she was doing so because she had spent more on her sons' education than on her daughter's. In reality Silvia was acutely anxious about Manon's future – for who would look out for the girl's interests when she was no longer around to do so?

On Saturday 16 September Silvia died in her bed in the rue du Petit-Lion, cradled between Manon's and Casanova's arms. Manon's future preoccupied her until the very end. 'Ten minutes before she died, she commended her daughter to my care,' Casanova recorded. 'I promised her truly from my soul that I would make her my wife; but Fate, as one always says, was against it.'[33] Two days later the idol of France was buried at her local church, Saint-Sauveur. No one was more devastated than her daughter. Casanova remained with the family for the next three days, but after that his business interests took him away. No date had been set for his marriage to Manon, and it is doubtful if anyone but the two of them even knew about their relationship.

A nightmarish month of legal formalities followed. The house was sealed up so that an inventory could be taken of the contents, and Manon was forced to deal with a steady stream of officials. By the time the seals were removed on 18 October, she was at her wits' end. To make matters worse, Casanova was sent to Holland on financial business by the French government, and did not return until the New Year. While he was away (and busy wooing a fourteen-year-old Dutch heiress named Esther) the grief-stricken Manon wrote him nineteen letters, numbering each one carefully at the top. 'If you knew how much I've been crying, my dear friend,' she wrote in letter number one. 'I have not stopped since you left; I'm really frightened that on your return you'll find me so ugly that you will no longer love me.'

Now that her mother was not around Manon was being pressed by her brothers and the Marquise de Monconseil to return to the Saint-Denis convent where she had been educated, or to take temporary refuge in the convent of Bellechasse until her future could be decided. She had little say in the matter, and was close to breaking down: 'The convent frightens me,' she confided in Casanova, 'your fickleness makes me tremble, I'm frightened that during your trip you will find objects more loveable than I am, who will make you forget how dear I am to you, and how much you are so to me. All this makes me despair, and I will not live until I receive assurances of the liveliest tenderness from you.'[34] Her only hope lay in believing Casanova's promise that, if he made sufficient money during his trip, he would fulfil Silvia's dying wish and marry her on his return. This alone could make Manon 'the most joyful, the merriest, the happiest of all creatures . . . You see my dear friend only these castles in Spain distract me from my misery, and whenever I think that they are only castles in Spain, blackness overwhelms me and everything distresses me.'[35]

Plans to put Manon in a convent alternated with the Marquise de Monconseil's desire to marry her off to a wealthy Provençal whom the girl had not yet met. 'Now appreciate this, my dear,' Manon reported to Casanova, 'they would send your poor little one in a

bundle, through the customs, with my harpsichord and my guitar (for that is part of the bargain) I would arrive or rather I would be unpacked; and this man would be told, here is the wife you have been sent.' Her humorous tone belied the fear she certainly felt at being out of control of her own destiny. The only thing she wanted, she told Casanova, was to be 'your little wife, yes, your little wife'.[36] Luckily the idea of the convent had been abandoned by November, but pressure was still being put on her to accept the proposed match. Summoned before M. Jonel, who was acting as intermediary, Manon nervously refused the man. Jonel washed his hands of her: she had already jilted one suitor, Clément, and her seemingly inexplicable refusal to accept a second brought the opprobrium of society down on her. It was suggested that she follow in her mother's footsteps and go on the stage – not at the Comédie-Italienne, where Mario and Antonio worked, but at the French theatre. The situation was becoming so complicated and agonising that Manon even contemplated confiding in the Marquise de Monconseil. Desperate to be permanently united with the man on whom all her hopes depended and whom she already regarded as her partner, she ended her eighteenth letter to him with a plea: 'always remember that you have a very loving little wife who expects the greatest fidelity from her husband.'[37] One can almost hear Casanova grind his teeth as he read this.

His return to Paris during the first week of January 1759 did not end Manon's unhappiness, but exacerbated it. Though he had made an absolute fortune by his share- and currency-dealing, and had bought Manon a pair of expensive diamond earrings from Holland, Casanova did not keep his promise to marry her, he did not act wisely to secure their future and he did not even visit her often. Since he was the richest he had ever been – probably the equivalent of a modern-day multi-millionaire – the one-time fugitive intended to enjoy himself and to shine in Parisian society. 'In less than a week I acquired a good coachman, two good carriages, five horses, a groom, and two good lackeys in half-livery,'[38] he boasted of his spending spree. Within days of his

return to Paris he was spotted 'making a magnificent appearance' at the Comédie-Italienne by an acquaintance from Italy, Giustiniana Wynne, the beautiful twenty-year-old daughter of a Venetian mother, Anna Gazini, and British baronet Sir Richard Wynne. 'He came to greet us and now is with us every day, although his company does not please me and he thinks this does not matter to us,' Giustiniana wrote of Casanova to her secret lover, his Venetian friend Andrea Memmo, on 8 January. 'He has a carriage, lackeys, and is attired resplendently He has two beautiful diamond rings, two different snuffboxes of excellent taste, set in gold, and he is bedecked with lace. He has gained admittance, I do not know how, to the best Parisian society. He says he is interested in a lottery in Paris and brags that this gives him a large revenue, although I am told that he is supported by a very rich old lady. He is quite full of himself and is foolishly proud; in brief, he is insupportable except when he speaks of his escape which he recounts admirably.' Unbearably full of himself Casanova might be, but this did not make him any less attractive to women, and Giustiniana finished off her account of him with a tantalising 'I talk with him about you very often . . .'[39]

While keeping on his rooms in the rue du Petit-Lion, Casanova also rented grand apartments in the rue Comtesse d'Artois, and a large, elegantly furnished country house, Cracovie en Bel Air, at La Petite Pologne, a hamlet just outside the city limits. With its terraced gardens, baths, cellars, kitchen, and suite of master's apartments, the hillside property also had stabling for up to twenty horses, and the rent of one hundred louis a year included a cook/ housekeeper – Madame Saint-Jean, or 'The Pearl' as Casanova referred to her. Taking advantage of The Pearl's culinary talent and La Petite Pologne's situation (because it was outside Paris's customs barrier, one could buy the best quality food and wine free of duty), he used the house to entertain his new friends with an international cuisine for which he soon became famous, and which included *pilau ris in cagnoni, macaroni al sughillo* and specially-raised chickens with the whitest flesh.

Needing something to do with all his spare money – aside from what he had made in Holland, he was now getting a huge income from the lottery and, as Giustiniana Wynne had heard, was also being supported by an elderly widow, the Marquise d'Urfé – Casanova opened a factory which produced hand-painted, Chinese-style silk panels similar to those currently being imported from Peking, but at a fraction of the cost of the imports. Housed in the Temple district, his factory employed some twenty young women aged between eighteen and twenty-five. When he took Manon to visit it she 'quaked when she saw me the owner of this seraglio'[40] – and she had good reason to do so. The beautiful all-female workforce were modest and 'of good reputation' until, one by one, their employer seduced them. Since he could never be bothered to bargain for women's favours and had plenty of money at the time, Casanova acceded to all their demands and set up each of them in turn in a separate furnished house. When, one by one, he lost interest in his workers, he generously continued to support them.

There was no end to Casanova's womanising at this time, and on occasions he derived vicarious pleasure from carrying it out right under Manon's nose, for example when he invited both her and Giustiniana Wynne – or Mlle XCV as he discreetly called her in his memoirs – to the same dinner party.

Soon afterwards, Casanova began a passionate affair with seventeen-year-old Madame Baret, a shopkeeper's wife, whom he believed he loved more than he had ever loved any woman – a frequently repeated phrase in his memoirs. While Madame Baret's lanky, unappreciative husband fussed over his stock of pantaloons and waistcoats, Casanova took the beautiful young bride to bed, or out on shopping trips to the Palais Marchand. When Madame Baret was taken ill, he offered her a week's stay at his country house in La Petite Pologne so that she could recuperate. While her grateful husband was taking care of their shop, Casanova spent eight days of ecstasy exploring Madame Baret's perfectly proportioned body and attempting to straighten her curled, golden pubic hair. She re-

ceived his attentions 'with the greatest calmness, and did not give herself up to the empire of Venus until she felt she felt every element of her charming self in tumult'.[41]

Was it any wonder that Manon complained Casanova had no time for her? Unfortunately her litany of justified reproaches was guaranteed to make him want to be with her even less. 'She could not conceive how I could defer marrying her, if I truly loved her,' he wrote disingenuously. 'She kept saying that I was deceiving her.'[42] Manon was too young to have any perspective on the unpleasant situation: although her fiancé made her increasingly miserable she was still fixated by the idea that her only chance of a happy future lay with him.

Carried away by his seemingly unstoppable success both with women and in business, Casanova continued to spend and woman-ise with reckless abandon throughout the first half of 1759. His outgoings would have financially crippled the richest aristocrat, not least the cost of maintaining each one of his twenty-strong factory workforce in their own establishment. By now the wallpaper business itself was in dire trouble: the continuing war with England over their American possessions had been ruinous for the French luxury goods business, leaving Casanova with a huge stockpile of unsold chinoiserie panels. He was spending what he did not have, and the tradesmen, who until now had allowed him almost un-limited credit, were at last becoming nervous and demanding to be paid. When, on 23 August, he was suddenly arrested for debt and imprisoned in the city's Fors L'Evêque jail, Manon loyally sent him the valuable diamond earrings he had given her on his return from Holland. Their worth was not enough to secure his freedom, and in the end it was the wealthy Marquise d'Urfé who bailed Casanova out two days later to the tune of 50,000 francs, and carried him off from prison in her gold carriage.

Slightly subdued by this salutary experience, Casanova returned Manon's earrings to her and promised her that he would give up his silk-painting business and its female workforce – a financial neces-sity, as it happened. But selling the factory was not as simple as he

had anticipated: three days after he sold off his shares in it to a man named Jean Garnier, one of the employees ran off with the liquid assets, and Casanova was faced with a legal suit for the return of Garnier's money. At about the same time, he was presented with a court action over a dubious bill of exchange in which he had been involved. Whether or not he was guilty of this particular crime, he knew that his period of grace was passing and that the time had come for him to leave France for a while. Promising a tearful Manon yet again that he would do his best to earn a great deal of money and then invest it wisely for their future when he returned, Casanova left Paris for a second trip to Holland at the end of September on another financial mission for the French government; despite the legal proceedings against him, France's ministers continued to trust him to negotiate loans on their behalf. Although he led Manon to believe that he would be back before December, Casanova's actions spoke otherwise: before leaving the city he resigned from his position as director of the lottery, gave up his apartments and sold off his carriage and his horses. He arrived in Holland with at least 100,000 francs in his strong box and an equal amount in jewellery.

Convinced that she would see him again in a matter of weeks, Manon was nevertheless distraught at his departure. Her whole world seemed to be collapsing around her. On 13 September her brother Antonio had been seriously injured by a stray bullet during a performance of Veronese's *Camille Magicienne* at the Comédie-Italienne. A fortnight later he was only just well enough to be lifted from his bed so that the sheets could be changed, and although he was starting to take a little soup he would never make a complete recovery. Manon visited him regularly, but at night she took refuge at La Petite Pologne, where Madame Saint-Jean looked after her, preparing nutritious meals to help her regain all the weight she had recently lost. Despite the rumours that were now circulating in Paris about Casanova's financial dealings, Manon's belief in him remained unshaken. Her 'dear Giacometto' could rest assured that 'bad talk, postponements, lies, nothing can change my heart, which is all yours, and which has no wish for a change of master.'[43]

The rest of Paris was less forgiving. Once it was known that Manon was staying at La Petite Pologne, a rumour spread that she was living there with Casanova, who was not in Holland, but rather in hiding. To a young woman who had kept her reputation and perhaps her virginity intact for two and a half years – rather miraculously, given the nature of her secret fiancé's sex-drive – this was an outrageous slur on both their characters. Manon was 'in a rage, an indignation, a misery which cannot be described,' she wrote to Casanova 'from petite pologne on 23 8bre 1759 for the last time', as she scribbled incandescently at the top. For honour demanded that she immediately leave the country house where she had all too briefly found contentment: 'I'm dying of misery,' she confessed, 'I have it on all sides, I can't hold out any longer I have to give into it; my heart aches. They wish to rob me of my honour. Finally everything contributes to make me pitiable, if I did not love you as much as I do I'd go and stick myself in a convent and never come out again. How evil the world is. How unhappy I am.'[44] Manon was friendless and inconsolable. If Casanova were to abandon her now it would be the worst thing that could happen to her. She reassured herself that he was incapable of such a betrayal, but his evasive reply to her laments slightly dented her confidence in him. Instead of being sympathetic, her 'husband' sounded bored by her complaints, and demanded to know the latest political news from Versailles.

November came and went, but Casanova did not return from Holland, where he was preoccupied with renewing his courtship of the teenage heiress, Esther. Back in Paris, Manon could not sleep. Her reputation was in tatters, but even after so many years of let-downs and disappointment she still hung on her supposed fiancé's every word. His letters had the power to turn her mood from depression to elation to guilt in an instant. When jealousy caused her to write a cold letter to him and he wrote back accusing her of doubting his love, she was overwhelmed by contrition. 'I am ready to make all the reparations you wish,' she wrote to him in the middle of December. 'Melancholy was the author of my

letter, and not me at all.'[45] Casanova was clearly manipulating her from a distance, but Manon did not seem to realise it. She lived only for the moment when 'my dear Casa, my dear jiacomo (sic), lover, husband, friend, whatever pleases you'[46] returned to Paris and made an honest woman of her, as he had been promising to do for years.

The end of 1759 saw no let-up to Manon's suffering. A rumour reached Casanova that she had married an adviser at court – or so he wrote to her, perhaps in an attempt to end their relationship, for by now he was deeply in love with Esther, whose future fortune would be considerable and whose intelligence and charm were, he declared 'designed to make me forget a thousand Manons'.[47] Quick to disabuse him, Manon replied on 20 December that she loved only him. Three months had been too long without him, and she begged him to return in January. Life in the rue du Petit-Lion was unbearably miserable. Antonio was still seriously ill, and she was being shunned by good society. At Christmas very few visitors came to see her, and the only present she received was an almanac. During the final days of the month Manon felt more isolated than ever. 'You speak to me of your solitude, my dear friend,' she wrote to Casanova on 3 January 1760, 'but mine has got to the point that I scarcely paid any visits on New Year's Day.' Sadness emanated from every line of her letter, yet by now Manon knew better than to complain: 'As for me, my very dear husband, I'm keeping well enough since the New Year, I only lack one thing which is really essential to me, and that's my very dear friend whom I love one hundred times more tenderly than I know how to say . . . Farewell, my dear friend, I kiss you with all my soul and love you with all my heart.'[48]

Manon's one remaining pleasure lay in receiving Casanova's letters, letters which, despite his passionate feelings for Esther, were as loving that January as they had ever been. Enchanted by them, Manon reassured him on 20 January that her heart was uniquely his: 'Farewell my most lovable husband,' she wrote, 'always be like your last letter and you will be madly loved by

nena, nenotola Ballettina. Farewell, my being, my heart, my heart, my heart.'[49] All her hope rested on Casanova's expected return at the end of that month, and in order to distract herself in the meantime she decided to stage a series of plays at home with a cast of amateur actors cobbled together out of her few remaining friends, who included the son and daughter of Louis Lambert, the chief of the Bureau de Poste; although Manon had not been allowed to go on the stage professionally, the theatre still ran in her blood.

Casanova did not return at the end of January as he had promised. Instead, at the beginning of February, Manon received a melancholy letter from him informing her that, as his business dealings in Holland had been unsuccessful, he was leaving for Germany and would not be back in Paris for at least another two months. She attempted to sound stoical when she replied on 7 February, filling her letter with comical tales about her rehearsals, but she was unable to hide her deep disappointment, and began her letter with a resigned 'So my dear husband it is at last decided that I am going to spend a very long time without seeing you.' By now Casanova had been away for more than three months, and she was 'beginning to grow furiously weary' with his long absence. She had no idea how long it would be until they were together.

In fact, Manon would never see Casanova again. But all the broken promises in the world could not make her stop adoring her beloved Giacometti. 'You remember very well that I love you, don't you?' she wrote at the end of her letter. 'Well never forget it my dear friend. Farewell. I kiss you with all my heart and think of you all the time, even when I am studying my roles. 3 kisses for jiacomo.'[50]

On 29 July 1760, five months and three weeks after writing this loving letter to Casanova, Manon Balletti married François-Jacques Blondel, one of the most influential architects of his day. Like his uncle François Blondel, who had become director of Paris's

Academy of Architecture in 1672, François-Jacques was passionate about providing would-be architects with a broad and thorough education. In 1737 he had published an important folio on pleasure palaces and interior design, *De la Distribution des Maisons de Plaisance et de la Décoration des Edifices en General*; in 1740 he had opened his own private school of architecture, L'Ecole des Arts, which was to influence a whole generation of French architects; and between 1752 and 1757 he had published a seminal two-volume work on building design and interior decoration, *L'Architecture française*, one of the first written documents on French architectural theory. Appointed architect to Louis XV in 1755, five years later Blondel was at the very top of his profession, with commissions in Metz and Strasbourg as well as Paris. He had money, status, and a house in the city's rue de la Harpe where he gave well-attended lectures on architecture. But despite his professional success, Blondel was by no means an ideal husband for Manon. At fifty-five years old to her twenty, he was a widower old enough to be her father. He had grown-up sons from his first marriage, one of whom, Georges-François, was an architect and a professor himself, and may already have been married with children of his own.

Casanova's version of events casts little light on the mystery of why Manon married François-Jacques Blondel. The heading to Chapter I, Volume Six of his memoirs, in which he reports the marriage, contains the bald statement *Manon Balletti is unfaithful to me* – this from the man who had been consistently deceiving her with other women for three years. He goes on to describe how, on Christmas Day 1759, he received a large packet from Manon, along with the following letter from her: 'Be reasonable, and receive the news that I give you calmly. This packet contains all your letters and your portrait. Send me back my portrait, and if you still have my letters, burn them. I count on your honour. Do not think of me any more. For my part, I will do everything in my power to make myself forget you. Tomorrow, at this time, I will be the wife of M. Blondel, Architect to the King, and a Member of his Academy. You

will greatly oblige me if, when you return to Paris, you will pretend not to know me wherever you may meet me.'[51]

The news that he had been jilted by Manon was, Casanova wrote, a 'great grief' which crushed his soul and sent him into a two-hour trance followed by a jealous fury in which he contemplated going to Paris to murder Blondel 'who had dared to marry a girl who belonged to me, and who everyone believed to be my wife'.[52] Yet, after only a few hours with Esther, to whom he now showed Manon's love letters (there were then more than 200 of them altogether, of which forty-one now survive) he was already certain that he could begin to forget his fiancée, whom he had already begun to despise and think 'unworthy of all that I had wanted to do for her'.[53] Once again, Casanova could not bear the humiliation of being rejected by a woman. As he later admitted, his pride was hurt more than his heart.

That Casanova received news of Manon's imminent marriage on Christmas Day 1759 in Amsterdam is either poetic licence on his part or a genuine mistake made when he wrote his memoirs more than three decades later. Manon's letters of January and February 1760, which were in his possession, prove that she was not only still in contact with him at that particular time but was also still madly in love with him.

Between 7 February, when she wrote her last love letter to Casanova, and the end of July, when she married Blondel, something had caused Manon to give up the dream she had been nursing since her seventeenth birthday to unite herself for ever with the love of her life. Perhaps she had finally realised that he did not love her, and never had. But now there was a pressing need for her to marry somebody. By 1760 the Comédie-Italienne, with which her family was so closely associated, was in debt to the tune of some 400,000 livres. They had lost Silvia, their main attraction, in 1758, Antonio had never recovered from the accident which had crippled him a year later, and Mario was in personal financial trouble with a number of his creditors. On 26 March 1760, a bailiff entered the Ballettis' house to seize the actor's possessions.

Claiming that everything belonged to his daughter, Mario managed to get rid of him, but the threat of losing their home continued to hang over the family.[54]

Manon's future had never been more precarious. The Marquise de Monconseil, among others, had been urging her to make a sensible marriage ever since she had broken off with Clément in the spring of 1757. Three years on, though still relatively young and beautiful, she was a far less marriageable proposition than she had been when the marquise and M. Jonel had attempted to marry her off soon after Silvia's death. Thanks to Casanova, she had already jilted one suitor and turned her nose up at various others. Added to this, rumours of her long, inconclusive relationship with the adventurer – including the brief period when she was supposed to have been living with him at La Petite Pologne – had not enhanced her marital prospects. Taking all this into consideration, the king's architect was quite a catch for Manon, despite the large disparity in their ages. From Blondel's point of view, he was getting the great Silvia's daughter as his wife, a young beauty who came with a substantial dowry of 24,000 livres.

If she had not already met Blondel through her parents and their large circle of artistic friends, it is likely that Manon was introduced to him at the beginning of 1760 by his friend, Louis Lambert, whose son and daughter were part of her troupe of amateur actors. Lambert was a signatory on her marriage contract on behalf of the groom, and may even have brokered the match. The marriage contract was drawn up on 20 July, and the couple were married nine days later, at which point Manon moved from her father's house to Blondel's home in the rue de la Harpe.

It was a good thing that Manon had not waited for Casanova to return to Paris. By the end of February 1760 he was in Cologne. By the end of March he was in Stuttgart, from where he fled at the beginning of April to Zurich, and then on to Baden, Lucerne, Fribourg and Berne. By the time of Manon's marriage that July, Casanova was in Geneva, discussing the merits of the sixteenth-century poet Ariosto with the great Voltaire. Since leaving Esther

in Holland he had become entangled with a wide variety of women including Madame Dubois, a respectable French widow who had fallen on hard times and taken a job as his housekeeper. Besides falling deeply in love with Dubois, Casanova slept with countless prostitutes, cavorted with lesbians in the bathhouses of Berne, and was tricked into having sex with a woman he despised and from whom he caught a bad dose of the pox. Put off sex by this experience, he even flirted briefly with the idea of becoming a monk.

Casanova next visited Paris in the summer of 1761. During his brief stay in the city he was invited to dine at Madame Vanloo's house, but when he heard that Manon, now Madame Blondel, was to be among the guests he made an excuse and absented himself. As Madame Vanloo reported the following day, Manon had asked her to thank Casanova for his discretion in the matter. By now she was pregnant. Her first child, a boy, was born on 19 November 1761, and died the following day. Her second child, also a boy, was born shortly before Christmas 1764, and baptised Jean-Baptiste Blondel on 24 December. In time he would become a famous architect like his father and great-uncle.

Casanova never forgave Manon for breaking off with him, and he did not resist the temptation to pass on salacious gossip about the state of her marriage. If Blondel had found his wife a virgin, he told Madame Vanloo, he owed that to no one but Manon herself. And he had heard that Blondel resided alone in the Louvre, he reported, while his wife lived in a house in the rue Neuve-des-Petits-Champs. Though they lived separately, they supped together every evening, which was 'a strange sort of set-up!' Having failed to find a mistress worthy to be his wife, Blondel 'was very happy to have found a wife worthy to be his mistress'.[55]

As a member of the Academy and Louis XV's architect, Blondel was indeed granted the use of an apartment in the Louvre, but not until 1767, when he moved there with Manon. In 1770 he began to publish his lecture notes as an architecture course; when he died on 9 January 1774, leaving thirty-three-year-old Manon a widow, this

mammoth task was still incomplete. Manon applied to the king to stay on in the apartment with their nine-year-old son, but permission was refused. Granted a pension of 800 livres, she spent the rest of her short life in the kind of artistic milieu in which she had grown up, surrounded by architects, artists and writers. She died in December 1776, aged just thirty-six.

EIGHT

The Marquise d'Urfé

*To trick a fool is an exploit
worthy of an intelligent man.*[1]

IN HER MANSION on Paris's quai des Théatins, overlooking the River Seine and the Palais du Louvre, Jeanne de Lascaris d'Urfé de Larochefoucauld, the fifty-two-year-old Marquise d'Urfé, stands at a table in her private laboratory, engaged in her favourite occupation, which is experimenting with chemicals. Using a key which she keeps on a long gold chain around her neck, she unlocks the wooden casket in front of her and spoons tiny nuggets of the pure platinum it contains into four clear glass vessels of equal size. Next, carefully removing the stoppers from three heavy bottles, she elegantly trickles sulphuric acid into the first vessel of platinum, nitric acid into the second, hydrochloric acid into the third, and into the fourth a mixture of the latter two known as *aqua regia*.

The chemicals bubble and hiss, releasing noxious gases into a room which already reeks of alcohol and sulphur, as well as coal-smoke from the perpetually burning furnace in the corner. These heady fumes do not bother the marquise; on the contrary, they act like smelling salts on her spirits. Jeanne de Lascaris d'Urfé de Larochefoucauld lives for her filtrations, her distillations and her chemical transmutations, in short for her search for the most elusive substance on earth – the fabled philosopher's stone, that which can prolong life for ever and turn base metal into gold.

Her alchemy laboratory is the marquise's refuge from the world.

Being a clever woman with interests that rise far above every day matters, she would far rather spend her mornings here among her grinding bowls, her burning mirrors, her blowpipes, her phials of salts and her caskets of silver, phosphorus and mercury than suffering under her hairdresser's curling tongs or making small-talk with sycophantic courtiers whose interests never go further than the paste buckles on their shoes. Luckily she can afford to do exactly what she likes in life. A widow with no children – well, none living that she cares to acknowledge – a position of unrivalled grandeur and a fortune so great she could not spend the half of it if she tried, the marquise has both the means and the time to indulge her every whim. Instead of being ruled by fashion like lesser mortals, she is guided by an invisible spiritual being she refers to as her 'Genius', whose every word she listens to slavishly, and in whom she puts her entire faith.

That is, until Giacomo Casanova walks into her life.

Jeanne Camus de Pontcarré was the daughter of Pierre-Nicolas Camus de Pontecarré, first president of the Rouen parliament, and his second wife Marie-Françoise de Bragelonne, who died giving birth to her in 1705. Brought up by a succession of stepmothers, Jeanne grew up into an intelligent beauty who was soon noticed at court by Philippe II, the Duc d'Orléans and Regent of France during the minority of Louis XV. By the time she was eighteen, Jeanne was known as Philippe's most beautiful mistress, but her lover appears to have valued her as much for her mind as for anything else, for, as she was never tardy in reminding her acquaintances, he nicknamed her Egérie, after the Roman goddess Egeria, the trusted adviser of King Numa Pompilius.

In September 1724, nine months after Philippe's death, nineteen-year-old Jeanne was married to Louis-Christophe de la Rochefoucauld de Lascaris, Marquis de Langeac, colonel of the regiment of Roche-Guyon and the last remaining descendant, through his mother's line, of the d'Urfés, one of France's most illustrious families. Louis's ancestors included the famous Claude

d'Urfé, representative of France at the Council of Trent and the trusted guardian of Henri II and Catherine de Medici's children, and his two literary sons: the improbably-named Anne, who was a poet; and the more famous Honoré, the author of *L'Astrée*, an internationally-popular pastoral novel.

Immensely proud of the d'Urfé heritage, Jeanne, along with her husband Louis, set about re-establishing the family name. Over the next nine years she bore him two daughters and a son: Adélaïde-Marie-Thérèse, born in 1727; Agnès-Marie, born in 1732; and Jean-Antoine-François, born in 1733. There was to be no happy family life for them. In January 1734 Louis died of smallpox while on active duty near Milan, leaving twenty-eight-year-old Jeanne one of France's wealthiest widows. For she had inherited the entire d'Urfé fortune including extremely profitable shares and invest-ments, properties in and around Paris, and country estates that brought in an annual income of some 80,000 livres. With no financial need to remarry – she spent less than 30,000 livres a year, much of it on augmenting Claude d'Urfé's famous library of ancient books and manuscripts which she had inherited along with her husband's fortune – Jeanne concentrated on astutely investing her money and raising her three children alone.

They brought her little joy. Jean, her only son, died at the age of nine, and her elder daughter Adélaïde grew up to be troublesome and extravagant. By the tail-end of 1753, Adélaïde, aged twenty-six, was still unmarried and deeply in debt. Worried about her losing her money, Jeanne took the drastic measure of applying to Louis XV to have her daughter's Paris mansion and country château sealed up to protect them from being seized by her creditors, and she requested that Adélaïde herself be forcibly enclosed in the convent of Sainte-Marie in Saint-Denis.[2] Locked up in a convent cell, forbidden to communicate with her friends or to use the income from her farms to pay off her debts, Adélaïde railed against her mother who, in return, claimed that her daughter was out of control and disinherited her. When Adélaïde was offered the chance to leave the convent on condition that she marry

straight away, she declared that she would accept the first suitor who came along to get away from Jeanne, even if he were the devil himself.

Though no devil, sixty-year-old widower Alexis-Jean, the Marquis du Châtelet-Fresnières, whom Adélaïde married on 7 May 1754, was nevertheless a highly unsuitable husband, because he was just as improvident as she, and by the following September creditors were snapping at the heels of them both. In dire straits, the poverty-stricken Marquis and Marquise du Châtelet-Fresnières, daughter and son-in-law of Paris's richest widow, were forced to flee from one lowly lodging house to another in the remotest, least fashionable arrondissements of the city while Jeanne lived in luxury near the Louvre. Their first son, born in April 1755, died when he was seven months old; their second, born in August 1756, died the following January. By 1765 the bereaved couple's debts totalled more than a million livres.

Meanwhile, a month before Adélaïde's marriage, Jeanne's younger daughter Agnès had married Paul Edouard Colbert, the Comte de Creuilly and Duc d'Estouteville. Sadly Agnès, who was said to be one of the most beautiful women in Paris, died two years later on 1 July 1756, leaving no children. Jeanne had now lost a husband, a son, a daughter and two grandchildren, and her one remaining offspring brought her nothing but grief. That she began to put so much faith in alchemy, mysticism and the supernatural is perhaps understandable given these circumstances. Her scientific experiments, some of which lasted for years, filled her otherwise empty life, and the hope of making new discoveries, coupled with the existence of a spiritual world in which it was possible to communicate with the dead, was perhaps more bearable to her than reality.

The forerunner of modern-day chemistry, alchemy had its roots in a short text known as *The Emerald Tablet of Hermes*, thought to date back to the ancient Egyptian era and studied by intellectuals as diverse as the thirteenth-century English monk Roger Bacon, the sixteenth-century Swiss-German doctor Philippus Paracelsus, and

even Sir Isaac Newton. Newton's translation of the *Tablet*, found among his papers, included the most important tenet of alchemic philosophy: 'That wch is below is like that wch is above & that wch is above is like yt wch is below.' Everything in nature, alchemists believed, ripened towards purity and perfection, even metals, which ranged from the impure tin and iron to the purest form, gold. Given the right catalyst – a secret substance known as the philosopher's stone – people could speed this natural process up, transmuting base metals into gold at will and producing a universal panacea or 'elixir of life' which kept people from ageing and indefinitely prolonged existence.

The marquise had taken an interest in alchemy ever since her affair with the regent, a liberal man who had been a disciple of the science himself. By the 1750s she had studied all the ancient books and texts on the subject in the d'Urfé library – they included Paracelsus's encrypted formula for the philosopher's stone and original manuscripts by the thirteenth-century Catalan mystic theologian Raymond Lully, also known as 'Doctor Illuminatus'. Although she approached her experiments with the dedication of a true scientist, she elevated her results to the realms of fantasy. In her laboratory she had 'a substance that she had kept on the fire for fifteen years, and which still needed four or five more', which she believed to be 'a powder of projection which could transform all metals into gold in one minute' – a process that alchemists described as the *opus alchemicum* or Great Work, and the highest goal in alchemy. Jeanne also experimented with *Plantina del Pinto* or platinum, a substance given to her in 1743 by the English chemist Charles Wood, who had discovered it two years earlier in Peru. By mixing silver, mercury and nitric acid the marquise created a silver dendrite known as a 'tree of Diana', and she claimed to be able to make one 'that would be a true tree of the sun, which would produce golden fruits that one could harvest'.[3]

'The philosopher's stone may be an inlet into another sort of knowledge that will allow us to have intercourse with good

spirits,' wrote the seventeenth-century Irish-born pioneering chemist Robert Boyle, author of *The Sceptical Chymist*. The marquise
certainly believed so. Over the years she had constructed a
personal Hermetic occult philosophy which encompassed elements of alchemy, magic, the planetary hours, Gnosticism and
arithmancy, a method of prediction which she based on Paracelsus's system of seven magic squares. She applied herself to the
Kabbalah, an ancient form of Jewish mysticism that also studied
by Christians, and she joined the Rosicrucians or Order of the
Rosy Cross, a secret metaphysical organisation usually only open
to men which was dedicated to understanding the principles of
the universe. The marquise would have loved to have been a man;
and one of her most bizarre fantasies was to believe that she could
be 'regenerated' or reborn as one with the help of her spiritual
guide or 'Genius'. Her other great folly was to believe that it was
possible for humans to converse with undines, sylphs, gnomes and
salamanders, the spirits which the Kabbalah assigned to the four
elements of water, air, earth and fire. Jeanne would have given all
her worldly possessions to accomplish these two aims. And thanks
to Casanova, she nearly did.

Acutely clever about investing her money, the Marquise d'Urfé
was gullible to the point of stupidity when it came to alchemy and
mysticism, the new-age beliefs of her time. A contemporary
memoir, *Les Souvenirs de la Marquise de Crêquy*, painted her as
'the most stubborn of alchemists, determined to find the philosopher's stone . . . She was a lost woman, my aunt the baroness told
us, her mind was in a whirl and all her wealth was blown away on
the search.'[4] The Landgravine of Hesse described her in slightly
more generous terms as 'a woman of wit, but who believes in
communication with sylphs and spirits' and novelist Jacques Cazotte, author of *The Devil in Love*, called her 'the doyenne of the
French Medeas'. The drawing-room of her Paris mansion 'was
always choked with quacks and people stampeding after the occult
sciences', Cazotte noted. 'She had been in communication with the
spirits throughout her life. Myself, I portrayed them with a master's

hand, and we found each other as learned as each other, that's to say, very obscure.'[5]

The Enlightenment was an age divided 'between the two extremes of rationalist doubt and mystic credence, between the most audacious scepticism and the most absurd superstition'.[6] As people sought to gain a new scientific understanding of the world, to prolong their lives and make themselves healthier and richer, alchemy, freemasonry and the occult became all the rage in the aristocratic circles of Paris. There was no shortage of pseudo-scientists, magicians and *voyantes* or mediums ready to milk the rich of their money; and the Marquise d'Urfé's potpourri of blind beliefs, coupled with her wealth, made her a prime target for them. Charlatans and con-artists of the time included Madame Bontemps, a fashionable fortune-teller and spiritualist consulted by the likes of Madame de Pompadour, the Abbé de Bernis and even Casanova (her name, 'Madame Good Times', suggests that she specialised in telling people what they wanted to hear); Jacques Cazotte, who enslaved the Marquise de la Croix with his prophecies of the future; the Count of Cagliostro, a chemist and hypnotist who, in the 1780s, would captivate the court with his séances and promises of miraculous cures; the extraordinary Comte de Saint-Germain; and of course Casanova himself.

The Marquise d'Urfé was introduced to Casanova in 1757 or 1758 by her nephew Nicolas-François-Julie de la Tour d'Apchier, the Comte de La Tour d'Auvergne, a man as prone to flights of fantasy as she was: in 1751 he had been thrown into the Bastille prison for frequenting witches and participating in '*parties de diable*', in which he and his aristocratic friends had run through the fields at night in the hope of seeing the devil.[7] Suffering from bad sciatica, the suggestible Nicolas declared himself miraculously cured after Casanova, as a prank, painted a mystical pentacle on his thigh using an amalgam of nitre, flowers of sulphur and mercury mixed with his patient's own urine, and he immediately told his aunt about his new acquaintance. The marquise responded by saying that she had already heard of Casanova and was dying to

meet him, that she believed she already knew him, and that he was not the man the whole of Paris believed him to be.

What was Casanova's reputation in Paris at the time? In January 1757, at thirty-one years old, he had arrived in the city armed with nothing except his heroic reputation. With the help of de Bernis, he had quickly established himself as one of the founders of the lottery and an adviser to the French government. Through the minister and the Balletti family he soon met everyone in the city worth knowing and, thanks to his brilliant mind, his ability to befriend a wide range of people and his overwhelming need to insinuate himself into their hearts, he was soon welcomed in all the best circles. But there was something else too that made Casanova sought after as a companion: his reputation as a magician and alchemist. Although he claimed that he abhorred being famed for these skills, in reality he was happy to trade on them. Fascinated by medicine since his youth, and well-aware of the power of sugges-tion, he possessed an intuitive understanding of the human mind and body which had already won him the worship of Senator Bragadin and his friends in Venice, and the gratitude of the Duchess of Chartres, whose disfiguring pimples he had helped cure during his first sojourn in Paris in 1750. At that time Casanova was already rumoured to be 'connected with fortune-telling and horoscope drawing', or so the French minister at Cologne wrote to the Duc de Choiseul.[8] Seven years on, the duchess and her ladies-in-waiting Madame de Boufflers and Madame du Blot continued to consult him on matters of health and prediction.

Casanova had no illusions that he was a magician. He had been aware of the power of magic since the day his grandmother had taken him to Murano to consult the witch about his nosebleeds, but unlike many of his contemporaries he was a rationalist who did not believe in the supernatural. Witnessing first-hand Bettina Gozzi's so-called demonic possession and exorcism in his early teens, he had seen through the ritual and rhetoric and come to the healthy conclusion that everyone concerned, including Bettina herself, was simply acting a role. Nevertheless, magic and illusion fascinated

him, perhaps because it fascinated others. Over the years he had taught himself the basics of alchemy, studied arithmancy and cryptology, and gained a working knowledge of the Kabbalah. As the Venetian spy Manuzzi had discovered, he had been initiated into the secret society of Freemasons in 1750 when he had joined a masonic lodge in Lyon. Like the Marquise d'Urfé, Casanova had also joined the Order of the Rosy Cross, or Rosicrucians, an occult order which combined, among other movements, Gnosticism, alchemy and Kabbalism.

As his relationship with Bragadin had shown, Casanova shamelessly used all this knowledge for his own ends and amusement. If the senator and his friends chose to believe his story that an ancient Spanish hermit had taught him how to predict the future, who was he to disillusion them? Not for nothing had one of Manuzzi's secret reports to the Venetian Inquisitors stated that Casanova 'cultivates people who are ready to believe anything . . . He is an exaggerator and by dint of lies and a witty tongue he lives at the expense of this, that and the other.'[9]

Refined, convincing, intellectual, with the reputation of being a mystic and a healer and the added bravura of being the only man ever to have escaped from The Leads in the Doge's Palace, by the time he returned to Paris in January 1757 Casanova's ability to enchant both men and women was unparalleled. He had no moral scruples about taking in fools or relieving them of their money, and even in old age he was certain 'that my readers will not condemn me when they see me emptying my friends' purses to satisfy my whims. They had chimerical plans, and by making them hope for their success I hoped at the same time to cure them of their folly by disillusioning them. I deceived them to make them wise; and I did not believe myself to be guilty, for what prompted me was not avarice. I was merely paying for my pleasures with money which was destined to acquire possessions that nature makes it impossible to obtain . . . It was money destined to be spent on follies; I merely diverted its use by making it pay for mine.'[10] Like all the best charlatans, he listened carefully to what others told him about

themselves, stole glimpses of their private documents, made his own deductions and then fed their own information back to them, pretending that he had discovered it by supernatural means. He was not above donning the white robes of a magician, drawing 'magic' symbols on the ground and chanting make-believe spells in order to raise buried treasure from under the earth if he felt there was something in it for him, as he had once done in Cesena in 1748 (this, his first magical operation, had coincided with a terrible thunderstorm, and had been so frightening that Casanova had even terrified himself).

The Marquise d'Urfé was 'famed for being learned in all the abstruse sciences', her nephew La Tour d'Auvergne told Casanova before he introduced them.[11] She was also fabulously rich and dying to meet the adventurer, whom she said she could introduce to the best people in Paris. All this made her an irresistible prospect for a man who was determined to make his fortune by any means. Their first meeting took place in the marquise's riverside mansion, and even before he arrived Casanova seized the reins of power by insisting that no other guests be present that day. In the presence of her nephew, the marquise and Casanova circled each other warily, exchanging polite small-talk while secretly studying one another. It was not until La Tour d'Auvergne left that the marquise opened up the subjects so dear to her heart. Eager to show off her occult knowledge in front of a man she was already convinced was an adept, she boasted with a gracious smile that she already possessed the philosopher's stone, and was experienced in all the great alchemic operations. Although she demonstrated that she was a skilled chemist she could not stop herself from revealing some of her most foolish fantasies: for example, that both the thirteenth-century monk Roger Bacon and the eighth-century Arabian physician Jabir ibn Hayyan were still alive and in communication with her, and that she frequently received letters from the author and philosopher Benoît de Maillet, who had died some twenty years previously.

When the marquise turned her back for a moment, Casanova

secretly stole a look at one of her notebooks, where he found a drawing of the same mystical pentacle he had painted on her nephew's thigh, surrounded by the names of the Planetary Gen-iuses, spirits assigned to the planets by the Kabbalah. A few minutes later, when the marquise asked him to write down the words he had spoken when he had drawn the pentacle, he cannily copied out the same names. Convinced that he had divined them by mystical means, the marquise immediately fell under Casano-va's spell. At nine o'clock that evening, when her nephew returned to the house, his aunt and friend were still deep in conversation. Jeanne believed that she had at last found a soul-mate in the intellectually impressive and handsome younger man, and she was reluctant to let go of him.

Casanova was eager to comply. Though, as yet, he had no specific plan to take advantage of the gullible marquise, he was happy to enjoy what was a rather malicious joke at her expense. From then he dined alone with her every day, for she sacrificed her other friends in order to enjoy his company, and she spent so many private hours with him that her servants presumed that he was her husband. Were they lovers? Casanova hinted as much. At the time he was conducting his secret liaison with Manon Balletti, sleeping with Parisian prostitutes and his female workforce, and pursuing countless other women, but this did not rule out his having an affair with the marquise in order to ingratiate himself further with her.

Despite being twenty years his senior, the marquise was still a beautiful woman. More important than any sexual attraction she might have felt for Casanova, she considered him her kindred spirit, the one person who truly shared her spiritual beliefs. She discussed her search for the philosopher's stone with him. They conducted alchemic experiments together. A fluent Latin speaker, Casanova helped her to translate ancient Latin texts she could not understand. Unwilling to recognise that he might have an ulterior motive in befriending her, the marquise convinced herself that Casanova was 'a genuine adept under the mask of a man of no consequence',[12] an independently wealthy young man who had

only taken his position with the French Military Lottery in order to disguise his real identity as a magician.

The marquise was deceiving herself, and Casanova did his best to encourage her. A few weeks after they first met he consolidated his hold over her by successfully decoding a manuscript she had given him. It purported to contain Paracelsus's formula for the philosopher's stone, written out in a secret code to which she believed only she held the key. Casanova worked out the code by using simple cryptography, but instead of telling her so 'the fancy took me to tell her that a Genius had revealed it to me'. Little did the Marquise know that Paralis, this invisible genius, was a being he had invented years back to impress Senator Bragadin and his friends. 'It was this false confidence which put Madame d'Urfé under my control,' he admitted. 'That day I made myself the arbiter of her soul.' He had successfully hijacked 'her heart, her mind, and all that remained of her common sense',[13] and for the next six years he would shamelessly abuse his power over her.

From now on, the marquise hung on Casanova's every word. She truly believed that he was omnipotent, and that he had the power and knowledge to fulfil her greatest wish by performing an operation which would 'regenerate' her by transferring her soul into the body of a male infant born of the philosophical union of a mortal with an immortal. She was aware that she might die in the process, she informed him in all seriousness, but she was prepared to risk death in order to be reborn as a man. Casanova, who could barely keep a straight face when she confessed this, would in time make the marquise's 'regeneration' the basis of a drawn-out con-trick he perpetrated on her, by which he hoped to gain control of her entire fortune. In the short term, he was flattered to be thought the greatest of all Rosicrucians and alchemists and the most powerful of all men by a lady of such high rank; and he was aware that, if he was ever in need of money, she would refuse him nothing.

For the next six years the marquise was Casanova's '*grand trésorier*', a source of frequent and extremely generous hand-outs. Her lackeys, horses and the sumptuous golden d'Urfé carriage lined

with red Utrecht velvet were permanently at his disposal and, as soon as he condescended to meet them (if only one at a time), she introduced him to her influential family and friends. They included her brothers, councillor Geoffroy Camus de Pontcarré and Jean-Baptiste de Viarmes, the provost of Paris's special mercantile courts, the ninety-year-old Chevalier d'Arginy, a pomaded, be-wigged high-ranking cavalry officer known as Paris's 'dean of the fops', and Anne Languet, the Comtesse de Gergi who brought with her the legendary Comte de Saint-Germain, a man who fascinated the marquise and Casanova alike, and whose outrageous claims put Casanova's in the shade.

Called 'Der Wundermann' in Germany and 'the man who knows everything and never dies' rather ironically by Voltaire, the Comte de Saint-Germain was an international celebrity. No one knew how he obtained his seemingly bottomless purse of money, or where he came from; he was rumoured variously to be the son of a Portu-guese Jew, an Alsatian Jew, the illegitimate son of Marie de Neubourg, widow of Charles II of Spain, or a child of Francis II Rákóczy, the Prince of Transylvania. Stockily built, with the refined dark looks of an aristocratic Spaniard, Saint-Germain claimed that he was anything between three hundred and two thousand years old. People believed him because he had an ageless appearance: the Comtesse de Gergi, who befriended him in Paris in the 1750s, insisted that she had met him decades earlier in Venice where her husband had been French ambassador, and that he had looked no different then.

Saint-Germain was a polymath and a savant. There seemed to be nothing that he did not know or could not accomplish. A brilliant linguist, he spoke every modern European language including German, Italian, English, Spanish, Portuguese and French and he also knew Latin, Greek, Arabic, Chinese and Sanskrit. He was a virtuoso violinist but said that he had given up music because he had no more to learn on the subject. He was a talented portrait-painter, and was an extremely learned alchemist who claimed, like the Marquise d'Urfé, that he could turn base metal into gold and

transform a handful of small diamonds into a single large flawless stone. His love of jewels was legendary. 'He wore very fine diamonds in his rings, watch, and snuffbox,' according to the memoirs of Madame de Pompadour's maid, Madame du Hausset. 'He came, one day, to visit Madame de Pompadour, at a time when the Court was in full splendour, with knee and shoe-buckles of diamonds so fine and brilliant that Madame said she did not believe the King had any equal to them.'[14] Saint-Germain was sought after and accepted in the most exalted circles in Europe, even more so than Casanova. But although he was constantly invited to dine at people's houses and was happy to join the company at table, he never ate or drank in public, and in private lived on a simple diet consisting almost exclusively of oatmeal. A mine of amusing anecdotes and dazzling knowledge, he often delivered them in a didactic tone which no one seemed to mind for he always appeared to know what he was talking about and spoke to everyone in the same way. As Madame du Hausset wrote, 'Nobody could find out by what means this man became so rich and so remarkable; but the King would not suffer him to be spoken of with ridicule or contempt.' In fact Saint-Germain became one of Louis XV's close advisers, setting up a laboratory for him and probably working as his spy. 'If he isn't God himself, a powerful God inspires him,' the Comte de Milly wrote of Saint-Germain.[15] Women in particular adored him, and he was known to have many lovers as well as female friends to whom he gave advice on dyeing their hair (he was a specialist on the subject of dyes), face paints to beautify their complexions and a secret 'water of youth' which he told them was very expensive yet gave to them free of charge, claiming that it would preserve their looks for ever.

The Marquise d'Urfé was among Saint-Germain's devotees; she even commissioned a portrait of him. He became a frequent visitor to her Paris hôtel, and despite the unspoken rivalry between them he was one of the few guests whom Casanova was happy to dine with there. The two adventurers had plenty in common, not least the habit of encouraging their admirers to swallow their tall stories.

'Sometimes I amuse myself, not by *making* people believe, but by *letting* them believe, that I have lived in the most remote periods,' Saint-Germain is reported to have said to Madame de Pompadour when she laughed at one of his more outlandish claims.[16] By his own admission, Casanova worked in exactly the same way.

Despite his suspicions about the Comte de Saint-Germain, Casanova was almost indulgent towards him when he met him at the Marquise d'Urfé's home: 'This man, instead of eating, talked from the beginning to the end of dinner, and I listened to him with the greatest attention, for nobody spoke as well as he did. He made himself out to be a prodigy in everything, he wished to amaze, and he really did amaze . . . This very singular man, born to be the most brazen of impostors, said with impunity, as if by the by, that he was three hundred years old, that he possessed the universal panacea, that he could do whatever he pleased with nature, that he melted diamonds, and that he could make one large one of the finest water out of ten or twelve small ones without diminishing the weight. For him these things were trifles. Despite his pretentious boasts, his eccentricities, and his obvious lies, I could not bring myself to find him insolent, but neither could I consider him respectable; I found him astonishing despite myself, for he amazed me.'[17]

However impressive Saint-Germain was, it was Casanova to whom the Marquise d'Urfé was in thrall. She trusted him implicitly, even with her financial investments: when he was sent to Holland by the French government in October 1758 she handed him 60,000 francs worth of shares she owned in the East India Company of Gothenburg, and asked him to sell them there on her behalf. If this was a test of his honesty, Casanova passed it, for after he had sold the shares for 72,000 francs he sent the marquise a bill of exchange for the entire amount, delighting her so much that she made him a present of all the profits she had made on the deal. However, most of the letter she wrote thanking him was taken up with her spiritual delusions: her Genius had informed her that Casanova would return to Paris with a young boy born of the philosophic union of an

immortal with a mortal – the very being into whose body she believed he could transfer her soul and thus regenerate her as a man.

Fate played into Casanova's hands when he ran into his old friend and lover from Venice, Teresa Imer. Since their brief affair in the early summer of 1753, the fortunes of the singer and *femme fatale* who had once captivated both Casanova's mentor Malipiero and the Margrave of Bayreuth had slipped inexorably downhill. She had returned to Bayreuth from Venice pregnant by Casanova; their daughter, Sophia Wilhelmina Frederica, had been born in the early months of 1754. When the margrave's court had moved south to Italy later that year, Teresa had left her long-suffering husband, choreographer Angelo Pompeati, and, taking her children with her, had travelled to Paris where she had attempted to make money by singing at private concerts, and later by staging musical evenings in her furnished apartment. Within two years she had been made bankrupt and imprisoned for debt. Bailed out by one of her many admirers, Teresa had fled to Flanders where yet another lover, the powerful Prince Charles of Lorraine, had set her on the road to becoming a theatrical impresario.

For two seasons, the plays and concerts Teresa had staged in Ghent and Liège had been as artistically successful as her father Giuseppe Imer's had once been at Venice's San Samuele theatre. However, financially they had been disastrous for her. Always a perfectionist in her work, Teresa had spent far more on her productions than they had earned – a problem that would dog her throughout her business career and lead to her eventual ruin. Leaving a trail of debts in her wake, she had fled from Flanders to the Dutch Republic, where she now rented dilapidated rooms in a tenement in The Hague and scraped a living by travelling to Rotterdam and Amsterdam and singing at concerts under the assumed name of Madame de Trenti or Tranti. Since they knew that she was in financial trouble, the music impresarios such as M. Van Hagen in Rotterdam refused to pay her any fees. Instead she was allowed to carry a collection plate through the audiences after each performance like some kind of beggar, with her young

daughter Sophia trailing after her in the hope of garnering more money by eliciting people's sympathy.

At a concert in Amsterdam on New Year's Day 1759, Teresa noticed Casanova in the audience. He was clearly as shocked to see her as she was to see him, and the sight of their daughter, whose existence he had not known about but who bore an unmistakable likeness to him, left him nonplussed. Although he put a generous amount of money on Teresa's collection plate Casanova would not acknowledge that he knew her in front of his wealthy companions. Later that night, the desperate and determined soprano sought him out at the inn where he was staying. During the last few years she had lost two of her four children. Scarcely able to feed Sophia, who was now nearly five years old, and too poor to provide for her son, twelve-year-old Giuseppe Pompeati, whom she had left 'in pawn' in Rotterdam with some of her creditors, Teresa threw herself on her old friend's mercy. But when Casanova offered to take their beautiful daughter off her hands she refused to part with her. Instead, she begged him to redeem her son from her creditors, take him to Paris and bring him up for her.

Casanova readily agreed to do so. He already had a hidden agenda: to pass the boy off as the half-immortal being whom the Marquise d'Urfé had predicted he would bring back to Paris with him. The suggestible marquise needed little encouragement. As soon as Casanova arrived in Paris with Giuseppe, she snatched the child from under his nose, took him home, made him sleep in her bed and, for the next four years, insisted on bringing him up at her own expense. Three years older than her son Jean had been when he died, Giuseppe Pompeati – or the Count of Aranda as he quickly reinvented himself in order to impress his rich foster mother – was an intelligent if rather lazy youth who gave new purpose and meaning to the marquise's life. Since Agnès's death in the summer of 1756 and her estrangement from Adélaïde she had had no one but herself to think of. Now she again had a child who depended on her. While her own daughter and son-in-law were all but starving in their dismal lodgings on the far side of the city, the

marquise plied Giuseppe with gifts of clothes and jewels, bought him a pony and enrolled him at Viard's, the best boarding school in Paris. 'A prince could not have been better lodged, better treated, better dressed or better respected by the entire household,' Casanova reported after visiting him there.[18] M. Viard taught Giuseppe all that a young French aristocrat was supposed to know about the world, and his pretty sixteen-year-old daughter, whose job it was to look after the boy, instructed him in the facts of life just as Bettina Gozzi had instructed Casanova during his schooldays.

Giuseppe had lived a hard hand-to-mouth existence with his critical and demanding birth-mother. Thanks to the Marquise d'Urfé his life in Paris was an earthly paradise. But while he gloried in his new identity as the adored and indulged protégé of Paris's richest widow, the marquise's relations with her daughter and son-in-law deteriorated sharply. Still unable to access Adélaïde's property, the couple brought a legal action against the marquise, claiming that she was withholding large sums of money from them. The loss of two children of her own, coupled with years of living in terrible poverty, took its toll on Adélaïde, who now fell ill. Suffering, perhaps, from postpartum depression, she believed that her late second son had been born with claws on his toes instead of nails.[19] Pregnant for a third time in 1759, she grew so deranged that her husband applied for permission to separate from her – reluctantly, the Marquis de Châtelet insisted, since he still loved his wife dearly. The couple's third child, Achille-François-Félicien, was born with a withered right arm at the ancient d'Urfé château of La Bâtie le Forez on 3 November 1759. The following year his desperate parents were ordered to surrender all their remaining property to their thirty-three creditors, who included a lemonade-maker, a master tailor, water carriers, butchers, horse riders, wood-sellers and even chair-men. Since they had nothing to live on, Louis XV granted the du Châtelets a generous pension of 10,000 livres. But the marquis died on 6 May 1761, and the half-deranged Adélaïde was extradited to the convent at Conflans for the rest of her life.

After his triumphant return from Holland at the start of 1759 Casanova had gone out of his way to flatter and court the Marquise d'Urfé in a fashion more suited to a lover than a platonic friend. When he rented his country villa at La Petite Pologne she was his very first visitor, and he encouraged her to believe that he had arranged the entire house with her happiness in mind. He had his portrait painted on a medallion with the intention of giving it to her (she never received it, though, for he kept it and had it made into a snuffbox which he eventually gave to Teresa Lanti when he ran into her in Florence in November 1760). When the marquise expressed a desire to meet the enlightenment philosopher and writer Jean-Jacques Rousseau, Casanova accompanied her to the château in Montmorency where he was then staying, and they both came away with the same impression – that the famous philosopher was entirely undistinguished and rather rude.

How much did the marquise know of Casanova's other amorous activities? Without doubt he was discreet about his other women and, with equal discretion, she never questioned him about what he did when they were not together, a quality he considered a great virtue on her part. She would not have been aware of his secret engagement to Manon Balletti, or of his crush on beautiful, twenty-one-year-old Giustiniana Wynne, whom he was intent on seducing.

Happy to flirt with him as she was, Giustiniana was not really interested in Casanova. Although her Venetian mother was trying to marry her off to a wealthy man she detested – France's Farmer General, arts patron Alexandre le Riche de la Pouplinière, she was already pregnant by her secret lover, Venetian nobleman Andrea Memmo, whom she had been forced to leave behind in Venice. Since she knew that Casanova was a friend of Memmo's Giustiniana turned to him for advice about procuring an abortion – a mark both of her desperation and of the confidence the adventurer inspired in women. He discreetly consulted the Marquise d'Urfé who gave him Paracelsus's recipe for an aroph or unguent made of powdered saffron, myrrh and honey, which, she said, smeared on to a cylinder of the appropriate size and inserted into the vagina so

as to sexually excite a woman, would infallibly bring on menstruation. Aware that this advice was ridiculous, it suited Casanova's purpose – to pass it on to the seven-months pregnant Giustiniana. On the spur of the moment he added that the aroph was most effective when mixed with sperm that had not lost its body-heat and administered three or four times a day for five or six days; and because Memmo was not available to administer it, Casanova offered to move into the Hôtel de Bretagne, where Giustiniana was staying with her family, and administer it himself. At first she laughed at him. Several days later, however, she consented, and the aroph was duly administered, with evident sexual satisfaction on both sides, two or three times a night in her chambermaid's garret under the hôtel's eaves. But despite repeated applications, it did not bring on a miscarriage.

Rather than abandon Giustiniana to her fate – and fearing perhaps that he would be blamed for her pregnancy – Casanova arranged through his well-connected friend Madame du Rumain both for the Venetian to take refuge during her confinement in a convent outside Paris, and for her proposed marriage to de la Pouplinière to be dropped. He pressed a gift of 200 louis on the pregnant woman, and, at great risk to himself, even helped her to abscond from the Hôtel de Bretagne. The whole Giustiniana affair, which could have led to Casanova's downfall, shows him at his most manipulative, but also at his most generous. He was capable of remarkable friendship and selflessness when he truly liked a woman – though perhaps not great honesty or loyalty towards his old friend Memmo.

The Marquise d'Urfé, in turn, would do anything for Casanova, but she would not lift a finger for her own flesh and blood. When Casanova was imprisoned overnight for debt in August 1759 she personally went to Paris's Fors L'Evêque prison, bailed him out for the sum of 50,000 francs, and then used her influence to ensure that the case was quashed. Yet when her only surviving grandson Achille was effectively orphaned on his father's death two years later, the marquise refused to accept responsibility for him, and he

remained at the d'Urfé château of La Bâtie in the Loire valley with a lawyer acting as his guardian. By now wearing a large magnet around her neck on the Comte de Saint-Germain's advice in the belief that it would draw lightning down on her and thus raise her up to the sun, the marquise thought only of her spiritual regeneration, Giuseppe and her guru Casanova. When he suddenly left Paris for Holland again at the end of September 1759 – his purpose was as much to escape Manon and his mounting debts as to do business for the French government – his departure must have been a blow for her; her relatives, on the other hand, who had by now become highly suspicious of Casanova's power over the marquise, were relieved that he had gone.

As he travelled restlessly through Holland, Germany, Switzerland, Italy and France over the next few years, the marquise supplied Casanova with letters of introduction; used her influence at court to intrigue on his behalf; bought him expensive diamonds, watches, snuffboxes and lace when he briefly returned to Paris in the summer of 1761 (unfortunately for him they were stolen by his faithless servant Costa); provided him with an elegant apartment in the rue du Bac, which she furnished with ancient tapestries depicting the Great Work; and, most importantly, bank-rolled his travels to the tune of hundreds of thousands of francs. None of this made Casanova grateful. On the contrary, he described her in his memoirs as 'the miserly Mme d'Urfé, who was obsessed with preaching economy to me'.[20]

Comic, pathetic, criminal and cruel in equal measure, Casanova's 'divine operation' to regenerate the Marquise d'Urfé as a man began in January 1762 when they spent three weeks closeted together in the rue du Bac making 'the necessary preparations'. These began with 'paying the appropriate devotions to each of the seven planetary geniuses on the days which were consecrated to them':

After these preparations, I would go to a place which would be made known to me by the inspiration of the geniuses, and take a virgin, the daughter of an adept, and impregnate her with a male

child by a method which was only known to the brothers of the Rosy Cross. This boy would be born alive, but with only a sensitive soul.[21] Mme d'Urfé must receive him into her arms at the instant he came into the world, and keep him with her in her bed for seven days. At the end of seven days, she would die, with her mouth glued to that of the child who, by this means, would receive her intelligent soul.

After this permutation, it would fall to me to care for the infant with the mastery that was known to me, and as soon as the child had attained its third year, Mme d'Urfé would become conscious again, and then I would begin to initiate her into a perfect knowledge of the Great Doctrine.

The operation must take place on the day of a full moon in April, May or June. Above all, Mme d'Urfé must make a will in due form leaving everything she had to the child, whose guardian I was to be until his thirteenth year.[22]

In short, Casanova's plan consisted almost entirely of quasi-mystical mumbo-jumbo spiced up with a smattering of Aristotelian philosophy and large dollops of thinly-disguised self-interest on his part. His intention was not merely to pander to the marquise's whims but to seize hold of her entire fortune, and during his travels he acquired a motley collection of accomplices to help him do so. They included Giuseppe Bono, a corrupt banker and silk merchant resident in Lyon; Giacomo Passano, a Genoese adventurer, actor and painter of erotic miniatures whom he met in Livorno; and Marianna Corticelli, a talented young Bolognese dancer he picked up in Florence.

La Corticelli, Casanova's *petite friponne de Bologne* or 'little Bolognese rogue' as his friend Count Trana called her, was scarcely more than a child when he first encountered her in November 1760. Yet she was already heading down the short road that led from dancing to prostitution. In the city to perform alongside Casanova's old love, Teresa Lanti, at the Teatro della Pergola, Corticelli was accompanied by her brother and her mother, Laura

Gigli, a woman so poor that she could not afford enough bedcovers for her children and was consequently willing to exploit them at the first opportunity. Pushy, cocksure and full of spirit, 'the little madcap', as Casanova described Corticelli, won his interest as much by her sense of humour as by the fact that 'she was thirteen years old, and only looked ten'. But even though he had obviously not lost his fondness for very young girls, the young dancer did not inspire any great passion in Casanova; her main attraction was that she made him laugh. For her part, she seems to have tolerated their sexual relationship without enjoying it: in bed with him she was humorous, compliant and yet passionless. Casanova had his uses, the greatest of them being as a provider of food, wine, a brazier to heat the freezing cold inn room where she slept naked under thin sheets beside her brother, and hard cash, with which she immediately bought herself a warm fur cloak. Rich enough to make people bow to his every whim, Casanova also intervened on Corticelli's behalf with the impresario at the Pergola, who had pledged to give her a pas-de-deux to dance in the second opera, but had not honoured the contract.

Sought by the Florentine authorities because of his involvement in some shady business deal in the city, Casanova carried Corticelli off towards Bologna without telling her mother; when Laura caught up with the fugitives she complained that his behaviour was beyond a joke. In Bologna, the family's home and a city well known for its prostitutes, Corticelli acted as Casanova's pimp, procuring him girls of her own age who provided him with such delicious pleasures that he still remembered them wistfully in his old age. He left Bologna seven days later, promising Corticelli that he would visit her in Prague, where she was engaged to dance for a year, and then take her to Paris with him.

After a year in Prague, Corticelli received a letter from Casanova asking her and her mother to meet up with him in Metz. There, in February, he informed them of his plan to involve Corticelli in the Marquise d'Urfé's regeneration operation by passing her off as a virgin countess descended from the Lascaris family, with whom the

d'Urfés had intermarried during the sixteenth century. After a few weeks spent coaching his protégée in her new role, and with Laura reluctantly posing as a servant, Casanova conducted mother and daughter to Pontcarré, thirty kilometres east of Paris, where he had arranged to meet the Marquise d'Urfé at one of her many homes. The Château de Pontcarré was an ancient fortress with turreted corners, surrounded by a moat teeming with vicious gnats. Warned to expect their arrival, the marquise had the drawbridges lowered and stood under the gateway surrounded by her household 'like an army general ready to surrender the place to us with all the honours of war'.[23] Surrender was unnecessary – Casanova had already conquered her. She greeted her long-lost 'relative' the Countess of Lascaris with effusive tenderness, ran through their genealogy to explain just how they were related, and had a bed made up for her in her own room. Corticelli behaved as if to the manner born, chattering away graciously in French to her hostess and captivating Giuseppe Pompeati, now known as the Count of Aranda, whom the marquise had brought to Pontcarré with her. Since it was immediately apparent that Corticelli had fallen for the youth, Casanova decided to get rid of him.

On the fourteenth day of the April moon, the first stage of the marquise's regeneration went ahead as planned. Casanova, the charlatan orchestrating it, went to bed and ordered the marquise to bring Corticelli to his room. Having undressed the so-called virgin countess, anointed her with perfumes and draped her in a magnificent veil, the marquise watched while Casanova 'deflowered' her and supposedly impregnated her with the male child into whose body her own soul was eventually to be transferred. But when, on the last day of the moon, Casanova consulted his numerical oracle, it declared – for safety's sake – that the countess had not become pregnant after all because Aranda had been watching the secret ceremony from behind a screen. The oracle went on to predict that the ceremony could be repeated successfully outside France during the full moon in May, but only if Aranda was sent at least one hundred leagues away from Paris for a

year, accompanied by a tutor, a manservant and all the appropriate
appurtenances. Since she was determined that nothing should
stand in the way of her regeneration, the marquise immediately
sent Aranda to stay with one of her relatives in Lyon.

Never able to support a rival in the bedroom, Casanova had used
his oracle to separate his godson from Corticelli. She was furious.
From now on she decided to look after her own interests. As,
accompanied by a retinue of liveried servants and retainers, they
made their way towards Aix-la-Chapelle, where the mystical
operation was to be repeated, the strained relationship between
them grew worse. Outwardly, Corticelli continued to behave like a
countess, charming everyone she met including Teresa Imer's old
lover the Margrave of Bayreuth and his daughter the Duchess of
Württemberg. Towards Casanova, however, she was hostile and
difficult, and at a ball in Aix she deliberately embarrassed him by
dancing more like the showgirl she was than the aristocrat she was
pretending to be. The marquise noticed nothing amiss: following
the ball she gave Corticelli a casket containing diamond earrings, a
jewelled watch and a ring set with a fifteen-carat rose diamond.
Together these were worth in the region of 60,000 francs – a vast
amount to a penniless theatrical family. Afraid that the dancer and
her mother would abscond with the jewels before the second
operation, Casanova confiscated everything. Incandescent with
rage, Corticelli, who now claimed she was already pregnant by
one of her admirers in Prague, threatened to tell all to the marquise
and expose Casanova's criminal intentions. Casanova threatened to
keep the jewels himself – which in fact he did; having dared to
stand up to him, Corticelli would never see her valuable diamonds
again. Furthermore he immediately convinced the Marquise d'Urfé
that her relative the Countess Lascaris had been bewitched by a
black spirit and had gone mad; nothing she said was to be believed
any more. Consequently, when Corticelli carried out her threat to
denounce him, the marquise merely laughed at her.

Since Corticelli had become such an unreliable accomplice,
Casanova decided to postpone the regeneration operation until a

replacement for her could be found. He advised the marquise that they must write for guidance to a spirit named Selenis who lived on the moon. In an elaborate hoax ceremony conducted in a house outside Aix, the marquise and Casanova bathed naked together by moonlight in a large bath filled with perfumed water, then burned aromatic herbs and recited mystical prayers. Spouting meaningless words which she devoutly repeated after him, Casanova burned her letter to Selenis in a juniper-scented flame. Ten minutes later, an answering letter appeared as if by magic on the surface of the water (Casanova had written it out earlier in silver ink on green glazed paper, and had smuggled it into the bath). The spirit informed the disappointed marquise that her regeneration would finally take place in Marseille the following spring, with the aid of a being named Querilinte, one of the three leaders of the Rosy Cross and yet another of Casanova's inventions.

The marquise left Aix to join Giuseppe in Lyon, and Casanova despatched Corticelli and her mother to Turin with no remuneration other than a letter of introduction and twenty-five louis. He then travelled on to Geneva where he made several new conquests including two cousins, one of whom, Hedwige, was an intellectual prodigy. Since both Hedwige and her cousin Helena were virgins, Casanova deliberately seduced them together – a tactic that, as he admitted in his memoirs, never failed him in his long career as a libertine: 'If the friend permits the slightest favour to be stolen from her, in order to stop herself blushing she will be the first to push her friend to grant a greater favour, and if the seducer is skilled the innocent will have gone too far to pull back. Then, the more innocent a young woman is, the more ignorant she is of the ways and aims of seduction. Without her knowing it, the appeal of pleasure entices her, curiosity adds to it, and opportunity does the rest.'[24]

Ignorance of his aims was also Casanova's best weapon when it came to the Marquise d'Urfé. Intent on keeping her in his thrall, he briefly rejoined her in Lyon where he mystified her with yet more talk of oracles and spirits. Fearing perhaps that if she returned to Paris her relatives would blacken his name, he made his oracle,

which took the form of a pyramid of numbers, predict that she should remain where she was until he sent word for her to meet him in Marseille. After lightening her purse of a further 50,000 francs in travel expenses, Casanova left for Turin to pacify Corticelli, who was by now a loose cannon loaded with dangerous ammunition against him. Catching her with another man, he walked out on her and refused to go back. In retaliation she told her story to the Comtesse de Saint-Giles, a popular society hostess in the city. Days later, Casanova was sent a manuscript containing almost the whole story of his plan to defraud d'Urfé, and in November he was expelled from Turin, probably through Saint-Giles's influence.

He arrived in Marseille in April 1763 with three accomplices: Giacomo Passano, a semi-literate crook whom he had taken on as his 'secretary'; his youngest brother, Gaetano Casanova, a dishonest priest and failed womaniser whom he had run into in Genoa; and Gaetano's great love, Marcolina. Casanova, who felt little affection for any of his brothers, despised Gaetano for being weak and stupid. So, it seemed, did Marcolina, a respectable girl whom Gaetano had lured away from Venice with false promises that he would marry her. Haughty, bright and tempestuous, Marcolina was so angry with Gaetano for deceiving her that she resorted to physical violence, and it did not take much effort on Casanova's part to seduce her himself – sibling rivalry at its most base. In bed, he found Marcolina voluptuous, accommodating and as insatiable as she was at table and, true to form, he fell in love with her. Soon she, too, was roped in to play a part in the Marquise d'Urfé's regeneration, along with Gaetano, whose status as a cleric – albeit a disgraced one – would hopefully lend some weight to the proceedings, and Passano, who was to play the part of Querilinte, the invented leader of the Rosy Cross.

The marquise had arrived in Marseille an impatient three weeks early, and she was eagerly awaiting Casanova's arrival at the best hostelry in town, the Swiss-run Auberge des XIII Cantons. Their initial conversation consisted of absurdities on her side, and on his

'nothing but falsehoods which had no trace of either truth or plausibility'.[25] Yet again, she was fooled into thinking that she was about to be regenerated as a man. In preparation for meeting Querilinte, she had prepared seven gifts for him, each dedicated to one of the seven planets and each containing seven pounds of precious metal and a seven-carat jewel. Since Casanova had no intention of letting Passano get his hands on these valuables, he persuaded the marquise that they must be placed one by one in a special casket which he himself would look after for safe-keeping.

Now, more than at any other time, Casanova cynically played on the marquise's gullibility. The operation which was about to take place was the culmination of five years' work on his part, and, since it might be his last chance of getting hold of her money, he was determined that nothing should go wrong. But his carefully-laid plans started to unravel during the marquise's first meal with Passano/Querlinte, who was so thrown by her bizarre line of questioning that he was rendered almost speechless. Two days later, he fell gravely ill with a venereal infection, took to his bed and announced to Casanova that he 'didn't give a f . . . for the marquise'. Meanwhile Gaetano acted like an imbecile in public and, in private, ranted against his brother for having stolen Marcolina from him. Insisting that he had won the beauty by the right of the strongest, Casanova threatened to have Gaetano arrested, then changed his mind and blackmailed him into boarding a Paris-bound diligence instead. 'That was how I got rid of him,'[26] he wrote with evident satisfaction in his memoir, unconsciously echoing the same phrase he used to describe how his mother Zanetta had disposed of him on his ninth birthday.

Passano may have been out of action, but that did not prevent him from issuing threats from his bed when he discovered that Casanova had kept the precious gifts which the marquise had intended for him. He demanded a thousand louis to keep quiet, and when Casanova called his bluff he wrote the marquise an eight-page letter telling her everything. This was the second time that she had heard the truth from one of Casanova's accomplices. But, as in

the case of Corticelli, Casanova took the precaution of blackening Querilinte's character in the marquise's eyes, again with the help of his oracle. Passano's letter, which the marquise gave to Casanova to read, may well have planted suspicions in her mind, but she was so eager for the operation to go ahead that she brushed them aside, saying that the letter was gibberish: she did not understand it, and moreover 'she did not choose to understand it'.[27] Casanova used the reprieve to get rid of Passano, whom he forced to leave for Lyon even though he was so ill he could scarcely stand up.

Left only with the compliant and adoring Marcolina to help him, Casanova fixed a date for the second regeneration ceremony. This time he was to impregnate the fifty-seven-year-old marquise while Marcolina, in the guise of an undine, or elemental spirit, conjured up out of nowhere, danced about naked in the background. Her purpose was as much to arouse Casanova as to impress the marquise, for the great lover doubted his own ability to perform to order with the older woman: 'I might find myself incapable. At the age of *thirty-eight* I was beginning to see I was often subject to that fatal misfortune.'[28]

The marquise was as nervous of the encounter as he was himself, though for different reasons. It is likely that Casanova had become her lover when they first met in 1758, but during the five years since they had often been apart, and she was perhaps now more conscious of the difference in their ages. Beautiful as she was, she was by no means young any more, and when she prepared for her part as the spirit Seramis, she sought to disguise her age by wearing an exquisite gold and silver dress, a pale lace mantle over her exposed bosom and too much rouge on her cheeks. Awed by the sudden appearance of the silent undine (since Marcolina spoke only Italian, Casanova had thought it best if she pretended to be a mute), she let the spirit undress and bathe her before Casanova – or rather Paralisée Galtinarde, as he had named himself for the occasion – made love to her three times, urged on by Marcolina who cavorted lewdly in the nude behind the marquise's back. Casanova's fears of impotence were almost realised. Though the marquise, 'tender, amorous, clean, and

not at all disgusting', did not displease him, by 'the second assault' he himself was tiring: 'I get in the lists, I work for half an hour, groaning in a sweat, and tiring out Seramis without being able to come to a conclusion and feeling ashamed to cheat her; she wiped my brow of the sweat mixed with pomade and powder which dripped from my hair; the undine, by giving me the most provocative caresses pre-served what the old body I was obliged to touch was destroying, and nature disavowed the effectiveness of the means I was employing to reach the finishing line. Towards the end of the hour I finally determined to finish having counterfeited all the usual signs which appear at that sweet moment.'

This, the first faked male orgasm in literature and a description as cruel as it is hilarious, was later followed by another: 'I decided to cheat for a second time by an agony accompanied by convulsions which ended in motionlessness, the necessary outcome of an agitation which Seramis, as she told me afterwards, found unexampled.'[29]

The marquise was convinced that she was pregnant with the male half-mortal into whom her soul would one day be transferred. To believe otherwise would have meant acknowledging Casanova's immense betrayal over the course of some five years. However, Passano's letter, coupled with the story that the Countess Lascaris/ Marianna Corticelli had told her in the past, planted doubts in her mind which would not go away. And now that the operation was over, Casanova was almost too sure of himself. In Lyon a fortnight later (he had sent the marquise on before him, and trailed behind with Marcolina in his own carriage, which, as we have seen, broke down outside Henriette's house on the way) he pressed the marquise into making legal arrangements for her confinement. These included drawing up a will in his favour and making provi-sion for herself to be looked after financially, presumably by him, once her soul was transferred into the body of the infant she believed she was carrying.

Casanova had not reckoned with Passano's persistence. Lying ill in bed in Lyon, he decided that Casanova had poisoned him. By

now he had become the adventurer's implacable enemy, intent on exposing him as 'the greatest scoundrel on earth . . . a sorcerer, a falsifier, thief, spy, coin-clipper, traitor, card sharp, slanderer, an issuer of false letters of exchange, a forger of handwriting, and in short the most despicable of all men',[30] as he told the local banker Bono. Roping in Gaetano to testify against his own brother, Passano attempted to bring Casanova to court, and only dropped the case when Casanova threatened to counter-sue him. Eventually Casanova blackmailed his brother into leaving Lyon for Paris, and Passano settled out of court for the sum of 100 louis, a mere tenth of the amount he had originally demanded.

It seemed that Casanova was going to get away with his deception after all. In his memoirs he claimed that, back in Paris at the very end of May, he and the marquise were on the best of terms, laughing together at her doctor's amazement that a woman of her age could be pregnant. Yet by 10 June he had abruptly left France for England, taking Giuseppe Pompeati, now known as the Count of Aranda, with him. He had been summoned to return Giuseppe to his mother, Teresa Imer, who was by now a successful impresario living in London and wanted her son back – but was that the only reason why Casanova left in such a hurry? Had he perhaps got wind that the marquise was suspicious of him and that Passano was not only on his tail but already in the marquise's pay? During the first week of June Passano wrote to Teresa Imer in London warning her against the adventurer, soliciting information about him and promising her in return 'a detailed account of his character'. He had heard that she and Casanova were married, he said, and he wanted to know whether this was true and to find out what she knew of him. Teresa's reply, written on 28 June, very likely with Casanova sitting beside her in her London mansion, Carlisle House, Soho Square, assured Passano that Casanova was not her husband but a dear family friend whom she had known all her life, and that she knew 'nothing of him other than honour and integrity, and towards me (as I do not doubt towards everybody) the actions of an honest man'.[31]

Teresa's letter reached Passano in Lyons on 7 July. Copying it out on thinner paper – the original being too heavy, and therefore too costly, for him to send on – he forwarded it to 'my adorable patroness' as he now addressed the Marquise d'Urfé. Throughout his letter he referred to Teresa as a strumpet, and to the dark-skinned Casanova as Goulenoire – a misspelling of Gueulenoire, meaning Blackface – calling him a thief, a liar and a debauched rogue given to ridiculing others. 'I forgot to tell you that Goulenoire wrote to M. Bono that he is never coming back,' he added as a postscript, 'and that he will pay for the calash and his debts with a bill of exchange.'[32]

Passano had indeed been to see the banker Bono that very day to show him Teresa's letter, for the banker immediately wrote to Casanova: 'It is true, and I hold it certain that the marquise is not at all pleased with you.'[33] Casanova could scarcely have been surprised at this news. He had lied to, cheated and stolen from the marquise for years. He had humiliated her in her own eyes as well as the eyes of the world, and he had now taken back the one tangible thing he had given her: her beloved Count of Aranda. Sadly, instead of coming to her senses, the marquise fell straight into Passano's slippery hands. She sent him an antidote to cure him of the poison that he believed was still afflicting him; she let him make purchases on her behalf; and she trusted him to pursue her grievances against Casanova. Rather than bewitching her as Casanova had done, Passano was fawning, pathetic and over-obsequious. 'I wish to have the honour of kissing your hand before I die,' he wrote to her on 11 July. 'My adorable patroness, you can make me happy; but maybe my crimes are so great that they make you disposed to hate me rather than do me a service . . . I am guilty but innocently. Chastise me by depriving me of your amiable self. I deserve it. Goulenoire, in one of his letters to M. Bono, calls me a monster. He is not right to give me such an epithet. You, madame, who find yourself deceived by a deceived wretch, have more reason to call me a monster. Oh well, I deserve to die, and your murderer has been my executioner. I will leave this world, and I will leave it

with all the resignation and happiness of having in part contributed to your not being sacrificed by this monster who calls me a monster . . . I have always found you generous, do not abandon me at the moment where I am either going to die or return home. Here and elsewhere I will do everything I can to show you marks of my repentance and devotion, my divine patroness . . .'[34]

Brutally honest in his memoirs about many unflattering aspects of his life, Casanova could not bring himself to tell the truth about the end of his relationship with the Marquise d'Urfé. In order to explain it, he took the well-trodden path of many writers of fiction and killed off his heroine prematurely. 'The first of August was an ill-fated day . . . for me,' he wrote of his stay in London in 1763. 'Among others, I received a letter from Paris, announcing the death of Mme d'Urfé.'[35] The cause of her death was a self-administered but accidental overdose of her own medicine, the universal panacea, he claimed, and all Paris was agog at her will, which bequeathed her fortune to a child she claimed she was carrying, and which also named Casanova as the baby's guardian. Casanova insisted that he was dumbfounded by the news of her death. Well he might have been, for the marquise was very much alive at that time. The letter he received would have informed him only that she now knew the truth about him and was dead *as far as he was concerned*. As he admitted elsewhere in his memoirs, 'I learned that my good Mme d'Urfé had died, or had become wise, which for me would have had the same result.'[36]

Not only was the relationship that had sustained him financially for more than half a decade at an end, but from now on Casanova had to avoid Paris, his favourite city. Due to his own greed he was finished there. When he next visited it, briefly, in 1767, he ran into the Marquis de Lisle, one of the marquise's nephews, who loudly remarked to his friends that the adventurer had stolen a million francs from his aunt. Two days later, Casanova received a letter of cachet ordering him to leave Paris within forty-eight hours and, furthermore, expelling him from France. He did not return to Paris again until 1783, and then only for another brief stay.

The Marquise d'Urfé's last years were spent at one of her many Paris addresses, a house in the rue des Deux-Portes, where she was looked after by a vast retinue of servants and where she eventually brought her one surviving grandson, Achille, to live with her. Her experience with Casanova may have taught her to be less trusting of the living, but she still stubbornly retained her belief in the dead. Among her papers was found a letter she wrote to her husband's ancestor, the writer Honoré d'Urfé, who had died in 1625. Although it is undated, it appears to have been written after the end of her relationship with Casanova. The marquise assured the dead author of *L'Astrée* that she had 'the pleasure of learning that you are still among the living' and unwittingly revealed not only her ambitions but also the depth of her disappointment and loneliness:

'What would I not do to have the pleasure of seeing you, and of trying to merit your friendship, which is more precious to me than life itself . . . You know how to scrutinise the depths of hearts. How happy I would be if you found in mine the qualities necessary for entering into the sublime company of sages for which I have sighed for such a long time. You have not ignored all my misfortunes. You know that the attachment and the respect that I have always had for your illustrious blood has caused the greatest part of them, losing in them everything which attached me to life. Come, monsieur, heal all my losses by taking the place of a father (I hope I am allowed to call you by this sweet name), and deign to enlighten someone who would sacrifice everything for the happiness of spending her days near you. Receive me like the prodigal child. Forget all my aberrations, which have only been caused by the desire to learn the true science. You know the critical situation I find myself in today. Deign to honour me with your advice, and do not suffer that she who has the honour of bearing your name should be tricked into mistaking black for white, and that the thing which should lead to supreme happiness by bringing us close to the All-Powerful should prove a fatal stumbling block to virtue. I dare to hope that you will not refuse

me this mercy and that of adopting me as your daughter and regarding me as the most submissive of your slaves. JEANNE, marquise d'Urfé.'[37]

Casanova, and alchemy, continued to preoccupy the marquise's thoughts. On 5 May 1769, she wrote out a list of questions to her late husband. They were 'a testimony of the enigmas that Casanova should solve with the help of his pyramids'. She wanted to know what had become of the powder of projection that had once belonged to the d'Urfés, and how she could get hold of it. Were any other members of the d'Urfé family still alive in the world? What did she have to do to understand the Kabbalah? What was the name of her good spirit? Who could put her magic mirror together again?[38]

The Marquise d'Urfé died just after midnight on 13 November 1775. Among her papers were found two sealed packets, on which were written: 'I pray that my executor should set fire to this packet without opening it. I have given my word about this, and I beg him to redeem it. They do not contain papers which relate to me nor to anything of mine.' On 19 December, these packets were opened in the presence of her nephew the Comte de Lastic, and the contents were immediately burned. Her will had been made the previous February. In it, she completely disinherited her daughter Adélaïde, who was still imprisoned in the convent of Conflans after thirteen years, in favour of Adélaïde's son, Achille.

His grandmother had belonged very much to the *ancien régime*, but Achille de Châtelet, who had just turned sixteen when he inherited the vast family fortune, grew up to be distinctly modern and egalitarian in his outlook. His wastrel parents had personified some of the most decadent aspects of the French aristocracy. By contrast, Achille joined the army, put his name to Anglo-American political philosopher Thomas Paine's call for royalty to be abolished, and fought and was gravely wounded during the 1789 Revolution. Arrested in 1793 because of his Girondine friendships, Achille wrote an impassioned letter to the Convention: 'Repre-

sentative Citizens, when the king was powerful, I dared to have it posted up that royalty should be abolished, and when he offered me favours, I rejected them with disdain. At the beginning of the war, I shed my blood for my country. After thirteen months of suffering, and with my wound still open, I demanded to take up my army post again, and I did not ask to retire until I saw through experience that I was too crippled to be able to carry out my duties and that my wound was deteriorating in the most dangerous way. After this conduct, I am rather surprised to find myself arrested by the surveillance committee of the town of Aire, whose motives are impossible for me to divine. I have perhaps a right to claim favours from the republican government. I ask for none, only for justice. So I beg you to make me acquainted with the reasons for my detention, to punish me promptly if I am guilty, and, if I am not, to allow me to be taken home, to Auteuil, to receive medical assistance, of which I have the greatest and most pressing need. *Salut et fraternité*. A. Duchastellet.'[39]

Achille died before his trial, on 10 or 11 April 1794, amid rumours that he was poisoned. 'This century was not worthy of him,' wrote one of his fellow-prisoners. 'His lights, his talents and his virtues would have honoured the finest days of Athens and Rome.'[40]

Such praise could not have been heaped on Marianna Corticelli, whom Casanova also killed off prematurely in his memoirs, claiming that she died in 1763 during a cure for venereal disease that he himself had paid for. This was a lie. After falling out with him over the marquise's gift to her of a casket of jewels – the value of which could have changed her life for the better – the giggling, reckless Bolognese dancer Casanova had seduced when she was just thirteen years old lived on for years. She danced her way through the theatres of Paris, Berne, Venice and Turin, and became embroiled in a series of abusive relationships with a succession of violent men who stole from her, took advantage of her, and promised her money but gave her none. A brute named Masson de Pressigny, with whom Corticelli lived in Paris in 1767, gagged her and beat her up so badly

that she had a miscarriage When she went to law to prevent him from harming her any further, Pressigny counter-claimed that he had paid off her huge debts, that she had run off with other men, and that she had been debauched before she met him.[41]

Corticelli had no cushion of wealth to stop her from hitting rock bottom. A life of poverty, violence, prostitution and its inevitable consequences – frequent pregnancies and venereal diseases – took its toll on her. Her death in Turin on 14 December 1773 earned a mere postscript in a letter to Casanova from his friend, the Comte de Perouse. 'P.-S. Corticelli, whom you knew long ago, died here yesterday of a high fever after only a few days of illness, she was engaged as third dancer at the Grand Theatre. Be calm, for she edified everyone. In her convulsions she made her last nude appearance in front of her confessor, for before she died she walked about completely naked in her room.'[42]

At the time of her death Marianna Corticelli was twenty-six years old. She had been a prostitute for half her life.

NINE

Marianne de Charpillon and Pauline

All women, respectable or not, are for sale.
When a man has the time, he buys them
with his attention, and when he is in a hurry
as I am he makes use of gifts and gold.[1]

THIRTEEN-YEAR-OLD Marianne de Boulainvilliers stood beside her aunt in a jewellery shop in Paris's Palais Marchand, and gazed with longing at a pair of shoe-buckles in one of the display cabinets. Set with small pieces of *strass*, glass tinted and cut to resemble precious stones, the buckles were not the most expensive ones in the shop, but they were pretty and colourful and sparkly, and Marianne coveted them.

The shopkeeper broke off her conversation with Marianne's Aunt Julie, opened the cabinet, took the buckles out and handed them to the girl with a smile. They cost only three louis, she simpered, and are a bargain at the price. Marianne gazed wistfully down at them, knowing full well that Julie would never buy them for her. Other people in Paris were veritably dripping with wealth – there were two in the shop now, a grown-up lady with a trilling laugh and her gentleman companion, a dark giant bristling with diamonds and lace – but her own family lived a hand-to-mouth existence. Along with the great number of gentlemen callers who knocked at their front door there came a never-ending stream of

creditors demanding payment. If there were ever louis to spare in their all-woman household they were spent on meals and wine, or on paying off nosy police inspectors, or on pretty clothes for Marianne's mother Rose, so that she could go out and earn money for all of them.

Marianne turned over the buckles with her surprisingly long, slender fingers, then looked up wistfully into her aunt's disapproving face. A petite child with a mass of chestnut hair, delicate bone-structure and startlingly blue eyes set in a pale china-doll face, she had a sweet, open countenance that gave her an almost noble air. If she owned these buckles she would be really happy, she muttered. But it was no good – with a movement as rough as her voice, Aunt Julie snatched them away from her, banged them down on the counter and pulled Marianne towards the shop door. 'I'll give you a better price – just two louis!' the shopkeeper called after them. Aunt Julie ignored her.

As she was hauled past the smart lady and gentleman, Marianne stopped and dropped a low curtsey as she had been taught to do. To her surprise, the lady bent down and kissed her, told her that she was as pretty as an angel and asked her name. The child was Mademoiselle Marianne de Boulainvilliers, her niece, Aunt Julie answered before she had a chance to speak. The giant gentleman looked down on her admiringly, then smiled at her aunt and said, 'Are you so cruel that you would refuse such a pretty niece these buckles, which she insists would make her happy?' And then he said, 'Will you allow me to make her a present of them?' And before Aunt Julie could say anything he plucked the buckles off the counter and pressed them back into Marianne's hands.

The astonished girl looked up at her aunt beseechingly. After a hesitation which seemed to last for ever, Julie told her in a gentle voice that yes, she could accept the present and that she should give the kind gentleman a kiss. The shopkeeper beamed. 'Those buckles only cost three louis,' she told Marianne's benefactor. 'What?' Aunt Julie said, her face suddenly clouding with anger. 'But you just told me I could have them for two!'

As the two women began to haggle furiously over the price of the buckles, the bottom dropped out of Marianne's world. For a brief moment the beautiful trinkets had been hers; now Aunt Julie was making a scene about the price and it seemed they were already slipping out of her grasp. She tightened her grip on them. 'Put them down, Marianne,' Aunt Julie said in a tone of voice that could not be disobeyed. She would not allow the kind man to be taken advantage in this way, she said. If he really wanted to spend three louis on her niece, why didn't he give the money directly to her, and they would go to another shop where they could buy buckles twice as pretty as these for the same price?

After she finished speaking there was a moment of awkward silence. Then the gentleman smiled with amusement and slowly put some coins on the counter: first one louis, then a second, then a third. Before Aunt Julie could object again, the shopkeeper snatched them up and pushed the buckles back towards Marianne. The bargain had already been struck, she said, the money was hers and the buckles belonged to the girl. But Aunt Julie was not in a mood to let this go. As insults flew through the air as thick and fast as mud splattering behind carriage wheels, a crowd of curious onlookers gathered outside the door. The shopkeeper was a cheat! Aunt Julie yelled. And she was a bawd! the shopkeeper shouted back.

They would have come to blows had not Marianne's benefactor – Giacomo Casanova – taken Aunt Julie's arm and gently led her out of the shop. Then he strolled off through the crowd arm-in-arm with his lady friend, Madame Baret, having taught Marianne one of the most valuable lessons of her life: if rich men like you, they give you nice things.

This was the first meeting between Casanova and Marianne Geneviève de Boulainvilliers, later known as Marianne de Charpillon. When they met again four years later she thanked him for his generous gesture by becoming his torturer. He wrote of their second meeting in London, 'It was on that fatal day at the beginning

of September 1763 that I began to die and I ceased to live.'
Casanova was thirty-eight years old, wealthy, successful and, he
had presumed until then, highly attractive to women. Sixteen-year-
old Marianne de Charpillon would show him otherwise. As a lover,
she almost destroyed him.

Marianne was born into a family of unscrupulous prostitutes.
Catherine Brunner, her grandmother, came from a respectable
family in Bern, Switzerland, where her father was a devout pastor.
After his death, Catherine and her three younger sisters found
themselves short of money, and in order to keep themselves in style
they took up a life of easy virtue in the brothels of the town.
Though Bern was a relatively small city, thousands of foreigners
passed through it and, along with the famous bear-pits, there were
plenty of bawdy inns to cater for them, as well as several dis-
reputable bath-houses along the banks of the River Aare. As one
French tourist reported, 'While you are preparing for your bath,
the house-girls arrive in succession, each carrying something, one
some wine, another some bread, a third the cheese. She who seems
to please you most stays with you and, putting no limits on her
compliance, gets right into the bath with you.'[2]

Catherine Brunner became the mistress of a married man named
Michel Augspurgher. She took his name and had several children
by him, including Marianne's mother Rose, who was born around
1721. Had Catherine played her cards right, she could have
married her lover after his wife died, but she appears to have
preferred her libertine lifestyle to respectability, and their relationship foundered. So, instead of being recognised as the legitimate
daughter of a Swiss burgher, when still a child Rose Augspurgher
was exploited by her mother and forced to follow her into what
would eventually become a three-generation family business.
'Scarcely was she able to burble her first words than she was
corrupted,' a French police inspector later wrote of Rose's childhood. 'The cabarets of the Bear, the Star, the Savage and the
Golden Key in and around Bern were the temples wherein the
premises of this young victim were sacrificed to Venus. Under her

mother's eyes and guidance, she made great progress and had so little choice in the matter that by fourteen years of age she had become the leftovers of the grooms and lackeys of the town.'[3]

By 1739, the Bern authorities had had more than enough of the Augspurghers' outrageous behaviour. So eager were they for them to leave the city that they gave them a hundred écus to speed them on their way. Armed with the recipe for a cure-all tonic which she called her *baume de vie* or 'balm of life' and intermittently sold to make money, Catherine led her motley family troupe to Paris via the Franche-Compté, where it is thought that twenty-five-year-old Rose gave birth to Marianne on 1 November 1746. According to Ange Goudar – adventurer, gambler, writer and a friend of both Casanova and the Augspurghers – the baby's father was the Marquis de Boulainvilliers, a well-known libertine from that area.

Once they reached Paris, Catherine Augspurgher rented furnished rooms above a cobbler's shop in the rue Pagevin. Her sister Julie was sent out to reel in punters, young Rose was put to work satisfying them, and Catherine fleeced them for all they were worth. Rose's most illustrious lover at this time was the Prince of Lichtenstein who set her up in an apartment and settled an income on her; but when he realised that he was being taken for a ride by her aunts and mother he soon abandoned her. 'It would be difficult to put a number here to those to whom they have distributed their favours,' stated a police report on the Augspurgher women compiled about ten years after they had settled in Paris. According to gossip, both Rose and her mother Catherine had slept with the same merchant who had made both of them pregnant at the same time. The inevitable consequence of so much promiscuous sex was venereal disease, and at least one of the women's clients was so badly infected by them that he was left 'in a state of never being able to hope for a recovery'.[4]

By 1750, the five Augspurgher women – Catherine, two of her sisters, her daughter Rose, and young Marianne – were living together in rooms in Paris's rue et porte Saint-Honoré. Marianne was now four years old, her grandmother and great-aunts were in

their forties or early fifties, and Rose was estimated to be some-where between twenty-eight and thirty years old, 'tall, good-look-ing, brunette, with beautiful slanting eyes, and with the exception of rouge and the white paint which she slathers on the pimples and growths on her face, she would be a tasty enough morsel.' Their household caused nothing but trouble to the authorities: out of vengeance or professional jealousy they shopped other women to the police for living off immoral earnings; they pretended to be duchesses in order to trick aristocrats out of their money; and they falsely denounced their creditors for being traitors to Louis XV. All in all, the Augspurghers were a bunch of 'dangerous females' who spun 'an abominable web of calumnies and falsehoods'.[5] Despite this Rose had a string of devoted admirers, several as crooked as her family, including a Swiss rascal named De Thormann, who offered to take the Augspurghers around the courts of Europe, conning wealthy men out of their fortunes, and Comte Antoine-Louis-Alphonse-Marie de Rostaing, the black sheep of a noble family from the Vendôme.

Rostaing was a professional gambler and a crook. At the same time as he was seeing Rose he was also involved with Marguerite Brunet, the female pimp who acted as Casanova's procuress in Paris. Forced to flee France in the late 1750s because of his debts, Rostaing persuaded Rose to accompany him to England. Like a close-knit troupe of gypsies, her grandmother and aunts de-camped with her to London where, using the name Deschar-pillon, they settled in Denmark Street in the crowded parish of St Giles, on the fringes of fashionable Soho. Here Rose underwent a mercury cure for a terrible case of syphilis she had caught from Rostaing. Her health was permanently ruined by it. From now on, the family she had once supported would increasingly have to support her.

Her daughter Marianne had already begun to blossom into the woman whom Casanova would describe as 'a beauty in whom it was difficult to find a single fault'.[6] The child who had caught his eye in Paris's Palais Marchand had grown tall and slender, with

delicate bone-structure, unusually elongated fingers and tiny feet. Her bright blue eyes appeared bluer because of her great pallor, which was set off by glossy light auburn hair. This beauty proved Marianne's curse, for now that Rose was too ill to work, the ageing Augspurghers looked to their youngest member to keep them. Like her mother before her, Marianne was to have no choice in the matter. Whether she liked it or not (and at times she clearly found it highly distasteful), she was forced to use her charms to reel in dupes for Catherine's shady business schemes and Rostaing's crooked games of cards. From her mid-teens onwards, Marianne's *raison d'être* was to be milked by her family as if she were a cash-cow. Unpleasant as this burden was, her affection for them ensured that she never shirked it. As her future lover, the MP and popular hero John Wilkes, would later write of Marianne 'Her whole life has been sacrificed to others.'

'Not yet on the wide streets'[7] when George III came to the throne in 1760, fourteen-year-old, fresh-faced Marianne was nevertheless being touted around the vast metropolis by her Aunt Julie in the hope of attracting a wealthy, generous benefactor. There were plenty to be had. London, with its population of three-quarters of a million people, was a magnet which drew in everyone from wealthy aristocrats to foreign artists, and from diplomats to poor country girls trying to better themselves. Since there was no professional police-force to speak of, the streets were thronged with petty criminals. From the labyrinthine old City in the east to the new, spacious residential districts of Marylebone, Soho and Westminster, pickpockets and cut-throats crowded the pavements, relieving the nobility of their diamond watches and lace hand-kerchiefs and the poor of their loaves of bread and parcels of laundry. Violent muggings were commonplace, even during the daytime, and anyone who walked around in court dress was liable to be attacked by the rebellious mob.

Sex was readily available on the streets. Prostitutes, whores and bawds were everywhere – it was estimated that as many as 30,000 them worked in the Marylebone district alone. They sold them-

selves in the backrooms of taverns, solicited on almost every corner, and had their names and addresses listed in well-circulated publications such as *Harris's List of Covent Garden Ladies*, a pamphlet freely available under the porticos of Covent Garden market – another favoured haunt for prostitutes. Designed primarily for out-of-towners, *Harris's List* gave the women's names and addresses along with their histories, their natures, titillating sexual details and even their faults. Miss Hamon of York Street had entered the business after having been 'debauched by a Scotch gentleman in the army'. Miss L– of Castle Street, though uneducated, was a 'lovely fountain of Transport . . . Her yielding limbs though beautiful when together are still more ravishing when separated.' The predominant passion of Miss R–ad of Queen Anne Street 'seems for horses, hounds and the delights of the field. No one is more emulous than our heroine to be in at the death.' Miss W–ll–ms of Upper Newman Street had 'a peculiar art in raising them that fall and bringing the dead to life. Two pounds Two shillings is the price of admission to enter her un-furnished parlour, which we are convinced is at a moment's notice ready for the reception of any gentleman.' Miss Godf–y, a lively twenty-two-year-old 'very fond of dancing', who resided in the same street, was 'a kind of boatswain in her way and when she speaks every word is uttered in a thundering and vociferous tone . . . extraordinary good companion for an officer in the army as she might save him the trouble of giving word of command.'[8]

The Augspurghers did not intend Marianne to become a common prostitute but instead a high-class courtesan who could command a good price for her favours. Some of the best places to attract a rich man were London's pleasure gardens – Chelsea's Ranelagh House, the Marylebone Gardens and the New Spring Gardens at Vauxhall – which were the only venues in the vast metropolis where Londoners socialised regardless of wealth and rank. Relatively cheap to get into – entrance fees ranged from a shilling to half a crown – the gardens were one of the city's main leisure attractions. With their heated dancing pavilions, lantern-lit

walls, mock classical ruins and tree-bordered paths they formed the perfect backdrop for young beauties to make an impression on gentlemen, and provided endless opportunities for making assignations – and even, in the dark shadows behind the trees and shrubs, for consummating them.

It was at Vauxhall Gardens in the summer of 1762 that Marianne de Charpillon was spotted by Francesco Lorenzo Morosini, the new Venetian ambassador to the Court of St James, and former ambassador to France. In her mid-teens, perfectly-formed, stunningly beautiful and no doubt with the highly-prized commodity of her virginity still intact, Mademoiselle de Charpillon appeared to be just what Morosini was looking for to amuse him during his one-year sojourn in London. Using the adventurer Ange Goudar as his intermediary, he paid a formal visit to Marianne's home, then summoned Goudar to his official residence in Soho Square and set out his conditions in a written document – a common practice at the time, not dissimilar to modern-day prenuptial contracts. In it, Morosini proposed renting a small furnished house where Marianne was to live and receive no one but himself, in return for which he would pay her fifty guineas a month. To this agreement, which had to be signed by Marianne's mother, Goudar added his own coda: when the ambassador left England at the end of his posting, he himself was to enjoy Marianne's charms for one night. (Months after Morosini left England, Goudar complained that Marianne had laughed in his face when he demanded his recompense, and that he had yet to enjoy the promised night in her arms. Goudar threatened to have Rose arrested for breaking the terms of their agreement.)

Within days an appropriate house was rented, and Marianne was moved into it and handed over to the Venetian, a man more than thirty years her senior. The liaison could not have been a great success, for when he left London the following spring Morosini did not even say goodbye to her properly – it appears that she avoided him. On his way back to Venice via Lyon, he happened to cross paths with Casanova, who was at the time en route to London, and

he entrusted him with a rather ambiguous note addressed to Marianne, which simply said that 'The Procurator Morosini is annoyed to have left without having been able to take his last leave of Mlle Charpillon.'[9] Casanova had no idea that the ambassador's Mlle Charpillon was the same Mlle de Boulainvilliers for whom he had impulsively purchased a pair of shoe buckles in the Palais Marchand four years earlier. When he asked Morosini where in London this Mlle Charpillon resided, the man replied that he had no idea, indicating a remarkable degree of indifference to her. It was left to Casanova to find her or not – it was an unimportant commission, Morosini insisted.

Unaware of the fate that awaited him in Marianne de Charpillon's long, dimpled hands, and with his pockets still overflowing with the Marquise d'Urfé's money, Casanova arrived in London on the afternoon of 13 June 1763 accompanied by his French servant, Clairmont, and Giuseppe Pompeati. After living for four years with the marquise, Giuseppe was to be delivered back to his real mother, Teresa Imer, who needed him to help her run the successful entertainment business she had recently established in Carlisle House, Soho Square. Proudly rejecting the modest accommodation she had rented for him in Soho, Casanova installed himself in a furnished house in Pall Mall, near the court of St James. After only a few weeks of enjoying the capital's many attractions he began to feel bored: what he lacked was a relationship to give meaning to his life. The thousands of readily available London prostitutes would not do. Casanova wanted something more than a brief sexual encounter – a woman he could relate to body and soul. Unsure how to meet one, he conceived the novel idea of advertising for a woman by offering cheap accommodation in return for some female companionship. 'A small Family or a single Gentleman or Lady, with or without a Servant, may be immediately accommodated with a genteel and elegantly furnished first floor, with all conveniences,' read his advertisement for a tenant in the *Gazetteer and London Daily Advertiser* of 5 July 1763, 'to which belong some peculiar Advantages; it is agreeably situated

in Pall Mall, with boarding if required; it may be entered on immediately, and will be let on very reasonable Terms, as it is no common Lodging House, and more for the sake of Company than Profit. Please to enquire at Mrs Redaw's, Milliner, exactly opposite Mr Deard's Toy Shop in Pall Mall, near the Hay Market, St James's.'[10]

The notice caused a minor furore among the fashionable *ton* and brought Casanova to the attention of two extraordinary women. One was Marianne de Charpillon, who, as she later told him, burst out laughing when she read it. The other was a refined Portuguese beauty in her early twenties, to whom Casanova gave the name Pauline in his memoirs.

Refined, chaste, modest and well-educated, Pauline was the daughter of an illustrious Portuguese aristocrat, the Marquis X . . . mo, as Casanova dubbed him (the abbreviation probably stood for Xostimo, a surname pronounced and later written as Cristostomo). On the run from an unwanted arranged marriage, she had fled Lisbon and eloped to England with the man she wished to marry, a low-ranking diplomat named Count Al. . . . Their elopement was discovered almost as soon as their frigate set sail for England, and a fast craft was dispatched to intercept them. By the time the couple disembarked at Plymouth, each disguised as the other, Portuguese officials were already waiting on the dock to take Pauline back home. Since she had swapped identities and clothes with her fiancé, the officials mistook them for each other, and, believing that the count was Pauline, forced him on to a boat back to Lisbon, taking Pauline's trunk of dresses with them. Left alone in England with nothing but the male breeches and shirt she was wearing, Pauline bought herself a few plain but respectable dresses and tried to survive on a pittance until such time as the count rejoined her in London or sent word for her to return to Portugal. Since she could scarcely afford to rent lodgings or eat, the offer of an 'elegantly furnished first floor' in smart Pall Mall to be let 'on very reasonable terms . . . more for the sake of Company than Profit' was too good an opportunity to pass by. Though she must

have been aware that she risked being molested by her landlord, Pauline saw no alternative but to move in.

Virginal Pauline was just the kind of challenge that Casanova relished. Seducing her was not enough for him: the compliance of a woman who was financially dependent on him would have given him as little satisfaction as seducing a woman who was drunk. After knowing her for only one day, he resolved to do everything within his power to win her away from her absent fiancé. The effort that this would involve only increased Casanova's desire, and he did not for a moment doubt his ability to succeed. 'I knew,' he wrote, 'that there was not a woman in the world who could resist the assiduous care and constant attentions of a man who wished to make her fall in love with him.'[11]

Pauline had staked her reputation on marrying Count A1. . . . Although she had shared a cabin with him for two weeks on the voyage to England, they had behaved with such strict propriety that they had never even glimpsed each other naked, let alone made love. Yet soon after she moved into Pall Mall, she allowed Casanova, a virtual stranger, to collect, as he described it, the 'blood-stained sacrifice'[12] of her carefully preserved virginity. By the following morning, when he made his third assault on her – the word is his own – he claimed that Pauline had grown as ardent as he was, and that she was longing for more pleasure. Casanova had accomplished what he had set out to do. It was moments like this that he lived for: a perfect physical union such as he had experienced with Henriette, an emotional experience which filled the unbearable void inside himself. The exquisite pain of knowing that his idyll was finite not only added to his pleasure, it was 'the true foundation' of it.[13]

By the time Pauline was summoned back to Portugal three weeks later, the man who had once meant everything to her and whom she was now to marry had been eclipsed in her heart by Casanova, his formidable, determined, more sexually experienced competitor. Assiduous to the end, Casanova accompanied Pauline across the Channel, parting from her at Calais on 11 August and sending

her on to Portugal under the protection of his trustworthy valet Clairmont. It was Clairmont who became the real victim of the affair: it is believed that he was shipwrecked on his return journey on the *Hanover*, an English vessel that sank on 2 December 1763 en route from Lisbon to England.

'I will never love another woman,' Casanova told his English friend Henry Herbert, Lord Pembroke, three days after parting from Pauline at Calais. The libertine Pembroke was rightly dismissive: Casanova would find another woman within a week, he predicted. In fact it took Casanova three weeks to find Marianne de Charpillon. This time, love would not be a pleasant experience for him. He was due to get a taste of his own medicine. He had deliberately destroyed Pauline's feelings for the man she had loved. Now it was his turn to have a great love ousted from his consciousness by a far less worthy rival.

As soon as her lover the Venetian ambassador had left England, Marianne de Charpillon was sent out to reel in another wealthy punter. The Augspurghers were more in need of money than ever, for their London household had become a sizeable one to support. Since 1762 Ange Goudar, the man who had introduced them to Morosini, had become a regular visitor to Denmark Street, where he had teamed up with Rose's lover Rostaing, and a Frenchman named Coumon whose job it was to bring in dupes he met at London's coffee shops so that they could be cheated out of their money at the Augspurghers' card table. The profits of these card games, and Marianne's conquests, were divided up between the gang of eight.

By now, Marianne had learned how to retain some control over her life by promising the men she attracted far more than she actually delivered. She needed them, but she did not want them, and consequently she enjoyed teasing and even punishing, them for wanting her. Her admirers during 1763 included Frederick Calvert, Richard, Earl of Grosvenor, and the Portuguese envoy Senhor de Saa, but it is unlikely that any of them had more luck with her than

Lord Pembroke himself who, one night at Ranelagh, paid Marianne twenty guineas in advance to go for a stroll with him in a shady walkway – a euphemism for having sexual intercourse or at least indulging in heavy petting. As soon as they left the main path, however, Marianne dropped Pembroke's arm and disappeared into the bushes before he had a chance to take the slightest liberty with her.

One night in September 1763, Marianne and her Aunt Julie turned up at the home of a Flemish officer named Malignan, where Casanova happened to be spending the evening. Marianne sized up the new addition to the London scene immediately. With his fashionable Parisian clothes, his showy jewellery, his enamelled snuffbox and diamond watch, the Italian was clearly a man of means and, it followed, a prospective source of income for her. Yet oddly, given his effect on women in the past, she did not find him in the least attractive. Twenty years her senior, Casanova, at thirty-seven, was beginning to show his age, and though he did not yet realise it he soon would.

When Marianne recognised the Chevalier de Seingalt (Casanova had adopted the French title in 1759 and used it in England), as the man who had given her a pair of buckles in Paris's Palais Marchand four years earlier, she took advantage of this stroke of luck to recall the story. Raising the hem of her dress, a seductive gesture in itself, she showed him that not only did she remember the occasion, she was still wearing the very same buckles on her shoes. Going even further, she reminded him that 'encouraged by my aunt, you did me the honour of kissing me'. The feeling that their meeting was fated was compounded when Marianne told Casanova her name, and like a magician, he produced from his portfolio the letter addressed to her from Morosini. By passing on the note from her ex-lover, Casanova made Marianne aware that he knew her position. Without a trace of embarrassment, she flirtatiously chided him for not having sought her out and delivered it sooner, and she invited him to dine with her family the following day. When he refused because Lord Pembroke was due to dine with him in Pall

Mall, Marianne invited herself and her aunt along, indicating that she was not only available but actively pursuing a relationship with him. She teased Casanova about his infamous newspaper notice advertising for a lodger, and said she had felt like applying for the position herself, because she 'wanted to punish the audacious author of such a notice . . . by making you fall in love with me, and afterwards making you suffer the torments of Hell by the way I treated you. Ah! How I should have laughed!'[14]

As an opening gambit this was daring stuff, guaranteed to put off the faint-hearted. But Marianne had pitched her tone perfectly. Although he responded in a similar fashion, declaring that hers was 'the project of a monster'[15] and that he would stay on his guard, Casanova was fascinated by her. Coming from the smiling lips of a sixteen-year-old whose sweet, seemingly transparent expression seemed to indicate delicacy of feeling as well as nobility of birth, her wicked words seemed little more than a tempting challenge, a teasing slap across the wrist with a velvet glove. Casanova would have done better to have taken Marianne more seriously. When she quipped that the only way for a man to resist her was to not see her at all, she spoke nothing less than the truth.

The following day Lord Pembroke, who had already had his fingers burned by Marianne, warned Casanova that she was 'a little strumpet who will do everything she can to entrap you'. His words fell on deaf ears. Marianne's brazen tone, combined with her innocent beauty, had already captivated Casanova who was confident that he would soon enjoy her charms and quickly tire of them. 'How could I imagine that she would make things difficult for me?' he wrote with hindsight. 'Without even flattering myself that I could please her, I knew that I had money, that I wasn't a miser, and that she would not resist.'[16] When he was invited to Denmark Street a few days later to meet her family, he became even more certain of making an early conquest. For, ill and haggard though Rose Augspurgher was – the mercury cure she had taken for venereal disease had ruined her looks – Casanova remembered her from a previous encounter. He had once sold her some

jewellery through a Swiss goldsmith in Paris. In return, she had given him two bills of exchange for six thousand francs which had never been honoured, and consequently she still owed him the money. Taking this and everything else into account, Casanova assumed that it was a foregone conclusion that Rose's daughter would soon become his mistress.

A relationship with Marianne was always very much a family affair. Seeking safety in numbers on Casanova's first visit to her home, she surrounded herself with her mother, her aunts and her grandmother. Later that night the party was joined by Ange Goudar, Rostaing and Coumon, and against his better judgement Casanova found himself roped in to several rubbers of whist with them. Even though he lost a small fortune at the card table, he still believed that he had his eyes wide open and was risking nothing as long as he concentrated his thoughts on Marianne. He was under-estimating the courtesan, who was as determined as he was to wield the power in their relationship. In her opinion, the Italian was behaving like a classic dupe, and she and her aunts intended to play him for all he was worth.

A protracted game of pursuit and evasion began. But who was pursuing whom? Without letting Casanova have a say in the matter, Marianne invited herself and the entire company to dine at his house in a few days' time. On the appointed day she turned up at Pall Mall at nine o'clock in the morning with her aunt, and insisted on speaking to Casanova privately. Coming straight to the point, she admitted that her family's finances were in chaos, and invited him to invest the sum of a hundred guineas in her aunt's 'balm of life' medicine; in return, he would receive a half-share of any profits, and the capital sum would be refunded to him in six months' time. One hundred guineas was a substantial amount – the equivalent in modern terms is about £10,000. Taken aback, Casanova said he would think about it, and concluding that this was the sum needed to buy Marianne, he sat down beside her on the sofa and moved in to kiss her in a lighthearted manner. To his astonishment, she turned her head away. Eventually she stood up,

smiled, and rejoined her aunt in the next room, leaving Casanova with a clear message: he would get nowhere with her without first showing her the colour of his money.

When the party came to dine with him that evening, Casanova took Marianne aside and promised to give the one hundred guineas to her aunt at the end of the evening. But when he then tried to kiss her she evaded him again. He would get nothing from her with money or by force, she scolded him; in fact she would only give him what he wanted when he behaved as gently as a lamb when they were alone together. Casanova was angry at being teased like a naughty child, and angrier still when Marianne then behaved towards him in front of the other guests with the kind of freedom that seemed to indicate that they were already lovers.

After this, Casanova decided to avoid Marianne in future. She did not pursue him. But when three weeks passed and he failed to appear in Denmark Street, Aunt Julie was dispatched to Pall Mall to tell him that Marianne loved him, but that she feared that his love for her was nothing but a caprice. Her niece, she said, 'only gives herself when she is sure of being loved'. She was at that very moment lying at home in bed with a cold and, Julie assured him, if Casanova came to see her he would not leave unsatisfied. Certain that he was being offered the opportunity to have sex with Marianne, Casanova arrived at Denmark Street fifteen minutes later only to be told that she could not see him because she was upstairs naked in her bath. When he lost his temper, Julie agreed to take him up to her room, adding that if her niece was furious with her she could criticise her all she liked after the event.

Though Casanova presumed that the two women had plotted the scene together, Marianne's behaviour showed that she was genuinely shocked when he suddenly appeared at her bedroom doorway. Cowering down in the bathtub, she warned him to get out, and ignored his command for her to spread her limbs so that he could see more of her. Though he promised not to touch her, Casanova then began to masturbate in front of her. Marianne might not have been a virgin, but at sixteen she was scarcely a woman of

the world. Horrified by this crude behaviour, she turned her back on him as best she could. When he had satisfied himself – the thing was quickly over – Casanova stormed out of the house, throwing a one-hundred-pound banknote at Julie as he left.

Angry contempt and vengeful fury were aspects of Casanova's personality that the women he truly loved rarely saw. Slightly embarrassed, perhaps, by what he had stooped to, he avoided Marianne at the Vauxhall Gardens later that week. To his aston-ishment, she came up to him and flirted as lightheartedly as if the ugly scene in her bedroom had never taken place. Casanova, who had been drinking quite heavily, was captivated by her again and suggested that they take a stroll in one of the darker walkways. Marianne cleverly side-stepped the issue: she wished to be fully his, she said with seeming sincerity, but in the daylight and only after he had called on her every day like a true friend of the family.

Marianne was establishing a pattern which would continue throughout their relationship: she ran away when Casanova pur-sued her, and ran after him whenever he rejected her. Ordered by her family to cultivate Casanova for his money, she preserved her dignity by becoming a tease of the first order, a past-mistress in the seductive arts of flirtation and titillation. With hindsight, Casanova would see how foolishly he behaved in allowing himself to be manipulated by her, but at the time he was too much in her thrall to help himself. He could think no further than that he wanted the tricky, elusive sixteen-year-old and that he was determined not only to have her but to conquer her heart just as he had conquered Pauline's. Used to having women of all classes fall at his feet, he simply could not tolerate the fact that a mere courtesan whose family owed him a great deal of money would consistently reject him. So far he had spent more than one hundred guineas on Marianne and had not received so much as a single kiss in return. Instead of turning him off her, the challenge only added to his determination to succeed with her. He would not be humiliated. Fooled by her constant promises that she would be his entirely *if only he would behave in the right way towards her*, he tried time and

again to please her. But for once the great lover seemed to have lost his touch. Nothing he did was right – or rather, no matter what he did, Marianne somehow managed to wrong-foot him.

With Ange Goudar acting as intermediary, Casanova offered Rose another one hundred guineas for a single night with her daughter; but he refused to pay the money in advance. Marianne was indignant. Appearing at his lodgings in tears early the next morning in tears, she berated Casanova for trying to buy her from her mother; it was an insupportable insult. If he wanted her he should not bargain for her, but rather woo her. He was handling the intrigue atrociously, treating her at first like a prostitute 'and yesterday as if I was an animal without a will of my own, a base slave of my mother's'. The phrase had the ring of bitter truth. If Casanova had dealt directly with her, she said, Marianne would have made him happy without the one hundred guineas. Her only condition would have been 'that you would have paid court to me for just two weeks, coming to my home without ever asking the least compliance from me, we should have laughed, you would have become part of the family, we should have attended promenades and plays together, and at last, having made me madly in love with you, you would have had me in your arms as you would have deserved to have me, not out of compliance, but out of love.' Casanova should try conquering her heart 'like a reasonable lover, and not like a brute'.[17]

As Marianne intended, her reprimands chastised and enslaved Casanova. During the next fortnight he visited Denmark Street every day without so much as trying to kiss her; he arranged outings to the theatre and day trips to the countryside; and he gave her expensive presents, for which she thanked him by letters written in charmingly misspelled French. She did not, she said in one of them, understand why he believed it was her fault that he was filled with bile towards her when she was 'as innocent as a new-born babe' and when she wished only to put him 'in such a sweet and passionate state that your blood will turn into a real clarified syrup, that would surely happen if you follow my advice.'[18] Tantalising promises like

these ensured that Casanova remained well and truly hooked despite his lack of progress with her. Later, he estimated that this period of their courtship alone cost him a hefty four hundred guineas.

His eventual reward was a night spent with Marianne on a mattress on the floor of the family's front parlour, a distinctly unromantic setting. It was an appalling experience for both of them. First Casanova undressed and got into bed. Then Marianne took off everything but her linen shift and, to his chagrin, blew out the candles before slipping into bed beside him. As soon as she lay down, he tried to clasp her in his arms, only to find her as rigid as a corpse. 'Curled up in her long shift, her arms crossed and her head buried in her breast, she lets me say whatever I want, and never answers me at all. When I run out of words, I make up my mind to act, she remains motionless in the same position, and she defies me to do it. I take this game to be a joke, but in the end I am convinced that it is not. I realise that I've been tricked, taken for a fool, the most despicable of men, just as the girl is the most abominable of trollops.'[19] It would have been far easier for Marianne to have let Casanova make love to her, but she continued to resist him. After a futile struggle to unfurl her rigid body, his anger turned into a violent rage. Grabbing hold of her as if she were an inanimate bundle, Casanova tore open the back of her shift from top to bottom and attempted to rape her. Marianne suffered his prolonged attack in silence, never calling out for help and only uncurling once, when she suspected, rightly, that he was trying to penetrate her anally. At the end of three terrible hours, Casanova's hands were around Marianne's throat. Realising that he was about to kill her, he suddenly let go of her, dressed and slammed out of the house, leaving her feverish, badly bruised and covered in scratches.

Despite his violent attack on their youngest member, the Denmark Street coterie still had no intention of letting Casanova slip away. The following morning, Rose threatened to bring legal proceedings against him. The day after that she wrote again, this

time saying that Marianne had admitted that she might have been at fault in the matter too. Next, Marianne was made to write to Casanova, promising to explain her actions if he would receive her. Leaving nothing to chance, the meddling Goudar was dispatched to Pall Mall to inform Casanova that Marianne's resistance had been Rose's idea, and to show him a rapist's armchair, a device which automatically clasped the arms and legs of any woman who sat down in it, forcing their lower back forward and their legs apart. The chair, Goudar said, could be Casanova's for the sum of one hundred guineas; and if he could get Marianne to sit in it, his business would be accomplished in seconds. Casanova balked at the idea. He was aware that the crime of rape carried the death penalty in England, although prosecutions were rare; and he would have derived no satisfaction from obtaining a woman in this way.

Eventually Marianne turned up at his lodgings and, acting the contrite tease to perfection, put out her face for Casanova to kiss (he refused), then lifted her dress to show him where her body was still scarred by the livid bruises and scratches he had inflicted on her. The erotic effect of small glimpses of bruised, naked flesh was too much for Casanova: although he had made up his mind to have nothing more to do with Marianne, he lacked the strength of mind to turn her away. Determined to gain control of the situation, the following day he went to see Rose and offered to establish her daughter in a house of her own on the same terms on which she had lived with the Procurator Morosini, that is for fifty guineas a month. Rose agreed, with the proviso that he pay her an extra one hundred guineas the instant Marianne left Denmark Street.

Now that she was finally to be his, Casanova did not waste another moment. Through Goudar he quickly rented a house at Chelsea, produced a written contract which was signed by both women and, giving Marianne no time to prepare herself, ordered her to throw her possessions into a trunk and leave Denmark Street with him immediately. As their carriage rumbled off down Soho's narrow streets, into spacious Mayfair and out into what was still countryside on the edge of Hyde Park, the victorious Casanova

anticipated the pleasures he imagined lay ahead. What was Marianne feeling? She was being taken away from her beloved family by a man for whom she felt absolutely no desire. A man whose behaviour in the past had revolted her. A man who had recently beaten her black and blue. Although his attack on her had not been entirely unprovoked, she feared Casanova's temper and what he might do to her. Once again she was in a position where she must sacrifice herself on her family's behalf.

When they arrived in Chelsea, Marianne put on a brave face, explored the house that Casanova had rented for her and declared herself delighted with it. They took a walk, chatted in a light-hearted manner and dined together in high spirits. But the moment they went to bed, her resolve to do what she was being paid to do faltered. Though she allowed Casanova to kiss and embrace her, she simply could not bring herself to let him make love to her. Using the excuse that her period had started, she cleverly overcame his objections and put him to sleep 'with caresses'. The following morning she awoke to find him in the process of unlacing her corset to check if she was indeed menstruating. She was not. Infuriated, Casanova tried to rape her for a second time, but Marianne successfully fought him off. As she scrambled out from under the covers and began to throw on her clothes, her 'impertinent mockery', as he described it, provoked him to hit her across the face and kick her off the bed. With blood streaming from her nose, Marianne screamed and stamped her feet until the caretaker came rushing upstairs. Advised that he would be risking arrest if he forced her to remain in the house, Casanova lay in bed fuming while Marianne washed her bloodied face and finished dressing. The caretaker called a sedan chair, Marianne left, and a stupefied, bewildered Casanova returned to Pall Mall and shut himself up in his rooms.

Through Goudar, Rose sent a message to her daughter's attacker that, if he did not immediately return her trunk of clothes to Soho and relinquish all claims on the Augspurgher family, Marianne would accuse him of rape or perhaps even pederasty, a crime which

also carried the death penalty. Rather than face ruin, Casanova capitulated, specifying only one condition: that Marianne receive her trunk from him in person. As he later reflected, he was acting like 'the greatest of fools' by insisting on seeing her. The mere sight of her swollen, bandaged face and tearful blue eyes made him so repentant that he put aside his grievances and once again became a slavish visitor to Denmark Street, where he sat in contrite silence watching his injured victim weep over her needlework.

Casanova had never before encountered such resistance in a woman. The challenge to win her heart was becoming an obsession. During the following weeks he sent her more expensive presents, including an elaborate pier glass and a Dresden tea service for twelve. When he described himself in a note to her as 'the most cowardly of all men'[20] Marianne appeared to forgive him, and invited him to sup with her in her bedroom, where, she said, she would show him unmistakable tokens of her gratitude.

Up in her bedroom that night, before they undressed, Casanova gave Marianne the two unpaid bills of exchange for six thousand francs which he had received from Rose years back in Paris; as soon as Marianne became his mistress, he told her, he would endorse them to her order. Marianne must have been amazed by his foolishness in handing them over before their affair was consummated. As if they were what she had wanted from him all along, she locked them safely in her jewellery case, then immediately burst into tears and refused to have sex with him. If she had ever had any intention of satisfying Casanova, the time had long since passed.

Casanova could not believe that he had allowed Marianne to make a fool of him yet again. When she arrived alone at Pall Mall the following day and offered herself to him he turned her away out of anger and pique, a reaction she may well have been gambling on. Though his pride let him believe that her remorse was genuine, his confidence had received a blow it would never recover from. The great seducer felt demoralised, unmanned, and, he was convinced, cured of his addiction to the tease. 'Such was the state to which Love had brought me in London . . . at the age of thirty-eight,' he

wrote of the moment in his memoirs. 'It was the end of the first act of my life.'[21]

The dangerous dance that the two of them were locked into was far from over, for by now Marianne was as caught up in its intricate steps as Casanova was. Annoyed that he ignored her when they next encountered each other by chance at the home of M. Malignan, under whose roof they had first met, Marianne invited herself along on an expedition to Richmond Palace which Casanova was organising the next day. Situated in a 2,500-acre park twelve miles outside London, the palace had been built by Henry VII in the sixteenth century, and although the turreted brick buildings were no longer a royal residence, the substantial gardens and several of the apartments were open for visits by special arrangement. As their party toured the park, Marianne clung on to Casanova's arm, undeterred by his flood of insults. Once they reached the maze and were separated from the others she pulled him on to the grass and launched what he described as a full-scale, tender amorous attack on him. After resisting her for a while, his desire got the better of his judgement, and he deluded himself into believing that Marianne was offering herself to him then and there. It was the triumph of self-confidence over experience. For just when Marianne seemed to invite him to 'gather the laurel of victory . . . at that very moment, just as I find myself certain of seizing hold of it, she becomes recalcitrant and turfs me off'.[22] Infuriated beyond measure, Casanova refused to be placated by her loving promises that she would spend the night with him at his house. This time he wanted immediate satisfaction – or revenge. He held her down, took out a knife, unsheathed it with his teeth and held it to her throat. With remarkable sangfroid, Marianne declared that if he raped her she would remain lying on the grass afterwards and tell everyone in the party what he had done. The ignominy would have been too much for Casanova, who got to his feet and stomped furiously away. To his amazement Marianne followed him and, when they met up with the others, took his arm and behaved as if nothing had happened.

If Marianne's intention was to torture Casanova, as she had so lightly threatened to do when they were first introduced, she was succeeding admirably. At the end of his tether, he vowed never to see her again and sent a note to Rose, threatening to prosecute her if she did not return his two bills of exchange. The Augspurghers must have laughed when they read it; they had no intention of letting the valuable papers leave their hands. Rose wrote back, expressing surprise at the request, and saying that Marianne would return the bills to him in person 'when you have grown wiser and have learned to respect her'. This effrontery was too much. Armed with two pistols, Casanova made his way to Denmark Street, determined to put an end to the business. But when he saw Marianne's hairdresser enter her house, as he did every Saturday night to put her hair in curl-papers, he decided to wait in the street until the man left.

Casanova hung about impatiently in the cold. Shortly afterwards, he observed Rostaing and Coumon leave the building, but not Marianne's hairdresser. The long minutes turned into hours. The dark street grew even darker. The cold intensified. Still Casanova waited, an angry stalker hovering in the shadows. After what seemed like an age the watch who patrolled the parish every night cried the hour – it was eleven o'clock. Three-quarters of an hour later, a maid opened the Augspurghers' front door and came out into the street. Unable to control himself any longer, Casanova slipped into the hall and opened the parlour door. Inside he saw, 'as Shakespeare put it, the beast with two backs, stretched out on the couch'.[23] The woman who had kept him waiting for sex for months was making love with her hairdresser.

Marianne screamed. As her half-naked lover broke away from her, Casanova mercilessly attacked him with his walking stick. Soon every female member of the household came rushing into the parlour, all of them yelling at him to leave the man alone. When the hairdresser ran off, Casanova turned his fury on the pier glass and Dresden tea set he had given Marianne, while she cowered beside the sofa, sheltering from the explosion of sharp glass and china

shards. When Rose still refused to return his bills of exchange, Casanova dashed the chairs to pieces and threatened to attack the women if they did not stop screaming.

The night watch, whose job it also was to keep the peace in the parish, heard the din and came rushing back to Denmark Street with his stick and lantern. Using the prerogative of the rich, Casanova paid him off with a handful of gold crowns. Meanwhile, taking advantage of the distraction, Marianne fled from the house. This was the fourth time she had suffered from Casanova's violent temper, and she was understandably terrified of what he might do to her. Her disappearance reduced her hardened family to tears. The streets around Denmark Street were dark and treacherous, they wept. Anything might happen to a young woman out alone at midnight. Overcome with remorse, Casanova bribed the maids to go out and find Marianne. He promised the Augspurghers he would pay for the furniture he had broken, and swore that, when she was found, he would beg forgiveness at her feet.

According to her maid, Marianne turned up the following morning in a sedan chair, feverish and in a pitiable state, having taken refuge all night in a shop near Soho Square, a short distance away from Denmark Street. For the next few days Casanova besieged her front door to enquire about her health, only to be told that she was desperately ill. Convinced that he had caused her irreparable harm, he shut himself up at home and neither ate nor slept. On the third day, half crazy with fear and exhaustion, he returned to Denmark Street only to be informed that Marianne was dying.

Determined to commit suicide, he went back to Pall Mall and put his affairs in order, then took his pistols, weighted his pockets with lead balls and headed for the lethal currents of the Thames. On the way, he bumped into Sir Wellbore Ellis Agar, an amiable twenty-eight-year-old acquaintance who, sensing that the foreigner was desperate, dragged him off to an inn for a typical English dinner of roast beef, Yorkshire pudding and oysters followed by a few hours of watching naked young whores dance the hornpipe. After-

wards, Agar insisted that Casanova spend the rest of the evening with him at Ranelagh. Although the adventurer believed that Marianne must be dead by now, the thought of London's pleasure gardens still lured him, and he decided to put off his suicide until the following day.

Marianne was not dead, nor even close to dying. Her spirit was not as easily broken as Dresden china. Having recovered quickly from the shock of Casanova's latest attack on her, she had been wreaking revenge on him by making him suffer. That night she, too, accepted an invitation to go to Ranelagh, in her case with eligible bachelor Lord Grosvenor, the racing-mad owner of a famous horse stud. At the Chelsea Gardens, always one of her favourite haunts in London, Marianne and Grosvenor made their way past the Chinese pavilion to the Rotunda, a huge covered pavilion heated by a vast central brazier which provided essential warmth during cold weather. Here they joined the fashionable crowd in dancing minuets. In the middle of one of the dances, Marianne looked up with smiling eyes, only to see a horrified Casanova staring at her. This time she did not wait for him to attack her, she immediately disappeared into the crowd.

Their chance encounter on the dance floor finally cured Casanova of his desire for Marianne, or so he told himself. But it did not curb his desire for revenge. He went to law and had the older Augspurgher women arrested for refusing to return his bills of exchange. Swearing that she would never grovel to him even to secure their release, Marianne retaliated by seducing the man who had saved Casanova from suicide. Sir Wellbore Agar immediately became her besotted lover, and even paid Casanova 250 guineas to cancel the bills of exchange and secure the release of Marianne's mother and aunts.

'Cursed be the moment when you came to England to make us all unhappy!' Julie Augspurgher had shouted at Casanova on the night he had caught her niece making love with her hairdresser. Thirsty for revenge, Marianne now brought her own legal complaint against her persecutor: she accused him of having attempted

to disfigure her with a knife. Arrested in the early hours of 27 November 1763 on his way home from a glamorous subscription ball at Carlisle House, Teresa Imer's premises, Casanova found himself dragged in all his finery to a bailiff's premises, then hauled before London's most famous magistrate, Sir John Fielding, brother of Henry Fielding, the novelist and author of *Tom Jones*. A brilliant social reformer and legal brain who had been blinded in a childhood accident and was consequently known as the 'Blind Beak', Sir John had such a remarkable ear that it was said he could recognise three thousand London criminals by the sound of their voice alone. It was probably his knowledge of Italian that saved Casanova from a long spell in prison. Able to talk fluently to the accused man in his own language, Fielding bound over 'James Casanova of Pall Mall, Gentleman' to keep the peace 'especially towards Mary Ann Charpillon and Elizabeth Augbour (sic) Charpillon'. Having ordered Casanova to appear in court in mid-December, Fielding released him on bail.[24]

To Marianne's chagrin, her case against Casanova was eventually adjourned from December until the following April, by which time he had fled England, partly to avoid standing trial, and partly because of his involvement in trying to cash an illegal bill of exchange. Over the New Year period in London he continued to persecute Marianne, this time through the mouth of a parrot which he taught to say '*Miss Charpillon is more of a whore than her mother*'. He dispatched his black servant, Jarba, to the Royal Exchange in the City with instructions not to sell the parrot for less than fifty guineas, a sum he was certain that no man would be prepared to pay for it. Day after day, Jarba stood in the Exchange with the talkative parrot. Its repetitive cry, followed by its cackling laugh, attracted a large, amused audience but no buyers, and it was not long before news of the insult filtered down to Denmark Street, as Casanova had hoped it would. The older Augspurgher women were horrified by the scandal but, rather than give Casanova the satisfaction of thinking that he had upset her, Marianne let him know through Goudar that she found the incident extremely

amusing. It is doubtful that she did. Marianne valued herself highly, and the last thing she would have wanted was to become a public laughing stock. When the parrot was eventually purchased, it was by her admirer Lord Grosvenor, who no doubt bought it to spare her further embarrassment.

The parrot's right to free speech would certainly have been championed by Marianne's future lover, John Wilkes, the famous dissident Member of Parliament and rake. In the spring of 1763 Wilkes had published an attack on the king's speech at the opening of parliament in his irreverent opposition newspaper, the *North Briton*, and he had subsequently been incarcerated in the Tower of London for publishing 'a false, scandalous, and seditious libel'. By claiming the privilege of his position as Member of Parliament for Aylesbury, Wilkes prevented the case coming to trial and at the same time turned himself into a national champion of liberty.

On 19 January 1764, while Casanova's parrot was singing Marianne's praises at the Royal Exchange, Wilkes was expelled from the House of Commons. After fleeing to Paris, he was convicted in absentia on two further counts of seditious, obscene and impious libel and declared an outlaw, a move which made him more popular than ever with freedom-lovers on both sides of the Atlantic. Wilkes's warning to Parliament, 'Do not underestimate the sons of liberty', was taken up by an American revolutionary group who thereafter called themselves the Sons of Liberty: their members included John Hancock and John Adams, and such was Wilkes's standing with them that the men asserted that 'the fate of Wilkes and America must stand or fall together'.

By the time he returned to England from France in the early months of 1768, Wilkes had become a popular hero and the Establishment loathed him more than ever. Determined to be a thorn in their side, he immediately stood as Member of Parliament for Middlesex, and won a clear majority. Instead of being allowed to take up his seat, Wilkes was thrown into the King's Bench, a prison usually reserved for debtors. The election was annulled, and the

vote was held again – and then again. Each time Wilkes won a clear majority. When the poll was held for a fourth time with the same result, the government declared their lackey Henry Lawes Luttrell to be the victor even though he had polled fewer votes. Fifteen thousand Wilkes supporters gathered outside the walls of the King's Bench on 10 May to demonstrate on behalf of their imprisoned hero. Troops fired on them, killing seven people and sparking violent protests throughout London.

Three weeks later, Wilkes was sentenced to a further twenty-two months. Protests about his continued imprisonment, co-ordinated by a group of radicals calling themselves the Bill of Rights Society, continued until his release two years later. On 27 February 1770, several months before he was due to be freed, these culminated in a near-riot outside Carlisle House, Soho Square, where a huge masquerade ball was being attended by every aristocrat and government member of any importance, including George III's newly-appointed prime minister, Lord North. Later that year Wilkes was finally released from prison, allowed to take up his seat in the Commons and, at the same time, appointed a sheriff of the City of London. In order to be close to the centre of power, he moved into lodgings in Prince's Court, Great George Street, Westminster with Polly, his daughter from a short-lived marriage.

Marianne de Charpillon was introduced to Wilkes during the autumn of 1773. Nine years had passed since her disastrous entanglement with Casanova, and her attitude to the men she was forced to cultivate had changed. She was now twenty-six, and the mother of a young boy, Tommy Lee. With a son as well as a grandmother, aunts and an ailing mother to support, Marianne's financial responsibilities were greater than ever. For the last four years 'Polite Tommy' Panton, the son of a well-known Newmarket race-horse breeder and half-sibling of the illegitimately-born Duchess of Ancaster, had been her lover; since Marianne's young son bore the same Christian name, he may well have been his child. Although Panton adored Marianne, he was not wealthy enough to keep her, leaving her little choice but to cultivate other admirers.

They included the voluptuary Chase Price, John Wilkes's close friend.

Wilkes's appetite for women was so legendary that posthumously he acquired a reputation as England's answer to Casanova. In his youth he had been a member of Sir Francis Dashwood's infamous Hellfire Club, whose devotees dressed up as monks and held orgies at Medmenham Abbey, an old Gothic monastery on the Thames near Marlow; the club's motto, *Fay ce que voudres* – Do what you will – is still carved on one of the abbey walls above a wooden grating which allowed voyeurs to glimpse the sexual shenanigans taking place inside its great hall. Separated from his wife Mary, Wilkes took numerous lovers including one of his housekeepers, by whom he had had a son in 1760. But although they absorbed his abundant sexual energy, his feelings for them were never deep. As he wrote touchingly to his daughter in 1778, 'I have since (my marriage) often sacrificed myself to beauty, but I never gave my heart except to you.'[25]

With her bright blue eyes, white skin, flowing auburn hair and refined, perfect features, Marianne de Charpillon immediately attracted Wilkes when he met her at a dinner held by Chase Price at the Old Swan Inn in Chelsea on 24 September 1773. In turn Marianne could not fail to have been impressed by him. Born in 1725, making him Casanova's direct contemporary, forty-seven-year-old Wilkes was a notoriously ugly man. As well as having dark bushy eyebrows and a shock of white receding hair, he was almost blind in one eye, and his marked squint gave his face a rather twisted expression. However, his personality more than made up for his lack of good looks. Witty, charming and a great conversationalist – his company was said to be a 'perpetual treat'[26] – Wilkes had a fabulous sense of humour and a great line in repartee: when Lord Sandwich criticised his morals, remarking that Wilkes would either die of venereal disease or on the gallows, Wilkes famously retorted, 'That depends, my lord, whether I embrace your mistress or your principles.' Despite his odd appearance, Wilkes never had any trouble attracting women; he boasted that it took him only half

an hour 'to talk away his face'. And although by the time he met Marianne the one-time romantic dissident was well on his way to becoming an establishment figure (the following autumn he would elected Lord Mayor of London) Wilkes was still very much a public hero.

A fortnight after meeting Marianne at the Old Swan Inn, Wilkes accompanied Chase Price to Black and White Lands Lane, Chelsea, where Marianne was then living. Five days later, on 12 October, he was back there again, this time without his friend. Though her family were always present – Marianne, it appears, still sought safety in numbers – Wilkes's courtship was swift and decisive, as his diary entries for that period show. On the twentieth, he took Marianne and her friend Miss Ratsell on an outing to Chiswick. Within a few days of this, he proposed a deal somewhere along the lines of Marianne's arrangement with the Procurator Morosini, but sensitively taking account of her close relationship with her family. In order to secure her exclusive services, Wilkes would install the entire Augspurgher clan in a house in Great Titchfield Street, just north of Oxford Street and much closer to his own home. Marianne agreed, and the move was made that same week. On 1 November, the MP joined Marianne, Rose, Aunt Julie and Miss Ratsell at number thirty Great Titchfield Street to celebrate both the move and his lover's twenty-seventh birthday. From then on, the busy MP visited Marianne as often as he could.

Was La Charpillon still up to her old tricks of withholding complete sexual fulfilment, even from a man of Wilkes's calibre? The family that had annoyed Casanova so much in the past still surrounded her like a human chastity belt. Within a fortnight of the move, her letters to Wilkes, though full of flattery, already hinted at misunderstandings between them. In one she thanked him for his 'good advice' but added that she considered him 'too kind to reproach me for my ideas since they are in your favour.'[27] In another, she hoped that the next time they met he would be in a calmer, quieter mood, indicating that he had left Great Titchfield Street in a temper. Soon afterwards Marianne warned Wilkes

against putting her in an awkward situation: if he took her advice, she wrote, it was impossible that he would not profit from it, and she wished him 'good health and much pleasure, something that you cannot possibly lack, seeing that you are so much admired by so many people'.[28]

If Marianne did manage to keep Wilkes waiting for sex, it was only for a short period, for on 9 January 1774, his diary entry recorded meaningfully and for the first time that he had 'dined in Titchfield Street with Madam de Charpillon alone'. By then, he had forced Marianne to break definitively with Tommy Panton, with whom she still enjoyed a close relationship. On New Year's Eve she wrote Panton two poems in the French language in which she always communicated. Each of them was charming, humorous and full of affection. The first, in which she referred to herself as 'preti thing', was a catalogue of good wishes for 1774:

> *je souhaite que pour la venir*
> *que vous ne trouvier pas martir . . .*
> *et vous trouverai que preti thing a dis des conseilles*
> *qui son san pareil*

> (I hope for the future
> That you will not be a martyr . . .
> And you will find that pretty thing has given you advice
> That is without equal.)

The second poem pushed him away in the most delicate fashion: if she had cut loose from him, it was for the pleasure of not seeing him ruined by their liaison:

> *je l'ai déchenné*
> *s'est pour le plaisir de ne plus vous voir ruinée.*[29]

Prey to the same insecurities as other men, Wilkes carefully copied out these poems in his own hand and kept them among his papers.

In February, he also copied out a letter Marianne wrote to Chase Price, in which she assured her old friend that she had made the right choice in choosing Wilkes over him.

For the next four and a half years, Marianne and her family enjoyed an unprecedented period of domestic and financial security at the expense of her 'vrais honnorable My Lord Mayor', as she addressed Wilkes after his election to the office in the City of London the following October. Marianne relished having such an important man as her lover, and in order to keep him interested she flirted with him, learned by heart the poems he wrote her from the Mansion House, the Lord Mayor's residence, and sent him charming letters full of domestic details, wit and suggestive remarks. 'Concerning my capricious health, my bizarre wit, and my baroque physiognomy they are all a little better than yesterday.'[30] 'If you are curious to know if I have gained anything from your little lesson this morning, come and experience it for yourself tonight.'[31] She also proved herself staunchly loyal to him. When in July 1775 Wilkes was briefly imprisoned in the King's Bench she wrote on his release, 'you will never go back there, at least I will do everything within my power to make sure you never again speak of the king's banch(sic)'.[32]

Wilkes lapped up the intimate, adoring attentions of this younger, irresistibly beautiful woman. Though he was extremely busy, he saw Marianne as often as he could, sanctioned a correspondence, though not a meeting, between her and his beloved daughter Polly and, aware of the importance of the dreaded Augspurgher entourage, he courted her aunts and mother with almost as much attention as he did her. Within a year, however, cracks started to appear in their relationship. Wilkes simply did not have enough time for Marianne. When he was in London, his business in the City preoccupied him. During the winter months he spent weeks on end far away in the county of Somerset, taking the spa waters in Bath. The domestic routine of Great Titchfield Street continued in his absence. It pleased Catherine, Julie, Rose and Tommy, but Marianne found the way of life claustrophobic and frustrating.

By the summer of 1775, she sensed that Wilkes's interest in her was waning. Though he continued to finance her modest lifestyle, and to send presents for all the family, he seldom came to see Marianne any more. While he went out on the town every night, she was expected to stay at home within the ever-suffocating bosom of her parasitic and increasingly elderly family and await his occasional visits. Too young and spirited to be fobbed off, like her grandmother, with a few chickens, cheeses and 'sugar candy . . . the best I have ever seen' as Catherine Brunner wrote to thank Wilkes after he sent her some, signing herself in her clumsy handwriting 'Charpillon grandmerre',[33] Marianne longed to enjoy all the pleasures London had to offer: the opera, the theatre, concerts and masquerade parties at Carlisle House, and, most of all, the glories of the pleasure gardens where she had, in former days, played cat-and-mouse with the likes of Lord Pembroke and Casanova. But her activities were severely circumscribed by her position as Wilkes's mistress. Although he occasionally allowed her to accompany him to 'Rennella', as she misspelled the name of the famous Chelsea pleasure gardens in her letters, for the most part he went everywhere without her, and disapproved strongly of her going out alone. This resulted in frequent squabbles. Marianne felt torn. She could not decide whether to go to the pleasure gardens alone 'or to make the sacrifice on your behalf', she wrote to Wilkes on 25 June 1775, adding plaintively that she believed 'our long acquaintance has lessened your feelings, and that you have changed your ideas concerning me.'[34]

Since she could not afford to quarrel with Wilkes – her entire family depended upon him – Marianne kept his interest in her going through a mixture of flattery and jealousy. Over the summer of 1776 she hinted that she had a new admirer, but this failed to have the desired effect on him. Though she and Wilkes still corresponded regularly, Marianne rarely saw him. 'As my destiny today is to live a monastic life, I wish to at least break the rules by a correspondence in this style,' she wrote to him with carefully judged wit on 17 February 1777, including with her letter some

of her aunt's *baume de vie*. 'I send you some of the convent's balm; it will do you good but be cautious, it is charmed . . . Adieu my dear father confessor.'[35]

Given that Wilkes so rarely visited Marianne, and was in debt himself, how long would he continue to support her? Marianne attempted to control her anxiety about the future, but on Sunday 11 May 1777, her fears broke through her usual reserve. It was the first time for months that Wilkes had come to dine *en famille* at Titchfield Street, so potentially the occasion was an opportunity for her to win him back. But after they had eaten, an acrimonious row broke out between them, which culminated in Marianne losing her temper completely. *'Monsieur,'* she yelled at the famous John Wilkes, *'Vous m'êtes devenu aussi odieux que ma Mère!'* ('Monsieur, you've become as hateful to me as my mother!') He immediately stormed out of the house, never to return there. His matter-of-fact diary entry for that evening – 'Supped at Madame De Charpillon's in Titchfield Street with Mademoiselle, Madame Topin, and Tommy Lee' – gave no hint as to what had really taken place. But the following morning he wrote Marianne a chillingly cold letter, throwing her last words back at her and breaking off their affair. His letter ended with a short rhyme:

> La plainte est pour le fat, le bruit est pour le sot,
> L'honnête homme trompé, s'eloigne et ne dit mot.[36]

> (The impertinent complain, fools shout,
> An honest man tricked, gets away and says nowt.)

Realising that she had gone too far, Marianne attempted to back-track. Wilkes, she wrote to him hastily that afternoon, had badly misinterpreted what she had said to him. 'I am honest,' she declared, 'that's the interpretation that you should have given to my last words.'[37] If he had only been less suspicious and had had more confidence in her, he would never have written her such an abominable letter. Wilkes was unmoved. He had been seeking an

excuse to shrug off his hefty financial and emotional responsibilities towards the occupants of Titchfield Street, and now Marianne had unwisely handed him one. Although she continued to plead with him for weeks, chiding him at the end of May that 'The amiable Mr Wilkes has become so capricious that I'm in doubt as to whether my writing to you would please you or pain you',[38] by mid-June her tone was downbeat and apologetic. Her spirits, she admitted, were very low, for Wilkes had taken an 'infamous resolution of indifference' towards her. Marianne had almost, but not quite, given up hope of winning Wilkes back. In her irrepressibly flirtatious style she let him know that she had attended a masked ball at Ranelagh where the only pleasure she had had was in seeing 'a gentleman with Wilkes and Liberty written on his cap' – or, as she wrote in French, 'un Mr. que avoit écri sur son chapo Wilkes et Liberta'. The masquerader disguised as Wilkes had played his role to perfection, and Marianne had heard the man say that the laws of England would have been lost had it not been for his hero.[39]

No amount of flattery could win Wilkes back; the former *femme fatale* who had been Casanova's nemesis in matters of love had at last met her match. Gradually, an intermittent correspondence resumed between them, but their love affair was finished. In Bath the following winter, Wilkes began two lengthy liaisons with other women. Even so, La Charpillon had not entirely lost her fascination. Although he never dined with the occupants of Titchfield Street again, he continued to note down his ex-lover's various changes of addresses: first to number fourteen Winchester Row, near Paddington, and later to number thirty-one Upper Seymour Street, near Portman Square.

From there, Marianne de Charpillon slipped quietly into obscurity. To Casanova she would always remain a vivid and uncomfortable memory. For him, a manipulative tease would for ever be 'une Charpillon'.

TEN

Sophia Williams and Teresa Imer Cornelys

*I have never been able to conceive how
a father could tenderly love his charming daughter
without having slept with her at least once.*[1]

ON 24 JUNE 1820, sixty-six-year-old Sophia Williams, a grey-haired lady with a nose so long and thin that it overshadowed her chin, stood at the threshold of numbers thirty-two and thirty-three Mornington Place, a street of nondescript terraced houses off the Hampstead Road, in the London parish of St Pancras. During the next half-hour, fifteen plainly-dressed young women wearing poke bonnets filed past her into the building, pausing only to drop her a small bob-curtsey. Mrs Williams, as Sophia was known despite her spinster status, responded with a thin, humourless twitch of the mouth that belied her turbulent emotions. Within its cage of tightly-laced stays her heart pounded with excitement. Today she was witnessing the culmination of a dream which she had been toiling for years to turn into a reality: the opening of the Adult Orphan Institution, her refuge and school of further education for vulnerable young women, women such as she had once been herself.

Inside the house the new wards, as the girls were termed, were each issued with half a dozen towels, two sheets and two spoons, and sent off to place their possessions in the simple, curtainless dormitories upstairs. Octavia Langhorne, Harriet Williams, Amelia

Kendall, the three Ross sisters, Arabella Batley, Amelia Bennet, Clara Bingham, Mary and Frances Bussell, Eleanor Cambell, Emma Middleton, Eliza Elliott and Alicia Sills – all of them had lost fathers who were middle-class clergymen or military or naval officers; and seven of them had lost their mothers as well. Some had guardians, others were friendless, still others completely destitute. In the absence of private incomes and dowries, all faced an uncertain future in which one of the few respectable options open to them was to obtain a position as a governess or lady's companion, and the dire alternative was to descend to a life on the streets. Mrs Williams's Adult Orphan Institution would equip them for the former occupation, while safeguarding them from the kind of unscrupulous people who might push them into the latter. The formidable Mrs Williams would protect them from exploitation. She would fight the world on their behalf, and equip them to fight for themselves.

This was not the first educational establishment that Mrs Williams had opened. In 1806, under the patronage of George III's wife Queen Charlotte, she had founded the Cheltenham Female Orphan Asylum, a school which prepared poor local orphans to take up positions as domestic servants. But the Mornington Place school, which she had got off the ground with the help of her friend Princess Augusta, was much closer to her own heart, and quite revolutionary in concept. For during the next few years Mrs Williams's fifteen wards, who ranged in age between fourteen and twenty-one, would receive the kind of well-rounded education that was usually only available to upper-class men. They would learn to 'be made perfect Mistress . . . of the English language and Arithmetic, to write and read French grammatically, to be well grounded in sacred and profane History, Chronology, Ancient and Modern Geography and the use of the Globes, perfect in the rudiments of Drawing and Theory of Music, so as to be capable of teaching others'.[2] In short, Mrs Williams's Adult Orphan Institution was the first academic school of further education for women in England, a training college for governesses and female

schoolteachers which predated the more famous Queen's College in London's Harley Street by twenty-eight years.

Since Mrs Williams's own childhood had been blighted by a mother who had thrust her opinions on her, she was determined not to mould her charges' minds against their will. Her aim was 'not to give talents, but to cultivate them; not to combat bad habits, but to encourage and confirm good ones; not to correct erroneous ideas but to instil just ones'.[3] False pride was to be avoided at all costs: as respectable girls who had fallen on hard times, those under her care must know their place in the world and yet be proud of it; for, as Mrs Williams later reported with heartfelt feeling to the wealthy subscribers who supported her school, 'nothing is below the Dignity of a Gentlewoman but doing wrong'.[4]

For all her prim and proper appearance, wrong-doing was something that Mrs Williams knew all about, though not through any action of her own. As a child she had known poverty, destitution and what it was like to live on the wrong side of the law. Later she had experienced temptation, abuse and the bad influence of those who would exploit her. Like her charges, Mrs Williams had experienced first-hand all the indignities and fears of being a young woman alone in the world. Only by putting her faith in God had she survived what she described in her last will and testament as a life of 'wonderful affliction'; and, almost certainly, survived it a virgin, in stark contrast to her promiscuous parents.

Now, through the Adult Orphan Institution, Mrs Williams would help other young women to resist evil as she had done. Showing the same entrepreneurial spirit that her despised mother had once possessed, she had worked tirelessly for years to enlist the hundreds of subscribers who were to support the Institution, and as chief governess, honorary secretary and sub-treasurer, she now had complete control of running it. Until her death four years later, the Adult Orphan Institution would be Mrs Williams's world, and one she would rule like the most benign of tyrants. When the last of her new charges had entered its portals that morning, she closed the front door and fastened it with a heavy

chain, cutting off her wards, and herself, from the bad influences of the outside world.

Sophia Wilhelmina Frederica Pompeati, later known as Sophia Cornelys and Sophia Williams, was the daughter of Giacomo Casanova and his childhood friend, Teresa Imer. After meeting Casanova at Senator Malipiero's palazzo in Venice, Teresa had become a famous opera singer, an impresario, a high-class courtesan and an adventuress every bit as unscrupulous and daring as he was. Their brief flirtation, which had cost Casanova his relationship with the senator, had eventually been consummated in June 1753, and Sophia was the result of it. Born the following winter in Bayreuth, where Teresa was then living with her husband, Venetian choreographer Angelo Pompeati, and their two other children, Giuseppe and Wilhelmina, Casanova's daughter had been named after Wilhelmine Friederike Sophie von Hohenzollern, the Margravine of Brandenburg-Bayreuth and the wife of Teresa's lover, the Margrave.

By the time Sophia was four her mother had left Bayreuth, and her husband, and dragged her through France, Flanders and the Dutch Republic. During their travels the little girl had seen the death of her sister Wilhelmina, and observed her mother on the arms of countless lovers, some important, others not; they included Alexandre le Riche de la Pouplinière, Louis XV's Farmer General and the one-time suitor of the pregnant Giustiniana Wynne, and Prince Charles of Lorraine, the Regent of the Austrian Netherlands. Sophia had lived through Teresa's riches-to-rags decline in Paris, and her subsequent arrest and imprisonment for debt. She had witnessed her quarrels with scores of creditors, men and women from whom Teresa was forced to flee time and again. During the first weeks of 1759, Sophia's brother Giuseppe was taken away from the Dutch Republic to Paris by Casanova, a man who, during his brief stay in The Hague, devoured her own half-naked body with kisses and who, so her mother told her, was her real father. Nine months later, thirty-five-year-old Teresa dragged Sophia

across the Channel to London in order to join yet another man, an independently wealthy English clergyman named John Fermor, who had fallen in love with Teresa after hearing her sing at a concert in Rotterdam and who had promised to help her re-establish her singing career in England.

In London mother and daughter had at first lived together in an uneasy, claustrophobic alliance. Teresa was totally dependent on Fermor. She knew no Englishman except her lover, and neither she nor her daughter spoke the English language. Almost as soon as they arrived in the sprawling metropolis, Teresa and Fermor began to squabble over money; besotted as he was by the sophisticated singer, the married father-of-two and school rector had not thought through the reality of keeping his extravagant foreign mistress and her child. As he had promised Teresa in the Dutch Republic, he arranged a debut concert for her at the Little Theatre in the Haymarket, but her singing career did not take off as they had both hoped that it would.

Teresa was by now posing as a widow and calling herself Mrs Cornelys (a name she had adopted from one of her many Dutch lovers, a man named Cornelis de Rijgerbos). Undaunted by her dire situation and past failures, she decided to reinvent herself as a music impresario, a career she had plied in Paris and Flanders with disastrous financial consequences. Though several concert rooms already existed in London – most notably the Great Room in Soho's Frith Street – they were lacklustre venues which did not attract the aristocracy in any great number. What the city lacked, Teresa realised, was an exclusive set of assembly rooms where the nobility and gentry could listen to high-class Continental music and, more importantly, socialise and gamble just as they had done in her father's theatre in Venice. Teresa hoped to make concert-going as popular an activity for the English nobility as was attending an opera at the famous King's Theatre in the Haymarket, where Zanetta Casanova had made her debut in 1726, and she herself had performed on a trip to London twenty years later.

All the odds were against the enterprise becoming a success. Teresa was an Italian Roman Catholic, which put her beyond the

pale in the eyes of the staunchly Protestant Hanoverian monarchy. Moreover she was a woman, with few legal rights, no status and absolutely no money of her own. Nevertheless she manipulated the doubtful Fermor into bankrolling her business and signing all the contracts on her behalf; and, using him as an intermediary, she took a lease on premises in the well-situated London parish of St Anne's, Soho. Built in the 1680s for Edward Howard, the second Earl of Carlisle, after whom it had been named, Carlisle House was a double-fronted four-storey mansion on the east side of fashionable Soho Square. Since the Howards had moved out of the building in 1753 it had been rented to the Neapolitan envoy, and later used as a tapestry factory and furniture warehouse. Now in need of renovation, Carlisle House was nevertheless a beautiful structure large enough to host assemblies in, and it came with substantial outbuildings which included a disused Roman Catholic chapel where Teresa could stage her concerts.

Exhibiting a natural flair for interior design, Teresa moved into Carlisle House with Sophia and, with Fermor's money, quickly transformed it into a fitting backdrop against which the aristocracy could display their jewels and finely honed wit. With the help of several fashionable society women whom she had somehow befriended – most notably the scandalous yet highly popular Miss Elizabeth Chudleigh, lady-in-waiting to Augusta, the Dowager Princess of Wales – the singer drew up a list of wealthy aristocrats who would be invited to subscribe to a private concert club which was to be known as The Society in Soho-square. The exclusive nature of the membership list, the high price of the society's subscription tickets, the novelty of the venture and Teresa's extraordinary powers of self-promotion ensured that Carlisle House became a success even before it opened. Thanks to Miss Chudleigh, the founder members even included a royal prince – Edward Augustus, the Duke of York, who would remain one of Teresa's staunchest supporters until his death in 1767.

Teresa's first concert meeting, which took place on 27 November 1760, was a sensation. Bored by life at the somewhat dull

Hanoverian court which inhabited St James's Palace, the English aristocracy had an inexhaustible appetite for novelty and were hungry for enjoyment, something that Carlisle House provided in good measure. Never before had a London concert been given with such style, or in such a glamorous semi-public setting. Never before had music attracted such a glittering audience. And with her charming continental manners, her sophisticated savoir-faire and her innate Venetian zest for life, the 'singular Mrs Cornelys', as Teresa was thereafter talked about by the fashionable *ton*, proved a huge hit as a hostess.

During the next decade almost every member of the royal family would frequent her Carlisle House assemblies, concerts and masquerade balls, with the exception of King George III and his queen. As well as the Duke of York and Miss Chudleigh and her friends, Teresa would number among her patrons the likes of the Duke and Duchess of Devonshire, the Duke of Portland, the Duchess of Northumberland, the Countess of Harrington, the Earl of Carlisle, Lady Spencer, Sir Horace Walpole, novelist Fanny Burney, the Duchess of Bolton, the Earls of Huntingdon, Sandwich, Falmouth and Chomondley, and most of the British government including Lords Palmerston, Bolingbroke and North. Anyone who was anyone, as well as anyone who aspired to be someone, wanted to join The Society in Soho-square and was prepared to pay heavily for the privilege: from half-a-guinea for a single afternoon concert ticket to five guineas for a ticket to a gala masquerade ball. Those who did not make it on to the list of eligible members attempted to gatecrash the front door or scrambled to buy stolen or counterfeited tickets on the black market, where they changed hands for as much as fifty guineas each.

Teresa's head was immediately turned by her instant success. Instead of saving for the future, or paying back the money Fermor had laid out on her behalf, she decided after only weeks in business to expand her new enterprise on an extremely grandiose scale. By the spring of 1761 she had engaged a builder, Samuel Norman, to refurbish the entire mansion and, furthermore, to pull down all the outbuildings at the back including the old chapel, and to replace

them with a purpose-built ballroom and dining-room. At thirty feet high, eighty feet long and forty feet wide, the Concert Room, as her ballroom was called, was three-quarters the size of the Banqueting Hall at Whitehall Palace, and had its own banqueting hall underneath it of almost equal dimensions where four hundred guests could be seated at one crescent-shaped table. Both rooms were adorned with pillars and furnished with the latest fashion in silk sofas and armchairs. This was just the start of Teresa's extravagance: she installed octagonal glass doors worth a hundred pounds each in the refurbished main house; commissioned chinoiserie furniture from society carpenter Thomas Chippendale; hung heavy velvet curtains at the huge windows; and adorned the panelled walls with scores of elaborate and expensive rococo candle sconces and burnished mirrors, the largest of which cost her £262 – the equivalent of £25,250 in the modern day.

The effect was fabulous. For the next eleven years the concerts and parties that Teresa held in the sumptuous surroundings of Carlisle House were among the most memorable events in London's packed social calendar. On gala nights Soho Square filled with crowds of onlookers who came to watch the jewel-bedecked aristocracy arrive in a continuous crush of carriages and sedan chairs that lasted from nine in the evening, when the house opened its doors, until well past midnight. The chaos in the square, which included the occasional overturned carriage and smashed window, was so terrible that Teresa soon instituted London's first one-way traffic system: in her frequent newspaper advertisements for her assemblies she ordered all the coachmen to pull up outside Carlisle House only 'with their horses' heads pointing towards Greek Street'.

Inside the candle-lit mansion guests danced, ate sweetmeats and drank French wine and champagne, or non-alcoholic beverages such as tea, coffee and orgeat, a cold drink made from almonds or barley mixed with orange-flower water. They listened to concerts by London's most celebrated musicians (they included Johann Christian Bach and viola da gamba maestro Carl Abel), danced to a full-scale orchestra, gambled into the early hours, made

assignations and occasionally even consummated them on the premises. Often her patrons did not leave Soho Square until well after dawn. And while they were enjoying themselves on the upper floors of Carlisle House, their hundreds of servants lived it up below stairs.

With Carlisle House, Teresa succeeded in bringing the magic and excitement of the Venetian carnival to the very heart of London. Her house became an essential stop on any out-of-towner's visit to London and the subject of gossip in newspaper columns as far afield as the American colonies. Only a few years previously she had been desti-tute; now she was a celebrity – London's 'Mother of Masquerades' and 'Empress of Magnificent Taste and Pleasure' as the newspapers called her. By 1763 she was hosting twenty-four full-scale balls a year, each for between 400 and 1,000 paying guests, and Carlisle House was taking some £24,000 in revenue – more than £2.5 million in modern terms. As befitted a woman in her position, its proprietor lived in grand style, keeping her own private carriage and six horses and employing upwards of thirty-two servants in the house, including a private secretary. As well as her apartments in Carlisle House she rented a country villa in the Thames-side town of Hammersmith, where she and Sophia went whenever they had the time.

To the outside world, Mrs Cornelys's 'fairy palace', as Horace Walpole called Carlisle House, appeared to be a phenomenal success. Few people were aware that it was a palace built out of playing cards which could collapse at any time, bringing down Teresa and Sophia with it. Contrary to appearances, by 1763 London's most famous impresario was already deeply in debt, and getting more so with every passing day. She had fallen out with Fermor over the huge cost of building the new ballroom, and the one-time lovers were now engaged in a bitter, costly four-year battle in the Courts of Chancery over both the ownership of the building and the business that was conducted within it. Fermor claimed that Carlisle House was entirely his and that he and Teresa shared a fifty-fifty partnership in the business. Teresa counter-claimed that the building and its profits were wholly hers: she had

paid the builders, therefore in law she owned the house; the thousands of pounds which Fermor had laid out had been given to her as a present; and seeing that they were lovers, this kind of generosity was only to be expected from a rich English gentleman.

Oddly, considering its huge turnover, Carlisle House was not making any profits. The reason was clear to anyone who worked there: Teresa's talent was only for arranging events; she had no head at all for the machinations of business, and knew nothing of the relationship between profit and loss. If the tickets to one of her balls netted her 1,000 guineas she would spend far more than that arranging the event. Furthermore, she was completely ignorant of bookkeeping, seldom paid her servants or suppliers on time, and had a disingenuously careless attitude to money, which she continued to borrow in large amounts, even from the hapless Fermor, and seldom paid back. With no one keeping a close watch on her finances, people stole from or cheated Teresa whenever they had the opportunity. Carlisle House veritably leaked money. Any coins or notes taken in at the front office immediately disappeared out the back door.

Three years after arriving in London, Teresa's daughter Sophia appeared to be living a far more settled life than she had ever done before. Her home was a smart London mansion rather than a crumbling Dutch tenement, she never lacked for food, and she was receiving the best education that her mother's money could buy. Yet, despite all this, nine-year-old Sophia's life was as insecure as it had ever been. Though her mother seemed to be wealthy there were still bailiffs in the wings waiting to confiscate the furniture at a moment's notice or to cart Teresa off to a debtors' gaol if she dared to step outside Carlisle House other than on Sundays, the one day of the week when English debtors were free to walk the streets without fear of arrest. Every rap of the shiny brass door-knocker was a potential threat to their settled existence. Every meeting between Teresa and her one-time lover ended in another bitter argument or expensive legal writ. Anxiety gnawed at Sophia's heart, like a mouse slowly nibbling away at a piece of cheese. One day there would be nothing left.

Teresa was far too preoccupied with her business affairs to notice her daughter's unhappiness, let alone understand it. Hounded by the prospect of destitution, she had since her youth pursued her various careers – singer, concert impresario, courtesan – with a gusto that left little time for the niceties of motherhood, an activity for which she never had much aptitude. Like most parents of the day, she believed that her task was to provide financially for her children and to equip them for the life they must eventually lead; the concept of caring for their emotional well-being did not enter her head. When Casanova had run into Teresa in The Hague in 1759 he had been shocked by what he interpreted as the oppressive manner with which she dealt with her children. Under her bad guidance, he had shouted at her in front of Sophia and Giuseppe; they were growing up false, deceitful and overly obsequious. If Teresa 'had brought them up to be actors, she had succeeded, but for polite society they were little monsters in the making'.[5] His criticism had reduced Teresa to tears.

At the time Casanova had presumed that Teresa was grooming their daughter to be a high-class courtesan so that she could keep her in her old age, in the same way that Rose Augspurgher, and later Marianne de Charpillon, kept their family. This was untrue. Unlike the Augspurgher women, who lived close by Carlisle House, Teresa had no intention of exploiting her precious daughter for her own gain. On the contrary, she was determined to use her unexpected success in London to turn Sophia into a respectable, cultured young lady who might, perhaps, make a good marriage – and if that meant sacrificing the child's present happiness for her future good, so be it. Miss Cornelys, as the staff of Carlisle House were instructed to call Sophia, was force-fed a thorough education by a steady succession of tutors. By the age of nine she could already speak and write fluently in Italian, French and English (a language which her mother had yet to master properly), she was knowledgeable in History and Geography, and she could draw skilfully and talk with precocious intelligence on any number of subjects. Musically, Sophia was even more talented than her

mother: her singing voice was as cool and clear as silver, she could play the guitar and the harp, and she danced superbly.

On assembly nights, and afternoons when her mother's patrons called at Carlisle House, Sophia was summoned downstairs from the nursery to show off her precocious abilities, to be praised, doted on, cuddled and kissed by the powdered, perfumed and bewigged nobility; and on Sundays she was allowed to dine with her mother and her private guests. The rest of her time was spent studying at an academy of art, or up in her room at Carlisle House where she was isolated from other children. Materially, Teresa made sure that she had everything that a child could need. What Sophia lacked was the companionship of her peers, the freedom to express herself, and her mother's understanding. She tried her best to please Teresa, but it was a struggle. One minute her volatile and over-stressed mother was laughing and cuddling her; the next she was shouting at her angrily for some wrong she had done.

Given her precarious financial situation, it was perhaps under-standable if Teresa was inconsistent, bad-tempered and preoccupied with business. Her losses were getting out of hand, so much so that over the winter of 1762/63 she decided that she could no longer cope with running Carlisle House alone. She needed a trustworthy man to help her – and who would be more trustworthy than her own son? She immediately wrote to Casanova in Paris, asking him to return Giuseppe to her, for at sixteen the boy was now old enough to take an active part in her business affairs. Hopefully his presence would leave Teresa free to do what she did best, which was to deal with the creative side of running her concerts and balls.

Since the arrival of Teresa's letter in the spring of 1763 coincided with the Marquise d'Urfé's failed 'regeneration' operation, and the wealthy widow was on the point of losing faith in Casanova, it suited him at that moment both to leave France and get rid of his charge at one and the same time. But Giuseppe, who had been living as d'Urfé's adopted son for more than four years, had no desire whatsoever to leave his life of luxury or to see his real mother

again, and in the end he had to be tricked into leaving France. When he and Casanova arrived in London on 13 June 1763, accompanied by Casanova's servant Clairmont, they made straight for Soho Square, where Casanova left his companions in the carriage and entered Carlisle House alone. Though he could not fail to be impressed by the magnificence of Teresa's premises, his pride was wounded when he was kept waiting in the entrance hall by one of her lackeys, only to be given a message that she was in a meeting with her lawyer and far too busy to see him just then. Led by another of her servants to the Soho lodgings she had rented for them, Casanova was further insulted when Giuseppe was given the best room and he was shown to what appeared to be valet's quarters. His landlady's eulogy on how successful and famous Mrs Cornelys had become in London and how marvellous her daughter was made him feel even more resentful of Teresa. The scene was set for a fight between the erstwhile lovers, and Sophia would be their battleground.

Casanova's presence in London had already caused trouble in Soho Square. For when Sophia had heard that the party had arrived from Paris, she had made the mistake of asking her mother if Casanova was well before enquiring about Giuseppe. Teresa had flown off the handle: the ties of blood and good manners decreed that Sophia should have asked about her brother's health first, she shouted. As punishment for this apparent display of bad manners, the girl was forced to stay at home that night instead of accompanying Teresa to visit the travellers. Casanova was not to see his daughter until the following Sunday, when Teresa invited him to join her for dinner at Carlisle House.

There was little pleasure for Sophia in this occasion either. Instructed by her mother to ignore the man she had once been told was her father, she negotiated the rocky ground between obedience and following her own natural inclination, which was to be friendly towards him. During the meal both adults shamelessly manipulated their daughter in order to score points off each other in front of Teresa's four other guests, and as her parents traded

veiled insults over her head Sophia was left with the feeling that she could do nothing right. When at last her mother instructed her to 'say something to M. de Seingalt', she was too tongue-tied to do so. She eventually summoned the courage to ask Casanova if he would like to look at her drawings, as he reported:

'I shall look at them with pleasure; but I beg you to tell me in which way you believe you have offended me, for you look guilty.'

'I! I've certainly not behaved wrongly towards you!'

'You speak to me without looking at me. Are you ashamed to have such beautiful eyes? And now, you're blushing. So what crime have you committed?'

'You're embarrassing her,' her mother says to me. 'Answer him that you've committed no crime, but that it's out of respect and modesty that you don't stare at the people to whom you are talking.'

She says nothing.

After a short silence the company rose, and the little one, after dropping a curtsey, went to fetch her drawings and came to me.

'Mademoiselle, I don't want to look at anything until you look at me.'

'Go on,' says her mother, 'look at Monsieur.'

'Oh, now I recognise you,' I say to her. 'And you, do you remember having seen me before?'

'Even though it was six years ago, I recognised you the moment you came in.'

'How could you have recognised me if you did not look at me? If you only knew, my angel, what unforgivable rudeness it is not to look at the person to whom you are talking! Who could have taught you such a bad lesson?'

The little one then looked at her mother, who went over to the window. When I saw that I had avenged myself enough, and that the English people had understood everything, I began to examine her drawings, congratulating her on her talent, and complimenting her mother for having procured for her such a good education.[6]

In Sophia's face Casanova 'saw a beautiful soul, and I secretly pitied her for having to live under the domination of her mother, who was a fool'.[7] His caring attitude belied his own secret intentions towards his daughter, which were scarcely honourable: as he admitted in his memoirs, one of his main motives in coming to London was 'to get my daughter out of her mother's hands'.[8] In part this was because Casanova believed that Teresa was bringing Sophia up badly; and in part it was for dubious and extremely selfish reasons. Casanova wanted his daughter for himself.

The idea of adult men having sex with young children, so shocking to us in the present day, was so common, particularly between the daughters of the poor and wealthy men, as to be almost unremarkable during the eighteenth and nineteenth centuries. Although the romantic idea of childhood innocence existed, the concept of childhood as being a state different from adulthood was scarcely recognised at the time. In France, although the average age of marriage grew higher during the eighteenth century (settling at about twenty-eight years for men and twenty-six years for women) there were nevertheless no provisions in law regulating having sex with children until the 1830s. In Britain the age of consent – that is, the age at which a child could legally consent to having sex – was just ten years old throughout the eighteenth century; in 1763 Sophia was only nine.

By his own admission Casanova had a strong predilection for pubescent and even pre-pubescent girls. When he was nineteen he had slept with Teresa/Bellino's adopted sisters, Marina and Cecilia, virgins aged eleven and thirteen respectively. Four years later he had been forced to leave Venice after beating and attempting to deflower a young virgin on the island of Giudecca. In 1747, when he was twenty-two, he had stealthily taken advantage of fourteen-year-old Genoveffa, the daughter of a peasant in the city of Cesena. Caterina Capretta, also aged fourteen, had been just half Casanova's age when he seduced her in 1753. The following year Casanova had seduced fifteen-year-old Tonina, the daughter of his Murano landlady, as well as Tonina's pre-pubescent sister

Barberina, whom he described as 'not yet a grown girl; the roses of her burgeoning breasts had not yet budded'.[9] More young girls had followed: thirteen-year-old Sara, whom thirty-five-year-old Casanova deflowered in Berne in 1760; and Marianne Corticelli who 'was thirteen years of age, and looked only ten' when he slept with her that same year.

In the future there would be more young girls. After leaving London in the spring of 1764, Casanova would persuade an anonymous French eleven-year-old to perform fellatio on him through the iron grating separating them in the visiting-room of a French convent. In Moscow he would deflower Zaire, a twelve-year-old virgin Russian serf whom he purchased as a personal slave from her parents for a hundred roubles; although she cowered in a corner 'like a rabbit scared that the dogs it saw would devour it'[10] when he negotiated to buy her, the thirty-nine-year-old adventurer soon convinced himself that she was in love with him.

Though not illegal, there was nevertheless a transgressive element to his relationships with young girls, as Casanova became increasingly aware as he grew older. In 1771, in the town of Frascati where he had once been consumed by his passion for Donna Lucrezia, an erstwhile lover of his named Mariuccia lifted the covers on a bed where Giacomina, her own nine-year-old daughter by Casanova, and Guglielmina, the thirteen-year-old illegitimate daughter of his brother Giovanni, were sleeping. Each little girl had a hand curved over 'the signs of their puberty which were beginning to show. The middle finger, even more curved, was held motionless over the little piece of small, rounded, almost imperceptible flesh.'[11] With trembling hands, Casanova quickly replaced the covers, horrified by the betrayal of spying on the girls at such an intimate moment. It was, he later wrote, 'the only moment in my life when I knew for certain the real calibre of my soul, and I was satisfied by it.' Nevertheless, he was so sexually aroused by the sight of them that he immediately had sex with Mariuccia and found himself unable to get the two children out of his mind. After a few days of flirtation and exchanges of kisses, he seduced his niece

and, in the same bed and at the same time, all but deflowered his nine-year-old daughter. He was forty-six years old at the time.

When he had first encountered Sophia, his daughter by Teresa Imer, in the Dutch Republic, Casanova had showered her with kisses, 'charmed to be the man to whom this little creature owed her existence'. He noted rather pruriently that the four-year-old had only been wearing the lightest of shifts at the time. Three and a half years later in London, he began to desire his small daughter with a complete disregard for the taboo of incest – a taboo which, though condemned by the Church, was not made a criminal offence in England until as late as 1908. Yet during his first two months in London, Casanova rarely saw Sophia. Teresa stood between them, and she was in such deep financial trouble that she seldom left Carlisle House. The mansion had become her prison, and the threat of arrest and bankruptcy stalked her every day, especially during the summer season when the aristocracy left London and her business was forced to close, cutting off her only source of income. That July, Teresa was forced to pawn her crockery and cutlery in order to stave off her creditors, and from Mondays through to Saturdays she did not dare to leave the sanctuary of her home in case she was arrested.

One weekday in mid-August, however, a canny bailiff slipped through Carlisle House's open front door, which he was legally entitled to do. Once inside the house, he arrested Teresa for having failed to redeem one particular bill of exchange for 200 guineas. As he carted her off to his own house to await either release on bail or transfer to one of the city's notorious debtors' prisons, Teresa wrote in desperation to Casanova, begging him to 'Prevent my ruin and that of my innocent family'[12] by bailing her out of trouble before her other creditors got wind of the situation.

Teresa entrusted the letter to Giuseppe and instructed him to deliver it by hand to Casanova's Pall Mall lodgings. But the son she had pinned her hopes on to help her to turn her business around proved as unenthusiastic a messenger as he had been a worker. Exchanging his former decadent lifestyle for that of an unpaid clerk

in his mother's business appalled him. Teresa had presumed that Casanova had prepared Giuseppe for the working life ahead of him, but the boy seemed to have learned nothing in Paris other than the effete manners of a French aristocrat. He spoke no English, was hopeless at mathematics and geography and was by nature lazy, spoiled and reluctant to work. Though six years his junior, Sophia was far brighter and better educated – but then, as Teresa told Casanova in no uncertain terms on the day he arrived from Paris, it was *she* who had brought her up. Instead of being a help to Teresa, Giuseppe was just another burden, one she would need to re-form in her own mould if he was ever to be of any use to anyone, even himself.

When the youth left Casanova's lodgings empty-handed, Teresa appealed to Sophia as her last hope: only she had the power to persuade Casanova to help her. Weighed down by this huge responsibility, and accompanied by her mother's portly friend Madame Raucour, Sophia hurried to the Pall Mall house, forced her way into Casanova's room where he was then dining with his lodger Pauline and threw herself tearfully at his feet. Was her emotion genuine or was Sophia merely acting the part of a distraught child? Her mother had schooled her in how to alter her emotions at will in order to manipulate people into doing what she wanted them to. And the moment Casanova promised to provide the bail money, Sophia not only cheered up but, egged on by her father, spent the rest of the evening criticising Teresa, probably because she sensed that this was what her 'dear Papa', as she now called him, wanted to hear. Although her mother had once told her that Casanova was her father, the child confessed, Teresa now insisted that she was the daughter of a man called the Marquis de Montpernis, the one-time impresario of Bayreuth's opera house and another of Teresa's past lovers. Sophia was aware that she looked the image of Casanova – the Duchess of Harrington who had seen them together at a Carlisle House ball had mischievously and repeatedly pointed the likeness out to all and sundry – but when she now bluntly asked Casanova if he was her father he

denied it. At the same time, he treated Sophia in what appeared to her to be a fatherly manner, sitting her on his knee and giving her the kind of warm hugs and kisses her mother did not. He praised Sophia's beauty and talents, and he seemed delighted when she called him her father.

Casanova's genuine fatherly feelings towards Sophia were complicated by two things: his dislike of Teresa, and his predilection for young girls. The compulsive seducer was deliberately stirring up trouble between Sophia and her mother to make sure that their daughter loved him more. And now that he had rescued her from the bailiff's clutches and Teresa was in Casanova's debt, honour demanded that she comply with his wishes – to be allowed to spend more time with Sophia. After being released from the bailiff's house on his surety, the impresario gratefully took Sophia to dine at Pall Mall, and even left her there to spend the night in Pauline's rooms at the top of the house. Casanova promised his daughter that he would come upstairs the next morning and have breakfast with her and Pauline 'on condition that she waited for me in bed, for I wanted to see if she was as pretty in bed as she was when dressed'. The following morning he deliberately went upstairs early so that he would find the child undressed. 'Sophia, all smiles, hid under the covers when she saw me appear,' he wrote, 'but as soon as I'd thrown myself down on the bed next to her, and begun to tickle her, she put out her little face, which I covered in kisses.' The kisses did not stop there: he 'took advantages of a father's rights to see exactly how she was formed all over, and to applaud everything she had, which was as yet very immature. She was very small, but ravishingly built.' Casanova knew exactly what he was doing. Furthermore he knew that it was wrong: 'Pauline watched me give her all these caresses without suspecting a shadow of evil, but she was mistaken. If she had not been there the charming Sophia would in one way or another have extinguished the flame that her little charms had kindled in her papa.'[13]

During the rest of the summer Sophia became deeply depressed and stopped eating. Her weight dropped away. By the beginning of

autumn she was skeletally thin and had developed a high fever. With no one else in London to call on, the distraught Teresa once again turned to Casanova for help. Summoned to Carlisle House, he found Sophia in bed 'looking at me with eyes that said she was dying of grief. Her mother was in despair for she loved her madly; I thought that she was going to batter my skull in when I told her in the presence of the invalid that if the girl died it would be she who had killed her. At that the little one cried "No, no!" and threw her arms around her mother's neck and pacified her; but before I left I took her aside and told her that Sophia was dying because she made her too afraid of her and ruled over her with an unbearable tyranny.'[14]

Yet again, Casanova was driving a wedge between Sophia and Teresa. He had come to London with the express intention of separating them, and he now succeeded by suggesting that their daughter be sent away to boarding school. As soon as she was well enough, Sophia was duly enrolled at a Roman Catholic boarding school in Hammersmith which had been recommended to Teresa by the Duchess of Harrington. Since Teresa still had no money, Casanova paid the first year's fees of one hundred guineas in advance. Though a sizeable sum, it was much less than the 300 guineas he lost at a London gaming table a few days later.

Run by the Roman Catholic Institute of Mary, an order of teaching nuns dating back to the seventeenth century, the Nunnery, as the school was locally known, was under the direction of a worldly, aristocratic sixty-year-old Mother Superior. Being there improved Sophia's life immeasurably. At last she was far away from the emotional pressures of Carlisle House, and in a secure environment where she was surrounded by girls of her own age. Casanova visited her there all the time. If the truth were known he did not come to see Sophia but her beautiful schoolfriends, whom he described as 'angels incarnate'. Dressed in a uniform consisting of 'brief dresses with an English whalebone corset that exposed all their breasts'[15] the young girls – all of whom were under thirteen years of age – sent him into ecstasies and distracted

him from his tortuous relationship with Marianne de Charpillon. At one point his visits to the Nunnery became quite obsessive: even though the journey from Pall Mall to Hammersmith took an hour and a quarter he undertook it almost every day, bringing with him baskets of sweetmeats and trinkets to give away as presents. 'I brought joy to Sophia's soul,' he wrote, 'and at the same time to all her schoolfriends, with whom she shared everything. But the pleasure that I felt surpassed theirs . . . Her ladyship was extremely courteous to me, and my daughter, who openly called me her dear papa, made me more convinced every day that I had just cause to be called so. In less than three weeks I congratulated myself on having forgotten La Charpillon, and on having replaced her by innocent affections, despite the fact that one of Sophia's school-friends pleased me a little too much for me to find myself completely exempt from amorous desires.'[16]

In mid-March 1764, Casanova abruptly left London for reasons that are still unclear. He had been involved in a financial transaction concerning a forged bill of exchange for 520 guineas, he was deeply in debt, and he had a court case pending against him brought by Marianne de Charpillon. Sophia, into whose heart he had deliberately insinuated himself during his stay in the city, would never see him again; and it is unlikely that he ever wrote to her. She remained at boarding school for another three years before returning to Carlisle House. 'Short, but very pretty, and full of talent', as an old school friend described her in her teens, she had by then grown far apart from her difficult but talented mother, just as Casanova had hoped that she would. By now London's most famous impresario was even more celebrated than she had been at the time of Casanova's visit to London and yet, at the same time, even more deeply entrenched in debt. In 1765 she had attempted to buy the famous King's Theatre in the Haymarket, the only theatre in London licensed by the Lord Chamberlain to stage Italian opera, and when she had failed to raise the required sum of £14,000 she had calmed her restless spirit by opening a second, smaller assembly room in Soho's Greek Street. In 1771, Teresa

staged her own highly popular but unlicensed opera at Carlisle House, and ran foul of the law. Competitors tried to drive her out of business. Her enemies accused her of running a bawdy house. Her many legal cases against John Fermor dragged on interminably, and expensively, through the Courts of Chancery. Arrested by creditors five or six times a year, Teresa was occasionally allowed out of prison on bail to run the concerts and balls which would help her to pay off the money she owed. Despite her dire situation, she still did her best to look after her children: in 1770, she even sent Giuseppe off on a grand tour of Europe, warning him to live within the modest allowance of one hundred guineas which she had scraped together for him and making him a promise to accept favours from no one.

Teresa finally went bankrupt in 1772, squeezed out of business by competition from the newly opened Pantheon assembly rooms on nearby Oxford Street – a building which was 'the wonder of the XVIII Century and the British Empire' and 'the most beautiful edifice in England' according to historian Edward Gibbon. In a humiliating, fixed auction, which she herself was forced to witness, Carlisle House, complete with its precious contents, was sold off to a consortium of her creditors for a fraction of its true worth. Thomas Chippendale, who had supplied her with rococo and chinoiserie furniture, was among the buyers.

Until then Sophia had remained at Soho Square, where she gave concerts herself and 'enjoyed the protection and the esteem of all the greatest ladies in London'. Since being enrolled at The Nunnery she had grown to despise her mother 'who mortified her every day, who reduced (her) to tears over nothing'[17] and whom she later accused of trying to push her into the arms of a local rake, Lord Piggott. As soon as Teresa went bankrupt Sophia abandoned her and fled into the welcoming arms of the Roman Catholic Church. Charles Butler, one of the most prominent Catholics of the day, gave her a small stipend with which she rented modest rooms for herself near Bedford Row, Bloomsbury. In a bid to distance herself further from her infamous mother, she immediately changed her

name from the all-too-distinctive Miss Cornelys to the anonymous-sounding Miss Williams, an anglicised form of her second Christian name, Wilhelmine. Following her example, Giuseppe, who had by now returned from Italy, changed his surname to Altorf and took a job as tutor to Lord Pomfret's son.

Sophia Williams had no intention of following in her mother's footsteps by going into commerce or becoming a courtesan. Instead, like her brother, she became a paid companion to the nobility who had once frequented her mother's house. For a woman to go into service in this way was an unenviable occupation 'considered in the light of a degradation' in the opinion of Mary Wollstonecraft, author of *Vindication of the Rights of Woman*, but it suited Sophia's nature. The education Teresa had drummed into her from her earliest years now paid off in full measure. Musically gifted, cultured, intelligent and, more importantly, as adept in her own way at ingratiating herself with the aristocracy as her mother had been, Sophia was taken in by Lady Harrington, who had always liked her, and became a companion and governess to her daughters. From the Harringtons' house in Stable Yard, St James's, Sophia eventually passed to Lady Cowper, and later to the Duchess of Newcastle, the Duchess of Beaufort, Lord Newhaven, the Marchioness of Tweeddale and finally to Margaret, the Dowager Lady Spencer.

Through these aristocratic connections, all of which she owed directly to Teresa, Sophia was introduced to George III's wife Queen Charlotte and her second daughter, Princess Augusta. Oddly, the governess and the princess had something in common: each had endured a miserable childhood under the rule of a repressive and temperamental mother against whom she had had to struggle for her freedom. An unlikely relationship developed between them – the princess signed her letters to Sophia as being from 'Your very sincere friend Augusta'[18] – and in time she appointed Sophia as her private almoner.

In many ways Sophia was the opposite of both her parents. Where Teresa and Casanova were both brave and adventurous, she

was fearful. They lived their lives on a grand scale; she played out hers on a small stage. While they were both sexually promiscuous she died a childless spinster and, almost certainly, a virgin. While they were both unscrupulous, disingenuous, and even dishonest if it was in their interest, she devoted her life to God, to the righteous (perhaps even self-righteous) path, and to selfless good works.

What she had inherited from her parents was her father's intellect and her mother's entrepreneurial spirit. And it was these qualities which helped her to start the Cheltenham Female Orphan Asylum in 1806, and the Adult Orphan Institution in Mornington Place, St Pancras, in 1820. Sophia's fifteen wards in the latter institution became her children – neat, orderly, grateful and well-behaved. All of them had 'come into the Institution at their own requests and have implicitly followed the regulations laid down for them with the greatest Cheerfulness', as she noted in her first report to the charity's trustees. 'They behave with infinite cordiality and affection to each other and appear fully convinced that, being equally the children of misfortune, it is an indispensable Duty to assist and feel for each other. . . . The certainty that if the Institution succeeds, and they are deserving of its Protection, they will at all times find an asylum in it endears it to them and makes them delight in lending their assistance in every way that can promote its prosperity.'

Having no position in life need not be a tragedy, Sophia seemed to be telling the world: if they looked after one another women could survive and even find fulfilment and happiness without marriage, a lover, an income or a family. Sometimes one was even better off without parents. By now she was a bona fide orphan too. Casanova had died in 1798, Teresa a year earlier. Bankruptcy in 1772 had not dented Teresa's enthusiasm for business. After getting out of prison, she bought a hotel in the south-coast town of Southampton, but the project ran into trouble through no fault of her own. Back in London in 1775 she organised a fabulous Venetian regatta on the River Thames, and soon afterwards wormed her way back into Carlisle House, this time as its manager.

To the amazement of fickle society, the seemingly indestructible Mrs Cornelys eclipsed her former success by holding two seasons of sensational 'Rural Masquerades'. Her imagination, and spending, ran riot over these parties. She transformed her old Soho mansion into an indoor Arcadia by covering the wooden floors in fresh turf and importing banks of hedges and armfuls of exotic, out-of-season flowers. As the newspapers reported in glowing detail, on one occasion Mrs Cornelys created an indoor arbour 'filled with greenhouse plants and pots of flowers, and in the centre stood an elegant pavilion hung with festoons of silk; on the top (to which the company ascended by a temporary staircase,) was spread a table for a dozen persons, in the middle of which was a fountain of water, and a reservoir, with gold and silver fish swimming about in it'. Upstairs, in the vast Concert Room, 'lofty pines stood at equal distances along the sides, and branched to each other at the top' while underneath them a luxurious picnic of crayfish, hot fowls, asparagus and strawberries was laid out on 'an elegant erection of Gothick-arches' decorated with coloured lanterns. Meanwhile, at the end of the Concert Room, the orchestra's dais was surrounded by orange trees and illuminated by 'a moving spiral pillar of lights, which terminated in a brilliant sun'.[19]

In the summer of 1776, Teresa was again termed 'the Mother of Masquerades, Taste and Elegance' by fashionable society. But her brilliant skills were not enough to keep her in business. Eighteen months later she was broke again. She clung on to Carlisle House as if to a life raft, returning there for a brief spell in May 1779, but it was a life raft more liable to sink her than save her. Later that year she was committed to the King's Bench prison by order of her many creditors, who no doubt congratulated themselves that this time the slippery Mrs Cornelys would never get out. They were wrong: on 6 June 1780 the gaol was set on fire during the anti-Catholic Gordon Riots, and fifty-seven-year-old Teresa escaped along with hundreds of other prisoners; she remained on the run until the end of August, when she was recaptured in Westminster.

Carlisle House was finally sold by auction five years later.

Nothing more was heard of its former owner until May 1792, when a letter appeared in *The Times* informing the public that she had remarried and was now the widow of a certain Mr Frederick Smith. A few years later Mrs Smith briefly took over The Grove, an old country villa in the village of Knightsbridge, near Hyde Park, which had extensive gardens and came with a flock of goats and asses. Determined to get back into the business she loved, Teresa tended the beasts, sold their milk, and, with the small profit she made, filled the house with books and musical instruments in order to open it to the public as a venue for female archery and country breakfasts. This ambitious plan collapsed when she fell into debt yet again. Injured by the bailiffs who came to arrest her, she was hauled off to prison, bleeding at the breast.

This was one blow Teresa would never recover from. 'Reduced to abject misery and want' and in agony from breast cancer, she lay dying in a series of terrible prison cells, first in the notoriously frightening Newgate Prison and later in the Fleet. Here she received a rare condescending visit from her daughter. Devoutly religious as Sophia was, she offered Teresa no words of comfort. On the contrary, she told her that she believed she was not her daughter, or Casanova's, but the illegitimate child of Prince Charles of Lorraine and 'a lady of quality'. When she had got this off her chest, Sophia left the gaol, never to return there. She sent her mother a meagre weekly income, but it was not enough to pay even for a proper bed or good food. When Teresa died on 19 August 1797 Sophia refused to pay for the funeral, priggishly informing the authorities that a pauper's burial was 'good enough for a woman who had led such an improper life'.

Haughty, bitter and cruel towards her mother, to the outside world Sophia was self-effacing and concerned only with doing good. Although her childhood had scarred her indelibly, she came to believe that 'every affliction has been a blessing in the end . . . Were my life to (start) over again there is not one single circumstance or event however bitter it has been that I would wish not to have occurred.' That she was in many ways the opposite of both

her parents – religious, upright and chaste – was certainly no accident, and to the end of her life she was haunted by the fear of following in her mother's profligate footsteps. As she wrote in her will, 'It will be my endeavour as long as life is spared not to owe any money.'[20]

Sophia died suddenly on 25 June 1823 at the Mayfair home of the Dowager Countess Sidney, three days after presenting her latest report on the Adult Orphan Institution to its benefactors. 'Most sincerely do I lament the loss of that excellent good Mrs Williams,' Princess Augusta wrote to her friend Lady Harcourt a fortnight later. 'Her worth was great. She was humble and yet persevering in doing good.'[21] Not everyone thought so well of her: in the eyes of writer John Taylor, who had known Sophia in her youth, she was 'an artful hypocrite . . . totally devoid of sensibility' who, while pretending to care for others, had looked out only for herself.[22]

She left few possessions – some books, a watch chain, a writing desk given to her by Queen Charlotte, an ink stand, a turquoise ring, a seal with a sphinx on it, and a silver teapot which she bequeathed to her faithful servant Catherine Troy. Her real legacy was the Adult Orphan Institution, the first academic school for the female sex in England, still going strong in the twenty-first century as the Princess Helena College, an independent school for girls in Hertfordshire. A huge portrait of its founder, donated by Princess Augusta, still hangs in the hall. Dressed in a white Regency-style frock and a turban-like head-dress, Sophia is playing the harp in a pair of open-toed sandals. In her face one can just make out the shadow of her father's features: the dark hair, the arched eyebrows, the long nose and the slightly receding chin. However, there is nothing of her father's or mother's visceral *joie de vivre* in her pose or her expression. As she stares up at the single shaft of sunlight breaking through the stormy sky above her, Casanova's daughter looks resigned to her fate, careworn, lonely, and more than a little sad.

ELEVEN

4 June 1798

SHADES OF NIGHT are closing in around Casanova. A blanket of darkness has settled around him in his bedroom in Dux Castle, not unlike the thick fog that he remembers once hung over Venice. From time to time the shape of a face looms up at him through the mist, the features hazy and unclear even at close quarters. He is aware of people tiptoeing across the creaking parquet floor, but he cannot see them. They mutter about him as if he is already dead and shuffle around his bed as if not to disturb him. But Casanova, who faces an eternity of peace, has grown frightened of silence, an absence of sound into which one could so easily slip away. He wants to be disturbed, to hear the off-key scratchy sound of violins playing outside the cafés in the Piazza San Marco, or the merry laughter of a crowd of gossiping women, or even Magda the maid's guttural voice, for at least that would be a sign that he is still alive. But Casanova cannot tell anyone this. He for whom words were formerly weapons of seduction and manipulation, the vehicles with which he manoeuvred himself so easily in and out of the finest salons in the world, is now too feeble even to ask for a chamber pot when he needs one. It is all he can do to keep breathing.

His bedroom, which once seemed as claustrophobic and hateful to him as his cell under The Leads, has suddenly become a place that Casanova never wants to leave. The coffered ceiling with its cobwebs that are never dusted to his liking, the hard-backed

armchair with its faded chintz seat in which he has fidgeted away so many restless hours, the mean little desk from which, jealous of their freedom, he has sent off so many hundreds of letters to travel the roads of Europe – all these things which have caused him endless grief since he arrived at Dux thirteen years ago are suddenly beloved to him. He has even developed a sentimental attachment to the charmless Magda, whose rough hands occasionally straighten the rumpled sheet he is lying under, tucking it tightly under the mattress as if she was a torturer binding him to the rack, with no regard as to the pain she causes him.

But these things are now under threat. There is scarcely a glimmer of hope left in the embers of the tiled stove, and the long-case clock in the corner, the hands of which once moved so inexorably slowly, is ticking away the last minutes of Casanova's life all too fast. All he can do is lie here, isolated in his pain, and wait for Death to claim him.

Even though his nephew-in-law from Dresden has come to look after him, Casanova has never felt so lonely. He aches for the touch of a tender hand, or to experience just one more time the comfort of warm, naked female flesh pressed against his own. But these are things of the distant past. For as far back as he can remember he has slept alone in this narrow bed, his feet warmed by the body heat of his only flesh-and-blood female companion of the last three years – Finette, his young fox terrier bitch who this afternoon keeps vigil on the rug beside him, whining softly for him to play with her, and staring up at him with her moist, black, uncomprehending eyes.

The man who was once surrounded by admirers and adored by so many women, and who in the future will be remembered as the greatest lover in history, is dying alone among strangers, mourned only by a dog.

How did the young fearless Adonis fired by lust and ambition come to this? When did success forsake him? When did old age – 'sad and weak, deformed, hideous old age'[1] as he so succinctly described it – catch up with him? Casanova's first intimation of mortality, a more-than-occasional failure to perform between the

sheets, visited him extraordinarily early: in his mid-thirties, soon after the London courtesan Marianne de Charpillon dealt his self-confidence those blows from which it never fully recovered. As if she had put a jinx on him, his luck changed swiftly. Senator Bragadin died, leaving him without a private income. The striking looks he had taken for granted since his youth became raddled by illness and age. His appearance lost its sparkle along with the diamond buttons that he sold to pay off his debts; it grew as faded as the gold embroidery on his once-glorious waistcoats. Despite his height and build, Casanova no longer stood out in a crowd of men as the most handsome among them. Instead, like his rivals, he had sallow skin, receding hair, rotting teeth and painful haemorrhoids.

He tried to ignore the change in his appearance. But he was aware that women did not. 'I still loved the fair sex,' he wrote of himself at this time, 'though with much less passion, much greater experience, and less courage for daring enterprises, for, looking more like a father than a lover, I no longer believed I had either rights or justifiable claims.'[2] Even the greatest love of his life, Henriette, did not fall into Casanova's arms when he turned up in Aix-en-Provence for a second time in 1768; and he was then only forty-three years old. In her mid-forties herself, Henriette was still living apart from her husband, and had grown prettily, contentedly plump. As was her custom, she spent the winter of 1768/69 in the city, receiving no visitors at home but often going out in company. Sometime in February 1769 she became aware, probably by seeing him at one of the many social gatherings she frequented, that her old lover was in town once more, this time alone. She made no move to contact him. The vicissitudes of life had clearly taken their toll on him, he was not ageing flatteringly, and he had the air of a downtrodden man. Forced for the first time since his early twenties to earn a living by his own abilities, both literary and at the gaming table, Casanova no longer had enough money or self-confidence to sustain his role as a rich nobleman. Instead of being taken in by his cultivated air and extraordinary story-telling skills, the aristocrats he mixed with frequently suspected that he was a lower-class

impostor. He had begun to smell of failure, of an early promise never fulfilled. In his youth he had got away with living on the very edge of legality through sheer force of personality, but over the past five years his dubious friendships and frequent brushes with the authorities had made him *persona non grata* in a host of cities and countries. In March 1764 he had fled London. In July 1766 he had been ordered to leave Poland after wounding General Branicki in a duel. The following January he had been banished from Vienna for illegal gambling, and in November 1767 he had been expelled from France. After spending a year in Spain, Casanova had wound up in a Barcelona prison for eight days after a series of indiscretions that had made him many enemies culminated in an ill-advised love affair with the mistress of the Captain General of Catalonia. Freed on 28 December 1768, he had crossed the border back to France and made his way, via Perpignan and Montpellier, to Aix-en-Provence where he planned to spend the carnival season, and perhaps find work with the local judiciary body or Parlement.

While diminished, Casanova's ability to seduce both men and women with his personality and intellect had not entirely deserted him. In Aix he was befriended by the Marquis d'Eguilles, the president or presiding judge of the Parlement, and his brother the Marquis d'Argens, a philosopher and writer who since 1744 had been Director of the Academy of Sciences in Berlin. Through their connections Casanova was invited to numerous balls and assemblies at which he always looked out in vain for Henriette. Although he occasionally heard her real name mentioned, he did not enquire after her 'for fear of suggesting that I knew the lady'; his loose tongue may have got him into trouble in Spain, but when it came to Henriette Casanova remained as discreet as ever. Convinced that she must be at her country château near the Croix d'Or, Casanova planned to call on her when he eventually left the city.

Before he could do so, events took an unexpected turn. After dining at the Marquis d'Argens' country house one night Casanova drove back to the city in an open carriage, in a strong wind and without an overcoat. By the time he reached Aix he was chilled to

the bone, but instead of going to bed he went out with an acquaintance and spent two hours attempting to deflower a four-teen-year-old virgin whose hymen had so far defied all other attempts made on it. Casanova was too old for such shenanigans, and the following morning he came down with a severe and dangerous case of pleurisy. Plagued by a terrible cough, he began to spit up blood – a sign of possible consumption – and a few days later slipped into a torpor. Eight days after taking to his bed he was at death's door, and a priest was summoned to hear his confession and administer the last rites.

Defying expectation, Casanova began a slow recovery. During the entire period of his illness and recuperation he was cared for day and night by a serving woman, who tended him so diligently that she probably saved his life. When he eventually paid her off, she told him that she had been hired by his physician. The physician, however, insisted that he did not know the woman, and nor did the innkeeper's wife. The mystery remained unsolved until Casanova finally left Aix for Marseille in late April or early May, by which time he believed he was well enough to arrive at Henriette's château in good health. He had written her a letter before he left the city, warning her of his arrival, and when his carriage reached the gates of her house 'a league and half before the Croix d'Or' he ordered the postillion to stop so that he could send it up to the château; aware that his visit might not be welcomed, he had no wish to foist himself on Henriette if she did not wish to receive him. Henriette, however, was not there: the manservant who came down to the gates told Casanova that she had been in Aix for the last six months, and was not expected back in the country for another three weeks.

Casanova had unwittingly been walking the same streets and attending the same social gatherings as his 'divine Henriette' and yet he had not recognised her. He was mortified. Invited up to the house so that he could write to her, he was surprised to see the same servant who had looked after him during his illness. The woman explained that she had worked at the château for the past

ten years. When her mistress had heard that Casanova was ill, she had sent her to his inn and told her to enter his room boldly and take care of him as well as if he had been Henriette herself. If anyone were to ask her who she was, Henriette had told her servant to say that the physician had sent her.

Convinced that Henriette must still love him, and upset that he had not recognised her, Casanova suggested in his letter that he immediately return to Aix. Her reply reached him in Marseille a day later. 'Nothing, my old friend,' she wrote, 'is more romantic than the story of our meeting at my country house six years ago, and our present encounter, twenty-two years[3] after our separation in Geneva. We have both aged. Will you believe that, though I still love you, I am nevertheless very content that you did not recognise me? It's not that I have grown ugly, but putting on flesh has altered my looks.' She was 'a widow, happy and comfortably enough off to inform you that if you lack money at the bankers, you will find it in Henriette's purse'; she had obviously seen or heard enough of Casanova to have noticed his relative poverty and, without wounding his pride, she generously wished to help him in any way she could. However, she was decisive that this was as far as she wanted the relationship to go. Although she was happy that she had perhaps helped to prolong his life by sending 'a woman whose good heart and fidelity I knew' to look after him when he was ill, Henriette was adamant that he should not rush back to Aix in case this gave rise to speculation about their relationship. If he were to return some time in the future, however, she assured him that they would be able to see each other 'although not as old acquaintances'; as in the past, her boundaries were clear. If Casanova wished to maintain a correspondence with her, she promised to do everything within her power to make it flourish. She was curious about his life and promised him, 'now that you have given me such strong proof of your discretion', that she would tell him the whole story of her flight to Cesena in 1749.[4]

As in the past Henriette maintained control over the relationship. She would always be grateful to Casanova for his impeccable

behaviour towards her, but a reunion between them was out of the question. 'Henriette had grown wise,' Casanova wrote. 'The force of temperament had diminished in her as it had in me. She was happy; I was not. If I went back to Aix for her, people would have guessed things that no one should have known; and what would I have done? I could only have become a burden to her.'[5]

Casanova's confidence with women was sliding inexorably downhill. He was to have one last great romantic adventure: in the arms of Leonilda. By 1770 his daughter by Donna Lucrezia was twenty-four years old and had been married for five years to an extremely wealthy man, the Marchese della C, one of the richest men in Salerno. She and her sixty-year-old husband divided their time between an immense palace in the city and a stunning villa in the country. In both homes Leonilda was waited on by vast retinues of servants. A French cook prepared her meals, more than a dozen pages served her at table, and whenever she strolled in the gardens she was followed both by a page who carried the train of her dress, and by a young female companion who walked half a pace behind her.

Widely travelled and highly intelligent, the Marchese della C appeared to outsiders to be a conventional man and a good Christian. In private he was a freethinker and a Freemason, but in the traditional moral climate of Salerno these things were best kept to himself. His general good health was marred by gout so painful that it made it impossible for him to walk and prevented him from making love properly to his beautiful young wife. Having remained a bachelor until the age of fifty-five, he had no children, which was his greatest sorrow. On his death his fortune would pass to one of the ten or so dislikeable nephews who hung around his palace like carrion crows, waiting for him to die. As Lucrezia, who had come to Salerno to live with her daughter, remarked to Casanova when he turned up in the city in 1770, 'if among the nobility of this city she could have found a man capable of pleasing her, the Marchese would have made a friend of him, and if it came to it he would not even have been sorry to see her become

pregnant.' Leonilda's husband would never be absolutely sure that a child she bore was not his, because 'when he is feeling well he comes to sleep with her, and from what my daughter has told me, he can flatter himself that he has done what he has effectively not done. But there is no longer any expectation that his fondness will have positive results.'

In 1761 in Naples, Lucrezia had stood protectively between father and daughter. Nine years on in Salerno, all she could do was to stand by helplessly while Casanova and Leonilda renewed and finally consummated their incestuous love affair. When, six months later, Casanova received a letter informing him that his daughter was pregnant, he shuddered at the thought of it. Three months after that, Leonilda gave birth to a boy who was almost certainly her half-brother as well as her son, and Casanova's son and grandson.

With this love affair Casanova's days as a great seducer were effectively over. By his mid-forties the once-irresistible lover had to talk hard to persuade a woman into bed. It scarcely seemed worth the effort. 'I had begun to find the pleasure of love-making less intense, less seductive than I imagined it to be beforehand,' he confessed, 'and my sexual prowess had already been diminishing little by little for eight years' – that is, since his late thirties. Women had once begged for his caresses. Now, if he was lucky, they tolerated them – an unbearable situation for a man who had always prided himself on giving pleasure even more than taking it. Discouraged by their indifference and his own financial circumstances from pursuing the kind of woman he could truly love, Casanova was reduced to paying for sex, or snatching his pleasures wherever he could. In Russia and Poland he bought small girls' virginities off their poverty-stricken parents. Wanting an easy life, he opted for the services of prostitutes. Anything else was too much trouble: when he tried to grope his landlady's nineteen-year-old niece in Spa, the girl punched him in the nose.

But relief sex was not enough for Casanova, who was bored by the mechanical emptiness of it. An 'intolerable void' occupied his

heart. Ironically, the pathological seducer wanted the act of love for, without love, both sex and life were meaningless to him. So he persuaded himself he was in love again: with Doña Ignacia, a devoutly religious boot-maker's daughter in Madrid, who stopped going to confession so that she could sleep with him without telling her priest; with Sophia's old schoolfriend Betty, with whom he had a brief fling in Siena; with Leah, a Jewess in Ancona; and with Charlotte, a pregnant young girl whom he befriended and selflessly, chastely looked after until she died in childbirth. Her death shattered him. Confronted so brutally by mortality, Casanova realised that he was now a different being from the man of his youth. Then he had been a happy, carefree hedonist with the prospect of a glorious future in front of him. Now he was 'forced to admit to myself that I had wasted all my time, which meant that I had wasted my life'.[6] He was forty-seven years old, 'the age scorned by Fortune' as he described it, and still had another twenty-six years ahead of him.

His love affair with love was not completely over. Having negotiated his pardon by the Venetian authorities, in 1774 the prodigal son returned to Venice, the 'beloved mother' of its citizens, where a last chance awaited him. Desperate for money as well as approval, he threw himself wholeheartedly into his literary career, translated the *Iliad*, wrote a three-volume history of Poland and published a literary journal. At the same time he became a secret agent of the Republic's Inquisitors. As poacher-turned-gamekeeper, he compiled at least fifty reports under the pseudonym Antonio Pratolini, including one which suggested burning impious and licentious books. And he did something else that would have been anathema to him in the past: he settled down with a woman.

For three years Casanova rented a house in Venice's Barbara delle Tole and shared it with a simple seamstress by the name of Francesca Buschini, her mother and her brother. He kept them all, bought Francesca fine dresses, and introduced her to the delights of the theatre and opera – grand gestures which cost him little but

which enslaved her heart. Although she was a far cry from the upper-class beauties who had captivated him in his youth, she seemed to give Casanova something he had never experienced before except fleetingly: a sense of security.

But over the summer of 1782 an act of self-sabotage on his part ended this domestic idyll, just as similar acts had brought to a close so many of his previous relationships with women. This time a humiliating row involving nobleman Carlo Grimani, the son of his old protector Michele, prompted Casanova to write *Ne' Amori, Ne' Donne*, a spiteful satirical pamphlet which suggested that Carlo was a bastard and that he himself was Michele Grimani's natural son. Its publication caused a furore and an outrage. Casanova took temporary refuge in Trieste, hoping that the disapprobation levelled against him would soon die down. It did not. Advised by his friend the Procurator Lorenzo Morosini to leave the Republic as soon as possible, he found himself reluctant to resume his peripatetic existence. The former drifter was feeling his age. 'I am fifty-eight,' he wrote to Morosini from Trieste that September. 'I cannot go on foot; winter approaches; and if I think of becoming an adventurer again I start to laugh when looking at myself in the mirror.'[7]

He had no choice but to go. On 17 January 1783 he returned to Venice just long enough to pick up a few possessions, then left for Vienna. Back in the Serenissima briefly that June to bid a proper farewell to Francesca, Casanova was too scared of being arrested to set foot on land, so he kissed her goodbye in a boat. Then he set off on the long downhill road into permanent exile. Though she would never see him again, Francesca's letters to her *Carissimo and Amatissimo* – her *dearest and most beloved* – Giacomo followed him along his route, reflecting his travels and changing moods, and giving him news of her own life in Venice. She was glad to hear that he was taking the waters in Spa, but sorry to hear that he was not sleeping enough. She took pleasure that he had enjoyed himself with a group of women, and laughed to think that he was contemplating going up in an air balloon. He had written to her that 'a man without money is the image of death, that he is a very

wretched animal',[8] and she regretted that he would not be coming back to Venice for the Feast of the Ascension. How sad she was to hear that his haemorrhoids had kept him in bed! She was sorry that he was still short of money, and she thanked him for the small sums he sent her. She hoped she would never hear him say again 'that you are disgusted with everything and no longer in love with life'.[9] She and her family had nothing to live on. Venice was ruinously expensive and she could find no work.

In June 1784, Casanova heard from a friend that Francesca had been seen out enjoying herself at a *casino*, and wrote breaking off with her. In a heartfelt reply, she pleaded her innocence and confessed that, four months earlier and desperate for money, her mother had sold off all his books. Casanova was so furious that eighteen months passed before Francesca heard from him again. By then his long journey into exile had ended at Dux Castle, where Count Waldstein had offered him the post of librarian.

Touchy, full of rancour, quick to be roused to anger and slow to forgive any slights against him, he prowled the vast library of 40,000 volumes like a beast in captivity. The feeling that he was trapped – that he had trapped himself – added to his frustrations, sexual and otherwise. 'Women and young girls preoccupy his thoughts,' wrote his good friend, Waldstein's uncle the Prince de Ligne, 'but that's as far as they can go nowadays. That distresses him, it rouses him to anger towards the fair sex, towards himself, towards the heavens, Nature and the year 1742. He takes his revenge for that on everything that it drinkable and edible; no longer able to be a god in the gardens or a satyr in the forests, he's a wolf at the table.'[10]

Half-philosopher, half-court jester, Casanova fulfilled his obligations to Waldstein by cataloguing his books and entertaining his visitors with witty, and erudite conversation. But the light had gone out of him. Although he made others laugh, he was slow to laugh himself. He retained the ability to befriend men and charm women when he wanted to, and even the desire to help them when they were in need, but now he preferred his relationships to be con-

ducted by letter only. He entered into a correspondence with a woman named Henriette de Schuckmann, who had met him whilst visiting Waldstein's library ten years earlier and who wrote to him in 1796 that 'I understand you perfectly and I love to distraction the lively and energetic manner with which you express yourself'. The following year he received a surprise letter from twenty-two-year-old Countess Cecile de Roggendorff, whose father he had once known and whose older brother Ernst sometimes stayed at Dux as Waldstein's guest. Orphaned seven years earlier at the age of fourteen, convent-educated Cecile had since suffered numerous humiliations and persecutions at the hands of her unscrupulous family. Badly scarred by a childhood attack of smallpox, and with no income of her own, she turned to Casanova for advice in desperation after her fiancé was killed at the Battle of Bassano in September 1796. Casanova's reply, and the practical help he subsequently gave her, soon seduced the vulnerable young woman and also steadied her on her rocky path. The septuagenarian became her confidant and her mentor, the one person she could totally trust. He sent her sound advice, and wrote a short, amusing précis of his life for her. They flirted with each other on paper, safe in the knowledge that her scarred face and his age would never matter because they were never going to meet. With Casanova's help and influence, Cecile secured a respectable paid position at the court of the Duke of Courlande, and in 1801 she married a count and had four children of her own. Without Casanova's disinterested friendship, she might well have ended her days in a poor-house or a brothel.

Even from his sickbed, Casanova continued his long correspondence with a dear female friend, Elisa von der Recke, to whom he wrote delightful poetry, and who, from her own sickbed in nearby Toplitz, sent him wine, crawfish soup far superior to the mess concocted by the castle's cook, and inspiring notes. They both knew that he was dying, for it was a fact that Casanova faced as unflinchingly as he had faced the other vicissitudes of his life. 'I swear that the idea of being separated from you cuts me to the

quick,' Elisa wrote to him, 'but the noble courage with which you approach the sombre gates of death elevates my soul.'[11]

Casanova believed that death was 'a monster which drives an attentive spectator from the great theatre before the end of a play which infinitely interests him. This alone is reason enough to hate it.'[12] The great unfinished drama of his own life had been abandoned in a corner of the library, its highs and lows inscribed on piles of dusty manuscript pages bundled up with ribbon and string. Writing it was a mammoth task – so overwhelming, in fact, that he never got beyond the year 1774, where his story abruptly ended with the middle-aged adventurer anticipating a tryst with a twelve-year-old girl. Although he was unable to face setting down the final, sad humiliating act – his life at Dux – the pleasure which he experienced whilst recalling the rest is evident on every one of the thousands of pages. He was unabashed about having written so much about himself: 'Worthy or unworthy, my life is my subject, my subject is my life. Having lived it without ever believing that I would want to write about it one day, it may be interesting in a way it would not have been if I had lived it with the intention of writing about it in old age and, what is more, publishing it.'[13]

In fact Casanova intended from the start that the work would eventually be published, and with that in mind he deliberately wrote in French, the lingua franca of Europe's educated classes, rather than in his native Venetian dialect or in Italian, a language which in the eighteenth century was spoken and read by few educated people outside Italy. Encouraged by the Prince de Ligne – who advised him to 'Put everything in print, believe me, in detail, year by year' and to 'Poke fun at your pleasures, if you want: but do not veil them'[14] – he held little back except a few names, and the details of his divine Henriette's story. Since false modesty was never one of his vices, Casanova believed that his memoirs would make him famous one day. But even in his wildest imaginings he could never have conceived just *how* famous, and for what reason.

For Casanova's name has echoed down the centuries and around the world as a synonym for a serial seducer of women. Nowadays

he is remembered not as a great writer or philosopher but as the greatest lover who has ever lived. Since it was first printed in 1822 – in a much edited and expurgated German translation – his long memoir has spawned a veritable academic and publishing industry. many scores of editions of it have been published, and it has been translated into at least twenty languages. By the dawn of the twenty-first century Casanova has featured as the hero of more than forty novels and has been the subject of twenty-five biographies. Scholars have written thousands of books, theses and articles about particular aspects of his life, including his correspondence, his methods of travelling around Europe, his knowledge of medicine, and his use of the Kabbalah. By 2006 twenty-four films and TV series have been made about Casanova in which he has been reincarnated by some of the most famous film actors of the twentieth century, including Donald Sutherland, Richard Chamberlain, Tony Curtis, Peter O'Toole, Marcello Mastroianni, *Dracula* star Vincent Price and, most recently, Heath Ledger. Casanova has inspired at least one ballet,[15] two operas[16] and a trio of musical scores, including a symphony for violencello and wind orchestra.[17]

Casanova has achieved the seemingly impossible by becoming both a male role model who is the very essence of *machismo* and, at the same time, a post-Feminist icon praised for his liberated attitude to women's sexuality. His name garners more than three million hits on the internet search engine Google, and has its own place in the Oxford English Dictionary as a term describing 'a man notorious for seducing women'.

And in Dux (now Duchcov in the Czech Republic) where for many years he felt so scorned and despised, Casanova is now the town's most famous celebrity and its main claim to fame. Academics come from around the world to consult the remarkable Casanova archive in the town's museum. Tourists who know little about the eighteenth century flock to Duchcov's annual Casanova festival, and visit Waldstein's grand baroque castle just to photograph their hero's armchair or touch the bed where he slept. And after they have searched for his unmarked grave and photographed

the simple plaque to him in the church, they toast his memory at the eponymous Café Casanova in the market square.

How amazed Casanova would be if he knew a fraction of all this! But as he lies dying he knows only that he has not a single friend at his bedside; that although his blood runs in the veins of at least three daughters and two sons he communicates with none of them; that the world which once fêted him has forgotten him; and that he has failed to find a publisher for his great work – at one point he even contemplated burning it. Having no legitimate heir, he has left the manuscript of *Histoire de Ma Vie* to his niece's husband Carlo Angiolini, who arrived in Dux recently to look after him in his dying days; and in 1821 Carlo's son will sell it to the German printer Brockhaus for the paltry sum of 200 thalers.

Tonight Casanova is beyond caring. An opportunist to the very end, his last words are reputed to be 'I have lived as a philosopher, but die as a Christian'. Will he be pulled down into the flames of Hell for his compulsive womanising like the anti-hero of Mozart's opera *Don Giovanni*, the premiere of which he almost certainly attended in Prague in October 1787 and the libretto of which he is rumoured to have collaborated on? Casanova thinks not. For despite his loneliness and his pain, his poverty and his bitter predicament, he is convinced that he has done good in the world, particularly to women, and he remains an optimist at heart. There are misfortunes in life, of course, as he is the first to know. But their very existence has proved to him over the last seventy-three years that the sum of good is greater. If pleasure exists, then life is a joy. And where there are women, there is always pleasure to be found.

'I am infinitely happy when I am in a dark room and see the light coming through a window which opens on to a vast horizon,' Casanova has written. Now, with a final, terrible effort that takes every last shred of his energy, he suddenly raises his head and gazes through his bedroom window, beyond the reflection of the old, gaunt, hollow-eyed stranger staring back at him, and out into the blank, black horizon of the Bohemian night. There are no stars out

there but, instead, a galaxy of women. The women who nurtured him. The women who toyed with him. The women he flirted with and seduced. The women who adored him. The women whose fortunes he made, and those whose fortunes he plundered, and the women whose lives he all but ruined. The women who, for better or for worse, have made Casanova the man he is.

Leaving his aching limbs behind him, Casanova rises from his bed and walks towards them. Here is Marina Morosini, propositioning him from behind her convent grating. And Bettina, holding up those unforgettable knitted stockings that started it all. There are Nanetta and Marta, giggling at him from their big bed on the top floor of their aunt's palazzo. And Marcia, his loving grandmother, come to rescue him from yet another debacle.

Here is Lucia, dancing her way to an early death in a sordid Amsterdam brothel. And there Marianne de Charpillon, still turning her back on him after all these years. And his mother Zanetta, as beautiful as she is impossible to please. And the mad, lonely Marquise d'Urfé, weeping secret tears over his betrayal of her.

Here is Sophia Williams sleeping the peaceful sleep of the self-righteous whilst her mother Teresa, the one-time famous London celebrity, dies alone and in agony in gaol. And Donna Lucrezia, resigned to being supplanted in his affections by their daughter Leonilda. And Leonilda, the mother of her own half-brother.

And here, waiting for him, is Henriette – his wondrous, mysterious Henriette – standing in front of Casanova on the windswept path to the unknown just as she once stood before him on the road leading up to her château, her body obscured by her hooded cloak and her face turned away from him.

NOTES

PREFACE

Casanova's twelve-volume *Histoire de Ma Vie* has appeared in countless editions. All quotations from it in this book are taken from the original French text, published in 1993 by Robert Laffont/Bouquins in a three-volume paperback edition, edited by Francis Lacassin. For simplicity, references in the endnotes refer to HDMV, followed by the Bouquins volume number (I, II, or III) followed by the page number in that volume.

PREFACE 2 APRIL 1798

1 Anon., *Onania – or the Heinous Sin of Self-Pollution, and all its frightful consequences in both sexes, considered. With spiritual and physical advice, etc.* London, 1737, p.137
2 HDMV, Bouquins III, p.672
3 HDMV, Bouquins I, p.346
4 HDMV, Bouquins I, p.847
5 Abbé Taruffi, cited in J. Rives Childs, *Casanova – A Biography Based on New Documents*, George Allen and Unwin, London 1961, p.220
6 Giacomo Casanova, cited in Arthur Symons, *Casanova at Dux*, An Unpublished Chapter of History

1 ZANETTA

1 HDMV, Bouquins I, p.171
2 HDMV, Bouquins I, p.23
3 HDMV, Bouquins I, p.20
4 Helmut Watzlawick, 'Les Vrais Débuts d'une Actrice, Naissance et Baptême de Zanetta Casanova', *Intermédiare des Casanovistes*, 2003, p.51, note 3
5 Maurice Andrieux, *Daily Life in Venice at the Time of Casanova*, George Allen and Unwin, London, 1972, p.183
6 Antonio Valeri, 'Casanoviana', *Fanfulla della Domenica*, 25 June 1899
7 HDMV, Bouquins I, p.25
8 HDMV, Bouquins I, p.29
9 Carlo Goldoni, *Mémoires*, Duchesnes, Paris, 1787, Vol I, p.273
10 Goldoni, op.cit., Vol I, p.275

11 Goldoni, op.cit., Vol I, Ch XXXV, p.277
12 Goldoni, op.cit., Vol I, Ch XXXV, p.277
13 HDMV, Bouquins I, p.51
14 HDMV, Bouquins I, p.638
15 HDMV, Bouquins I, p.101
16 The queen: Elizabeth Maria Josepha (1669–1757), wife of Augustus III and Queen of Poland
17 HDMV, Bouquins I, pp.100–101
18 *Beitrage zur Histoire und Aufnahme des Theaters*, Stuttgart 1750, I, p.278, – quoted HDMV, Bouquins I, p.969
19 HDMV, Bouquins II, p.712

2   VIRGINS OF THE VENETO

1 HDMV, Bouquins II, p.783
2 HDMV, Bouquins I, p.28
3 HDMV, Bouquins I, p.32
4 HDMV, Bouquins I, p.33
5 HDMV, Bouquins I, p.33
6 HDMV, Bouquins I, p.35
7 Anon, cited in Muriel Segal, *Virgins – Reluctant, Dubious and Avowed*, Robert Hale, London 1978, p.88
8 Wetenhall Wilkes, *A Letter of Genteel and Moral Advice to a Young Lady*, 1740, cited in Julie Peakman, *Lascivious Bodies – A sexual history of the eighteenth century*, Atlantic Books, London, 2004, p.27
9 Muriel Segal, *Virgins*, p.26
10 Voltaire, *Notebooks*, ed T. Besterman, 2nd Edn. 91968 Vol II, The Leningrad Notebooks (c.1735–1750), p.455
11 Casanova, *Confutazione della Storia del Governo Veneto d'Amelot de la Houssaie*, Amsterdam 1767, quoted in HDMV, Bouquins I, p.972
12 HDMV, Bouquins I, p.43
13 HDMV, Bouquins I, p.50
14 HDMV, Bouquins I, p.50
15 HDMV, Bouquins I, p.51
16 Charles de Brosses, *Lettres Familières*, Letter XIII, Paris 1931, I, p.155. Quoted in Rives Childs, p.5
17 HDMV, Bouquins I, p.52
18 HDMV, Bouquins I, p.57
19 HDMV, Bouquins I, p.58
20 HDMV, Bouquins I, p.103
21 HDMV, Bouquins I, pp.58–9
22 HDMV, Bouquins I, p.70
23 HDMV, Bouquins I, p.75
24 HDMV, Bouquins I, p.71
25 HDMV, Bouquins I, p.72
26 Archivo della Parrochia S. Giacomo dall'Orio, battesimi 1705–1715 (Anno 1707)
27 HDMV, Bouquins I, p.78
28 HDMV, Bouquins I, pp.80–81
29 HDMV, Bouquins I, p.84
30 HDMV, Bouquins I, p.85
31 HDMV, Bouquins I, p.89
32 HDMV, Bouquins II, p.129

33 HDMV, Bouquins II, p.129
34 HDMV, Bouquins II, p.233
35 HDMV, Bouquins II, p.130
36 HDMV, Bouquins I, p.134
37 'in the year 1776' Casanova adds, but he was mistaken. Bettina died on 29 June 1777
38 HDMV, Bouquins I, p.51

3 DONNA LUCREZIA

1 HDMV, Bouquins II, p.347
2 HDMV, Bouquins I, p.165
3 Thomas Nugent, The Grand Tour, London 1749, Vol III, p.36.ff
4 NB: Capuchin monks did not shave
5 HDMV, Bouquins I, p.172
6 HDMV, Bouquins I, p.173
7 HDMV, Bouquins I, p.179
8 Johann Goethe, Italian Journey, translated by W.H. Auden and Elizabeth Mayer, Penguin Classics, 1970, p.184
9 Charles de Brosses, Selections from the Letters of Charles de Brosses, translated by Lord Ronald Sutherland Gower, Kegan Paul, London, 1897, p.115
10 Thomas Nugent, New Observations on Italy and its Inhabitants, written in French by two Swedish Gentlemen, translated by Nugent, L. Davis and C. Reymers, London, 1769, Vol II, p.212
11 Jerome le Français de Lalande, Voyage d'une Française en Italie fait dans les années 1765 et 1766, Paris, 1768, Vol VI. p.339
12 Thomas Nugent, New Observations, Vol II, pp.212–213
13 Carlo Goldoni, Mémoires, p.386
14 Charles de Brosses, Selections, pp.119–120
15 HDMV, Bouquins I, p.174
16 HDMV, Bouquins I, p.174
17 HDMV, Bouquins I, p.175
18 HDMV, Bouquins I, p.176
19 HDMV, Bouquins I, p.177
20 HDMV, Bouquins I, p.177
21 Johann Goethe, Italian Journey, Translated by W.H. Auden and Elizabeth Mayer, Penguin Classics, 1970, p.133
22 Charles de Brosses, Selections, p.135
23 HDMV, Bouquins I, p, 179
24 HDMV, Bouquins I, p, 183
25 HDMV, Bouquins I, p, 184
26 HDMV, Bouquins I, p, 185
27 Johann Goethe, Italian Journey, p.138
28 HDMV, Bouquins I, p.195
29 HDMV, Bouquins I, p.196
30 HDMV, Bouquins I, p.196
31 HDMV, Bouquins I, p.203
32 HDMV, Bouquins I, p.204
33 HDMV, Bouquins I, p.205
34 HDMV, Bouquins II, p.579
35 HDMV, Bouquins II, p.627
36 HDMV, Bouquins II, p.636

37 HDMV, Bouquins II, p.637
38 HDMV, Bouquins III, p.310
39 HDMV, Bouquins II, p.639
40 HDMV, Bouquins II, p.639
41 HDMV, Bouquins II, p.640
42 HDMV, Bouquins II, p.644
43 Casanova, Letter to Opiz, January 10, 1791
44 J. Rives Childs, *Casanova – A Biography*

4 BELLINO

1 HDMV, Bouquins II, p.898
2 Cited in J. Rives Childs, *Casanova –A New Perspective*, Constable, London, 1989, p.33
3 HDMV, Bouquins I, p.225
4 Dr Charles Burney, *The Present State of Music in France and Italy*, cited in Angus Heriot, *The Castrati in Opera*, Secker and Warburg, London, 1956, p.42
5 Cited in Angus Heriot, *The Castrati*, p.26
6 Charles de Brosses: *Lettres Familières sur l'Italie*, Paris, 1931, cited in Angus Heriot, *The Castrati*, p.14
7 HDMV, Bouquins I, p.186
8 HDMV, Bouquins II, p.654
9 HDMV, Bouquins III, p.966
10 HDMV, Bouquins I, p.231
11 HDMV, Bouquins I, p.233
12 HDMV, Bouquins I, p.234
13 HDMV, Bouquins I, p.236
14 HDMV, Bouquins I, p.245, note 2
15 HDMV, Bouquins I, p.246
16 HDMV, Bouquins I, p.246
17 HDMV, Bouquins I, p.240
18 HDMV, Bouquins I, p.240
19 HDMV, Bouquins I, p.241
20 HDMV, Bouquins I, p.242
21 HDMV, Bouquins I, p.250
22 HDMV, Bouquins I, p.250
23 HDMV, Bouquins I, p.251
24 HDMV, Bouquins I, p.251
25 HDMV, Bouquins I, p.294
26 Archives de Dux, Marr 40–264. '*Il est ordonné . . . de laisser surement et librement passer: Jacques Cazanua Italien agé de trente deux ans, taille de cinq pieds dix pouces et demie ou Environs Visage long plain Bazanné Le nez long et gros. La bouche grande Les yeux bruns a fleure de teste Qui va en Flandre*'
27 HDMV, Bouquins I, p.253
28 HDMV, Bouquins I, p.264
29 HDMV, Bouquins I, p.264
30 HDMV, Bouquins I, p.264
31 HDMV, Bouquins I, p.271
32 HDMV, Bouquins II, p.575
33 HDMV, Bouquins II, p.574
34 HDMV, Bouquins II, p.577
35 HDMV, Bouquins II, p.579

5 HENRIETTE

1 HDMV, Bouquins II, p.909
2 HDMV, Bouquins I, p.501
3 HDMV, Bouquins I, p.374
4 HDMV, Bouquins I, p.380
5 HDMV, Bouquins I, p.384
6 HDMV, Bouquins I, p.448
7 HDMV, Bouquins I, p.473
8 HDMV, Bouquins I, p.477
9 HDMV, Bouquins I, p.478
10 Tartan: a small, two-masted sailing vessel
11 HDMV, Bouquins I, p.489
12 HDMV, Bouquins I, p.490
13 HDMV, Bouquins I, p.490
14 HDMV, Bouquins I, p.491
15 HDMV, Bouquins I, p.493
16 HDMV, Bouquins I, p.492
17 Louis Jean André, 'Sous le Masque d'Anne d'Arci: Adélaïde de Gueidan', Intermédiare des Casanovistes, No XIII, 1996, p.10
18 HDMV, Bouquins I, p.501
19 HDMV, Bouquins III, p.69
20 HDMV, Bouquins I, p.508
21 HDMV, Bouquins I, p.511
22 HDMV, Bouquins I, p.517
23 HDMV, Bouquins I, p.517
24 Horace Walpole cited in The Grand Tour 1592–1796, ed. Roger Hudson, The Folio Society, London 1993, p.70
25 HDMV, Bouquins I, p.520
26 HDMV, Bouquins I, p.520
27 HDMV, Bouquins I, p.522
28 HDMV, Bouquins I, p.521
29 Laurence Sterne, Tristram Shandy, cited in Roger Hudson, The Grand Tour, p.30
30 HDMV, Bouquins III, p.22
31 Casanova spoke French with a strong Italian accent
32 Letter of 28 May 1763 from Marie de Nairne to Baron Michel de Ramsay, cited in Compigny des Bordes, Casanova et la Marquise d'Urfé, n.p., Paris 1922, p.2
33 HDMV, Bouquins III, pp.63–4
34 HDMV, Bouquins III, p.65
35 Helmut Watzlawick 'Fata Viam Invenient, or Henriette Forever', Intermédiare des Casanovistes, No. VI, 1989
36 Jean Louis André, in the article ' "Sous le Masque" d'Anne d'Arci: Adelaide de Gueidan', Intermédiare des Casanovistes, No. XIII, 1996
37 'une foule de chambres et de cabinets obscurs'. Une Famille Provençale: Les Gueidan, Arts & Livres de Provence Bulletin No.29, Marseille 1956 p.81
38 Archives Départementales. Notaires d'Aix Series 303 E 486, p.1050
39 'une famille distinguée, qu'on pourrait même qualifier d'illustre': Gaspard de Gueidan, cited in Une Famille Provençale: Les Gueidan, p.74
40 Une Famille Provençale: Les Gueidan, p.75
41 Archive Gueidan. Bibliothèque de l'Académie d'Aix-Musée Arbaud, Aix-en-Provence, cited by Louis Jean André, 'Sous le masque', p.11
42 In French: 'pour le voiturier qui a porté la malle à Cannes'.

6 M.M. AND C.C.

1 HDMV, Bouquins III, p.649
2 HDMV, Bouquins I, pp.714–15
3 HDMV, Bouquins I, p.719
4 Pierre Gruet, 'M.M. et Les Anges de Murano', *Casanova Gleanings*, XVIII, 1975
5 Letter from Prince de Ligne to Casanova, cited in Bouquins I, p.1046
6 Dr Charles Burney on the profession of a young Roman noblewoman, cited in Hudson, *The Grand Tour*, pp.182–3
7 Arcangela Tarabotti, *Inferno Monacale*, cited in Mary Laven, *Virgins of Venice*, Viking, London, 2002, p.22
8 Arcangela Tarabotti, cited in Mary Laven, *Virgins of Venice*, Viking, London, 2002, p.31
9 James Howell, cited in James Morris, *Venice*, Faber & Faber, London, 1960, p.290
10 *Anecdotes Dramatiques*, Duchesne, Paris, 1775
11 François de Bernis, *Memoirs and Letters of Cardinal Pierre de Bernis*, translated by Katherine Prescott Wormeley, London, William Heinemann 1902, Vol I, p.172
12 François de Bernis, *Memoirs and Letters*, Vol I, pp.175–6
13 HDMV, Bouquins I, p.790
14 Pilatti di Tassulo, *Reisen in verschiedenen Landern von Europa in den Jahren 1774–5 und 1776*, cited in Maurice Andrieux, *Daily Life in Venice at the Time of Casanova*, translated by Mary Fitton, George Allen & Unwin, London, 1972, pp.225/6
15 HDMV, Bouquins I, p.750.
16 HDMV, Bouquins I, p.668
17 HDMV, Bouquins I, p.662
18 HDMV, Bouquins I, p.671
19 HDMV, Bouquins I, p.679
20 HDMV, Bouquins I, p.709
21 HDMV, Bouquins I, p.713
22 HDMV, Bouquins I, p.721
23 HDMV, Bouquins 1, p.732
24 HDMV, Bouquins 1, p.736
25 HDMV, Bouquins I, p.747
26 HDMV, Bouquins I, pp.757–8
27 HDMV, Bouquins I, p.760
28 HDMV, Bouquins I, p.771
29 HDMV, Bouquins I, p.798
30 HDMV, Bouquins I, p.799
31 François de Bernis, *Memoirs and Letters*, Vol I, p.177
32 *My house in the fields*: In March 1754, de Bernis rented a villa on the Brenta Canal which linked Venice and Padua
33 Cited in Rives Childs, *Casanova*, p.82
34 Letter from Lady Mary Wortley Montagu, 30 May 1757, cited in Rives Childs, *Casanova*, pp.83–4
35 Rives Childs, *Casanova*, p.84
36 Giovanni Battista Manuzzi, 'Report to the Inquisitors Concerning Casanova's Activities', 17 July 1755, cited in *Story of My Life*, translated by Willard R. Trask, Johns Hopkins University Press, Baltimore and London, 1977, Vol 4, p.357
37 Manuzzi, cited in Bouquins, I, p.1055
38 Rives Childs, *Casanova*, p.85

7 MANON BALLETTI

1 HDMV, Bouquins I, p.847
2 Emile Campardon, *Les Comédiens du Roi de la Troupe Italienne* – Slatkine Reprints, Geneva, 1970, p.12
3 HDMV, Bouquins II, p.16
4 HDMV, Bouquins I, pp.560–1
5 Archives de la Bastille, 10243 ff 187–9, and 10235 fol. 362 v°
6 HDMV, Bouquins I, p.866
7 HDMV, Bouquins I, p.868
8 Manon Balletti, letter to Casanova, Archives at Dux, Marr 8–139
9 HDMV, Bouquins II, p.15
10 HDMV, Bouquins II, p.31
11 HDMV, Bouquins II, p.55
12 HDMV, Bouquins II, p.57
13 HDMV, Bouquins II, pp.65–6
14 HDMV, Bouquins II, p.42
15 Archives at Dux, Marr 8–139
16 Archives at Dux, Marr 8–139
17 Archives at Dux, Marr 8–161
18 Archives at Dux, Marr 8–145
19 Archives at Dux, Marr 8–150
20 Archives at Dux, Marr 8–149
21 *Stronsegosse* – the invented word seems to be a mixture of Italian and French: *Stronse*: Ital: excrement and *gosse*: Fr: a kid, or brat
22 Archives at Dux Marr 8–142
23 Archives at Dux, Marr 8–156
24 Archives at Dux Marr 8–120
25 Archives de Dux, Marr 8–143
26 Archives at Dux, Marr 8–155
27 Archives at Dux, Marr 8–130
28 Archives at Dux, Marr 8–153
29 Archives at Dux Marr 8–135
30 Archives at Dux, Marr 8–136
31 Archives at Dux, Marr 8–141
32 Archives at Dux, Marr 8–144
33 HDMV, Bouquins II, p.199
34 Archives at Dux, Marr 8–137
35 Archives at Dux, Marr 8–148
36 Archives at Dux, Marr 8–121
37 Archives at Dux, Marr 8–132
38 HDMV, Bouquins II, p.148
39 Giustiniana Wynne to Andrea Memmo, 8 January 1759, cited in Rives Childs, *Casanova*, p. 102
40 HDMV, Bouquins II, p.191
41 HDMV, Bouquins II, p.209
42 HDMV, Bouquins II, p.199
43 Archives de Dux, Marr 8–129
44 Archives at Dux, Marr 8–152
45 Marr 8–147
46 Archives at Dux, Marr 8–147
47 HDMV, Bouquins II, p.247
48 Archives at Dux, Marr 8–126

49 Archives at Dux, Marr 8–137
50 Archives at Dux, Marr 8–159
51 HDMV, Bouquins II, p.242
52 HDMV, Bouquins II, p.242
53 HDMV, Bouquins II, p.247
54 Pierre Labracherie, *Silvia et Mario en Ménage, L'Illustre Théâtre, la Vie et l'Histoire de la Comédie Française, No 3.*, Editions du Tertre, Paris 1955, pp.29–32
55 HDMV, Bouquins II, p.706

8   THE MARQUISE D'URFÉ

1 Bouquins I, p.3
2 Archives Nationale de France, T47925
3 HDMV, Bouquins II, p.87
4 Renée Froulay, *Souvenirs de la Marquise de Créquy de 1710 a 1803*, n.p., Paris, 1842
5 Jacques Cazotte, letter of 8 May 1792, cited in Charles Samaran, *Jacques Casanova Vénitien*, Calmann-Lévy, Paris 1914, p.213
6 Edouard Maynial, *Casanova and His Time*, translated by Ethel Colburn Mayne, Chapman & Hall, London, 1911, p. 148
7 Arche de la Bastille, 11751
8 Letter from M. de Beausset to the Duc de Choiseul, cited in Edouard Maynial, *Casanova and His Time*, p.156
9 Report by Manuzzi of 11 November 1754, quoted Maynial, *Casanova and his Time*, p. 152
10 HDMV, Bouquins I, p.8–9
11 HDMV, Bouquins II, p.85
12 HDMV, Bouquins II, p.95
13 HDMV, Bouquins II, p.96
14 N. du Hausset, *Secret memoirs of the courts of Louis XV and XVI*, n.p., Paris, 1904
15 cited in Maynial, *Casanova and His Time*, p.7
16 *Memoires of Madame Hausset*, quoted in Edouard Maynial, p.13
17 HDMV, Bouquins II, p.95
18 HDMV, Bouquins II, p.184
19 Archives Nationales de France, Y 11337, comm Chenon. See also Samaran, *Jacques Casanova*, p.240
20 HDMV, Bouquins II, p.471
21 In Aristotelian thought, it was believed that people had two souls, one sensitive, one intelligent
22 HDMV, Bouquins II, pp.731–2
23 HDMV, Bouquins II, p.737
24 HDMV, Bouquins II, p.783
25 HDMV, Bouquins III, p.36
26 HDMV, Bouquins III, p.41
27 HDMV, Bouquins III, p.44
28 HDMV, Bouquins III, p.42
29 HDMV, Bouquins III, p.50–51
30 HDMV, Bouquins III, p.76
31 Letter to Passano from Teresa Cornelys, 28 June 1763, cited in Samaran, *Jacques Casanova*, pp.222–5
32 Letter from Passano to Marquise d'Urfé, cited in Samaran, pp.224–5
33 Cited in HDMV, Bouquins II, p.935
34 Giacomo Passano, letter of 11 July 1763, quoted in Samaran, pp.227–8
35 HDMV, Bouquins III, p.198

36 HDMV, Bouquins II, p.716
37 Marquise d'Urfé, Bibliothèque Municipale de Montbrison, cited in Samaran, pp.230/31
38 Archives at Dux, Marco-134
39 Archives Nationales de France, F7 4 648, cited in Samaran, p.246
40 Cited in Samaran, p.246
41 Archives Nationales de France, Y 11,577 and Y10894
42 Comte de Perouse, letter of 15 December 1773. Archives de Dux, cited in HDMV, Bouquins II, p.973

9   MARIANNE DE CHARPILLON AND PAULINE

1 HDMV, Bouquins II, p.670
2 Comte d'Espinchal, *Journal d'émigration*, n.p., Paris, 1913, pp.35–6
3 Report of 16 April 1750, Archives de la Bastille, 10238, fol.306–308
4 Archives de la Bastille, 10238, fol.306–309
5 Archives de la Bastille, 10238, fol.312–315
6 HDMV, Bouquins III, p.222
7 HDMV, Bouquins III, p.231
8 *Harris's List of Covent Garden Ladies*, n.p., London, 1793
9 HDMV, Bouquins III, p.85
10 Cited in J. Rives Childs, *Casanova*, p.188
11 HDMV, Bouquins III, p.165
12 HDMV, Bouquins III, p.195
13 HDMV, Bouquins III, p.198
14 HDMV, Bouquins III, p.221
15 HDMV, Bouquins III, p.221
16 HDMV, Bouquins III, p.222
17 HDMV, Bouquins III, p.234
18 Marianne de Charpillon, letter to Casanova, Archives at Dux, Marr 2–210
19 HDMV, Bouquins III, p.236
20 HDMV, Bouquins III, p.245
21 HDMV, Bouquins III, p.247
22 HDMV, Bouquins III, p.251
23 HDMV, Bouquins III, p.253
24 Records of Clerkenwell Court, Middlesex, cited in J. Rives Child, *Casanova*, p.189/190
25 BL, Add MSS. 30880B. fol.71
26 *Gentleman's Magazine*, 68, 1798, p.81
27 BL Add Mss. 30880A, fol. 36
28 BL Add Mss. 30880A, fol. 40
29 BL Add Mss. 30880A, fol. 36
30 BL Add Mss. 30880A, fol. 111
31 BL Add Mss. 30880A, fol. 75
32 BL Add Mss. 30880A, letter of 9 July 1775
33 BL Add Mss. 30880A, ff.99
34 BL Add Mss. 30880A, ff.83
35 BL Add Mss. 30880A. ff.139
36 BL Add Mss. 30880A. ff.141
37 BL Add Mss. 30880A. ff.143
38 BL Add Mss. 30880A. ff. 145
39 BL Add Mss. 30880A. ff.147

10 SOPHIA WILLIAMS AND TERESA IMER CORNELYS

1 HDMV, Bouquins III, p.310
2 Sophia Williams, cited in Donald Clarke, *A Daisy in the Broom, The Story of a School 1820–1958*, Julia London, Tweeddale, 1991, p.13
3 Sophia Williams, cited in Clarke, *A Daisy*, p.25
4 Sophia Williams, cited in Clarke, *A Daisy*, p.114
5 HDMV, Bouquins II, p.122
6 HDMV, Bouquins III, p.142
7 HDMV, Bouquins III, p.142
8 HDMV, Bouquins III, p.69
9 HDMV, Bouquins I, p.844
10 HDMV, Bouquins III, p.396
11 HDMV, Bouquins III, p.928
12 HDMV, Bouquins III, p.166
13 HDMV, Bouquins III, p.173
14 HDMV, Bouquins III, p.208
15 HDMV, Bouquins III, p.215
16 HDMV, Bouquins III, p.227
17 HDMV, Bouquins III, p.825
18 Clarke, *A Daisy*, p.15
19 Cited in Judith Summers, *The Empress of Pleasure*, Viking-Penguin, London, 2002, pp.255–6
20 Will of Sophia Wilhelmina Frederica Williams, PRO, Prob 11/1673
21 Cited in Clarke, *A Daisy*, p.17
22 John Taylor, *Records of My Life*, Edward Bull, London, 1832

11   4 JUNE 1798

1 HDMV, Bouquins I, p.245
2 HDMV, Bouquins III, p.767
3 In his manuscript Casanova first transcribed *twenty-one*, then crossed it out. In fact, they had parted in December 1749 or January 1750, nineteen and a half years previously
4 HDMV, Bouquins III, pp.731–2
5 HDMV, Bouquins III, 732
6 HDMV, Bouquins III, p.987
7 Casanova, letter to Lorenzo Morosini, 22 September 1782, cited in Rives Childs, *Casanova*, p.281
8 Francesca Buschini, letter of 14 April 1784
9 Francesca Buschini, letter of 29 May 1784
10 Prince de Ligne, *Pensées, portraits et lettres à Casanova et à la marquise de Coigny*, Rivages Poches, Paris 2002, p.86. The prince has written 1742, meaning the year of Casanova's birth. In fact, he was born in 1725
11 Letter from Elisa von der Recke, 29 April 1798, Archives of Dux, Marr 8–12
12 HDMV, Bouquins I, p.9
13 HDMV, Vol I Preface, Bouquins I, p.4
14 Prince de Ligne, *Pensées*, p.91
15 *Casanova*, music by Goran Vejvoda, choreography and costumes by Angelin Preljocaj, 1998
16 Dominick Argento, *Casanova's Homecoming*, 1984; and Daniel Schnyder, *Casanova*
17 *Casanova* by Johan de Meij, 1999

BRIEF CHRONOLOGY

1697:	birth of Gaetano Giacomo Casanova, Casanova's father.
1707:	27 August: birth of Casanova's mother, Zuanna (Giovanna) Maria Farussi, known as Zanetta.
1709:	marriage of Marcia Baldissera to Girolamo Farussi.
1724:	27 February: marriage of Zanetta Farussi to Gaetano Casanova. Death of Girolamo Farussi, Zanetta's father.
1725:	2 April: birth of Giacomo Girolamo Casanova in Venice. 5 May: Giacomo baptised in church of San Samuele.
1726/7:	Zanetta and Gaetano go to London, leaving Casanova with his grandmother.
1727:	1 June: birth of Casanova's brother Francesco in London.
1728:	Zanetta and Gaetano return to Venice.
1730:	4 November: birth of Casanova's brother Giovanni Battista.
1731:	28 December: birth of Casanova's sister Faustina Maddelena.
1732:	25 December: birth of Casanova's youngest sister Maria Maddelena Antonia Stella.
1733:	18 December: death of Gaetano Casanova, aged thirty-six.
1734:	16 February: birth of Casanova's youngest brother Gaetano Alviso. 2 April: Zanetta takes Casanova to Padua and leaves him with Signora Mida. She spends the summer in Verona with the San Samuele theatre company. 24 November: Goldoni's play, *Belisario*, is premiered in Venice, followed by *La Pupilla*, a play inspired by Zanetta. During the summer Casanova moves to Dr Antonio Gozzi's house in Padua and meets Bettina.
1735:	Easter: Zanetta leaves for St Petersburg, leaving her children with her mother.
1736:	20 August: death of Casanova's four-year-old sister Faustina.
1737:	Zanetta returns from St Petersburg. 1737/1738: she leaves for Dresden. Casanova enrolled at Padua University.
1739:	Marcia brings Casanova back to Venice.
1740:	14 February: Casanova takes the tonsure at the church of San Samuele. Meets Senator Malipiero and Teresa Imer.
1741:	22 January: Patriarch of Venice confers four minor orders on Casanova. He meets Angela Tosello, and Marta and Nanetta Savorgnan. Possible first trip to Corfu.
1742:	Casanova returns to Venice by 2 April. May: he meets Lucia on visit to Friuli.
1743:	18 March: death of Marcia Farussi. Casanova stays at the seminary on Murano for two weeks.

1744:   Casanova goes to Martirano, Naples and Rome where he enters service of Cardinal Acquaviva. Affairs with Donna Lucrezia and Bellino/Teresa Lanti.

1745:   17 January: marriage of Lucrezia d'Antoni, the sister of Casanova's 'Donna Lucrezia'. End January–beginning February: Casanova leaves Rome and returns to Venice. Teresa Imer leaves Venice for Vienna where she marries Angelo Pompeati. Marriage of Nanetta Savorgnan. Marta Savorgnan enters convent. Birth of Cesarino, Casanova's son by Teresa Lanti; and of Leonilda, his daughter by Donna Lucrezia. Casanova leaves for Corfu, travelling on to Constantinople in July and returning to Corfu in October. Leaves for Venice on the twenty-fifth where he is employed as a lawyer in the office of Manzoni.

1746:   Casanova employed as a violinist at San Samuele theatre during the carnival. April: meets Senator Matteo Bragadin.

1748:   6 November: premiere in Dresden of Zanetta Casanova's play *Le Contese di Mestre e Malghera per il Trono*.

1749:   early in year, Casanova compelled to leave Venice. Financed by Bragadin, he travels to Milan where he meets Marina (Teresa Lanti's sister) and Antonio Balletti. In the autumn he meets Henriette in Cesena and travels with her to Parma and Milan.

1750:   February: Henriette returns to France via Geneva. April/May: Casanova is in Venice. June: leaves for Paris, meeting up with Antonio Balletti en route. He is initiated into freemasonry in Lyon. July/August: Casanova arrives in Paris. His first meeting with Silvia and Mario Balletti and their young daughter Manon.

1751:   Casanova translates *Zoroastre* for the Dresden court.

1752:   October: Casanova and his brother Francesco leave Paris for Dresden to visit Zanetta.

1753:   April: Casanova leaves Dresden and returns to Venice via Prague and Vienna. Love affairs with Teresa Imer, Caterina Capretta, and the nun M.M. (Marina Morosini). December: meets the French ambassador, the Abbé Joachim de Bernis.

1754:   birth in Bayreuth of Teresa Imer's daughter Sophia.

1755:   April/May: De Bernis leaves Venice. 25/26 July: Casanova arrested and imprisoned under The Leads in the Doge's Palace.

1756:   31 October/1 November: Casanova escapes from The Leads and heads for Paris via Munich, Augsburg and Strasbourg.

1757:   5 January: Casanova arrives in Paris, talks his way into a job with the finance ministry and organises a state lottery in conjunction with Cazalbigi. His flirtation with Manon Balletti begins. August–September: Casanova sent on secret mission for French Government.

1757–1758:   Casanova meets the Marquise d'Urfé.

1758:   18 April: the first lottery draw. 16 September: death of Silvia Balletti. October: Casanova sent to Holland where he runs into Teresa Imer and their daughter, Sophia.

1758/1759:   Casanova opens a wallpaper factory.

1759:   January: Casanova returns to Paris with Giuseppe Pompeati. He adopts the name the Chevalier de Seingault, and rents a country house on the outskirts of Paris. First meeting with Marianne de Charpillon in the Palais Marchand. August: brief imprisonment for debt in the Fors L'Evêque. Late September: Casanova leaves Paris

for Holland. October: Teresa Imer and Sophia leave Holland for England.

1760: 5 February: last love letter from Manon Balletti. Casanova travels to Cologne, Stuttgart and, by April, Zurich. 6–8 July: meets Voltaire in Geneva. 20 July: marriage of Manon Balletti to Blondel. November: Casanova meets Teresa Lanti/Bellino and their son Cesarino in Florence.

1761: January: Meeting with Donna Lucrezia and their daughter Leonilda in Naples. Later he travels via Rome, Florence, Bologna, Modena, and Parma to Turin, returning briefly to Paris in July before leaving for Strasbourg, Augsburg and Munich.

1762: early January: Casanova arrives in Paris. Mid-January: He leaves Paris to prepare for the Marquise d'Urfé's regeneration operation. February: he meets Marianna Corticelli in Metz. April: the Marquise d'Urfé's first regeneration operation in Pontcarré. By May Casanova is in Aix-la-Chapelle. From there he travels to Liège, Metz, Basle, Geneva and Turin. November: Casanova expelled from Turin.

1763: January: Casanova is back in Turin. March/April: meeting with Marcolina. The Marquise d'Urfé's second regeneration operation. May: second encounter with Henriette. Early June: brief visit to Paris. 11 June: Casanova crosses the Channel to England with his servant Clairmont and Giuseppe Pompeati. 14 June: He arrives in London. Teresa Imer, Sophia, Pauline and Marianne de Charpillon. 27 November: Casanova is arrested on the orders of Charpillon.

1764: mid-March: Casanova flees London, and travels to Wesel via Calais, Dunkirk and Brussels. By July he is in Berlin where he meets Frederick the Great. September/October: leaves for St Petersburg via Riga.

1765: May: excursion from St Petersburg to Moscow. September: leaves St Petersburg for Poland, arriving in Warsaw in October.

1766: 5 March: Casanova loses Polish king's favour over duel with Branicki. 8 July: He is forced to leave Warsaw. Travels to Vienna via Breslau, Dresden and Prague.

1767: January 23: Casanova banished from Vienna. He travels to Augsburg, Cologne, Aix-la-Chapelle, Spa (August–September), Paris (by October). 14 October: Death of Senator Bragadin in Venice. November: Casanova expelled from France by Louis XV. Leaves for Madrid via Bordeaux and Pamplona.

1768: Casanova accused of illegal possession of weapons in Madrid. September: leaves for Barcelona. 16 November: imprisoned in Barcelona after a love affair. 28 December: released from prison, he leaves for France.

1769: February-May: in Aix-en-Provence, where he falls ill. Third encounter with Henriette. To Marseille via the Croix d'Or, then on to Antibes, Nice, Turin, Lugano and Turin.

1770: 15 March: Casanova leaves Turin for Parma, Bologna, Florence (by April), Sienna, Rome, Naples (June to mid-August). In Salerno in late August, with Leonilda and Donna Lucrezia. Naples. Rome.

1771: July: Casanova leaves Rome for Florence. Late December: banished from Florence, he goes to Bologna.

1772:	early October: Casanova leaves Bologna. 15 November: settles in Trieste. Bankruptcy of Teresa Imer in London.
1773:	14 December: death of Marianna Corticelli in Turin.
1774:	3 September: Casanova pardoned by the Venetian government. 14 September: he returns to Venice after an absence of eighteen years.
1775:	publication of the first volume of his translation of Homer's *Iliad*. 13 November: death of the Marquise d'Urfé in Paris.
1776:	November: Casanova undertakes occasional work for the Venetian Inquisitors. Death of Zanetta Casanova (29 November) and of Manon Balletti (December).
1779:	Casanova starts a three-year affair with seamstress Francesca Buschini.
1780:	January–July: Casanova publishes a monthly magazine. 7 October: he begins to file regular reports for the Inquisitors.
1782:	August: publication of Casanova's pamphlet *Ne' Amore, Ne' donne* leads to his disgrace. September: flees to Trieste.
1783:	13 January: Casanova returns to Venice for a few hours, then leaves for Vienna. 16 June: revisits Venice briefly before going into permanent exile. Travels to Augsburg, Aix-la-Chapelle, Spa, Paris, Brussels, Amsterdam, Vienna, Frankfurt and Vienna in search of employment, then on to Dresden, Berlin, Brno.
1784:	in mid-February he returns to Vienna, where he meets Mozart's librettist Lorenzo da Ponte. Accepts post as a secretary in the service of the Venetian ambassador, Sebastiano Foscarini. First meeting with Count Waldstein, who offers him a post as his librarian at Dux. Casanova declines.
1785:	23 April: death of Foscarini. Casanova travels to Brno, Carlsbad and Teplitz where, in September, he meets Waldstein again. This time he accepts Waldstein's offer of employment and travels to Dux.
1786:	publication of Casanova's *Soliloque d'un penseur*.
1787:	voyage to Prague. Publication of *Histoire de Ma Fuite*.
1788:	voyage to Dresden and Leipzig. Publication of *Icosameron*.
1788/1789:	possibly starts writing *Histoire de Ma Vie*.
1792:	July: finishes first draft of *Histoire de Ma Vie* and begins revising it.
1797:	19 August: death of Teresa Imer in London.
1798:	April: Casanova falls ill. 4 June: he dies. His nephew Carlo Angiolini takes the manuscript of *Histoire de Ma Vie* to Dresden.
1820:	24 June: Casanova's daughter Sophia Williams opens the Adult Orphan Institution in London.
1821:	January: manuscript of *Histoire de Ma Vie* is sold to the Leipzig publisher Brockhaus. 1822–1828: Publication of first edition of *Histoire de Ma Vie*, in an edited German translation.
1823:	23 June: death of Sophia Williams in London.
1826–1838:	first French edition of *Histoire de Ma Vie*, edited and much revised.
1960–1962:	first edition of the original text of *Histoire de Ma Vie* is published.

BIBLIOGRAPHY

ANDRE, Louis Jean, 'Sous le Masque d'Anne d'Arci: Adélaïde de Gueidan', *Intermédiare des Casanovistes* No. XIII, 1996

ANDRE, Louis Jean, 'Considerations Médicales sur la Variole de Bettina', *Intermédiare des Casanovistes*, No. XV, 1998

ANDRIEUX, Maurice, *Daily Life in Papal Rome in the Eighteenth Century*, translated by Mary Fitton, George Allen and Unwin, London, 1968

ANDRIEUX, Maurice, *Daily Life in Venice at the Time of Casanova*, translated by Mary Fitton, George Allen and Unwin, London, 1972

ANON., *Onania – or the Heinous Sin of Self-Pollution, and all its frightful consequences in both sexes, considered. With spiritual and physical advice, etc.*, N.P., London, 1737

BERNIS, François Joachim de, *Memoirs and Letters of Cardinal de Bernis*, translated by Katherine Prescott Wormeley, William Heinemann, London, 1902

BLEACKLEY, Horace, *Life of John Wilkes*, John Lane, London, 1917

BLEACKLEY, Horace, *Casanova in England*, John Lane, London, 1932

BOUCE, Paul-Gabriel (ed.) *Sexuality in eighteenth-century Britain*, Manchester University Press, Manchester, 1982

BOUDET, Micheline, *La Comédie Italienne – Marivaux et Silvia*, Albin Michel, Paris, 2001

BORDES, Compigny des, *Casanova et la Marquise d'Urfé*, n.p., Paris, 1922

BROSSES, Charles de, *Selections from the Letters of Charles de Brosses*, translated by Lord Ronald Sutherland Gower, Kegan Paul, London, 1897

BURNEY, Charles de, *The Present State of Music in France and Italy*, T. Becket and Co., London, 1771

CASANOVA, Giacomo, *Histoire de Ma Vie*, three volumes, edited by Francis Lacassin, Robert Laffont, Paris 1993

CASANOVA, Giacomo, *History of My Life*, translated by Willard R. Trask, twelve volumes, Johns Hopkins University Press, Baltimore and London, 1966

CLARKE, Donald, *A Daisy in the Broom, The Story of A School 1820–1958*, Julia London, Tweeddale, 1991

CAMPARDON, Emile, *Les Comédiens du Roi de la Troupe Italienne pendant les deux derniers Siècles*, Slatkine Reprints, Geneva, 1970

DAHOUI, Serge, *Le Cardinal de Bernis ou La Royauté du Charme*, Lienhart, Paris, 1974

ESPINCHAL, Comte de, *Journal d'émigration*, n.p., Paris, 1913

FLEM, Lydia, *Casanova, The Man Who Really Loved Women*, translated by Catherine Temerson, Farrar Straus Giroux, New York, 1997

FROULAY, Renée de, *Souvenirs de la Marquise de Crêquy de 1710 à 1803*, n.p., Paris, 1842

GOETHE, Johann, *Italian Journey*, translated by W.H. Auden and Elizabeth Mayer, Penguin Classics, London, 1970

GOLDONI, Carlo, *Mémoires*, Duchesne, Paris, 1787

GOLDONI, Carlo, *Memoirs of Goldoni written by himself*, translated by John Black, Henry Colburn, London, 1814

GREEN, Shirley, *The Curious History of Contraception*, Ebury Press, London, 1971

GRELLET, Pierre, *Les Aventures de Casanova en Suisse*, Editions SPES, Lausanne, 1919

GRUET, Pierre, *M.M. et Les Anges de Murano*, Casanova Gleanings XVIII, 1975

GUNTHER, Pablo, *The Casanova Tour. A handbook for the use of the private travelling carriage in Eighteenth-century Europe and America*, printed by the author, Lindau, 1999

HARRIS, John, *Harris's List of Covent-Garden Ladies*, H. Ranger, London, 1788

HAUSSET, N. du, *Secret memoirs of the courts of Louis XV and XVI*, n.p., Paris, 1904

HERIOT, Angus, *The Castrati in Opera*, Secker & Warburg, London, 1956

HUDSON, Roger, *The Grand Tour*, The Folio Society, London, 1993

LABRACHERIE, Pierre, Silvia et Mario en ménage: *L'Illustre Théâtre. La Vie et l'Histoire de la Comédie Française*. No. 3., Editions du Tertre, Paris, 1955

LALANDE, Jerome le Français de, *Voyage d'un François en Italie fait dans les années 1765 et 1766*, Desairt, Paris, 1769

LAVEN, Mary, *Virgins of Venice, Enclosed Lives and Broken Vows in the Renaissance Convent*, Viking, London, 2002

LEVER, Maurice, *Théâtre et Lumières. Les Spectacles de Paris au XVIIIe siècle*, Fayard, Paris, 2001

LEWINSOHN, Richard, *A History of Sexual Customs*, translated by Alexander Mayce, Harper and Brothers, New York, 1958

LIGNE, Prince de, *Pensées, portraits et lettres à Casanova et à la marquise de Coigny*, Rivages Poches, Paris, 2002

MASTERS, John, *Casanova*, Michael Joseph, London, 1969

MAYNIAL, Edouard, *Casanova and His Time*, translated by Ethel Colburn Mayne, Chapman and Hall, London, 1911

MCLAREN, Angus, *A History of Contraception From Antiquity to the Present Day*, Basil Blackwell, Oxford, 1990

MERCIER, Sébastien, *Le tableau de Paris*, Mercier, Paris, 1781–1788

MONVAL, Georges, *Le Molièreiste*, Paris, 1886

MORRIS, James, *Venice*, Faber & Faber, London, 1960

NUGENT, Thomas, *The Grand Tour*, n.p., London, 1749

NUGENT, Thomas, *New Observations on Italy and its Inhabitants, written in French by two Swedish Gentlemen*, translated by Nugent, L. Davis and C. Reymers, London, 1769

PARKER, Derek, *Casanova*, Sutton Publishing, Stroud, 2002

PEAKMAN, Julie, *Lascivious Bodies – A sexual history of the eighteenth century*, Atlantic Books, London, 2004

PIERRAT, Emmanuel (ed.) *Almanach des demoiselles de Paris, suivi du Dictionnaire des nymphes du Palais-Royal*, Arlea, Paris, c.1999

POSTGATE, Raymond, *That Devil Wilkes*, Constable, London, 1930

QUADRO, Francesco Saverio, *Della Astoria e della ragione d'ogni poesia*, Bologna, 1739–49

RAVA, Aldo, *Lettere di Donne a Giacomo Casanova*, Milan, 1912

REES, Gillian, 'The Italian Comedy in London, 1726–27, with Zanetta Casanova', *Intermédiare des Casanovistes*, 1996

RIVES CHILDS, J., *Casanova – A Biography Based on New Documents*, George Allen and Unwin, London, 1961

RIVES CHILDS, J., *Casanova – A New Perspective*, Constable, London, 1989

ROUART, Jean-Marie, *Bernis, le cardinal des plaisirs*, Gallimard, Paris, 1998

ROY, Jeanne-Hélène, Fashioning Identities: Casanova's Encounters with La Charpillon, *Intermédiare des Casanovistes*, Année XVIII, 2001

ROUSSEAU, G.S. AND PORTER, Roy (eds), *Sexual Underworlds of the Enlightenment*, Manchester University Press, Manchester, 1987

RUGGIERO, Guido, *The Boundaries of Eros. Sex crimes and Sexuality in Renaissance Venice*, Oxford University Press, Oxford, 1985

SAMARAN, Charles, *Jacques Casanova, Vénitien, Une Vie d'Aventurier au XVIIIe Siècle*, Calmann-Lévy, Paris, 1914.

SEGAL, Muriel, *Virgins – Reluctant, Dubious and Avowed*, Robert Hale, London, 1978

SUMMERS, Judith, *The Empress of Pleasure*, Viking, London, 2002

TAYLOR, John, *Records of My Life*, Edward Bull, London, 1832

THOMPSON, Grace E., *The Life of a Covent Garden Lady*, Hutchinson, London, 1932

VARIOUS AUTHORS, 'Une Famille Provençale, Les Gueidans', *Arts et Livres de Provence*, Bulletin No. 29. Marseille, 1956

VARIOUS AUTHORS, La Dernière Amie de Jacques Casanova, Cécile de Roggendorff, d'Après une correspondance inédite, *Pages Casanoviennes*, Vol. V, Paris, 1926

WATZLAWICK, Helmut, 'House of Childhood, House of Birth: A Topographical distraction', *Intermédiare des Casanovistes*, 1999

WATZLAWICK, Helmut, 'Fata Viam Invenient, or Henriette Forever', *Intermédiare des Casanovistes*, 1989

WATZLAWICK, Helmut, 'M.M. Was she a Michiel?', *Intermédiare des Casanovistes*, 1971

WATZLAWICK, Helmut, 'Les Vrais Débuts d'une Actrice: Naissance et Baptême de Zanetta Casanova', *Intermédiare des Casanovistes*, 2003

PICTURE CREDITS

FRONTISPIECE

Giacomo Casanova Pastel portrait by Francesco Casanova (1727–1802) Dashcov Collection, State Historical Museum, Moscow

p.23 *Zanetta Casanova* Silhouette of the actress found amongst Casanova's possessions at Dux

PLATE SECTION

Venice: The Doge's Palace and the Molo from the Basin of San Marco Francesco Guardi (1712–1793) Oil on canvas. 58.1 × 76.4cm. Photo © National Gallery, London

The Parlour of the Nuns at San Zaccharia Francesco Guardi (1712–1793) Oil on canvas. 108 × 208cm. Ca'Rezzonico Museum, Venice. Photo © Ca'Rezzonico Museum, Venice

Teresa Lanti Anonymous, 18th century Bolognese School. The Scala Theatre Museum, Milan

Manon Balletti Jean-Marc Nattier, 1757. Oil on Canvas. 54 × 47.5cm. Photo © National Gallery, London

Thalia, Muse of Comedy Jean-Marc Nattier (1685–1766) Oil on Canvas. 53½ × 49in. Fine Arts Museum of San Francisco, Museum purchase, Mildred Anna Williams Collection, 1954.59

Adélaïde de Gueidan and her Sister Polyxène at the Harpsichord 18th century French School. Musée Granet, Aix-en-Provence. Photo © Musée Granet, by kind permission of Bernard Terlay

Teresa Cornelys Permission British Library. Shelfmark 1889b.10/1–8

Mrs Sophia Williams Anonymous, oil on canvas. The Princess Helena College, Hertfordshire. Photo © Martin L. Thompson

View of Dux Castle Anonymous, 19th century. Photo © and permission Duchcov Castle, Duchcov, Czech Republic

A NOTE ON THE AUTHOR

Judith Summers is the author of four novels and two non-fiction books, *The Empress of Pleasure* and the prize-winning *Soho, A History of London's Most Colourful Neighbourhood*. Born and brought up in London, she studied Fine Art in Bristol and Manchester, and trained as a film editor with the BBC. After becoming a tourist guide, she discovered a passion for historical research. She has written widely on London, and lives in north London.

A NOTE ON THE TYPE

The text of this book is set in Berling roman. A modern face designed by K. E. Forsberg between 1951–58. In spite of its youth it does carry the characteristics of an old face. The serifs are inclined and blunt, and the g has a straight ear.

EASTON AREA PUBLIC LIB.

3 1901 00271 4485

BC 335 S

D1032129

NO LONGER PROPERTY
OF EASTON AREA
PUBLIC LIBRARY